2015

THE MYTHOLOGY OF THE WICHITA

THE MYTHOLOGY OF THE WICHITA

BY
GEORGE A. DORSEY
Curator of Anthropology, Field Columbian Museum

FOREWORD BY
ELIZABETH A. H. JOHN

UNIVERSITY OF OKLAHOMA PRESS
Norman and London

Library of Congress Cataloging-in-Publication Data

The mythology of the Wichita / George A. Dorsey.
    p.   cm.
    ISBN 0-8061-2778-3 (pbk. : alk. paper)
    1. Wichita mythology. 2. Wichita Indians—Folklore. 3. Tales—
Texas. 4. Tales—Oklahoma.
    E99.W6M98 1995
    299'.72—dc20   95-2857
                                                                         CIP

The paper in this book meets the guidelines for permanence and dura-
bility of the Committee on Production Guidelines for Book Longevity of
the Council on Library Resources, Inc. ∞

Published by the University of Oklahoma Press, Norman, Publishing
Division of the University. First edition published in 1904 by the Carnegie
Institution, Washington, D.C. Foreword by Elizabeth A. H. John copyright
© 1995 by the University of Oklahoma Press. All rights reserved. Manufactured in the U.S.A. First printing of the University of Oklahoma Press
edition, 1995.

                    1   2   3   4   5   6   7   8   9   10

CONTENTS.

CONTENTS.

THIRD PERIOD: THE PRESENT.

FOREWORD.

The Mythology of the Wichita is a priceless legacy from a formative period in American ethnology. George Dorsey was among the pioneers of that discipline who ventured into tribal worlds late in the nineteenth century to record Indian cultures then at risk of oblivion. Although their methods and even their motives are sometimes denigrated by current practitioners (anthropologists are notoriously wont to slay the fathers of their discipline), those pioneers and the institutions that sponsored them deserve boundless gratitude for preserving tribal traditions imperiled by a rapid change in lifeways. No less gratitude is due the tribes that mustered the vision and the patience to support such efforts.

No investigator could have wished for a more gracious reception than that accorded Dorsey by the Wichita. They won his admiration for their character as well as his gratitude for their cooperation. Welcoming him into their world, they told in great detail how Wichita people had behaved from time immemorial and why, showing him their extant material culture and explaining changes that had occurred over time.

Most importantly, they let Dorsey record the complex heritage of myths and legends that embodied the Wichitas' understanding of the universe and their sense of themselves. Respected elders of each of the tribe's extant bands presented the tales: six men and two women of the Tawakoni told twenty-nine; four men of the Waco told twenty-one; and five men and two women of the Wichita proper told ten. Their foremost leader, Tawakoni Jim, began with the Creation Myth, and he would contribute a total of thirteen by the time he recited the sixtieth, concluding story. Even more prodigious was the contribution of a Waco man, Ahahe, who told sixteen stories. The sum of their efforts comprises an immutable treasure for their posterity as well as a valuable resource for scholars.

Why such a generous response to Dorsey's project? Perhaps the recent ordeal of allotment of their reservation in severalty had sharpened the elders' realization that theirs would be the last generation to have lived the traditional Wichita lifeways based on communal domain. Perhaps even more telling was the Wichitas' growing awareness of many signs that, in their mythology, foreshadowed the approaching end of the world.

In contrast to his rich harvest of cultural data, Dorsey gleaned only a few, somewhat misleading fragments of historical context. In fact, for at least two centuries before Dorsey visited the Wichita, their history had been far more complicated and turbulent and had involved a more extensive arena than was indicated by any source available to Dorsey. *The Mythology of the Wichita* was published a decade before historian Herbert Eugene Bolton led the way into the wealth of information about Indians to be found in Mexican and Spanish archives, revealing to twentieth-century investigators a Wichitan village world once comprised of many more bands than the three—Wichita, Tawakoni, and Waco—still recognized in Dorsey's time.

Subsequent investigators have found—and published—enough information on the Wichita to sketch their history since 1541, when Spanish explorers first examined the agricultural villages of the Wichitas along the great bend of the Arkansas River. By the mid-eighteenth century, changes wrought by horses, European manufactured goods (particularly guns), and diseases made the Arkansas basin untenable for the surviving Wichitan peoples. Coalescing into four bands, they migrated southward to the Red, Trinity, and Brazos valleys, locating their new villages at appropriate distances westward from those of the long-established Caddo and Kichai peoples. Linguistically related through their respective Caddoan languages and culturally similar in many respects, the three neighbouring nations of agricultural villagers readily cooperated in trade and especially in war against their common enemies.

Within the new Wichitan homeland, the Tawakonis predominated in the southern reaches initially along the Trinity and later the Brazos rivers, and the Taovayas—usually in close association with the much fewer Wichita proper—predominated in the northern reaches, along the Red River.[1] The Yscanis apparently fluctuated between the Taovayas and the Tawakoni spheres. Yet to be explained is the obliteration of Taovayas and Yscanis identity, even from tribal memory, during the turbulent nineteenth century, and the eventual lumping of all surviving bands under the name of Wichita. In the same era, Kichai identity also blurred as that dwindling nation found refuge with the kindred Wichita. The final Wichitan migration, northward to the Washita Valley, occurred in 1859: a tragic exodus escorted by U.S. troops after a series of catastrophic experiences with hostile Anglo-Texans.

The "first contact with the United States Government" mentioned by Dorsey was the visit of a regiment of U.S. dragoons to a Wichita village on the North Fork of the Red River in 1834. But three decades earlier, Dr. John Sibley, the first U.S. Indian agent in the Louisiana Territory, had assiduously wooed the Wichita with gifts and trade as well as with his hospitality at Natchitoches. Nearly a century before Dorsey's mission, Sibley recorded the tribal migration tale that a distinguished Wichita chief told him at Natchitoches in 1811. Although that tale apparently was lost to the tribe before Dorsey's time, the version preserved by Sibley provides a useful complement to *The Mythology of the Wichita*.[2] It is included in the appendix to this new edition.

It is illuminating to compare Dorsey's observations of the Wichita with those reported by late eighteenth- and early nineteenth-century visitors. In addition to the migration tale, Sibley also preserved an intimate description of daily life by an Anglo-American trader who lived with the Wichitas for two months in 1808 at a pivotal cluster of three villages—Taovayas and Wichita on the right bank and Waco on the left bank of the Red River—just west of the Cross Timbers and just east of the ninety-eighth meridian.[3]

That 1808 account compares instructively with the first detailed report of the Taovayas and Wichita villages at the same strategically important location, written in 1778 by a French visitor, Athanase de Mézières, who was the Spanish crown's most effective agent among Indians of Louisiana and Texas.[4] Wichitan leadership and political process are vividly described in a 1785 report by a pair of envoys from San Antonio, a Frenchman and a Spaniard who had formerly lived at those villages on Red River and thus knew the language and customs of the inhabitants.[5] Also available are structural details of the extraordinary fort that the Taovayas built on the Red River in the 1750s and 1760s, together with a crude map, drawn in 1763, locating all Wichitan villages in relation to those of other Indians in the region as well as to the frontiers of Spanish Texas and French Louisiana.[6]

Access to those earlier reports surely would have deepened both Dorsey's appreciation of Wichita tenacity in preserving their culture to the end of the nineteenth century, and his gloom about the overwhelming loss that seemed inevitable at the turn of the century. The Wichitas weathered the challenges of the twentieth century, however, more sturdily than Dorsey dared hope. Most still live in the vicinity of their former reservation. Community activity centers in Anadarko, Oklahoma, around the tribal park and headquarters building of the Wichita and Affiliated Tribes, the government which they established under the Indian Reorganization Act of 1934. Although band distinctions no longer figure in Wichita life, some families remember Waco or Tawakoni forebears. While a few families have some Kichai blood, there may remain only one person who can still speak and understand the Kichai language. Eligibility for tribal membership hinges upon proof of at least one-eighth Wichita blood. Because the Wichita tribe does not permit dual membership, persons who also meet the blood quantum requirement for other tribes must officially waive those memberships in order to be enrolled as Wichita, which imposes a painful choice in some families.

As of early 1995, the official tribal roll numbers some 1800, of whom approximately half are less than seventeen years old.[7] Such a youthful population requires deliberate efforts to perpetuate tribal culture. As in times past, elders share with youngsters the stories and traditional knowledge and skills handed down by preceding generations. Further encouraged by tribal and intertribal dances and gatherings in the Anadarko area, the rising generation of Wichitas grow increasingly interested in the language, songs, and dances of their people.

Unfortunately, the Carnegie Institution's 1904 edition of *The Mythology of the Wichita* has proven much less durable than either Wichita culture or the substance of Dorsey's report. In fact, the volume exemplifies the physical vulnerability of publications from that era. The highly acidic paper has become so brittle that it may crumble with even the most careful turn of a page, forcing libraries increasingly to restrict use of such volumes. Some resort to photocopies to replace crumbling pages, but that process risks further damage to the book, and the outcome is not very usable.

Hence the timeliness of this new edition of *The Mythology of the Wichita*, which includes a lost migration tale not found in the original edition and also translates into English passages originally printed in Latin.[8] It is now conveniently available to Wichita families and general readers, as well as to scholars of Wichita culture.

ELIZABETH A. H. JOHN.

FEBRUARY, 1995.
AUSTIN, TEXAS,

NOTES

1. The Wichita experience to 1795 is traced in Elizabeth A. H. John, *Storms Brewed in Other Men's Worlds: The Confrontation of Indians, Spanish, and French in the Southwest, 1540–1795* (College Station: Texas A & M University Press, 1975; Lincoln: University of Nebraska Press, 1981). No comprehensive account of their extraordinarily complex nineteenth- and twentieth-century experience is yet available. A useful summary, however, appears in Gary and Ardina McAdams, "The Wichita Tribe," *Southern Plains Indian Museum Association News* 5, no. 1 (July 1994): 1, 5–6.

2. Elizabeth A. H. John, "A Wichita Migration Tale," *American Indian Quarterly* 7 (Fall 1983): 57–63.

3. Elizabeth A. H. John, "Portrait of a Wichita Village, 1808," *Chronicles of Oklahoma* 60 (Winter 1982–83): 412–37. This is the earliest documentation of the band name that Anglo-Americans later wrote as Waco; three years later a Spanish source reported that band to have moved south to settle near the Tawakonis on the Brazos River, where Anglo-Texan settlers came to know them in the 1820s.

4. Herbert Eugene Bolton, ed., *Athanase de Mézières and the Louisiana-Texas Frontier, 1768–1780*, vol. 2 (Arthur H. Clark Co., 1914), 200–209.

5. Elizabeth A. H. John, ed., and Adán Benavides, Jr., trans., "Inside the Comanchería, 1785: The Diary of Pedro Vial and Francisco Xavier Chaves," *Southwestern Historical Quarterly* 98 (July 1994): 26–56.

6. Elizabeth A. H. John, "A Case Study in the Interdependence of Archeology and History: The Spanish Fort Sites on the Red River," *Bulletin of the Texas Archeological Society* 63 (1992): 197–209.

7. Current population estimates and related information were supplied in January and February, 1995, through the courtesy of the President of the Wichita and Affiliated Tribes, Gary McAdams, and the Director of Enrollment, Cleta Attadlety.

8. In eight of the tales in this book, Dorsey offered passages in Latin—his effort to convey language of a sexual nature only to those whose education presumably made them impervious to prurient interests. The English translation of these passages is courtesy of Professor John S. Catlin, Department of Classics, University of Oklahoma.

PREFACE.

This collection of Wichita myths is largely the result of investigations begun in 1903, under a grant from the Carnegie Institution of Washington. In 1900 I began work of this nature for the Field Columbian Museum, and continued it interruptedly for three years. Throughout the three years I used as interpreter Burgess Hunt, a well-educated Wichita of full blood. For assistance in the final arrangement of the myths, and especially for a large part of the information embodied in the introduction, I am indebted to the well-known chief of the Wichita Towakoni Jim. To his great knowledge, always freely given, and for his unfailing kindness it is a pleasure to acknowledge my indebtedness.

Inasmuch as the present work forms but a part of my investigations among the tribes of the Caddoan stock, I have deferred until a later publication references to tales of a similar nature of other tribes, while in the "Introduction" I have confined myself to such matter as would assist in understanding the references made in the tales to the customs and beliefs of the Wichita. The music accompanying certain myths has been transcribed by Mr. Frederic R. Burton, who is also responsible for the comments made on the songs.

GEORGE A. DORSEY.

FIELD COLUMBIAN MUSEUM,
CHICAGO, October 1, 1904.

THE MYTHOLOGY OF THE WICHITA.

INTRODUCTION.

The Wichita, at the time of their first contact with the United States Government, occupied a village on the North Fork of the Red River, about four miles below its junction with Elm Fork, in Oklahoma. Soon afterwards they were removed to a place called Rush Springs, twenty-five miles east of Fort Sill, in 1882. The Wichita, with affiliated bands, were transferred to the north side of the Washita River, on lands a portion of which had been assigned to the Cheyenne and Arapaho in 1869. It is probable that they have now reached their final home, as they occupy their land in severalty and the tribal relationship has ceased to exist. It seems probable that, at least for a hundred years or more, their permanent villages were never out of sight of the Wichita Mountains. Their range may be said to have been confined by the ninety-seventh and ninety-ninth parallels, and to have extended south from the Washita to about that part of Texas where the city of Waco now stands. The territory occupied by them in general may be characterized as a high, rolling, broken prairie, fairly well watered in places, of a sandy nature, and in the main treeless, except for irregular clusters of scrub oak, with heavier timber, chiefly of elm, cottonwood, and willow, along the water courses.

According to Powell's classification, the Wichita form the third of five groups of the Caddoan stock, the other groups being the Pawnee, Arikara, Kichai, and Caddo. With the Wichita proper, therefore, according to this classification, belong the Waco and Towakoni, which may be regarded as sub-tribes of the Wichita. For a very long time, however, the Kichai have also been closely affiliated with the Wichita, and to-day are regarded as an intrinsic part of the tribe. According to the well-known chief of the affiliated Wichita of to-day, Towakoni Jim, there is but little difference in the language of the Wichita proper and the Towakoni and Waco, while neither of these three tribes is able to understand Kichai. The same informant maintains that but four full-blood Kichai exist. He is of the opinion that the Kichai is more closely related to the Hainai group of the Caddo and the Pawnee than to either the Wichita proper or the Towakoni or Waco.

The manners and customs of the four bands have been practically the same from very early times, and they have intermarried and lived

1

together to such an extent that it is no longer possible for one custom
or another to be considered as the exclusive property of a single tribe.
This holds good also regarding religion and mythology, and no attempt, therefore, has been made to group the myths according to tribes,
though in the note giving the name of the informant his tribal affinity
has been indicated.

The population of the four bands, according to the reports of the
Bureau of Indian Affairs, was as follows:

In 1874—Wichita, 300; Waco, 140; Towakoni, 125; Kechai, 106; total, 671.
In 1885—Wichita, 176; Waco, 64; Towakoni, 145; Kichai, 63; total, 448.

This total diminished slightly but steadily from year to year, until
1896, when the total for the four tribes was given at 365. The census
of 1903 gives the total of the four tribes at 433, but in this is included
the Delaware. It is evident that there has been a material falling off
in the number of the Wichita in the last thirty years. It is believed,
however, that at the present time they are almost, if not quite, holding
their own. But that they are to suffer a further decline seems probable,
owing to the fact that in the recent opening of their reservation they
suffered a decided change in their method of life, and especially to the
fact that it is possible for them to obtain whisky without great effort.
Previous to this time they kept up with great conservatism their ancient
method of living, and, on the whole, were in the enjoyment of a robust
and vigorous constitution.

In stature and color, the Wichita present a decided contrast to the
Plains tribes by whom they are surrounded, such as the Cheyenne,
Arapaho, Kiowa, Comanche, and Apache. They are decidedly of a
shorter and stockier build, with a somewhat darker skin. The men
pierced the lobe of the ear, generally in four places, from which were
suspended innumerable metal pendants. Both men and women in former times practiced tattooing, that of the man differing radically from
that of the woman. The men were tattooed both on the upper and
lower eyelids, and from the outer corner of the eyes extended a slight
line about half an inch in length. From this design the Wichita claim
is derived their name, owing to the resemblance of the eyes thus tattooed to those of the raccoon—Kidikides (Raccoon Eyes). These
marks about the eyes are made on a boy when young, at which time
he is told that they will prevent him in the future from having sore
eyes. The men bore two additional marks on the face, consisting of
short lines passing downward from each corner of the mouth. On the
back of each hand is tattooed a small design resembling the bird's foot.
This is made immediately after the boy has killed his first bird. Up

and down the arms and across the breast may be found additional marks in the form of a small cross. These indicate the number of times the individual has acted as a spy for a war-party which has been successful, one mark being made for each incident. These crosses are symbols of the stars and represent a well-known mythical hero among the Wichita called "Flint-Stone-Lying-Down-Above" (Tahanetski-hadidia), who, as is told in one of the myths, is one of the guardians of the warriors. The marks tattooed upon the women differ from those of the men, the entire group of designs differing but slightly among individual women. The most complete, as well as the most common design, is here given: A single line passes down the ridge of the nose and is carried on to the end of the upper lip, from which a line passes in each direction to the corners of the mouth, where each joins a short line passing downward and terminating in another line directed toward the center of the lower lip. Before these lines meet they turn downward to the chin. The space between these two lines is occupied by two short parallel lines, and all four terminate in a line which passes entirely around the jaw from ear to ear, and which is surmounted by a row of solid triangles. Similar rows of triangles pass across the neck and across the upper part of the breast. Down each arm are two series of four parallel zigzag lines, while four long lines pass down the middle of the breast. Above each of the breasts are three pairs of lines, each pair crossing at a wide angle, the open space at each end being occupied by V-shaped connecting lines. The nipple is also tattooed, and around it are three concentric circles. It is claimed by the Wichita that the chief object of the tattooing was to distinguish the woman, not only from other tribes, but especially from the slaves, of whom in former times they seem to have held many. The whole tattooed design is said to have been derived from the buffalo. The girls are told that by receiving these marks they enjoy a more perfect life. They are also told that the concentric rings about the breasts prevent them from becoming pendulous in old age.

In character, the Wichita stand high among the Plains tribes as regards morality. Their home life seems to have been exceedingly well regulated, and intertribal strifes were rare. They have given very little trouble to the United States, and from an early time they manifested a uniformly friendly disposition, from which, however, they have received no apparent benefit. Of all the tribes of the Plains they seem the best natured and most kindly disposed toward the whites; indeed it would be hard to find anywhere people of finer nature than that possessed by the Wichita.

In culture, the Wichita belonged to the southern Plains group, and the pursuit of the buffalo was secondary to that of agriculture. Even to-day their cornfields are not inconsiderable, and with encouragement would become a source of great profit to them; for apparently throughout their whole career they have been devoted to agriculture, raising large crops of corn, beans, melons, etc. The produce of their fields was, of course, supplemented by the flesh of the buffalo and other wild game, but unlike the more nomadic tribes of the north they were by no means dependent upon the buffalo. As among the Pawnee, many of their most important ceremonies were concerned with the cultivation of their fields.

The Wichita were village-dwellers, occupying substantial and spacious habitations of a bee-hive shape, commonly known as "grass-lodges," of which a few still remain, and the construction of which has not been entirely given up. In building this lodge, upright forks of cedar are erected, varying in number from eight to fourteen or sixteen, according to the size of the lodge desired. Transverse beams, also of cedar, connect these forks. Leaning against them, one end resting on the ground, and so placed as to form a circle, are long, slender cedar poles, which are united at the top. Transversely over this framework are placed long, slender, decorticated willow poles, held in position by thongs of slippery elm bark. A long, coarse, bunch grass is spread over the entire surface in layers, beginning at the bottom and continuing upward till the top is reached. The grass covering is held in place by additional slender willow poles. Where these poles cross the uprights bunches of grass are tied.

The lodges vary in diameter from fifteen to thirty feet. The beds are two or three feet from the ground and are arranged around the wall, the upright forks serving to mark the position of the beds. The number of beds varies according to the size of the lodge, six being the usual number, while twelve is not an extraordinary number. Houses of diminutive size are occasionally built to hold a single family. The lodge has two openings, about two feet wide and three and a half feet high, one on the east and one on the west side. Each opening is provided with a door made of grass over a willow framework. These doors do not move on hinges, but are easily set aside, either from within or from without. The eastern door is usually left open in the morning, while the western door is used in the afternoon. Generally a similar opening is found on the south side of the lodge. This at the present time is not used as a door, and seems to be a survival of a time when the lodges had both a north and south door, which, however, were used only during ceremonies, especially the ceremony of the medicine-men. In the center of the lodge is an excavation for the fireplace. The smoke makes its exit through a circular opening about eight inches in diameter on the eastern side of the roof, near the top. The top of the lodge is continued to a height of about three feet above the point where the upright cedar poles meet, by means of tightly wrapped bundles of grass, while from the base of this peak project four poles about three feet in length, one pointing east, another south, another west, and another north.

The four projecting poles outside stand for the four world quarters or gods, while the upward peak is symbolic of Man-Never-Known-on-Earth (Kinnekasus), the Creator in Wichita mythology. It is said that a door is placed on the east side that the sun may look into the 'lodge as it rises, and that the west door is so placed that the sun may look in as it sets, while through the small circular opening overhead the sun may look in at noon. The south door is still retained that the god of the south wind may enter. The fireplace is considered sacred, for here offerings are made, the food is cooked, medicines heated, etc.

The furnishings inside the lodge are not unlike those found in the Pawnee lodge. The beds consist of mattresses made of slender willow rods and coverings of buffalo hide. Over the bed and hanging down in front, is a long curtain of buffalo hide, which can be raised or lowered at will; this is often painted with war scenes. In the same place, between the west opening and the fireplace, stands the corn mill, consisting of the trunk of a tree about a foot and a half in diameter and four feet long, implanted in the ground. The pestles are long, with a heavy end. Usually two or more women engage in grinding corn at once.

Formerly, pottery was extensively manufactured by the Wichita, but its use was long since abandoned. Beautifully made wooden vessels of large size and buffalo horn spoons are still occasionally found. A small, flat granite rock was used for crushing seeds and medicines, and a small wood hand mortar was used for a similar purpose. The parfleshe, similar to that used by other Plains tribes, is found among the Wichita, together with long rawhide bags used as food receptacles. For dressing hides they used a flesher similar in shape to that used by the other Plains tribes; the handle, however, was of wood and beautifully fashioned. At one side of the lodge, in well-to-do families, was a large summer arbor, built like the grass-lodge, but of elongated shape, and with open sides to a height of about four feet. These arbors were often of great size, and were provided with a platform raised a foot above the ground. Here they worked and rested in the shade during the summer months. A third structure was the corn drying arbor, varying in size from ten to twenty feet square and reached by a ladder made of a single notched slender tree. Upon this was placed not only corn, but meat, etc., to dry, while from its sides and underneath were suspended great masses of pumpkins cut into long, thin strips and beautifully braided, for which purpose a specially constructed pounder was used. Reference is frequently made in the tales to a sleeping arbor, upon which it was formerly the custom to make beds for the maidens; these were usually smaller in size than the corn drying arbors. In addition to the structures described, the Wichita also made use of the skin tipi, when on the march, and the sweat-lodge. These differed in no essential particular from those used by other Plains tribes. The houses were grouped in villages, which occupied the lower levels of a hill slope in some well-watered valley.

The clothing of the men, as a rule, consisted of a loin cloth and moccasins. This was supplemented by leggings and the buffalo robe. The shirt, such as worn by the northern Plains tribes, was not known. The costume of the women consisted of a skirt, generally of buckskin or of young buffalo hide, tanned on both sides and wound around the waist and reaching below the knees. The feet and lower legs were encased in moccasin leggings. It has been said that the women formerly wore an apron made of bark, but the Wichita deny this.

The basis of the social organization of the four tribes was that of the village, at the head of which was a chief and a sub-chief. Election to the chieftainship was never through heredity alone, it being necessary that the chief's son should show not only marked ability, but bravery and generalship equal to that of his father. It was possible, as the stories themselves abundantly illustrate, for the youngest and meanest born boy of the village, through exhibition of bravery, to rise to the position of chieftainship. But more than bravery was necessary, for the aspirant to this high place must have won the love and respect of the members of his tribe by acts of generosity and kindness covering the entire period of his life. The power of electing the chief was in the hands of the head warriors, who virtually controlled the village, and could make or unmake a chief, as they wished. Next in rank to the chief was a leader, whose title was The-One-Who-Locates (Okonitsa), and whose duty it was to be constantly on the lookout for better village sites. It was he who was responsible for the removal and laying out of new villages and for everything, in fact, pertaining to the location of villages. Next in rank were the medicine-men, who were also priests of certain ceremonies, one of their number being known as the "crier," or "announcer." From the remaining inhabitants of the village were selected one or more known as "servants." Their duty was to do the bidding of the chiefs and of the medicine-men, especially in time of ceremonies. After years of apprenticeship they became medicine-men. Of the remaining inhabitants of the village the basis of rank was that of prowess in war, and wealth.

Although manifesting almost from the beginning a friendly disposition towards the whites the Wichita have never been accused of cowardice, and in spite of their small numbers, were probably as successful warriors as any of the Plains tribes. As is so often illustrated in the tales, the time and nature of the war-party was determined by some one who desired to lead an expedition, at which time he would invite his friends to his lodge, tell them his plans, and select a head leader and two second leaders, the latter serving as spies or scouts, while on the journey.

The chief object of war expeditions was the taking of scalps and the capturing of women to be used as slaves. The hereditary enemies of the Wichita were the Apache, Osage, and Tonkawa. These three tribes, in the order named, were considered the bravest of all their foes, and as a consequence, the taking of a scalp of an individual from one of these tribes was looked upon as a high honor. The Wichita had the usual grades of showing prowess in war; such were counting coup, stabbing, scalping, and killing. Their war records were usually depicted in detail on the robe, or the more salient features of the record might be indicated on the tipi. The significance of the marks describing these war records was always supposed to be known by the other warriors of the tribe, and when an individual misrepresented his record, either on his robe or on his tipi, he was at once proclaimed a liar throughout the camp, and his robe or tipi might be destroyed. It was also the custom of warriors to proclaim their prowess by contests in the lodges during the long winter evenings, when war tales exclusively were told. The return of a victorious war-party was always the occasion for great rejoicing in the village, the news being transmitted by the signs made by the leader of the party as he arrived at a certain high hill overlooking the village, which was always set apart for this purpose. Then followed days and nights occupied with scalp and victory dances.

Often before birth, a name was selected for the forthcoming child. This name might be due to some dream of its mother or some relative, the sex of the child being revealed at the same time, and the name would agree with its supposed sex. Naturally the dream did not always come true, as, for example, in the case of a certain well-known Wichita still living, who bears the name "Ignorant-Woman," although he is a robust man and is far from being ignorant. Should nothing occur to indicate to the parents a suitable name for the child before its birth a name was given it soon after birth. The name, however, was not hastily chosen, but they waited until the child itself had done something which the parents believed to be characteristic or indicative of deeds he was to perform during the course of his life. Again, the name might be deferred until the child could crawl, or walk, or until such time as it should have, done something, or manifested some peculiarity, which would suggest a name to the parents. This name the child usually bore until it was well-grown. Should the child continue to live and be prosperous it might retain this name throughout life. If, for any reason, it should seem desirable to change the child's name it was done, sometimes by women for the girls, or by men for both boys and girls, for it was supposed that a man, having been on the war-path, had a wider range of experience than a woman. Should the child be sickly and have much bad luck in its early years its name might be changed innumerable times. Several other men would be invited to the lodge, their names pronounced, and the child would be asked the name it liked best. The individual whose name was chosen walked up to the child, saying: "The name that I shall give you is the one you shall bear throughout life. As I give you this name you shall live to be as old as I am, for I myself have enjoyed life without sickness, and so you, too, shall enjoy the same sort of life that I have enjoyed, and you shall have my powers as well as my name." Instead of giving his own name to the child, the man might give it some name which had reference to some act or deed of his on the war-path, or of some particular enemy.

Should the man marry and have children, and be unfortunate with them, he would change his own name, thinking thus to bring about a cessation of sickness or death among his children. Thus he would call in an old man, spread robes on the ground and ask him to sit down, thereby presenting him with the robes. He then presented the old man with a pipe. The visitor now realized that he had been called for some particular purpose, and asked why he had been invited and what he might do that was in his power for the man.

Then the unfortunate man would reply about as follows: "I realize that you have enjoyed a successful life and good health and I wish that you may have good luck for the remainder of your life; and as you are getting old, I hope that your good fortune will continue. I have had bad fortune, and I desire to obtain your name." The old man then pronounced his own name and the other man bought it. The old man then stated that, for example, this name was given to him in childhood. He told how he got his name, and that throughout life he had always had good luck in everything, and he thought that as the young man took his name he also would enjoy good life. Then the name was transferred without ceremony, and the village crier was requested to go through the village and ask the people to give their attention. He then cried out that such and such a man had desired to have a new name to prevent sickness among his children; that he called an old man to his lodge and obtained the old man's name, and that hereafter he was to be known by this name. The old man either obtained a new name for himself or he went for the remainder of his days without a name, in which case he would be given a nickname, such as "Old-Man," "Old Woman," "Gray-Hair," "Dog Hair;" or he might say at once: "My name I have given to so and so, and I have given myself a new name."

Should a man meet death on the war-path, or die prematurely, his name was never mentioned. An instance is told of a man by the name of "Two," who died. After his death this word was never pronounced, but in expressing the numeral the sign language was used. If a person died through the influence of a witch, or if some one killed him because he had brought sickness upon some one, his name was not used, but he was referred to thereafter by a nickname, such as "Buffalo-Calf," "Corn-Bread," etc. Characteristic names in use to-day may be found in the names of the informants, given in footnotes to the myths.

During the early life of a girl she was closely watched, not only by the parents, but by relatives; as she grew older she was warned to have nothing to do with men, to keep away from them, and in the choice of a husband she was supposed to have no part. It being decided by the parents of some young man that a particular girl was desirable for a daughter-in-law, they asked some individual to go to the lodge to obtain the parents' consent. This go-between was usually a middle-aged woman and a relative of the boy. She asked of the girl's parents if they were willing that their daughter should marry, and in case of an affirmative answer the relatives of both families were called together. First, however, it was supposed that the parties had learned all about the boy, whether he was of good or bad reputation, and especially whether he was able to support a wife. The parents of the young man were informed that their proposition had been accepted, and the young man himself went to the lodge of the girl next evening. Should the parents of the girl still favor him he remained. Then, after this, the girl was watched, that she might not associate with other men. Should she prove unfaithful at any time she was beaten with a stick by her father. But should the parents of the girl at any time disapprove of their son-in-law they told the girl to send him home. This constituted divorce. The duty of the young man was to watch over the property of the family, and in the faithful fulfillment of these duties and in the providing of food rested his claim for favor with his wife's parents.

Again it might happen that the parents of a certain girl desired a certain young man for their son-in-law, in which case the girl's parents sent some middle-aged woman to ask the parents' consent for him.

Should the young husband die the girl's parents cut her hair, the length being determined by the favor in which they held the young man. The parents of the deceased husband might also visit her from time to time and cut off a portion of her hair. The girl remained single for a certain number of months, during which time she kept secluded and permitted her hair to remain uncombed. During this time she wore old clothes. After the requisite number of months had passed, the parents provided new clothing for the daughter. The parents of the deceased husband now went to the young widow's lodge. She, having been forewarned, had carefully swept the lodge. Upon entering, they washed her face, combed her hair, and painted her face, and then placed upon her, her new clothing. They then began to talk to her, telling her that they thought as much of her as when their son was alive, and now they had come to tell her that the period of mourning was over; that they had given her the things that they had brought; that she might laugh, eat heartily, and that now she might marry anyone she pleased. The woman, having her liberty, after the requisite period, might meet with some man whom she conversed with and who desired to marry her. She then reported the fact to her parents and to the parents of the deceased husband, in which case she was usually told that she might do as she liked. Should she have been faithful to her former husband during the time of mourning, her husband's parents then said that they thought just as much of her as when her husband was living, and they might take her and her new husband into their lodge. Occasionally a man might wish to marry a woman who had a brother, and who had been separated from her first husband by death, in which case, the suitor went to the brother and asked him if he might have his sister, taking with him a present, such as a robe or a bow and quiver full of arrows, on his pony.

The usual age of marriage among the girls was sixteen or more years, by which time she was supposed to be able to cook and look after the lodge, as well as to assist in the fields. The men were supposed to marry when old enough to be able to provide food and safety for a family.

During the period of the woman's monthly sickness the husband did not sleep under the same roof. She did not prepare food for him; otherwise he would suffer illness. Having recovered, the woman went at once to the river and bathed, and her relations with him were resumed as before.

Delivery was performed by old women especially trained for this purpose. After the birth of a child the husband did not enter the lodge of the child and mother until after four days; otherwise he would invite sickness, especially consumption, on his wife and child. Immediately after the birth some old woman was selected to take the child to the river and bathe it. She had to be well versed in the mythology of the tribe, and especially had to know the instruction given by the Moon to women when she instructed them about the birth of children. Arrived at the river she prayed to the Moon and Man-never-known-on-earth. Then she carried the child into the water, praying to all the gods in the water. She asked that the child might grow as fast as they did. The child's head was then sprinkled with water, after which it was immersed. On the appearance of the moon the child was taken outside of the lodge and held up to the moon, and a prayer was made that it might grow as she, the moon herself, grew from day to day.

The after-birth was always wrapped in a cloth and placed in a straight young elm tree—the elm because it produced splendid, straight offspring which grow well, and always seem prosperous. They prayed to the tree: "Keep this until it decays. I beg that the child which was in this may have power. May it grow like your children." The after-birth was never put on the ground, lest animals should harm it; nor was it thrown into the water, lest fishes should eat it, in which case the child would be sickly and die. In the story of After-Birth-Boy may be found another reason why the after-birth was never thrown into the water.

Shortly after the birth of the child the father looked about the village to discover some woman who had grown fast and who had always had good health. His choice having been made he went to the timber and cut twenty-four small, slender willow rods, the longest of which, to form the sides of the cradle, were cut first. Before the stick was cut he addressed it: "Now you were made to be used for many different purposes. I have now come to take your life. You are to be used for a cradle." Standing on the south, he cut the stick on the east side, then stepping to the west of the stick, he cut it on the south side. He then stepped to the north and cut it on the west side, and then he took hold of the stick and made it fall towards the north. He then trimmed the sticks and cut them into the proper length. During this time he neither sang nor made any noise. Having cut the twenty-four sticks, he returned home. He now decorticated the rods, carefully saving the bark. He dried and straightened the rods, and if any were too large he trimmed them down. The shavings also were carefully saved. The rods having been prepared he took them, together with the bark and shavings, to the woman he had selected. She took the bark and the shavings toward the north and hid them either in a tree or in the ground; otherwise the growth and health of the child would have been impaired. Returning to her lodge she took up the twenty-four rods, prayed to Man-never-known-on-Earth, then to the Moon, that as she made the cradle they would help her to make it in a proper manner, and that the child might grow rapidly. The sticks were then painted red or yellow and were bound together in the form of a flat mat by sinew from the back of the neck of a buffalo. As soon as the cradle was finished she took it to the parents, and handed it to the mother, telling her that she had finished the cradle; that while making it she had prayed to the maker of all things and to the moon; and that the moon would see to it that the child would grow rapidly and be healthy. As soon as the child began to walk the cradle was put aside and kept for future use in the same family. A cradle which had served for several children in one family, all of whom had been healthy, might be sought after by another family, believing that by the use of it their children would grow without sickness or any trouble. Should the child die during its cradle days the cradle was carried out and placed upon a tree, that it might never be used again.

A single form of burial was recognized among the Wichita. This varied slightly, according to the rank of the family of the deceased. Immediately after the death of a chief or of any prominent person, the parents or near relatives called upon some friend to take charge of the funeral. This friend invited three or four to assist him, and together they went to the burying ground, always situated on a near-by hill, and dug a grave, about four feet in depth. In the meantime the body had been bathed by other friends of the family and had been carefully dressed in suitable clothing, and the face was painted with the symbols which were the especial property of the individual in life. With the body were placed all war trappings except the shield, which was never buried, but was either turned over to some friend who might know its medicine, or was placed by the grave, or more generally, in a tree remote from the village. By the side of the body might be placed leggings by some relative or friend who asked the deceased to keep them for him. During this time the body had remained in the house, and was visited by all the relatives and friends of the family, who came to mourn over it. After two or three days' mourning the body was carried to the grave, the parents and near relatives remaining at home. Before placing the body in the grave a prayer was addressed to the earth by the one in charge of the ceremony: "Now you have been made to contain all things, to produce all things, and for us to travel over. Also we have been told to take care of everything which has come from your bosom, and we have been told that in your body everything should be buried. I now come to bury this man." The body was placed full length in the grave, with its head to the east, that when the spirit should rise it might without delay take the road which leads upward towards Spirit-Land. The body was then covered up. At each end of the grave was erected a forked upright about four feet in height, the forks being connected by a cross-bar. Against this cross-bar, with their lower ends resting against the sides of the grave, were uprights, thus entirely encircling the grave. The one in charge of the funeral rites then returned to the parents of the deceased and told them that he had finished, whereupon they might offer to take him into their family as son or brother, as the case might be.

Formerly it was the custom for one or more horses, especially the best horse of the deceased, if he had had many, to be slain by the side of his grave, or a horse, or many horses were given to his brother or to the one who assisted in the funeral rites. It is not known that slaves were ever killed at the time of the burial of a chief or prominent individual. It is told, however, that a well-known Wichita once lost his life in a fight with the Tonkawa, and that he was the owner of four Tonkawa slaves. One of these was put to death on the return of the war-party.

Death while in battle was held preferable to any other form of death among the Wichita. At least they preferred to die in full health and in some open place. Thus, a man injured in fighting would be told not to go into the timber to die, but to go out on the prairie, where the wolves would eat him. Should two individuals be about to die while in battle, they were told not to separate further than a crow could jump.

Immediately after burial the spirit of the dead was supposed to rise and ascend toward the east to Spirit-Land, the rank of the spirit in Spirit-Land being determined by that held by him while on earth.

To take one's own life was held to be the most dishonorable form of death, and the spirit of the suicide was supposed to wander just outside the entrance of Spirit-Land, not being able to enter and share in the pleasures of the village.

Between the time of the death and the burial the parents and friends continued to mourn, going about with uncombed hair and in ragged clothing. In the village no one was heard to sing or give evidence of joyfulness, and if the children were noisy they were hushed into silence. This continued for four days after the burial. On the morning of the fourth day a certain individual of the village, who must be of good character, informed the mourners that they must watch for them. He then selected two or three additional individuals of good character, and together they entered the lodge of the mourners, bearing a pipe and a wooden bowl. The inhabitants of the village had already been notified of the coming event and had gathered outside. As they entered the lodge the leader spread a robe on the ground, upon which he placed the mourners. Lighting the pipe he handed it to the father or next of male kin, and said: "I have come to tell you this. I have come to tell you to stop mourning. You have mourned long enough. Take my pipe and smoke. Thus you will signify that you have ceased to mourn." The pipe was passed to all the mourners, the father or the brother first. All of them smoked, thus signifying their assent, whereupon the leader turned to the people and told them that the mourners had accepted the pipe. He again talked to the mourners: "Now I want you to tell me what you have in your heart, to say how you feel. I want you to tell me that since you have smoked, the people in the camp may be allowed to sing and dance and be happy as heretofore; that you will release the camp from mourning; and that you yourselves will eat, enjoy life, and that we may enjoy life with you again." After giving their assent to this the whole village mourned for a few moments, then the leader wiped the tears from the mourners, told them to cease weeping, and took the bowl of water and washed their faces. Now followed the mourning feast, provided by friends of the mourners, after which the village returned to its normal condition. In case the deceased belonged to one of the singing societies, the members now at once went to the lodge of one of their number, sang four songs, mourned for a few minutes and then dispersed to their homes, and the entire village assumed its normal condition.

Often the leader of a returning war-party was obliged to admit to the village that he had not only failed to return with a scalp of the enemy, but that one of his own party had lost his life. Approaching the village, some man of the party was chosen to precede the war-party, and as he came within sight of the village he began to mourn. The village at once was on the alert and sent a servant to meet him, to see who had been killed. As soon as the servant learned the name of the unfortunate member of the party he returned to the silent village and called out the name, saying, "So and so has been killed in manly fashion." Immediately on such a return the head warrior went to the parents (or brother) of the warrior killed, and said to them: "I have been the leader of a party, and in this party was your son (or your brother) who lost his life. I failed to save him. Here I am. Do with me as you like, for it was my place to have brought him back to you alive." The person addressed said: "No, I do not deside to take your life," and going up to him, cut off the end of his hair and told him to go and live.

Everyone in the village now mourned, especially the near relatives of the one who was killed. The parents at once gave away all of their property, including that of the son, retaining only their oldest dresses for mourning costume. Now followed four days of mourning. Then a certain self-appointed man of the village, and he must be a brave man, undertook to bring about a cessation of mourning. He collected objects of various kinds, and clothing, for use in the forthcoming rite. On the morning of the fourth day he went with his bundle of clothing, etc., and a filled pipe, to the lodge of the mourners and seated them outside of the lodge. He took his pipe, lighted it and offered it to the head mourner, thus asking him to smoke, saying: "I want you to allow me to tell you that you must stop mourning. Tell me what you think in your heart. Shall the people go on mourning, or not? The people want to know. The people want you to tell them that you will stop mourning and permit them to sing and beat the drum and play." The head mourner took the pipe, smoked, and passed it to the other mourners, whereupon the leader said: "Here are your gifts, for your mourning has ceased. Now, then, mourn for a few minutes," whereupon he wiped away their tears and bathed their faces and then followed the feast as above. By so doing this individual had made it known to the village that within a short time he was going to lead a party on a war expedition, in which case, should he be successful in securing a scalp, he would give it to the mourners. In the meantime the life of all the members of the village was continued as before the death, except for the mourners. They continued to mourn in silence, however, and in their lodge, until he had returned victorious from a war expedition, with a scalp.

In the religious organization of the Wichita, the same liberality which is so characteristic of the tribe in general was strikingly manifested. While we find certain religious ceremonies in control of quasi-secret societies, they do not prove to be esoteric to the same extent as are those of the Pawnee. As a consequence, not only the salient features of their religious belief, but the mass of tribal lore constituting their mythology is open to all who can afford the slight compensation asked by the narrator of traditions.

While intensely conservative in many ways, as already pointed out, the religious ceremonies of the Wichita began many years ago to decline. This was largely due to the fact that the Wichita were a race of warriors, and their societies were largely concerned with acts of war. We do not find the extended and beautiful rituals, so characteristic of the Skidi and other bands of Pawnee, nor do we find, to any degree, extended ceremonies based upon the dramatization of myths, so characteristic of the tribes further to the west and south. Membership in all religious organizations seems to have been based almost entirely upon the wish of the individual. No organization is known to have existed the basis of membership in which was hereditary.

Standing at the head of the ceremonial societies was the deer dance, or the ceremony of the medicine-men. According to my informant, the last ceremony was performed in 1871. From my scant knowledge of the ceremony, it seems not to have been unlike that of the Skidi. No one could participate in the ceremony except medicine-men, each of whom had his own song or songs, in which was set forth the story of the origin of his magic power. In addition there were certain rituals sung, in connection with the opening and closing rites of the ceremony. The dance was held generally three, occasionally four, times a year; the first occasion when the grass had just appeared, the second when the corn was ripe, the third when the corn was harvested. The ceremony was never held in the winter. One of the special features of the ceremony was the administering to the novitiate of a small red bean, which produced a violent spasm, and finally unconsciousness, this condition being indicated by the inability of the novitiate to suffer pain when the jaw of a gar-pike was drawn over his naked body. During the ceremony offerings were made to the different gods, and at the end of the ceremony and following the feast was a ceremonial foot race, in which all members of the tribe, both male and female, were permitted to compete. This was followed on the part of those engaged in the ceremony by violent vomiting. The foot race was supposed to give the participants great endurance while on the war-path. The chief efficacy of the ceremony was the removal from the camp of all evil influences and the promoting of good health, long life, and general prosperity.

Next in importance was the ceremony of the calumet pipe sticks, during which feathered pipe-stems were carried to some chief or other prominent individual of the tribe or to some neighboring tribe. This ceremony abounded in ritual and had its origin in one of the early myths, and its performance was supposed to confer lasting benefit upon the tribe. It is claimed by the Wichita, and there is evidence that their claim is valid, that they originated this ceremony, and that it was obtained from them by the Skidi, who, in turn, passed it on to the other tribes of the Pawnee.

Next in importance, and having their origin in times comparatively modern in the legendary chronicles of the Wichita, were the rain bundle ceremonies, the first having to do with the maturation of the corn; the second with the propagation of the buffalo. The chanting of the rituals was the chief feature in both of these ceremonies, the time of the singing being marked by the drawing of a stick over a notched club, one end of which rested on a buffalo rawhide resonator. Both had their origin in the animal gods.

Next in importance were two ceremonies similar in nature, and known as "Surround-Fire," and "Small-Robes." These ceremonies also were of ritualistic nature, the first having its origin in the stars, and the second from the animals. The performance of both ceremonies was supposed to be efficacious in obtaining certain power or magic from various animals.

Next in rank were two societies, the first known as the Many-Dogs, and the second as the Horn. The time of the origin of these societies, like that of the rain and buffalo, was comparatively recent. They may be characterized as singing societies, in which ritualistic songs were sung, and they were preparatory to the setting out of a war-party.

Forming the last group were certain ceremonies or dances, all of which had more or less to do with the return of the successful war-parties. These were the Scalp, the "Etwats," the Rubbing-Bone, the Turkey, the Squng, the Singers, and the Flat, the last four being danced exclusively by the women.

In addition to the ceremonies just enumerated, the Wichita played the well-known forms of games common to the other Plains tribes, but always in a ceremonial manner. Among the most noted and sacred of these games were the shinny, the double-ball, and the ring-and-javelin games.

The religious system of the Wichita, like that of the Pawnee, though to a less extent, may be characterized as a star cult. The chief of all the gods is Man-never-known-on-Earth, who, as is related in the first myth, was the creator of the universe, and to him is made the first offerings, both of food and of smoke. Next in importance and dignity is the Sun, who not only gives his light, but assists in the growth of everything and in keeping the earth fresh and sweet.

Closely following the Sun in importance is the Morning-Star, whose duty it is to drive the stars along and keep them in place, especially to usher in the daylight.

Next in importance is the South-Star, the protector of warriors and of chiefs.

The next in rank is the North or Pole-Star, who stands still, and out of regard to the people on earth, at night, he shows them which way is north. He is the guardian of the medicine-men, who derive their powers from him, and who in their ceremonies give smoke to him before recognition is made of the other gods.

Next in importance are the stars of the Great Bear. Their powers are not unlike those of the Sun and the Morning-Star. They are made to circle about the North-Star, and are to be prayed to, for in their hands is placed power to be given to those who pray to them, especially to those who are about to undertake a war expedition. It is said that those who pray to them and follow their direction will have good luck and have a prosperous expedition.

Next in importance is a star in the north known as the "Ghost-Bear." This star is of comparatively recent origin, for it is said that a certain man who traveled in the far north saw a human being standing before him, who said to him: "This is my burial place. I live in the far north. There I live. Should you like some of my power, and should you accept whatever I offer you I will give you power. You shall have the power over the herbs to cure people, for I am a medicine-man. If an accident should happen, or if sickness should arise, I will give you a way to heal, and in your doctoring you should look to the Sun, for my powers are derived from him. Before you begin doctoring, offer me smoke." Thereupon the man was informed that it was the Ghost-Bear who was talking to him, and upon looking again he saw that it was a Ghost-Bear. The man looked back and the Ghost-Bear had become a star.

Flint-stone-lying-down-above is the next in importance in the Wichita pantheon. This star, which is said to be immediately overhead, and which can not be seen except in a moonless night, is always to be prayed to as one of the important gods. Smoke and food are also to be offered to him, inasmuch as we know, according to the tales, that while upon earth he took pity upon the people, that they might have good fortune, live long, be free from sickness, and have good success in war.

The Moon is the special guardian of the women, for she is a woman and possesses all the powers which women desire. She it was who taught the first woman on earth and gave her power. She instructs the women as to the time of the monthly sickness, informs them when they are pregnant, and when the child is to be born, and has told them that after birth the child must be offered to her by passing the hands over the child's body and raising it aloft, offering it to the Moon, at which time she is asked to bestow her blessing upon the child, that he may grow into power rapidly, for she herself has the power to increase rapidly in size. Furthermore, she regulates the increase not only of human beings, but of all animals, birds, and plants.

Somewhat similar in her power to the Moon is the woman known as "Woman-having-Powers-in-the-water (Otskahakakaitshoidiaa). She it is who has power over the water. She is chief of all water potencies and things living in the water. She not only furnishes drink, but cleanses and heals the people by the action of water. The child is taken to her at birth and she bestows upon it the power to grow to old age. She is also the special guardian of the wife left at home when her husband has gone on the war-path. She it is who encourages her to remain virtuous, and thereby make sure of the good fortune of her husband while on his journey. Thus the wife repairs to the river in the morning, just as the Morning Star rises, and also late in the evening, and bathes secretly. As she goes to the river she wears a new skirt of buffalo drawn up tightly over her shoulders and held at her waist by a buffalo hair lariat rope, while her feet are encased in moccasins tightly wrapped with rawhide strings. These she changes each night before retiring. Again, putting on her costume early in the morning, as before, she hastens to the river and during this time, at any meal, she eats only four spoonfuls.

Next in power and in reverence is Mother-Earth, who gives birth to everything, is mother of everything, who keeps everything, even her bosom for the people to walk upon. Prayers are offered to the earth before journeys: "As I start on this journey, and as I take this first step, carry me through to the end of my journey." She is also a great medicine chest, keeping upon her body various roots, etc., used in healing: "We are children of the earth, and as we go on a journey it means that we are like children crawling upon our mother, and as we exist upon the earth we are kept alive by her breath, the wind, and at the end of our time we are put in the ground in the bosom of our mother."

Prayers are also offered to the god of the Wind, which is breath, and hence life. Especially in case of sickness, prayers are frequently offered to the Wind god: "Now, good Wind, I ask you to come and breathe on me, so that I may be healed and feel comfortable. I pray you, good Wind, enter me, so I may breathe and be healed."

Finally, offerings and prayers are made to the animals, especially to those which are supposed to have magic power, and which are the special guardians of the medicine-men. Thus, in the ceremony of the medicine-men, after the novitiate has been placed in a trance, he usually holds speech with some fierce wild animal, who visits him and instructs him—should he prove brave and not become scared. Thus he obtains power which he uses in doctoring, and in his songs, sung during the medicine-men's ceremony, he tells of his experience with the animal.

In general, the gods of the Wichita are spoken of as "dreams," and they are divided into four groups: Dreams-that-are-Above (Itskasanakatadiwaha), or, as the Skidi would say, the heavenly gods; and (2) Dreams-down-Here (Howwitsnetskasade), which, according to the Skidi terminology, are the earthly gods. The latter "dreams" in turn are divided into two groups: Dreams-living-in-Water (Itskasanidwaha), and the Dreams-closest-to-Man (Tedetskasade).

The myths of the Wichita tell of the story of the origin of the world, its transformation, its present existence, and foretell its end. There are thus recognized four distinct eras or epochs in the history of this earth, these four to be replaced by another four in future years. In this scheme the succession of events in these four eras may be categorically stated as follows: In the first era, that of creation, appears the land floating upon water, the first man and woman, who were given an ear of corn and a bow and arrows. Darkness still wanders over the earth. The shooting of the third of three deer ushers in the daylight, and certain stars are seen. Then follows the promise of more people, and when day appears the promise is fulfilled, for villages are seen, and animals. Then the first creatures are instructed. The first man lives to become the Morning Star, and the first woman, having, like her husband, wandered from one village to another giving instruction and power, becomes the Moon.

In the second period, that of the transformation, the people scatter out over the earth. They again learn of their power and of their nature. Especially do they begin to give themselves names, turn by groups into the animals whose names they have taken, or, should they not give themselves a name, remain as human beings. Certain ones during this period forget their duties. Everything seems to have gone wrong, and both planets and animals overstep the bounds of respectability. This period of change and unrest and of transformation finally culminates in a woman giving birth to four monsters whose heads tower upwards toward the heavens. To destroy them and other insolent creatures is sent the deluge, which marks the termination of the second period.

The third period, or the present, was inaugurated by the survival of two individuals after the deluge. They again are provided with corn and the bow and arrows, and are taught the use of various implements, as well as the construction of the lodge. These two degenerate, and teach their offspring concerning the times of the ancients. People do as they were taught, and are given power by the animals. During the early days of this period the people were not only taught the mysteries of the animals, and were told that they could exercise great powers, but they were told that they would have to die, whereupon, on the return of a certain individual from a journey to Spirit-Land, they learned of the other world and the consequent belief in life after death.

The fourth period, or the end, which the Wichita suppose to be rapidly approaching, is known as "Things-running-short" (Wadawakahitstsiaitsquawaskina), or "When-everything-begins-to-run-out" (Dakawaitsakakide). The belief in the end of the world as now believed by the Wichita, has prevailed from early creation, for even then it was foretold. At the end, the supply of the necessaries of life will run short. People will no longer accomplish anything. As the time approaches Mother-Corn will cease to grow, and in her stead will appear some despised weed. At that time, animals will begin to speak to men, even the trees and flowing water will talk. Children of the same families will intermarry and cease to have offspring, and this is to be one of the indications of the approaching end, for they will lose their judgment. The animals will cease to reproduce their kind, and human beings likewise will give birth to animals. The old world will be completely worn out and no longer fit to be inhabited. Furthermore, the man who has been following the three deer throughout the ages, when the end approaches, will overtake the deer, for he has been following them since the beginning, in order to recover his arrow, and it is believed that he is drawing nearer to them.

The end having arrived, some great star will return to earth and will pick out some man who is of a kind disposition to explain to the people what is about to take place. Then all the stars and the sun and the moon will be human beings again, as in the first days. Thereupon will begin a new cycle of four eras; another world will be created; another transformation period will follow, and other generations will live as have lived the generations of the present era.

The belief that this period is approaching is strong among the Wichita, for they say they are no longer surrounded by the animals which they formerly made use of in so many ways. Everything seems to be different from what it used to be. There are no more wild flowers or green trees. Nothing seems to grow any more. Even the fowls of the air have disappeared, and they were forewarned that their disappearance would be a sign that the end was near at hand. Furthering this belief is the frequency with which the people in their dreams converse with stars. Another evidence that the world is getting old and going the other way, is the realization that the tribe is constantly growing smaller and that, like the offspring of the pair saved out of the deluge, they will soon be obliged to intermarry.

The myths of the Wichita naturally refer to the first two epochs of the world's history, and are spoken of as "old" or "true" tales; while those which refer to the present period are spoken of as "new."

In relating the various myths no order, as a rule, is followed, for, on account of their great length, generally not more than one or two are told in a night. Should it seem desirable, however, on the part of the teller, to follow some order, he bases his scheme not only upon what he considers to be good chronological order, but one which in its relation to the happenings of events preserves the order followed by the sun in its course, for this was the scheme of creation. Hence the gods of the east take precedence over those of the south, while those of the south take precedence over those of the west and north.

Instruction concerning the time of creation and transformation is considered by all Wichita parents as conferring a lasting benefit upon their children. Hence it is their custom to invite to their lodge some man, generally of advanced years, who is known throughout his life to have been upright, kind, and brave, to relate the deeds of the ancient heroes. Not only was the rehearsal of these tales looked upon as a form of worship, as a prayer to the gods and heroes which still exist, but by the relating of their acts the young men and women of the household were led to believe that they, too, might become great and good.

It was customary before the beginning of a tale to offer a sacrifice of smoke to all the gods as human beings, addressing them to the effect that the teller was about to relate the story of their life; for these gods had said while human beings that if anyone should tell correctly the story of their life, such narrators would receive benefit, and that on the following day a sign would be given them if they had not misrepresented their life, the sign being a light fog early on the following morning. Should a night of story telling in winter be followed by a day of excessive cold it would be said that the story teller had not told his tale properly, or that he had told a tale which he should not have told. At the end of the story the narrator, especially should he have followed as nearly as may be in the footsteps of the hero whose life he is recounting, often weeps, and the young listeners strike their front teeth with the nail of the thumb, thus indicating their desire that their teeth may always be sound, and that, having heard the story, they may live happily and enjoy good luck and live to old age and do wonderful deeds, such as were performed by the hero of the tale. Then followed the offering of food and smoke by the narrator to the heroes of the tales he had just recounted, the smoke offering being first made. Then, taking a pinch of food, he raised it aloft and asked Man-never-known-on-Earth to accept the offering. This he now placed at the foot of the fire crane. He then offered food to the east to the Morning-Star; to the south to the South-Star, the protector of warriors; to the west, the home of the meteors; to the north to the Pole-Star and the Seven; and then to Mother-Earth.

In general, it may be said that the object of relating stories of ancient times was that the listeners might have recalled for them the fact that evil creatures and monsters, and in general the evil spirits of the world no longer exist; that they were removed from the earth; that their destructive powers were taken from them by Wonderful-Man, who knew that the world was changing, so that human beings might be human beings and animals exist as animals, to serve as food for man. But above all, the value of the stories for the young, lay in the lesson taught by example that bravery and greatness were something which depended upon individual effort, no matter how low or mean might have been his origin, and at the same time, that there might descend upon him the same longevity and good fortune as was possessed by the hero of the tale.

THE FIRST PERIOD: CREATION.

1. THE FIRST CREATION.*

In the times of the beginning there was no sun, no stars, nor anything else as it is now. Time passed on. Man-never-known-on-Earth (Kinnekasus) was the only man that existed, and he it was who created all things. When the earth was created it was composed of land and water, but they were not yet separated. The land was floating on the water, and darkness was everywhere. After the earth was formed, Man-never-known-on-Earth made a man whose name was Having-Power-to-carry-Light (Kiarsidia). He also made a woman for the man, and her name was Bright-Shining-Woman (Kashatskihakatidise). After the man and the woman were made they dreamed that things were made for them, and when they woke they had the things of which they had dreamed. Thus they received everything they needed. The woman was given an ear of corn, whose use she did not know, but this was revealed to her in her heart; that it was to be her food; that it was Mother-Corn; that it was to be the food of the people who should exist in the future, to be used generation after generation; that from Mother-Corn the people should be nursed. Still they were in darkness, not knowing what was better than darkness.

Once upon a time it came into the mind of Having-Power-to-carry-Light that he should go toward the east. He went further and further, not knowing where or why, but still wanting to find out what he was after. He kept on until he came to a grass-lodge. He found somebody existing on the earth besides himself. As he entered the grass-lodge there was light. He saw the man of the grass-lodge. This man of the grass-lodge said to him: "Well, I have brought you here. I put it in your mind to come this way and visit me. Therefore, you are here, and I am told to tell you of some things that are to come to pass. You have always thought you were the only person living, but I am here too. I have been created the same as you. The man that creates things is about to improve our condition. Villages shall spring up and more people will exist, and you will have power to teach the people how to do things before unknown to them." While they were talking they heard a voice from the east, saying: "Hurry, you men in the grass-lodge! Come out with your arrows and shoot the deer that are now starting

*Told by Towakoni Jim (Towakoni.)

out to your shore!" The man of the grass-lodge replied to the voice: "All right, I will be ready to meet the deer, but I have not yet made my arrows, nor have I got my bow. I must cut and make these first." The man of the grass-lodge went and cut the bow and arrows. Again the voice came, saying: "Hurry, the deer are about to land on the shore that you are on. You are not to shoot the white deer or the black deer, but shoot the last one, that is half black and half white." The man replied: "All right, I will have my bows and arrows ready for him." The man peeled the bark off from his arrows and dried them. The voice came again, telling him to make haste and finish the arrows. The man of the grass-lodge again answered, telling how much he had done on the arrows, and that he was feathering them. After a time the voice came again, saying: "Hurry!" The man of the grass-lodge said: "I have my arrows ready, but I have yet to put on the string." After he had put on the string the voice came again, and said: "The deer are about to land." The two men went out and saw the deer coming out of the water toward them. When they got to the bank the white and black deer jumped out, and as it was jumping out the man of the grass-lodge shot it. After shooting it he heard a voice from above, saying he had done well. This meant that everything would move, that the sun would rise, the stars would move, and the darkness and the light would move on. After shooting the deer he followed all of the deer. Now the voice was heard from above, saying: "You have done the right thing." The white deer went ahead, then the black one, then the one that was wounded. The man of the grass-lodge followed them. This man now became Star-that-is-always-moving (Kinnihequidiki-dahis). Having-Power-to-carry-Light stayed there after the other man had left to follow the deer. By shooting the deer that was half black and half white it was signified that there should be days and nights. Having-Power-to-carry-Light, as he stood there, looked toward the east, where he heard the voice telling what to do, and there he saw a man standing across the water on the other shore, who said that thereafter he should be called Reflecting-Man (Sakidawaitsa), the sun. The man on the other shore thought that as he should be known as the sun, he would give light, that he would be seen at all times by the people and give them light, and by his powers he would aid them in having great powers. After looking, Having-Power-to-carry-Light looked back at the man who had been speaking to him and he was gone; but he saw the sun coming up. He then turned back to his home. As he went along he began to find out the object of his visit to the grass-lodge. This he liked very much. He had light to travel in and could see a long way. He found that light was better than darkness. On his way back home he found he could travel faster than he could travel in darkness. In a very short time he reached his home. When he got home the sun went down and darkness followed, and he saw up in the sky three stars coming up, followed by a single star. Having-Power-to-carry-Light made up his mind that the three stars were the three deer and that the other star coming behind was the man that had wounded the deer. The three stars represented the three deer as they had come out of the water, while the fourth star, which came later, represented the man who had wounded the deer.

This was a new start for the man and the woman. They enjoyed this kind of life better than living in darkness. Time went on, and Having-Power-to-carry-Light saw that the promises which were made by Man-never-known-on-Earth to Star-that-is-always-moving were being fulfilled. He saw villages springing up. There were more people existing, and this was as had been promised.

After these things had happened the man and the woman went from one village to another, showing the people how to use the things they had, how to make them, and what to use them for. The people in the village had things that they knew nothing about, and they did not hitherto know how to make or use them. They simply knew that they were existing as human beings. They knew neither where they had come from nor how to live. The woman and the man were greatly helped by the day. Having-Power-to-carry-Light then began his work among the men, teaching them what bows and arrows were; that the bow was a weapon of great strength; that the arrow was a thing to shoot and kill game with. He gave the men a ball, smaller than the shinny ball. He told them that this ball was to be used to amuse themselves with; that the men were to play together and the boys were to play together. Whenever a child was born, if it was a boy, this kind of ball was to be given to it, that he might observe it and learn how to move around. The ball had a string to it. The further the ball rolled— that is, the older the child should get, the faster it would move around. He went on and taught the men how to play the game, for the people were ignorant and did not know what the things were for. Finally the men were shown how the ball should be used. He showed them the clubs for the shinny game. He told them they should be divided equally in the game, one party on one side and the other party on the other side. Many men were interested, for the game was new to them. Many of the men were fast on their feet. The game was to be won by the side that should get the ball to the goal first. Having-Power-to-carry-Light also told them how to travel with the arrows and ball. This marks the time when they learned to travel fast from one place to another. The men went out hunting animals after they had been taught that animals existed for their use, and they traveled with their arrows and ball. They would shoot an arrow in the direction they wanted to go, then would go with the arrow as it went up. This is the way they traveled. They would hit the ball and as it flew the person would be on the ball. When the ball would hit the ground they would hit it again, and so they would go from place to place. Having-Power-to-carry-Light traveled like a spirit. When he heard of a place he would be right there, but the people who were made after him were a little slower in traveling. This sort of traveling was fast enough for these people. From this place he went to other places, and he taught the people how to use things. He would make the things for them at first, then would teach them how the things were made.

When the woman began her work among the women she gave them Mother-Corn, and told them that this was theirs, and this was their mother; that from this time they should be nursed; that with the use of Mother-Corn they could live and it would strengthen the young ones; that Mother-Corn was to be used as long as the world should last. There were no certain times for the women to plant the corn, because the time passed pretty fast. When the women planted their corn it would grow right up and they would gather their corn at once. The Moon told the women that whenever Mother-Corn was eaten by them, whether ground or dry, they must offer some food to Man-never-known-on-Earth. Then they were to eat of it, and as a prayer for blessing before eating of the food they were to take four kernels of corn and rub them over the child. These were the Moon's instructions to the woman. Things progressed very rapidly. The young ones grew quickly. The woman told the women that Mother-Corn should be used for many different purposes. She gave them the things that they should use to enjoy themselves—namely, the double-ball game. She showed them how to play the game and told them that the ball was for their use in traveling. Now she told them the time was drawing near when she would have to leave them, for she had gone from one place to another, showing the women what to do, how to travel, how to raise Mother-Corn, how they must eat it and offer it, in all the ways that Mother-Corn was to be used. She told the women that after she had become something else she would ask the people, especially the women, to look upon her once in a while. She said that by her face women should be able to tell their condition; by their monthly flow, whether they were pregnant or not. She was to show herself a certain number of times, and by keeping count they might know what time the child would be born. She said that when she made her appearance the parents of the young child should turn its face toward her, implying a prayer, and asking her that the child might grow as fast as she did. By keeping track of the days and the months and the seasons they could foretell what things were about to happen. After the woman had given all these instructions to the women, telling them how to make their offerings to her and to the stars and other heavenly bodies, and all the important supernatural beings of the earth, she told the women that she had all their powers and they were to know their conditions at all times, through her. She then told the women she would be seen after the sun had gone down, then she disappeared. Late that evening after the sun had gone down, they saw her in the sky, and she had become the Moon.

Now, the man told the men that they, in bringing their game from the hunt, must offer to the moon, to the stars, and other heavenly bodies and to the important supernatural beings on the earth. After he had told them how to use all the other things he said he would have to leave them and become something else. He had told them all the things they were to have, to use and to do, that there was a place for him to go and that he was about to go to that place. He told them that when he should go to his place he would show himself early in the morning, before daylight, and if, at that time, people should take their children to the nearest flowing water and put them in the water and bathe them (but they must drink before bathing them) he might help them to grow up and enjoy life. He told them that that place was the one at which they would get powers that he would give them. He then told them that he would sometimes be seen in the early morning as a star, and sometimes as a human being, and that his name was to be known as the First-Star-seen-after-Darkness-passes-by (Hoseyasidaa).

THE SECOND PERIOD: TRANSFORMATION.

2. THE DEEDS OF THE COYOTE AND YOUNG-STAR.*

At this time the Coyote was living out by himself with his family. Of course, he was the same as ever and would often go hungry, for he could not kill much game. Once upon a time when the Coyote was going out to wander around after food he found a boy. He asked the boy where he was going. The boy replied that he was going nowhere. The Coyote then asked if he might take him to his home to play with his boy and live with his family. The boy agreed to live with the Coyote's family. For a long time he lived with them. Through the powers of the boy, the Coyote did not have to go very far when hunting; everything seemed easier than before the boy had come to live with him. The Coyote, being smart in some respects, commenced to find out what sort of a boy it was that was staying with him. At times Young-Star would foretell what was going to happen, and it would come true every time. So the Coyote thought that the boy was wonderful, although he was about the age of his own boy. The boy would leave his home for a time, then come back again. Sometimes the Coyote would ask him where he came from before he came to his home. The boy would never tell him where he was from, but would tell the Coyote he thought he ought to know from the name he bore. The boy kept leaving his home with his little companion. One time while they were out playing they kept on going east, and there they found a black horse (kawara). The boy, being wonderful, caught the horse and using his bow-string for a lariat, rode it. But he was unable to get the young Coyote to ride the horse, for it was something he had never seen. They took the horse home with them. On their arrival the Coyote was frightened at sight of the wonderful animal. The boy tied the horse near their home and forbade anyone to go near it, for fear it would be scared by their scent. While all of the Coyote family were in the lodge the boy stepped out to see if his horse was still tied. When he saw that it was tied he stopped just outside for a moment and heard the Coyote talking about the horse, telling his family that it was a dangerous animal to be kept by their home. He was talking especially to the young ones, telling them not to go near the horse, for it had a long face and it surely must have long teeth, too, and that the horse's body was long enough to permit of its swallowing anybody. The Coyote also said that perhaps the boy had brought the fierce animal there to eat them up. The boy listened to the Coyote, and thought to himself, "What foolish ideas he has, and what a big coward he is to fear the horse." Now, the boy went in and the Coyote stopped talking about the dangerous animal. The boy then began to tell about the horse and what it was used for, for he and his brother (for so he called his young Coyote companion) had often been off a long way and got tired, but when the time should come for them to go again they could ride the horse, and that would be far better than traveling afoot, and perhaps the Coyote could ride it when going after game, for this horse was as good a runner as any animal living. The Coyote then began to tell his family about the horse and how harmless it was.

Long afterward, after the young Coyote had learned to ride the horse, the old Coyote commenced to think about moving to the village, just to show off his wonderful boy and the wonderful animal they had. The Coyote told his family that he wanted to leave their old home and move to the village to live. The family was now pretty well acquainted with the horse, and when the time came to move away the boy let them ride it. He intended that they should take turns riding the horse, for the family was very large. As they started off toward the village the boy said he would go off a while to see about something out toward the east. The Coyote family started toward the southeast. They took along the horse and put a big load on it, including the old woman and the children. They came to a steep canyon. The Coyote asked the boy's little companion whether the horse could travel over a steep place. The little Coyote said the horse could go over any kind of a place, very easy. So the Coyote allowed the family to remain on the horse while he whipped it to make it jump across the canyon. The horse did not want to go over the place, but the Coyote kept whipping it, and finally it jumped, and off went the Coyote's family, into the steep place, and the Coyote was left standing there. After a time the horse came out of the canyon and started toward the place where he was found. Just then the boy came in sight, but not near enough to call to the Coyote. He had forgot to tell the Coyote to look for a low place when he wanted to cross a canyon with a loaded horse, but now it was too late to say anything about it. When the boy came up with the Coyote he asked him why he had not looked for a better place to cross the canyon, but there was the Coyote's family lying in the canyon, all dead. The boy then told the Coyote to go right on to the village and he would go with him. He told the Coyote that it was his mistake and not that of the horse that he had tried to get the horse to cross. They traveled all day and reached the village in the evening. The Coyote knew all the time that he would be treated well, since he had a son that was wonderful. When they came to the edge of the village there was some one standing there whom the Coyote asked where visitors were received. The person directed him to the largest tipi, in the middle of the village, which was the chief's place. They went straight to the chief's tipi. When they got there the chief told them to sit on the west side of the tipi. It was the cusom of the chief to give visitors something to eat, so he fed them. The Coyote noticed that the chief had four pretty sisters, whom he desired for wives. At the chief's place, according to custom, men met to sit up at night and pass the time and talk about the past. There were a good many men at the place. About midnight all of the men went home, and the Coyote and his adopted son went to bed. The next morning, after they had eaten their breakfast, the adopted son told the Coyote to go to a certain place towards the north to some timber and there he would find a man and his sister living out by themselves, for whose power he should beg. The Coyote went as directed, and when he arrived at the edge of the timber he saw a tipi. In the tipi was the man and his sister, and they each had a blue complexion. The Coyote walked into the tipi and was asked to be seated and to explain the object of his visit. The Coyote said he had come that the man might take pity on him and give him the same powers he had, so that he might be like him. The man told the Coyote he must first have a bow and arrows; that he would have to go and cut dogwood for arrows; that he himself had a bow he did not use that the Coyote could have. The man told the Coyote to go into the dogwood timber and call out to the dogwoods, "Which one of you shall I cut?" saying that the one first to say "Me," he must cut; that he must do this four times, because he was to cut four arrows. The Coyote then went to the edge of the dogwood timber, stopped and called out, "Which one of you shall I cut?" The dogwoods all at once commenced to halloo, "Me! Me!" The Coyote did not know what to do, and in order to satisfy all of them he cut as many as he could and carried an armful of them to the man in the tipi. When he went into the tipi the man asked him why he could not tell which one of the dogwoods said "Me!" first. The Coyote said that all of them had hallooed at once. So the man selected four of the dogwoods himself, and he told the Coyote to take the remainder of them back and pitch them into the timber. The Coyote did as he was told. He then went back and found the arrows ready made for him. Then the Coyote was told what to do and what not to do. Besides the bow and arrows the Coyote was given a shield and a war-bonnet. The man told the Coyote that upon his arrival at the big tipi of the chief he should not think about any woman while he had these things that were given him; that four times, at daybreak, the enemy were to attack the village; that he and his son would have to do all the fighting, for the reason that he was given power to run faster than any man but his son; that he must not think about women until the end of these four days, when he might do as he pleased about the women. The man asked the Coyote if he was honest and brave. Of course, the Coyote could not deny that he was honest and brave, so he said he was the most honest and the bravest man he knew of. Now, the man told the Coyote to stand up. The man then touched the Coyote's eyes with his hands and rubbed them, and when he took his hands from the Coyote's eyes he asked the Coyote what he could see. The Coyote said: "I see everything." The Coyote was now like the man in countenance, and he had the blue complexion of the man. The man told the Coyote that he could not be hit by enemies, for he himself was that way. The man said to the Coyote, "It may be that you have heard about the Jay-Birds (Keats). I belong to that class of people." This was the man from whom the Coyote got his powers.

The Coyote now returned to the big tipi of the chief. Upon his arrival he put his things away. The chief told him he might stay in the same lodge with his sisters. The Coyote was glad of the privilege. His son was not pleased that the chief should give him the privilege of sleeping in the same place with the chief's sisters, lest the Coyote should disobey the orders given him by the man with the blue complexion; for the boy had already learned that the Coyote was dishonest, and he had no confidence that the Coyote would abstain from that which had been forbidden him. That night the Coyote went early to bed and the women commenced to talk about him and tell about their wishes, and they were full of wishes. The Coyote had it in mind to avoid the women until four days should pass. However, he lay awake a part of that night listening to the women tell about how good-looking he was, and saying there was no doubt but that they themselves were good-looking. Finally the Coyote went to sleep, and the next morning he heard some one crying that the enemy were attacking their village. He immediately rose from his bed, and as he was about to go through the door, there stood one of the women, who caught him and asked him his name. He told her that his name was Owner-of-Flint-Knife-Quarries (Tahanetshedaehetsiwe). He finally got loose and went on to the scene of the battle. He saw his son in front. When they each had killed four of the enemy's bravest men they turned back to the village. Each had a scalp, which they presented to the chief. As the sun rose higher everybody came in and the news began to spread about the chief's visitors doing the first part of the fighting and killing the enemy's bravest men. Of this the Coyote was very proud. There were three more battles to be fought. The Coyote began again to think about the chief's sisters and of what one of them had already done to him. He thought that the rest of the women would also do the same thing. The boy knew all about this, for he could read the Coyote's thoughts, and he also knew from the man who had given him his powers. As soon as the sun went down the victory dances commenced. The Coyote was in the midst of the dancing. When he was tired of dancing he went to bed. All the sisters of the chief were after him, as well as a good many other women, for they knew that he had had the largest share of the winning of the battle. All the songs sung were about him. When he went to bed he would pay no attention to the women, but he was not over mindful of the command he had received to avoid the women until the four battles were accomplished. He went to bed and to sleep. The women bothered him, but he would pay them no attention. Early the next morning he again heard the same alarm as on the preceding morning. He started out, and again there was one of the women who called to him and said: "Hanging-Knife (Tahatsawi) must remember me this time." The Coyote turned around, and said: "You are spoiling my name. That is not my name. My name is Owner-of-Flint-Knife-Quarries." The Coyote now went to the place where the fighting was and saw his son. They performed as on the day before, and each took four scalps, which they presented to the chief. About the same time the people began to come back and tell the people at home what the chief's visitors had done. The chief was proud of the visitors' good names and brought their names before the people. When it was dark they again had dances. The Coyote took part, and when he retired from the dance he got into the bed of one of the chief's sisters and slept all night with her. Early in the morning another alarm was given that the enemy were attacking the village. The Coyote went out and took his place with his son in the front, and again they killed four of the enemy's bravest men. When the enemy retreated the warriors on the Coyote's side began to chase them. The Coyote and his son turned back home, having secured each a scalp for the chief. On the delivery of the scalp to the chief the Coyote noticed on the body of the woman he had slept with, blue marks where he had lain upon her and where he had had his arms around her. He noticed at the same time that some of the blue had disappeared from himself. He thought that if he should sleep with all of the women all of them would turn blue the same as he was. Now, he wanted to lie with the other three women during the night. He waited patiently for night to come. The three women were thinking the same as did the Coyote, for they wanted to sleep with him. In the early part of the night the Coyote and his son both went to join in the dancing. The boy knew that the Coyote was doing wrong. The Coyote did not think his powers could be taken away from him unless the blue complexioned man saw him. He forgot that the blue complexioned man had told him that the bow and arrows had lives in them and that whatever he might do they would know about and that they would escape from him. While the dance was going on the Coyote slipped away and went right to the place where he was staying and got in bed. When the three women noticed that he had left the scene of the dance they also left. On the arrival at their place the Coyote told them that he was going to sleep with them one at a time during the night. Each took her turn in sleeping with the nice-looking man that they thought him to be. As he was lying with each of these women the Coyote heard his arrows and bow talking about his failure to keep his agreement and about making their escape. He heard every word they spoke. He was worried by what they said. The whole night he did not sleep a wink, and finally towards morning he heard the wind blowing. It seemed to him that the wind came inside of the lodge. He and the woman with him fell sound asleep. When the other women got up they saw the last woman to sleep with the Coyote sleeping with a real coyote. When they awakened their sister and asked her to look at what she was sleeping with she looked at him and there was this coyote lying on her side with his arm around her. She screamed and wakened the coyote. He arose from the bed, looked at himself and saw that he had a long tail, long ears, and was no longer a man. He escaped at once from the place. But he had already caused all of the women to be pregnant. The news spread of the Coyote losing his powers through disobedience. His powers went back to the man from whom he had obtained them.

The boy now told the chief to assemble his people. The chief called the people about his place. They asked the chief why he had called them. The chief told them that the Coyote's adopted son, who was known as Young-Star, had something to say to them. The chief told the people to listen to him. Young-Star was then asked what he had to say to the people. He told them that since he had been living among them he had done all he could to help them along on the war-path; but because of what his father had done he could no longer stay with them; that he was going to leave his bow, arrows, and other things and his powers, to be used by all the warriors; that they could pattern after these weapons in making others, which would be just as good; that when first they came to the village he had ordered his father to go to a certain place to secure what powers he had had, and which he had lost through foolishness, and that for this reason he was not to remain with them; that generation after generation they would see him mornings as the Morning Star, just as he used to be while human. Young-Star then left some of his powers upon earth for the people. He was a small boy and when on the war-path he would put on a white feather. This is the way Young-Star left the village. Early the next morning he was seen, and he has ever since been known as First-Star-seen-after-Darkness-passes-by (Hoseyasidaa), that is, Morning-Star.

3. THE COYOTE AND HIS MAGIC SHIELD AND ARROWS.*

Once upon a time there lived the Coyote with his family. He lived by wandering around, hunting all sorts of game, but he never was lucky enough to kill enough game to last long, for he had so many children that they ate the meat as fast as he could bring it. Once upon a time he went towards the west, where he found a man living by himself. He walked up to this place, stopped outside, and the man called to him to step in. The Coyote stepped in and was asked to be seated, so he sat down. The Coyote looked around inside of this man's lodge and he saw many things, such as meat of all kinds. The man asked him if he wanted anything to eat. The Coyote said that he would eat some meat. The man put a big pile of meat before the Coyote and he commenced to eat. When he had eaten all the meat he thanked the man for what he had eaten. The Coyote saw a pole stuck up outside of this man's place, and he asked the man what that was. The man replied that it was his shield. The Coyote begged the man to give him the shield or one like it. The man told the Coyote that he could direct him how to make one like it if he would come back the next day. Before leaving, he was given a big pile of meat to take home with him. He started back home with the load of meat on his back. He arrived at his place and told his old woman that he had had good luck, so

*Told by Ahahe (Waco).

that she need never go hungry any more. The old woman advised him not to do wrong to the one who had given him all the meat. The Coyote said to the old woman, "Never mind about my doing anything wrong to my friends."

The next day, the Coyote went back to the place where the man was living alone and walked right in. The man asked the Coyote many questions. He asked him if he was brave, and the Coyote said that he was born brave. He asked him if he was a fast runner, and the Coyote said that he was a fast runner. Then the man asked the Coyote to go toward the south, which was a good ways off. He told him to go until he came to a small hill, and that around this hill he would find three Buffalo sitting down. These Buffalo were of different sizes, so if he wanted a large shield or a small shield he was to select a large or a small Buffalo. The Coyote started, and when he came to the place, he went around the hill and saw the Buffalo sitting down and he walked up to them and wondered which he should choose. He finally decided that he would have a large-sized shield, and so he asked the largest Buffalo to go with him. The Buffalo arose and chased the Coyote, who ran to where he had started from. Once in a while he would look back to see if the Buffalo was gaining on him. The Buffalo was pretty near up with him when he finally reached the man's place. The man told the Coyote to go outside, to take the Buffalo by the horns and give it a jerk, and then he would have his shield. The Coyote went out and walked up to the Buffalo and started to grab it by the horns; but the Buffalo made a quick motion and made as if he was going to hook the Coyote. The Coyote dodged away quick. The man told him not to dodge. He walked up to the Buffalo a second time, but failed to have courage enough to go up and take it by the horns; so the man told him to try again. He walked up the third time, and failed again. On the fourth time he was told that if he failed again he could not have the shield. He walked up again and the Buffalo made another dash at the Coyote, but failed to scare him this time. The Coyote took the Buffalo by the horns and jerked it, and there was a shield. After this was given to him, bow and arrows were given him. He was directed to command his arrows to go out hunting, by shooting them in four directions; so that he need never go out hunting himself. The Coyote shot the arrows towards each direction—north, east, south, and west. It was not very long until he heard these arrows talking, saying that they had killed certain buffalo. All at once he heard something fall to the ground and he saw buffalo falling to the ground, each one of them having an arrow stuck in him. These arrows themselves brought the buffalo and the Coyote butchered them, took his arrows from them, and cleaned the blood from them. The Coyote was told to keep his shield as it was when he first got it, and then he would be protected by it. He was also told never to forget to rise early in the morning and jerk the buffalo by the horns, before sunrise; but not after the sun had risen high. He was also told that each of his arrows had life in it, the same as he himself had. So the Coyote took his shield, bow and arrows, and plenty of meat for his family and set out for home. When he got home he told his wife to go and cut him a pole on which to hang his shield, bows and arrows. The old woman cut the pole and hung up his shield and quiver, and unloaded his beef. He told his wife to make haste and cook him some meat, for he was hungry, and that he wanted to go out hunting. After he had eaten he stepped outside and commanded his arrows to go out hunting, shooting one in each direction. Then he waited until his arrows returned with their load. He told his wife to butcher the buffalo and clean his arrows, then he again commanded his arrows to go out hunting. He repeated this four times, so that they had plenty of meat.

The Coyote, being so proud of his wonderful arrows, decided to go out to a certain village. He told his wife that he thought he had enough meat to last until he should come back again. The old woman told the Coyote to hurry back. On his way, the Coyote met a man carrying a large bow and arrow, but the arrow had a blunt point. The Coyote asked the man if the arrow was any good. The man replied that he used it in killing all kinds of game, and everything else. The Coyote laughed over this man's arrow, telling him that it was too big to do anything with, and asked him if he thought he could hit him. The man told the Coyote that anything he shot at was killed. The Coyote laughed again, saying that he did not believe it, and he coaxed the man to shoot at him, but the man refused. Finally the Coyote got him into the notion. The man told the Coyote to go a certain distance away. The Coyote walked off a little way and turned back, telling the man to go ahead and shoot. The man told the Coyote to go on further, so the Coyote walked a good long way off and stopped. He saw the man point the arrow toward him and shoot it. All at once he heard the arrow coming, and finally he saw it coming, and he ran hard. He dodged around, but the arrow kept chasing him until it overtook him and shot him in the back and came out of his mouth. The man walked up to the Coyote, kicked him on his feet, and told him to arise. The Coyote got up and rubbed his eyes, saying that he had fallen asleep. The Coyote looked at the man and noticed that he was handsome. He had blue teeth and would spit out blue spit. This power the Coyote was bound to have, so he begged the man to give him the power to become fine-looking and have a large bow and large arrow. The man told the Coyote if he wanted to be fine looking he could be made so, and that he could be given the bow and arrows. They started to a small stream of water, and the man threw the Coyote into the water where it was over his head. When the Coyote came up he was as fine-looking as the man was. The man who appeared to the Coyote was the Sun (Sakida). The Coyote left the man and continued his journey, and when he came to a stream of water he looked around for a place where the water was still and looked at himself and saw what a fine-looking fellow he was. He kept on until he came to the place where he was going, and late in the evening he went into the village.

On reaching the place he met a woman and asked her to show him where strangers generally went for a night's lodging. The woman told the Coyote to go on until he should find a high tipi. He went on until he reached the high tipi. When he entered, the man who lived there told him that the place was not safe for any man to visit, for there was a man who would call in early in the morning for him to meet him at the river. On entering, the Coyote had asked for a place at the back of the tipi to erect his pole in the ground. Next morning, of course, the Coyote had a duty to perform when his shield was hung. In the morning he arose and went around back of the tipi to hang up his shield, and there was a Buffalo grazing. The Coyote took the Buffalo by the horns, jerked it, and there was his shield. Now, he was called to meet his enemy at the river. He and the chief both went to the river, where the Coyote and the other man were to meet. Great crowds gathered around the banks of the river. They were ready to dive in the river, to find out who could be under the water the longest time. In this way the other man had the privilege of killing his enemies if he stayed under the water the longest. He had killed many men before the Coyote came to the place. They both got on the bank of the river and both dived. When the Coyote dived he found under the water a beaver lodge, which he entered, just as if he were going into a tipi, and there he remained. The other man stayed under the water all day, until late in the evening. The crowds were still waiting on the bank of the river. The chief once in a while would go near the bank, to see who was still under the water. In the evening the Coyote's enemy appeared. Then the Coyote appeared. The other man now sat on the ground, begging the Coyote not to do anything to him, and he promised the Coyote that he should have the same powers as he himself had, and should become the head man of the village. To this the Coyote would not consent; for he knew how cruelly the man had treated the people who visited the chief. The Coyote took a rest for a while, and the other man spoke to the people, saying that the Coyote should not be in a hurry to kill him. The man was not going to offer his life to anyone, and so he went into the air. This man was Shadow-of-the-Sun (Ihakaatskada). The chief spoke to the Coyote and asked him why he had not killed the man before he got away. The Coyote asked to have his large bow and arrow brought to him. They brought his bow and arrow. He then went to the place where the man was sitting, and looking up, he shot his large arrow. He then told the people to look up once in a while in the direction in which the other man had disappeared. ˙ All at once the people got to stirring around and saying that something was coming down. They could just barely see it coming, but finally it came closer and closer, until it hit the ground. The Coyote then ordered the people to bring wood to that place. The people went for the wood and each one brought an armful and placed it on top of this man's body. The Coyote cut a stick with the sharp stone that he had for his knife, and set fire all around the body and burned it. When the body was burning he would poke the fire with the stick that he had cut, and to those that this man had before killed as he had tried to kill the Coyote, he said, "Your house (body) is burning." So one after another of the men jumped out, and there were a great many men saved.

After the fire went out, the chief who owned this village took the Coyote back home and made him one of the head men and gave his sister to him for a wife, because he had destroyed the cruel man. Of course, the Coyote was fine-looking, and so he was glad to marry the chief's sister. He lived here for a while. The people noticed that every morning the Coyote went out to take the Buffalo by the horns and jerked it, and then his shield would appear; and that he would remain outside and command his arrows to go out hunting, by shooting them in each of the four directions, until they had brought the buffalo to where he was, when he would call his wife to butcher them. On this account everybody liked the Coyote. One night some one carried off one of the Coyote's arrows. The arrow, having life in it, spoke out to the rest of the arrows, saying that he was being carried off to another place. The Coyote said to his brother-in-law that some one had stolen one of his arrows. This arrow was brought back to him, and he said that no one of his arrows could be stolen without his knowledge of it. Every morning the people gathered around this man's tipi, looking at the Buffalo that the Coyote called his shield, and they knew that he was a wonderful man. After a time he decided that he would let more of the people see his shield. He let the Buffalo stand there until the sun got up high, but the Buffalo began to back up and get angry. The Coyote finally stepped out and tried to do the same as he had always done, but failed. Before this his arrows got to talking among themselves and to the Coyote, saying that his children's and wife's food was nearly exhausted, and that they wished he would go back home. The Coyote would not pay any attention to them, for he had a good wife here and was content. When he let the people see the Buffalo, and when the Buffalo got angry with him, all of his arrows and bow left him alone, and let the Buffalo fight him. The Buffalo became so angry and fought so hard that he killed the Coyote. After he was killed he was changed into just an ordinary coyote, as he had been before. His wife and children starved to death. The people gathered around him and took his body and carried it off to another place outside of the village.

All the stories about the Coyote show that he always met men who could give him powers to do certain things, so that it would be easier for him to live and hunt; but he would always do wrong and have his powers taken away from him. In these times, any being who was as cruel as Shadow-of-the-Sun was killed, but always lived again, but would have less powers. So at all the times there were wicked people among the good.

4. THE COYOTE AND HIS MAGIC SHIELD AND ARROWS.*

The Coyote (Ketox) was once living out by himself with his family. There were no other people living near them. The Coyote wandered around looking for all kinds of game to feed his family. Early one morning he fixed himself up and resolved to go somewhere. He started out towards the west. As he went along, after having traveled a long way (and he was a fast traveler) he came to a tipi. He thought to himself: "I must first go and visit my partner" (naawada). The Coyote frequently used this word. As he went near the place he saw a large Buffalo standing out by the side of the tipi, and he was afraid to go near. The Swallow (Widtisgecha), the man that was living in the tipi, came out, and with his right hand grabbed the Buffalo by the hair between the horns and shook it, and

*Told by Ignorant-Woman (Man) (Towakoni).

there was no more a Buffalo, but a shield. Swallow then went into the tipi. The Coyote observed what the Swallow had done. He then approached and entered the tipi of the Swallow, who asked him if he was hungry. The Coyote said, "Of course I am hungry." Then the Swallow gave him something to eat. The Coyote noticed that the Swallow was fine-looking. When the Swallow spit, his spittle was blue instead of white. The Coyote also noticed that he had inside of his mouth a greenish-blue color. He also noticed that he had many things that he himself wanted. The Swallow told him to eat all he wanted and that he could take what meat he could pack on his back to his family, if he had a family. The Coyote said he had a family. He then asked the Swallow if he could not give him some powers. The Swallow asked the Coyote if he was brave. The Coyote said that he knew of no braver man. The Swallow told the Coyote to take home to his family the meat, then come back and he would equip him with the things as he wished. The Coyote then got what meat he wanted and took it on home to his family, and said: "I have now found a way so that you young ones and my old woman need never more go hungry." He told his family to go ahead and eat what they wanted, and that he had to go and see the Swallow. He then set out to go to the Swallow's place, and when he got there the Swallow asked him if he was a good runner. The Coyote said that he could run pretty fast. The Swallow told him to go towards the south until he came to a high point, and there he would find four large Buffalo bulls sitting down. "As soon as you get there," said the Swallow, "point to one of the Buffalo and tell him that you want him, then turn right back and the Buffalo will follow you." The Coyote started out for the high point, which was as far away as he could see. The Coyote traveled pretty fast and finally reached the high point. There he saw four large Buffalo sitting down. He called one of them, then turned right back and he saw the Buffalo coming after him. The Coyote had to run with all his might to prevent the Buffalo from catching up with him before he got back to the Swallow's place. The Buffalo kept gaining on him, and when he reached the place he was pretty nearly tired out. Now he was safe, and the Swallow told him that he was a pretty good runner. The Swallow then went with the Coyote to catch the Buffalo. He told the Coyote to walk up to the Buffalo and grab him between the horns. The Buffalo began to get angry and would go backwards and forwards, but the Swallow said that he would not be harmed, and that he must go through that ordeal if he would get a shield. The Coyote finally walked up and did as directed, and there it was, a shield. He took the shield, as instructed by the Swallow, and threw it up on the pole, and there it hung. The Swallow then told the Coyote to go out into the timber and cut four of the finest dogwood sticks he could find, from which to make arrows and a bow. The Coyote went out in the timber and cut the sticks, and when he brought them in they were prepared for him. When they were completed the Swallow instructed the Coyote how to handle his shield, bow, and arrows. Said he: "You see for yourself that your shield and bow and arrows have lives in them, the same as you have. The way to keep the shield, whether at home or away from home is to hang it on a pole. You must not forget this. In the morning you will see a Buffalo standing outside. You must then do as I tell you. Do not allow the sun to get too high before you put up the shield. As soon as the sun rises put it up." The Coyote said: "I can do that all right. I am too old to forget a simple thing." Said the Swallow: "In using the bow and arrows out hunting, all you have to do is to go a little way from home and shoot one arrow in one direction, another in another direction, the next in another way and the fourth in still another way, then remain where you are until they all come back to you. When they are coming back the arrows will talk to one another, telling what kind of a buffalo they have killed, and the buffalo will be brought to you instead of your having to go after them. The arrows will remain in whatever place they land on the buffalo. It is your place to take them off and clean them. Then you can butcher the buffalo and your family can have all the meat they want." After the shield, bow, and arrows were given to the Coyote he went to the nearest flowing water and looked for the deepest place. When he had found it the Swallow took hold of him and threw him into the water. When he came out of the water the Swallow said: "You are now just like me." The Coyote, just to prove it, spat, and his spittle was blue. The Coyote was satisfied and both of them went back to the Swallow's tipi, and the Coyote was permitted to go to his home.

On his arrival his wife and children did not know him. He told his family that he was the same old man, but that he had got powers from the Swallow. The Coyote asked his wife to cut him a pole to hang his shield on. The Coyote's wife did as she was told to do and the Coyote hung up his shield. He then called his wife, and said: "You need never go hungry any more, for I now have powers to kill what game we want." The old woman said to him, "Whatever powers you have, do as you are told and make no mistake." "Oh, no," said the Coyote, "you need not worry about my making a mistake; I am too old to do anything like that." That night the Coyote waited patiently for daylight to come. Just about daylight the Coyote went out to send out his arrows to hunt. He went out a little way, as he was told to do, before he sent his arrows to hunt. There he waited for a while and finally he sent his arrows out to hunt. He soon heard them talking to one another, telling how fat and how large was the buffalo they had killed. Finally all his arrows came in, each carrying a whole buffalo. The Coyote then pulled out all his arrows and cleaned them as he had been directed. He went back to his home and put up his bow and arrows and commenced to butcher the buffalo. While he was doing this the sun rose, and the old woman and the young ones all got up, and as they went out they were afraid of the buffalo that was standing at their door, and they ran back into their tipi. As soon as he heard the folks screaming the Coyote saw the buffalo and went right up to it. He grabbed it between its horns and there was no more a buffalo, but a shield. He pitched it up on the pole and it hung there. The Coyote then told his family to come out. When they came out they told him that there was a buffalo standing at their door, and the Coyote told them that it was his shield. Now they went where the Coyote was butchering. The Coyote was nearly through, and when he got through they commenced to bring the beef into the lodge. They had all the meat they wanted. The Coyote continued this right along every morning. Finally they had plenty of fresh meat and some dried meat. The old woman then had to put up a drying arbor for the meat.

The Coyote now began to think about going on a visit to some strange place, that he might be seen somewhere else, instead of staying at home all the time. While he had this in mind he kept on killing buffalo, so that his family would have enough meat until his return. Some time after, he told his family that he was going on a visit for a while, for they had enough meat to last until he should return. The Coyote set out to the tipi of the Swallow. On his arrival he told the Swallow that he was going out on a visit for a while, for he was tired of staying in one place all the time. The Swallow told the Coyote not to stay too long. The Coyote then said that he had enough meat at home for his family to live on during his absence. The Swallow told him that his arrows would let him know when the meat at home was all gone; that then he must at once return. The Coyote said, "All right, I will come whenever they tell me about that." The Coyote then started out on his journey. While on the way he saw some one coming. He thought he would find out who it was and finally he met the man. The Coyote saw that he was a fine-looking man, and this man had a large bow and a large arrow with a blunt point. He commenced to make fun of the man's arrow. He asked him if he could kill any-thing with it. The man said that he could. The Coyote asked why he did not have arrows like his, saying that if he just had arrows like his he would think that he had good arrows. The Coyote told the man that the arrow was too heavy to go very far. The man told the Coyote that his arrow could go as far as his arrow could go, and perhaps further. This the Coyote could not believe. He then said, "What if you should shoot at me? Would you kill me?" The man said, "The arrow could find you and overtake you wherever you might be, and it might kill you." The Coyote laughed, and said: "Well, I will go off to some distance and let you shoot at me to show me that your arrow can go far." The man told the Coyote that he did not want to kill him. But the Coyote kept coaxing the man to go ahead. He finally persuaded him to shoot at him. The Coyote went a good long way off, then stood facing the man, who shot at the Coyote. The Coyote heard the arrow coming and ran toward the man and the arrow over-took him before he got to the man and struck him in the arms. The man went to where the Coyote was lying dead, kicked his feet and told him to get up. The Coyote got up, rubbed his eyes, and said, "I was sound asleep." The man asked the Coyote if his arrow had hit him. The Coyote said: "O yes, it hit me. That is a good arrow of yours." The Coyote then asked the man if he could let him have the arrow. He also asked him who he was. The man told him that he was the Sun (Sakida). The Coyote said, "O, is that who you are?" The man gave the Coyote the arrow and his bow. The Coyote told the Sun that he was going out on a visit, and he wanted to be better equipped for meeting danger, to be ready to meet all troubles, for there was a good many bad people that he might happen to meet.

The Coyote then left the Sun and went on to the village. On his arrival he asked where visitors were allowed to stay. He was then told to go straight to the largest and highest tipi in the center of the village and there he would find a chief and would be allowed to stay there. So the Coyote followed his directions until he got to the chief's place. He left his shield outside and was asked to be seated on the west side of the tipi. He was asked where he had come from and he replied that he had come from afar and was tired. He told the chief to have some one cut him a pole so that he could hang up his shield. The Coyote was given something to eat right away, for the chief knew that he was wonderful. The Coyote stayed all that night, and early the next morning the people that were up in the village saw at the chief's a large Buffalo standing right at the door. The people then howled at the people to come out to the Buffalo standing at the door, but the chief was smart enough to know that his visitor was wonderful, and he knew that it must be the shield that was hung up there. Before long, many other people saw the Coyote step out and grab the Buffalo between the horns and shake it and pitch it up to the top of the pole, and there was nothing but a shield. The people began to find out that the chief had a wonderful man visiting him. That day, news began to spread about this wonderful man visiting the chief's place, and the people began to come to see the shield and the man. The Coyote felt prouder than ever, to have all the people in the village come around to see him. All the prominent men of the village came and stayed all that day, talking to him. The Coyote told them that the next morning he was going to give them all the meat they wanted. The men finally retired and went to their homes, and there was a man selected to announce that the visitor had promised to give them food. Early the next morning the Coyote took his bow and arrows and went outside of the village and shot the arrows to every direction and waited there for a time. This was pretty early, before anyone was up. Finally his arrows came around, the same as usual, talking to one another, and telling what kind of buffalo they had killed. The buffalo were laid before him. He took the arrows out and cleaned them, and at once he sent them off again to kill some more. Finally the arrows came back again, the same as usual, and again he took them out from the buffalo that they brought and sent them out the third time and the fourth time, then, having cleaned the arrows, he went back into the village. It was about sunrise. He went in and told the chief to have some one announce that he had killed the buffalo and to have them go over there at once to butcher them. The chief sent out a man at once, and the Coyote went to hang up his shield. There were many people there at this time, watching the Buffalo and waiting to see this wonderful man come out and hang up his shield. The whole village was fed by the Coyote's work. The chief now came to like the Coyote very well. He stayed at the village a good while and continued to perform his miracles right along. The chief liked the Coyote so well that he gave him his sister for a wife. The Coyote became the chief's brother-in-law. The marrying of the chief's sister caused him to get up late. Once upon a time while he was asleep his arrows woke him and told him that the people at home were running short of food and that he had better go on home; but the Coyote would not listen to them. That morning he got up still later, but he was yet able to hang up his shield. The next morning his arrows tried to coax him to go home, and this time, his bow, his arrows, and all the other things he had got from the Sun ran away from him. The next morning he thought he had better wait until everybody should see the Buffalo before he should hang it up, for he thought he had been hanging his shield too soon for everybody to see it. The sun rose higher and higher, and the Buffalo began to back off toward the north. When the Coyote thought everybody in the village was present he walked out of the chief's place and went toward the Buffalo. At this time the Buffalo began to get angry. It commenced to throw up dirt and would hook the ground, but the Coyote was not afraid to go up to it. But the Buffalo was angry at the Coyote, and as he went near the Buffalo it came at him and hooked him and threw him up, and as he went up he was no more human, but a regular old coyote. The people then understood the secret of the whole thing, that the Coyote had obtained powers from some one and had disobeyed his instructions. After the Buffalo had killed the coyote it turned toward the north and ran away, and left the coyote's body lying at the edge of the village. Since the Buffalo went north, that is where it is known to live. The chief of the village called on certain ones to announce to the people about moving their village. They moved away to the west and arrived at a place where they always lived thereafter.

5. THE GREAT-SOUTH-STAR, THE PROTECTOR OF WARRIORS.*

These are the names of the village where Healthy-Flint-Stone-Man (Tahadiidakotse) lived: Where-Blackbirds-lit-on-elm-Tree (Kasit-syukkari); Stone-Corn-Mills-lying-on-Hill-side(Nawishkatuk); Large elm-Tree-near-Edge-of-the-Village (Taatstatschiaheichitiwa); and Where-large-Ears-of-Corn-grow (Tastasitiwa). He had a family which consisted of father, mother, sister, and wife. He was a great hunter and warrior. He had a good many followers who would go along with him, when he went out with any war-party against the Trickster (Kinas) people, who were then their enemies. He was so brave that the men knew that it was always safe for them to go along with him, for he always returned victorious. This was one reason people liked to be with him. Once upon a time when he knew that his wife was pregnant he began to instruct her as to how the child should be born. He told her that when the time should come for the child's birth, the place where she was should be closed up and no one should be in there

*Told by Towakoni Jim (Towakoni).

but herself; that she should not open the door until after the child should be born; that the child must be called Young-Flint-Stone (Tahadia); that she must not let him know where his father was until he should become old enough, for he himself was going to a far distant place, and be there for all time; that he was tired of going out to the old scenes of wars; and that he was going where he could be near his enemies.

After telling all this he at once set out on a war expedition. Of course there were a good many followers who went along with him. He went towards the south. He kept on going, and it took him so long that some of the older men died on the way, of old age, until he had but four men left. He kept on going until one of these gave out and then there were three with him. They kept on going until another gave out and this left with him but two men. Continuing their journey, another gave out, and this time there was left but one man along with him, and this man finally gave out and this left him alone to seek for himself a place to live, and he went on nearer to his enemies. He kept on until he found a high cave-like place, and this he made his permanent home, and there were his enemies near his new home. Here he lived for a long while. Whenever he felt like fighting he would go and attack his foes and cut off their heads. Being a man with great power there was never an arrow that could hit him. He secured a long pole, which he stuck up in front of his place, on which he hung the heads of his enemies.

The time came when his son was born, and he grew rapidly, and finally he got to be a man. The child of the Healthy-Flint-Stone-Man began to ask his mother if he had any father, and she told him that his father had gone away a long distance to live, and was never to return. One time the boy asked his mother to grind enough meal for him to take along with him while he went out to look for his father. This was done, and the young man set out in search of his father. Young-Flint-Stone, being famous like his father, traveled fast, and he found the trail of his father. He was on the road for a good while, until he ran on to one of the men who had given out. When he got near to this man, he found him too angry to see him, and the man asked why he had come around him. He then took out a handful of meal and put it in the man's mouth, and then the man had to believe that it was some one from the village he himself had come from, and he said: "Oh, yes! This reminds me of being in Where-Blackbirds-lit-on-elm-Tree, or Stone-Corn-Mills-lying-on-Hill-side, or Large-elm-Tree-near-Edge-of-the-Village, or Where-large-Ears-of-Corn-grow." Then the man said to him: "You are Young-Flint-Stone. Keep going, and you will come to where your father lives.'" So Young-Flint-Stone went on, and on, until he came to the next man, and this man was angry like the first one. But this made no difference with Young-Flint-Stone. He went up toward the man, and took out a handful of meal and put it in the man's mouth. The man then replied, saying: "This reminds me of being in Where-Blackbirds-lit-on-elm-Tree, or, Stone-Corn-Mills-lying-on-Hill-side, or Large-elm-Tree-near-Edge-of-the-Village, or Where-large-Ears-of-Corn-grow. I am sure I can see the place in memory. Young-Flint-Stone, your father lives somewhere beyond, to the south. If you go that way you will meet another man, and he will give you more information about this place." Young-Flint-Stone continued his journey until he came to the next man, who was the third man he met after leaving home. This man also was angry at the sight of a stranger, because it had been such a long time since he had seen a human being. But Young-Flint-Stone went up to him and took out a handful of corn meal and put it in the man's mouth, to show he was from the same village the man was from. When he had done this, the man threw back his head, and said: "This puts me in mind of being in Where-Blackbirds-lit-on-elm-Tree, or, Stone-Corn-Mills-lying-on-Hill-side, or, Large-elm-Tree-near-Edge-of-the-Village, or, Where-large-Ears-of-Corn-grow. You are Young-Flint-Stone. You are going to see your father. By keeping on you will come to another man, and there you can secure more information from him. He knows more about your father, for he is near to your father."

Young-Flint-Stone went on again, traveling fast, until he came to one whom he knew to be the last man whom he would meet before reaching his father's place. When he made his appearance to this man the man was angry with him, for the reason that he had seen nobody for a long time, the Healthy-Flint-Stone-Man being the last man he had seen. Young-Flint-Stone went up to the man in order to show him that he lived at the same place the man had lived and which the man had left. He put a handful of meal into his mouth. The man threw back his head and laughed, and said: "Yes, this reminds me of being in Where-Blackbirds-lit-on-elm- Tree, or, Stone-Corn-Mills-lying-on-Hill-side, or, Large-elm-Tree-near-Edge-of-the-Village, or, Where-large-Ears-of-Corn-grow. Well, Young-Flint-Stone, you came in search of your father. Your father lives down further south where he is near to his enemies. He surely has great powers and you will have many dangers to overcome before seeing him. You will have to sneak around to get to his dwelling place, for if he sees you before you get up there he will kill you. He lives on a high point. Sometimes he is out, and there are times when he goes to sleep. When you do get there he will try to kill you, for he allows no one to come to his place; and there are times when I can hear him giving the war-whoop, when he goes out after his enemies." Young-Flint-Stone went on, leaving this man after he had given him information regarding his father's place and his habits and how cruel he was. He traveled on and on until he came to the place, and doing as he was instructed, he sneaked in, so as not to be seen. He finally succeeded in reaching the door, and entering, said to his father: "My father, I am now here in search of you." Just as he said that, Healthy-Flint-Stone-Man arose on his feet, and said: "I can not believe you. I know I have a son, but he is so far away that he could never reach this place, and you are trying to play a trick on me." He went to get his war-club, but Young-Flint-Stone got hold of him, saying, "I am your son." But Healthy-Flint-Stone-Man began to push him around and tried to throw him, and he pushed Young-Flint-Stone away from him. Young-Flint-Stone had only one hand to use, for he had to use the other to get the corn meal sack, so as to put some meal into his father's mouth. Young-Flint-Stone finally succeeded in untying his sack. He took out a handful of meal and put it in his father's mouth. Healthy-Flint-Stone-Man asked Young-Flint-Stone to release him, threw his head back, and said: "O yes, that is the way everything tastes in the place I came from. This puts me in mind of being in the village of Where-Blackbirds-lit-on-elm-Tree, or Stone-Corn-Mills-on-Hill-side, or Large-elm-Tree-near-Edge-of-the-Village, or Where-large-ears-of-Corn-grow. You are surely my son. I left home when you were in your mother's womb, and I gave you the name that you bear. Well, I am a good long way from home, and it suits me to remain here all the time. When I lived there where you are from I had to send out war-parties, and had to go a long way, so that I thought that it would be best for me to be where I could be near my enemies, just as I am now. I was tired of going a long way. So this is what brought me here. I can not go back with you when you feel like going back." Young-Flint-Stone, in looking at his father, saw that his hair was turning into flint stones.

Healthy-Flint-Stone-Man was surprised to see Young-Flint-Stone. Young-Flint-Stone then remained with his father, who showed him all his powers, and where he went to fight his enemies. Young-Flint-Stone noticed a pole stuck up outside of his father's place, on which there hung many skulls, old and fresh. The next morning Healthy-Flint-Stone-Man took Young-Flint-Stone along with him to help him fight some of his enemies. They both went on down the hill, traveling all that morning, until they came to a village, and there they met their enemies. Young-Flint-Stone was the first one to kill a man, and the old man next, and then they turned and came on home. Young-Flint-Stone did not remain here very long. He was asked to return home, for the people were looking for him to come home. Healthy-Flint-Stone-Man told him that it was very near time for the next generation to come, and that the place where he was then would be known as the Protector-of-Warriors (Netskatcitikitawe). He told his son to tell the people that he had seen his father, and that he was there, never to return home, and that in the next generation he would be seen as the Great-South-Star; and in the next generation, when any one sent out war-parties they should offer him smoke, and then he would take pity on whoever should make the offering, and give him good fortune of having an easy time in meeting enemies, and of always returning victorious. So Young-Flint-Stone was requested to take back with him a scalp for the man's wife and father, mother, and sisters. Young-Flint-Stone then departed from his father with the scalp.

On his way back he met the four men once more, and they asked the same as his father had done, that they might remain where they were, for it was so far from home and they were so old that they could never reach home. He traveled on, and on, and no one knows how long it took him to reach home, but when he reached home he delivered the scalp to his people. The people were surprised to see him once more, for they knew it was not safe to be off as far as he had been from home. When the whole village heard of Young-Flint-Stone's return they came about his place to see him, and to hear how he met his father. He then informed them what hard times he had had in traveling, and how he met the four men who were near to his father, and what they had said when he first met them on his way to see his father, and what hard times he had had introducing himself to his father, and how his father threatened his life when he met him, and how he accompanied his father on the war-path, and how the scalp was given by his father to be presented to his people. The people then began to move away to their homes and the news spread about the boy's visit to his father. When night came they had dances of all kinds in honor of Young-Flint-Stone and his father. So it is known that Young-Flint-Stone was the only person who ever went far enough south to see his father, the Protector-of-Warriors, and he was the last one ever to see him.

Young-Flint-Stone then became a famous man, and as great a warrior as his father had been when he lived at the village. He would send out war-parties against his enemies, the Tricksters. Having such great war powers he would always be victorious and bring home with him many captives, as well as scalps. This was what made him a famous man. Young-Flint-Stone told all of his followers that the Great-South-Star was his father, whom he had once been to see. Whenever this Star was seen Young-Flint-Stone would offer his smoke to it, as he had been told to do by this Star, who was his father. It was not very long before Young-Flint-Stone called forth the people. When the people gathered around his lodge and were all present they asked him why he had called them forth. He replied that since he had been with the people he had been well cared for by the young men who were his friends and his warriors, and that since he had seen his father as a Star he himself thought that he had better be like his father. Young-Flint-Stone then waited until night. When darkness came he went out up to the sky and became Flint-Stone-lying-down-Above (Tahanetskitadidia).

6. THE GREAT-SOUTH-STAR, THE PROTECTOR OF WARRIORS.*

There was a village named Large-elm-Tree-near-Edge-of-the-Village (Taatstatschiaheichitiwa), because there was a large elm tree at the edge of the village, where all the dances were had whenever the men came home from war. The village was also called Where-Black-birds-lit-on-Elm-Tree (Kasitsyukkari), or Stone-Corn-Mills-lying-on-Hill-side (Nawishkatuk), or Where-large-Ears-of-Corn-grow (Tas-tacitiwa). In this village was a man known as Wearing-Flint-Stone-on-top-of-Head (Tahadiidakotskitiwe), who afterwards became the Great-South-Star, as we call it. This man was famous in all ways. He was the leader of war-parties and had many followers who always followed him whenever he sent out war-parties. In his home his father was the chief of the village. He also had a mother and a sister. When he had become famous and a great warrior, his sister got married to a famous warrior. Once upon a time, before he undertook to leave home, his sister became pregnant. He told his sister that when the child should be born they should call him Flint-Stone-yelling-Boy (Tahanitsiaskase). He also said that this boy would follow the footsteps of his uncle and be a great warrior.

*Told by Towakoni Jim (Towakoni).

There came a time when he undertook to send out greater war-parties than had ever before been sent out. He called forth all his followers. When his followers came about, he told them that he would go out in a few days on an expedition, and that he would go towards the south, and that they should be ready at that time. When the time came, he set out on this great expedition. There were men who followed this main expedition, then traveled on and on, but never seemed to want to stop like other warriors, to send out spies, but kept on. When they had gone far away from home, some of the men turned back, and thereafter, every day, some more men would stop following their leader, for he was going too far. So finally all but four of the men had stopped, who thought that they would follow him until they should come to the end of their journey. But as they kept on going, one of these gave out, and had to stop, and when he stopped he found that he could not turn back, for his life was too short, and he knew that he could not get home. Having given out this man had to sit down and remain there for all time. The rest of them kept on going. Another man gave out, and he had to stop, for these other men were traveling faster at this time. The leader then told his last follower that the place to which they were directed was getting nearer. But this last man gave out, too, and had to stop. This man watched Wearing-Flint-Stone-on-Top-of-Head until he got clear out of sight. Wearing-Flint-Stone-on-Top-of-Head then found a place where he could live all alone. To live by himself was just what he wanted, for he was a single man. Near where he lived was a large village of enemies. He knew that he could have all the fun he wanted, for fighting was fun for him. Whenever he wanted to attack the village he would go down the hill from his home and he would fight the enemy, and this was the way he enjoyed life by himself. About this time there was born at his old home a nephew. His nephew grew fast, and he soon sent out war-parties, too. When he was old enough, the other men who followed him on his expeditions told him about his uncle. He was told that his uncle was down south somewhere; that he had once sent out a war-party and had never returned. Some time afterward, while the nephew was at home, he told his mother that he wanted to see his uncle; that he was going to that place, wherever it was; and that he was going to look for him, if it took him all of his life. So he told his mother to make him two pairs of moccasins and to grind some corn to take along for his uncle, to remind him of his old home. He said that if he could he would bring his uncle home. After these things were ready for him he took plenty of tobacco and other things that he had ordered and at once set out.

He was traveling alone, so he went fast, for he did not have to wait for any one. Some time afterward he came to the place where the four men had turned back, and he saw that there were but four men besides the one who had gone on further south. He kept on and on, until he came to one of the men who had given out. When he went near to this man, he found him to be pretty angry with him, for he was not used to seeing people. But the nephew told the man who he was, and that he had come a long way in search of them. But the man would not believe him, for he knew that the distance was too great for anyone to travel. So the nephew took out his pipe and made the man smoke his pipe. He lighted his pipe and gave it to the man. The man then took four puffs and then emptied the pipe. Then he drew back, and said: "O yes! It is a surprise to me to see some one come from my old home. This reminds me of being in my home in the village of Large-elm-Tree-near-Edge-of-the-Village, or Where-Black-birds-lit-on-elm-Tree, or Stone-Corn-Mill-lying-on-Hill-side, or Where-large-Ears-of-Corn-grow." He then put a handful of meal into the man's mouth. Then the man said: "Yes, that is just the way everything tastes back home, but I am so far away that I can not get back. But your uncle and his other followers went on, and you are now on the right road to them, and you will find another man further down, and he will tell you the same thing, and more, too." The nephew continued his journey to his uncle's place, and, as he went further, he came to another man sitting down and facing the south. When this man found that some one was coming, he was angry, too. But the nephew told the man that he had come from a long way, looking for them; and that he was the nephew to their leader. The man then replied, "Well, show me something, so that I may believe you, that I may know if you came from my home." The nephew filled his pipe for the man to smoke, lighted it and gave it to him. The man puffed only four times, then emptied the pipe. He drew back, and said, "Well, this is the way the old home smoke tastes." Then the nephew gave the man a handful of cornmeal, and the man said, "This reminds me of being in our old home in the village far to the north." Of course, he also named the village names. The man then told him that this was as far as he had been able to go, and that he had often wished that he was back at his former home, but that he never could get there. The man told the nephew that his uncle was further south and that there was another man further south that could tell him more about his uncle. The man said that this also was as far as he could go. All this man would do was to sit up. So the young nephew noticed that the man was about to turn into something.

The nephew continued his journey further south, with the expectation of reaching his uncle. He came to another man, whom he supposed had followed his uncle, and this man was as angry as he could be when he was approached, but the nephew was ready to talk with him, telling him that he was from their home village and was on his way to his uncle's place. But this man would not believe him, for it was too far for anyone to travel. Then this man told the nephew to show him something, so that he could believe him. The nephew filled his pipe full of tobacco and offered it to the man to smoke, and he took but four puffs, then emptied the pipe. He also gave the man some of the corn meal, and got a handful of it and poured it into the man's mouth. The man drew back, and said: "Yes, that is just the way everything tastes at our home village. I often think of my old home and wish I were there, but I can not get there; my life is too short for me to return home, but you go on and you will find one more man on the road, who, I think, is in the same condition I am in, because there are two more further north who gave out, and I gave out, too. So surely there must be another man down further to the south."

So the young nephew went further south, leaving this man behind. Of course, he traveled faster, in order that he might find his uncle sooner. As he went further south he came to another man, whom he supposed to be another of his uncle's followers. As soon as this man found out that some one was coming he was as angry as he could be. He was like the other men—he could not move, but could only shake his head. The nephew told him that he was from his old home, far away to the north; that he had come in search of them and his uncle, who was leading the great war-party. But this man said, "No! No! You can not be the one, for it is too far for anyone to come to look for us." The nephew then asked the man if he remembered his leader's sister, saying that he himself was the son of the sister of this great war leader of his. The man then told the nephew to show him something from their distant home. The nephew filled his pipe and the man smoked it, then drew back and said: "Yes, you are from that village, my former home. That is the same old smoke that I used to smoke among my home people of that village that you recently came from." Again he took a handful of the corn meal and put it into the man's mouth, and when this was put in his mouth, he said, "Yes! That is just the way everything tastes in my village far to the north." The man, of course, named the names of the village. It was a surprise to the man that he should see some one who had come from a place so far away. So he said: "Well, my boy, you are now right close to your uncle's place. Often I hear him yell on quiet days whenever he goes after his enemies, although it is a long way from here to his place." This man gave the young nephew instructions how to get there safe. The nephew was told to be sure and get there while his uncle was asleep; that his uncle generally slept at noon, and by getting there at that time of the day he would be safe, but he was not safe yet. Said the man: "If you are not strong enough your uncle is going to kill you. On the morning after you make it all right with your uncle, he is going to take you to his enemies and attack the village with you, and if you do not run fast enough, after he goes through the village, he is going to kill you." The young man thought that his uncle was perhaps getting old, and he, being younger, could outdo him in everything. The man then said that the uncle was changing from what he used to be and was about to turn into something else; that his head was covered with flint stones instead of hair.

The nephew thought he had better go on. So he went on, until he came to a high point whereon he had been told that his uncle lived. It was then about noon and he knew that his uncle was sound asleep about that time. As he went around he noticed the door facing east, and there he saw a long pole stuck up, and on it there was a long string of scalps. He then entered the place where his uncle was asleep. As the nephew entered, his uncle awoke. He got hold of his uncle, telling him that he had come, but his uncle said: "You do not need to tell me that you are my nephew, for my nephew can not come down this far to see me. You are trying to fool me." So they wrestled there for a good while, and while they were doing this the young man was trying to get some corn meal into his uncle's mouth, to show him that he was from the village where he once lived, and he finally succeeded in doing so. Then the uncle said: "Sure enough, you are from that village that I used to live in, and you prove to be my nephew. Yes, this reminds me of being in my old home in the far north, where the village is called 'Large-elm-Tree-near-Edge-of-the-Village,' or 'Where-Blackbirds-lit-on-elm-Tree,' or 'Stone-Corn-Mill-lying-on-Hill-side,' or 'Where-large-Ears-of-Corn-grow.' Now then do something else that the people do at that village." Again he filled his pipe with tobacco and gave it to his uncle, who took the pipe and took four puffs, then emptied the pipe, and said, "Oh, yes! That is the way the old home smoke tastes."

The uncle then said: "I came down this far because I wanted to be near to my enemies, where I would not have to go so far to look for them. Well, nephew, I guess you are as good as I was back in our home, in leading war-parties. I suppose you do the same things

I used to do. Everybody thought well of me, but I undertook to come down here and not live with our people any more, so here I am, out by myself, and I am that much better off, for I like this way of living."

The nephew stayed the entire day, until the next morning, when his uncle told him to accompany him and attack the enemy's village. So they went on, and when they made the attack they both ran, and the nephew was far ahead of his uncle. As they ran into the village the people began to run, but this nephew went on through them and got after one that was ahead of all the rest and who had white hair dyed with red dye. He killed this man, took his scalp, and turned back. He then met his uncle, who told him he was as good a warrior as he himself, so they went back to his home. When they arrived home the uncle began to tell his nephew all about his powers, for he was never going to return home. The uncle began to tell him what to tell all those who were once his followers; that sometimes when they should think of him while out on the war-path he would take pity on them and carry them through, for it was near time for the world to change, so that there would be nothing but human beings doing this, and others who had these powers would turn into something else and not have the same powers that they had had when existing as human beings. So he offered powers to the generations to come, but not so great as the powers that he had. He also told his nephew that he must always remember when going through Leader-of-War ceremonies—that is, the smoke ceremonies—that they must surely offer him some of the smoke, in order that he might help them. So he told his nephew that when he should get home he was to tell the people that he was still alive and that he was to be seen by them and by other generations to come. This meant that he was to become the Great-South-Star, and be known as having great powers of foretelling things in case of war. So the name he afterwards bore was given by the people. His real name was Wearing-Flint-Stone-on-Top-of-Head. After he went to where he was now he was called "Protector-of-Warriors" (Netskat-citikitawe), or Having-Powers-to-watch-out-for-War-Expeditions.

After staying with his uncle for a while, his uncle presented him with a scalp that was on the pole where the scalps were hung; it had red hair, like the one the nephew had, and it was turning white. This he was to give to his mother. At this time, the nephew made up his mind to go home. He told his uncle that he wanted to go home. He then went on home, and when he passed the four men again they told him that they could not get home, for their life was too short. So he went home, traveling day and night, in order to get home in haste.

The nephew finally reached home and presented the scalp given by his uncle, to his mother. At this time, when nights came this great bright Star was seen, and this Star, he told the people, was his uncle, whom they used to have for a leader. Of course, when he arrived home the crowds began to gather around his dwelling place when they heard about his return. He then told about his long trip to his uncle's place and how he met his uncle's followers, what they had said on giving them smoke and corn meal; also how he met his uncle and how his life was threatened, and how he came out safely after giving him smoke and corn meal; how he went to fight his uncle's enemies and what kind of a scalp he had secured when fighting his uncle's enemies. The people saw the scalp that was presented to his mother by his uncle. This kind of a scalp was hard to get. So afterwards, he showed other men his powers that had been given him by his uncle, and since that time his powers still exist. The ceremonies of the expeditions and songs are still sung by the people of the present time, and the ceremonies are carried on the same as in those times, whenever the songs are sung. Flint-Stone-yelling-Boy then told the people that he would do as his uncle had done—become something else, after he had shown all his powers to all men who were his followers. That night he was seen ascending into the sky, and he became a Star. But the village still existed, though some of the people became something else.

7. THE GREAT-SOUTH-STAR, THE PROTECTOR OF WARRIORS.*

There was once a village by the name of Where-Blackbirds-lit-on-elm-Tree (Kasitsyukkari), or Stone-Corn-Mills-lying-on-Hill-side (Nawishkatuk), or Large-elm-Tree-near-Edge-of-the-Village (Taats-tatschiaheichitiwa), or Where-large-Ears-of-Corn-grow (Tastacitiwa), and in the village there lived a man by the name of Protector-of-Warriors (Netskatcitikitawe). He had a family consisting of father, mother, sisters, and wife. He himself was a great hunter and warrior and had a good many followers, who would go along with him on the war-path against the Tricksters (Kinas), his enemies. His followers always knew they were safe with him, for he never returned except victorious, and this is the reason they liked to go with him.

Once upon a time, when Protector-of-Warriors knew his wife to be pregnant, he began to instruct her as to how the child should be born: The place they were in should be closed, and no one should

*Told by Kill-Enemy (Woman) (Towakoni).

be allowed to enter; the door should not be opened until after the child should be born; she should not allow the child to know where his father was until he should get to be of the proper age, for he (the father) was going to a distant place, to be there for all time, so that he might thereafter be near his enemies, for he was tired of going a long way to find them. After giving these instructions he set out on the war-path with his followers. He went towards the south. He kept on going until one of the men gave out, and there were three left. He went on again, and another gave out and there were two left. He went on again, another gave out, and there was one left. He went on again, and the last one gave out and then he was left alone. He kept on, looking for a place to live, where he would be near his enemies. He came to a high cave-like place, and this he made his permanent home. Here he lived for a long time, near his enemies. Whenever the Pro-tector-of-Warriors felt like fighting he would attack his foes and cut off their heads, for he was a wonderful man, who could not be hit with an arrow. He had a long pole, which he stuck up in front of his place, upon which he might hang the heads of his enemies.

The time finally came when the Protector-of-Warriors' son was born. The child grew rapidly and finally became a man; his name was Young-Flint-Stone (Tahadia). Young-Flint-Stone began to ask his mother if he had any father. She told him that his father had gone a long distance to live and was never to return; so he asked his mother to grind meal enough for him to take along with him while he went out to look for his father. This was done, and Young-Flint-Stone, being wonderful like his father, traveled fast and found his father's trail. When he had been on the journey a good while he came to one of the men who had given out. When he came near him the man was too angry to see him, and asked why he should come around near him. Young-Flint-Stone then took out a handful of meal and put it in the man's mouth; then he believed that Young-Flint-Stone must be some one from the same village he himself had come from, and said, "O yes, this reminds me of being in Where-Blackbirds-lit-on-elm-Tree, or Stone-Corn-Mills-lying-on-Hill-side, or Large-elm-Tree-near-Edge-of-the-Village, or Where-large-Ears-of-Corn-grow. Young-Flint-Stone, by keeping on going you will reach the place where your father lives." Young-Flint-Stone went on, and on, until he came to the next man who had given out, who, like the first, was very angry at being approached; but this made no difference to Young-Flint-Stone. He went up toward him, took out a handful of meal and put it in his mouth, and the man said: "This reminds me of being in Where-Blackbirds-lit-on-elm-

Tree, or Stone-Corn-Mills-lying-on-Hill-side, or Large-elm-Tree-near-Edge-of-the-Village, or Where-large-Ears-of-Corn-grow, which I still hold in memory. The Protector-of-Warriors, your father, lives somewhere beyond here, to the south. By going on you will meet another man." Young-Flint-Stone went on and came to the third man who had given out, and he was angry, not having seen a human being for a long time. But Young-Flint-Stone went up to him and took a handful of meal and put it in the man's mouth. The man drew his head back, and said, smiling: "This puts me in mind of being at Where-Blackbirds-lit-on-elm-Tree, or Stone-Corn-Mills-lying-on-Hill-side, or Large-elm-Tree-near-Edge-of-the-Village, or Where-large-Ears-of-Corn-grow. Young-Flint-Stone, you are going to see your father. You will come to another man, and there you can secure more information from him. He knows more about your father, for he is nearer to him." So Young-Flint-Stone traveled fast, until he came to the man whom he knew to be the last one who had given out. The man was angry because Young-Flint-Stone came around where he was, but Young-Flint-Stone went boldly up to him and put a handful of meal into his mouth. The man drew back his head, laughed, and said: "Yes, this puts me in mind of being at Where-Blackbirds-lit-on-elm-Tree, or Stone-Corn-Mills-lying-on-Hill-side, or Large-elm-Tree-near-Edge-of-the-Village, or Where-large-Ears-of-Corn-grow. Well, Young-Flint-Stone, you have come in search of your father, who lives further south, near to his enemies. He surely had great powers, and to go and see him you will have to sneak around to get to his lodge, for if he sees you before you get up there he will kill you. He lives at that high point; sometimes he is out, and then there are times when he goes to sleep. When you get there he will try to kill you, for he allows no one to come to his place. There is a time when I can hear him giving a war-whoop, when he goes out after his enemies. Now you may go on." So Young-Flint-Stone went on, after he had gained the information regarding his father's habits and lodge. He traveled on and on, sneaking so as not to be seen, as he had been instructed, until he came to the place where his father was.

He finally succeeded in reaching the door of the lodge, and on entering, said to his father, "My father, I am now here in search of you." Just as he said that, the Protector-of-Warriors rose on his feet and said: "I can not believe it. I know I have a son, but as far away from here as he is, I can not believe he could ever reach this place. You are trying to play me a trick." Then he went for his war-club. Young-Flint-Stone got hold of his father and said to him, "I am your son, Young-Flint-Stone." His father then began to push him around towards his war-club. Then Young-Flint-Stone pushed his father away from it, but his father kept pushing him towards it, still believing some one was trying to trick him. Young-Flint-Stone finally succeeded in untying the sack, and he took out a handful of meal and put it into his father's mouth. Then his father asked him to loose him, and throwing his head back, said: "O, yes; that is the very thing; it tastes just like what they had where I came from; this puts me in mind of Where-Blackbirds-lit-on-elm-Tree, or Stone-Corn-Mills-lying-on-Hill-side, or Large-elm-Tree-near-Edge-of-the-Village, or Where-large-Ears-of-Corn-grow. Surely you are my son. When I left her, you were still in your mother's womb and I gave you the name you bear. Well, I am a good long way from home, and it just suits me to remain here. All the time I lived at the place you are from I had to go a long way with war-parties, and so I thought it to be best for me to be where I am now. I can not go back with you." Young-Flint-Stone noticed that his father's hair was turning into flint-stone, and he noticed the pole that was stuck up outside his father's place, which had on it many skulls, old and fresh.

Next morning the Protector-of-Warriors insisted that Young-Flint-Stone should go with him to help him fight some of his enemies. They both went down the hill, traveled all that morning, until they came to a village, and there they met their enemies. Young-Flint-Stone was the first one to kill a man, when his father also killed a man, then they turned and came home with the scalps. Young-Flint-Stone did not remain here very long before his father asked him to return home, for the folks were looking for him to come home. The Protector-of-Warriors said: "It is very near time for the next generation to come, and, where I am, I will be known as the Protector-of-Warriors. Tell the people that I am here, never to return, and that I shall be seen as the South-Star; and in the next generation, when anyone sends out a war-party they shall make their offering of smoke, and then, if I take pity on whoever offers the smoke, he shall receive good fortune, easy times in meeting enemies, and shall always return victorious, like other people when I was living." He then asked Young-Flint-Stone to take back with him a scalp to his wife and father's mother, and his sisters. Young-Flint-Stone then departed from his father, and as he passed the men who had given out along the way they said that they would like to remain where they were. He traveled on and on, and no one knew how long it took him to reach home, but he finally arrived with the scalps, which he delivered to his folks for the Protector-of-Warriors. The folks were surprised to see him; for they knew that it was not safe for anyone to go so far away from home as he had gone.

When everybody had heard of Young-Flint-Stone's return they came to see him, and asked how he met his father. He then told them about the hard times he had had traveling, the four men who were near to his father, what they had said when he first met them on his way to see his father, how his father threatened to take his life, how he accompanied his father in a fight with the enemies in that part of the country, how he and his father secured scalps, what length of time he had remained there with his father, and about the scalp that was to be presented to his folks. Young-Flint-Stone showed the people the scalp that he had brought. When the people heard the news that Young-Flint-Stone had brought they began to move away to their homes, and the news of his return spread. When night came they had dances of all kinds, in honor of Young-Flint-Stone and his father. So it is known that Young-Flint-Stone is the only person who ever went far enough south to see his father, and he was the last one who ever saw him. Young-Flint-Stone then got to be a famous man, a great warrior like his father had been while he lived at the village. He would send out war-parties against his enemies, the Tricksters, and with the great powers he had he was always victorious and brought home with him many captives, as well as scalps. This was what made him a famous man.

At this time the South-Star could be seen, so Young-Flint-Stone told all his followers that the star was his father, whom he once went to see. Thereafter, whenever this star was in sight, Young-Flint-Stone would offer smoke to it, as he had been instructed by his father, who was now the Star itself. It was not very long before Young-Flint-Stone called forth the people, who gathered around his place. They asked him why he had called them forth, and he replied that since he had been well cared for by his young men friends and his warrior friends, and had seen his father as a Star, he thought he had better be like his father was at this time. Young-Flint-Stone then waited until night, and when darkness came he went up into the sky and became a star, which we call "Flint-Stone-lying-down-above" (Tahanet-skitadidia).

8. THE SEVEN BROTHERS AND THE WOMAN.*

In the time of the story, there were several villages, and in these villages there was always a head man or chief. In one of these villages there was a head man, who had a wife. Now, at this time there were all kinds of people living, good people and bad people, and there were people who had great powers of all kinds. There was a certain person who had the power to change his looks, so that sometimes he would appear to be a young man, and at other times an old, ugly man. His name was Mixed-Timber (Kilakilakawi). One time Mixed-Timber started for the village where the chief lived, expecting to carry off his wife. On arriving at this place, he changed his looks so that he appeared to be a young man. Late in the evening he reached the chief's place. When the chief's wife stepped out to bring in wood for the fire she saw a man standing in front of her. When she stepped out of the tipi she noticed a fragrant odor; this came from Mixed-Timber. She started to see who he was, and the man kept backing off, and the woman kept following him, until they reached the end of the village.

She found that she could not turn back any more, but had to continue following this man. They went outside of the village, and Mixed-Timber stopped to tell the woman that he had made a long journey for her; then they started off toward the west, traveling all that night, until the next night, when they stopped to rest and sleep. When they stopped to rest, the woman was told to lie down at a certain place. The man lay down in another place. Next day they continued their journey until darkness came, when they stopped again. The woman lay down again at a certain distance from Mixed-Timber, and at times she wondered why they did not lie together. The next day they started again to the place where they were going, and as far as the woman could see, she saw something in sight. As they came nearer to it, it changed into the shape of a lodge, and they finally reached the place, and the woman was told not to go in until bidden. She was finally asked in harsh words to enter. In the room there was an old, ugly man, sitting by the fireplace. There was also the mother of Mixed-Timber. After a while, the old man, who was Mixed-Timber, asked for something to eat, and he was given some meat. His mother, and also the woman he had brought, ate with him. After the meal Mixed-Timber started out on another hunting trip, and while he was making this trip, his mother told the young woman that on his return she would be asked to go and bring some water; that he had a drinking place all of his

*Told by Ahahe (Waco).

own, in which was human blood, and he had a human skull for a cup; that he was wicked and had human flesh for his meals; and that this was the worst of all places to be; that on her son's return, if asked to go and fetch water for him, she should look out for her hand, for if he got hold of it, she would be slain and butchered.

On the following day, late in the evening, this man returned from his hunting trip. Upon entering the place, the very first thing he asked for was something to eat. The old woman gave him human flesh for his supper, and then, after the meal, the young woman was asked to bring him some fresh water. She stepped out and went for the water. Arriving at the spring, she found a human skull, which she was to use for her cup. She dipped the skull in the blood and carried it to the man, remembering what the old woman had told her. When she entered the place she gave the blood water to Mixed-Timber, and in taking it, he reached for her hand. She jerked it away from him. He asked her why she did this; then she was told to go and put the skull back where she had found it. This was in the night, and they all went to bed and to sleep, the two women sleeping together and the man sleeping by himself. While Mixed-Timber was on his next hunting trip, his mother told the young woman that he did not mean what he had said about not killing any game; that he wanted an excuse for killing the young woman; that the next day the man would go on another hunting trip; and that he would say that he had not killed any game (for it was human beings that he hunted); and that the next time the man should start to hunt, the young woman should make her escape. The young woman stayed all that day, and Mixed-Timber returned from his hunting trip again and was as hungry as he could be. He asked for something to eat, and the old woman gave him something to eat. Then he asked for fresh water to drink, and the young woman went out to get him water. She took the skull again and brought him some blood water, and he made a quick jerk for her hand, but the woman was too quick for him. Then he asked her why she jerked away. Early on the next day the man went on another hunting trip. The young woman was told to make her escape, and to go south, where she would be saved. She was given power to get away. Early that morning she was given the double-ball and a stick to go on. The old woman stood on the north side of the fireplace, and the young woman took water, put it on the fire, and as the smoke went up she went up with it. The smoke of the fire went for a long way toward the south. The old woman had told the young woman that she would have to cross some river; that there would be some one there to take her across;

that she should then go to a place where there was a small hill, where she would see a little boy; that she should beg the boy to save her life, for this little boy's people had great power. After the woman had lighted on her feet, she ran along for a way, and then took the stick and tossed the double-ball towards the place where she was going. (In these times the double-ball would go a long way. They were used by women traveling.) When she tossed the double-ball she went with it up in the air.

The old woman now called for her son and told him of the young woman's escape. (The man had great power, to hear a long way off.) Then the old woman took a club and killed herself. When the man came home he saw his mother lying on the ground, dead. He made a circuit around the place, looking for the young woman's trail, then he went back again to the place where his mother was lying dead. He looked and looked, and wondered which way his prisoner had gone, and then went around the place again, always a little way off, to look for her trail. Mixed-Timber at last found her trail. While on the way, she could hear him talking, saying, "I will get you. You need not think you are going to get away from me." When he came to the place where she tossed the balls, he lost the trail again, and there he would have to spend some time in looking for it. Then the woman would light on her feet and go on the ground for a while, and when' she gave out again, she would use the double-ball. She tossed the double-ball four times, and then went on the ground for a while, until she came to the place where she was told to go. When she tossed the double-ball for the last time she could just barely see the place where she was going. Every time she tossed the ball the man would lose her trail, but she could always hear him talking. After getting on her feet she had to run a long way, but finally came to the river, where she went along the bank, looking for a certain person to take her across the river. She finally found the one she was looking for, and this was a Crane (Hakeakawi). The Crane stretched his neck across the water, so the woman could walk across. She told the Crane not to let the man cross over, but the Crane told the woman if he did not he would be killed. He also told the woman the same thing the old woman had told her, and so she went to the point, and there she found a boy walking around. His name was Big-Belly-Boy (Wikskatsitawaks). She begged him to save her life. She told him some one was after her to kill her. The boy still continued to go around. At this time Mixed-Timber came in sight of her, and he was telling the boy not to listen to her, but she begged the boy to save her life and he finally agreed to do so. They went into the place where the boy lived, and on their way the woman noticed that there was a great, big stone at the point they were going to. Big-Belly-Boy removed the stone and they entered. There was an old man in the room by the name of Man-with-supernatural-Powers (Nihosikiwarikit), to whom he said he had some one with him who wanted her life saved.

By this time Mixed-Timber had arrived, and he asked for the release of the woman, but he could not get those people to give her up. He went on ahead and began destroying the little hill which they were in. Beginning at the top, he tore off the rocks. The boy said to Man-with-supernatural-Power, "Make haste, that man is about to destroy our lodge." So the old man arose. Around his neck was tied a string which had something tied to it. He took the string off from his neck and threw it up, and killed the man outside instantly. When he threw it, it sounded like thunder and lightning. The old man then went outside to fix up the place again, and to replace the stones that had been torn up by Mixed-Timber. This lodge was at a high point, and the people had a big stone that was used for a door. When Mixed-Timber was dead, they told the woman that she could go where she was from, but the boy quickly spoke, saying that the woman had made all kinds of promises as to what she would do to relieve him of work, such as wood hauling and carrying, etc., if he would help her. The boy asked Man-with-supernatural-Powers to let the woman stay, because he himself was tired of doing all his work. The woman was allowed to remain. Man-with-supernatural-Powers told the woman that he had six sons; that they were out; but that they would be in soon, as they were now coming. Before reaching the lodge the sons all stopped and asked what it was they had in the lodge. They all said that it must be something unpleasant, for they could smell something. The boy was out begging his brothers to come, and to prevail upon them he told them they had always said they loved him; and he told them there was somebody in the lodge that the old man had saved from being killed, and that this one had made all kinds of promises to him to relieve him of his work. They all agreed to enter. One after another they entered, and died; for these men were used to living by themselves, and thus they could always tell when there was some stranger at the place. When the oldest one started into the lodge, he closed up his mouth and fell dead. The rest did the same thing, until they were all dead. So Big-Belly-Boy begged Man-with-supernatural-Powers to restore his brothers to life. The old man, having such great powers, raised these boys from the dead, and there they were again.

They were surprised to see what was there. They all thought, as they looked at the girl, that she was a funny kind of man, for she was of a different shape from a man, and they had never before seen a woman.

Time passed, and the six brothers were always on some kind of a hunting expedition; but Big-Belly-Boy, Man-with-supernatural-Powers, and the woman all stayed home. In so doing, all the work that the boy formerly did was to be done by the woman, while she was carrying wood or water. The woman told the boy what people where she was from did to bring forth children; but Big-Belly-Boy could not understand what she meant. The woman told Big-Belly-Boy that where there were people, man and woman became husband and wife. Big-Belly-Boy told his brothers of this, saying that people ought to increase in number, and so in the night, the oldest brother did the same as the young boy had done, and he told the rest of his brothers about it. Altogether, the woman had seven men to whom she was married. She was living with these folks, and Big-Belly-Boy stayed close to her every day while she went to haul wood and water. Soon she told the people that she was pregnant, and as time passed, again she told them that she was going to be confined, and that men were not allowed to stay where a woman was about to have a child. The six men stepped out of the lodge; but the old man and the boy remained. A child was born to these seven brothers; it was a boy. The old man fumigated the place with smoke, so that his boys could enter. Then the boys came in, and they were surprised to find the child. They passed around and around to examine it.

As the six boys were in the habit of going hunting, they all went out on a trip again. When they returned, they saw that the boy was sad, as if something were the matter with him. One of the six brothers asked why he was feeling sad, and he said, "Because we are to be attacked by somebody." They told the boy not to mind that. In a few days, while they were out of doors, there came two Double-Faced-Monsters (Witschatska) to attack them. The boys began to fight, but found that they could do nothing to these two monsters, and now all were killed. The boy asked his father to make haste in raising the boys from the dead. The old man went and brought them in, one at a time. When he had brought them all into the lodge, he brought them all to life again.

The six brothers went out hunting again, while the boy, the woman and the child went out to some place, walking around. While walking, they came to a cave, and in this cave they saw lots of young Double-Faced-Monsters. They were fierce looking creatures. Over head they saw a kind of line stretched across the cave, and something hanging on it. The boy asked what these were, and the children said that they were their lungs. These young ones also told of the story about the six brothers having a fight with their father and mother. Big-Belly-Boy had some arrows. He took one of these arrows and punched one of these lungs with the point of it, and one of the young ones fell dead. Then he stuck the point of his arrow through another, and another, until he finally stuck the arrow point into the last two, killing them. The boy, woman, and child then went back to the lodge and told what they had done. Big-Belly-Boy himself had great powers. They lived there for a long time.

Finally the woman began to tell the boy what fun there was where children were among children, and that where she came from there were games of all sorts. She told him that if there were more people, he and his little boy could play, and she finally persuaded him to move their lodge. She told him that the rest of his brothers could marry some girls, and be with many other young men of their age. The time came when the boy made out that he was feeling very bad over something. His people asked him what was the matter, and he replied that he was told that if they moved to where this woman was from he would have all the fun he wanted and that he could play with other children. They told the boy not to feel badly, because they always agreed to do whatever he asked. They finally moved toward the north. When darkness came on, Man-with-supernatural-Powers took a bunch of grass in his hand and blew upon it, and put it on the ground, and there was the first grass-lodge. They stayed all that night until the next day, when they continued their journey. When they started, Man-with-supernatural-Powers took a straw and carried it along. When darkness came again, the old man took the straw, stuck it in the ground, and there was a grass-lodge again. The next day they went on again. Man-with-supernatural-Powers took another straw and made another grass-lodge. The next day they traveled all day until late in the night, when they reached the village of the woman. The old man took the straw, stuck it in the ground and they had a grass-lodge to live in. No one knew of these strangers moving in. They remained for a long time. The boys did as the woman had told them, and they were married. Of course, the oldest of the brothers was married to the woman whom they brought with them. Big-Belly-Boy and the other little boy played with the rest of the children. Here they lived for a while, until some child made the little boy cry; and Big-Belly-Boy felt sad over it. On their way home the boy cried all the way, and Big-Belly-Boy himself began to cry, too.

At this time, the oldest brother sent Big-Belly-Boy to round up all his brothers who were living with other women. When they arrived, the old man told them that they had better move out again, for he did not like the way the boy was treated. They intended to leave the woman, but she begged to go along, too. Man-with-supernatural-Powers took his family and went up into the sky, but the village remained. If we look carefully at the Seven Stars (Ursa Minor), we can always find Big-Belly-Boy, second to the last, with the little boy. The old man himself became the Never-Moving-Star (Kasasaniki), or North Star; and another bright star below him, is the woman, mother of Big-Belly-Boy. So North-Star is the father of the Seven-Stars.

9. THE SEVEN BROTHERS AND THE SISTER.*

There was once a village. Some people lived within this village while some lived outside. There were seven brothers who had five sisters, and they with their father and mother lived in this village. The seven brothers were like other men of their time and went hunting and on the war-path. They were always out on some kind of a trip. When not on the war-path they had great powers. None of their enemies knew when they were near nor when they were about to attack. They blindfolded their enemies, as it were, so that they might easily do to them whatever they wanted to do. At home they had fun and played all sorts of games, the same as other men did. Their chief game was with the hoop. Each of the brothers had a certain power that the others had not, and they were named accordingly, as follows: Good-Sight (Otsnanaaiai), Good-Hearing (Gaatsia), Great-Strength (Netsia), Good-Shooter (Otsnaiwigaia), Fast-Runner (Nataquantsiki), Great-Prophet (Nadikakidilue), and Afraid-of-Nothing (Kakinaidari). They spent most of their time on the war-path, leaving their folks at home. Large crowds would go with these parties against the Trickster (Kinas) people of those times.

While the oldest brother was home, some one came to his bed nearly every night, and he knew it was a woman. He soon got tired of the occurrence, for he wanted to remain single all his life. He took white clay and water, mixed it, then put it away for use at night. When he went to bed again to sleep, a woman came to his bed. When the woman came he would always kick her off the bed; but this time, when the woman came to his bed he took the clay and water that he

*Told by Lodge-in-front-of-all-the-Lodges (Waco).

had mixed, then he grabbed the woman and put a mark on her back, then pushed her away. The next day he announced publicly that he wanted to see the women play the double-ball game. The following morning the women from every lodge came to the play-ground and played the double-ball game. The young man sat watching the game, looking out for the one he had marked. While the game was going on he noticed that one of his sisters bore the mark. She was his oldest sister. He then ordered the women to go home. When the game was going on, the rest of the women would ask the young man's sister why she had the hand mark on her. He, of course, felt sad that his sister should have treated him like this, so he decided to punish her when she should come to him again. The very next night, the sister came to his bed again, and this time he was ready for her with his arrows on his right side. When the woman came he took his arrows by the points, struck all over her and made her cry aloud. The woman, full of regret, left her parents behind, going north, and when she was by herself she became Woman-having-great-Powers (Widadadiakista), or Grisly-Bear.

Now, the seven brothers went on the war-path and were gone for a good while. The time came when Great-Prophet stayed behind the rest of the crowd. His brothers said among themselves: "What can be the matter with Great-Prophet. Surely he must have found out something." So they all stopped a moment to see if he had discovered some danger before them or at home. He answered them, saying there was danger at home; that some beast had killed all the people but their youngest sister. They asked Good-Sight to look and see if he could see anything at home. When he had looked he said to his brothers that surely there was a Bear going around their home. They at once turned back and made a straight journey to their home. They remained outside of their former village to avoid danger, but they kept close watch of the Bear and their sister. One day the seven brothers watched to see if their sister would come away from the place where the Bear was. They saw her coming toward the prairie; so they went toward her and asked her for information. The girl said the Bear was always looking for her brothers' return and wanted to do to them as she had done to the people; that she was sent out to get a sack full of Indian turnips. She had a short stick, to kill a jack-rabbit. Her brothers asked her if she did anything else during the day. She told them that the Bear always slept about noon, and part of the night, and woke up in the afternoon. They quickly dug the turnips, and filled her sack full, and ordered Good-Sight to take the stick and go quickly and kill a jack-rabbit. He took the stick and went to look for the rabbit to kill for the Bear. He finally succeeded in finding one, threw the stick and stuck it into the rabbit through its side. After they had done these things for their sister they again asked her if she had ever asked the Bear where a person should shoot her in order to kill her. She told them that all one had to do was to shoot the Bear in her hands and under her feet. The brothers again begged Good-Sight to give the girl power to shoot straight, for they knew the Bear would make her repeat the shooting of the rabbit. They knew that the Bear would not believe the girl had dug the turnips so quickly and that she had killed the rabbit. They started her off and told her to keep secret their presence around the village. The next time the seven brothers met the girl she told them that when she had arrived with the turnips and jack-rabbit at the place where the Bear was, the Bear had said to her: "Your brothers must be somewhere around the camp; I know that you could not have filled the sack so soon and could not possibly have killed the rabbit so easily." She told them that she had denied that her brothers were somewhere around their former camps; that the Bear had said to her: "I must see with my own eyes how you did when you killed the rabbit;" that the Bear had stood up the dead rabbit and given her the stick to prove that she had killed it; that she had thrown the stick at the rabbit and hit it right in the wound, so that the Bear had to believe her; that she had cooked the rabbit by the fire; that the Bear had fallen asleep, it being about noon, when she had come to her brothers. The seven brothers then consulted as to what must be done and what would be the best way to get away from the Bear. When the Bear went to sleep she could be heard a long way off. The brothers left the girl with Fast-Runner, who at once started for the north, going as hard as he could go. His brothers then went straight to where the Bear was, and on their arrival they saw her still sleeping soundly on her back, with her hands and feet up. This gave them a chance to shoot her under the feet. Four of them got around her, one at each foot, to shoot and kill her. They all shot at once, hitting her under the feet. Then they all ran toward the north, where Fast-Runner had gone with their sister.

They could hear the Bear talking, saying: "Who would ever believe anyone could kill me by shooting under my feet and hands! I knew the seven brothers were somewhere about the village; but never mind, I will get them." The Bear at once took after them and they could hear her talking, saying: "I will get you. You need not think you are going to make your escape from me. It is the hardest thing a person could do." By this time the brothers were a good way off, but they could still hear the Bear talking. They went fast, each taking his turn carrying their sister along. The Bear kept gaining on them, and came so near that they could see her coming. The oldest brother took a turtle shell, threw it on the ground, and there was a great, big bunch of turtles crawling around. Then they continued their escape. When the Bear came to the turtles she stopped quite a while, trying to get them to one place, so that she could get them. But the turtles kept crawling around. They were the Bear's main food, and this was a good chance for her to get all she wanted. The Bear forgot for a while all about chasing the seven brothers, who, with their sister, had gone a long way ahead of her. The Bear again chased the people, saying: "I will get you. You need not think you are going to make me forget to chase you." The seven brothers and their sister could hear the Bear talking, but she was a good way off yet. They still kept traveling as fast as they could. The Bear, having power to travel a good deal faster than the seven brothers, gained on them so that they could see her coming and could hear her voice, and they were frightened. The oldest brother took a piece of red colored stone and threw it on the ground and the place was full of red colored stones. This brother knew this to be the very thing that the Bear wanted for painting. When the Bear came to the place she stopped, thinking that was the very thing she had been wanting for a good while. The Bear commenced to pile up the red colored stones and almost forgot about chasing the seven brothers. The Bear did forget once in a while, but soon thought of it again. She now said to herself: "Well, when I come back I will have what I want." She then pursued them again. The seven brothers had gone a long way ahead of her. She commenced talking again, and this time they heard her saying that they were the people she was after, for they had done her wrong by pricking her with the points of the arrows, and she was bound to get them and get even with them. They traveled along, but the Bear kept gaining on them, and she got so near that they could see her coming.

The oldest brother now took his knife, cut out of his arrows a fine dust, threw it on the ground and there were great, big bushes that arrows are made of. When the Bear came to the place she stopped again and began to look for the best and straightest bushes, saying to herself, "Well, here are the things I have been wanting for a long while, and here is the best chance for me to get what I want." She commenced to cut them with her teeth. Whenever the oldest brother left something behind for the Bear, the Bear would forget for a while all about the seven brothers. The brothers and sister were now a good way ahead of her again, when the Bear remembered and began to pursue them. The people were traveling rapidly, but the Bear gained on them again and kept gaining until they were compelled to do something or die. Finally they saw the Bear coming. The oldest one said to the rest: "We will now have to die. There is only one thing left to be done. When the Bear succeeds in passing the next place we surely will have to die." He now took his bow-string off from his bow, passing it through his left hand four times, then threw it on the ground, and there was a deep canyon, but it had a place where the Bear could get down and get out on the other side. They commenced to travel again. When the Bear came to the canyon she went all round, looking for a place, going further and further, and finally came to a place where there was a high cedar tree standing over the canyon. She made a jump onto the tree, climbed down, got on the ground and commenced to look for a place to get out. She climbed onto another tree, then jumped on the other side of the canyon and commenced to chase the seven brothers. The party was now a good way off, but they could hear her talking. This being their last chance, the brothers and their sister had to give up traveling. They all stopped, sat in a row, and faced toward the south. The oldest brother was on the west end, their sister on the other end, next to Fast-Runner. Finally they saw the Bear coming, saying: "I thought I would finally get you. You thought I never would give up chasing you."

When the Bear arrived she sat down and rolled around, rolled up to each of them, kept rolling around, and would sometimes slap one of them, and say, "You knew that nobody could get away from me." When she rolled away from them, the oldest brother jumped up, called to his brothers to rise, took the feather off his head and blew it. As it went up the seven brothers and their sisters went with it. They went up in the sky before the Bear knew it, and they now live as the Seven (Kiowhits), or the Dipper. When the Bear rolled up where they had been, she finally noticed that she did not touch anyone. She opened her eyes and looked around to see where the people had gone, but there was no sign of them and no trail. She looked around, but could not see any trace of them. When she looked up in the sky she saw them above her, where she could never get them. She commenced to scold herself, saying: "Why did I not kill them when I arrived! Well, I can not help it now; they have got away from me." The Bear had to give up and went off to the canyon and never did go back where she had come from. In the north there can be seen worlds of these bears, because the Bear went there, and never returned. Before the Bear arrived where the seven brothers were the oldest one talked to the rest, saying: "The powers we have had and the things we have had are to remain on earth for the people of the next generation. If at any time anybody sends out any kind of an expedition and the leader wishes aid from us he can get it by offering smoke to us." These benefits they left on earth for generations to follow.

10. THE SEVEN BROTHERS AND THE SISTER.*

The Coyote was a famous schemer. He wandered about in the wilderness looking for food for his family, and there were times when he was lucky enough to get something. The Coyote worked all kinds of schemes and tricks on other people to make a living. Sometimes power was given him to become famous like those who had given him the power. The Coyote was living out by himself, where there was no one else. He had no neighbors, and was accustomed to prowl around, and wander from one place to another, hunting for food. Once upon a time the Coyote went toward the west. He kept going, and was getting far from home. He finally came to some thick timber, and in this timber there was flowing water. When he crossed the creek he saw a grass-lodge. He then decided to go and visit the place and find out who lived there.

When the Coyote reached the place he entered the grass-lodge, and he saw a young woman who was staying at her home all alone. The woman asked him to be seated. Then she asked him if he was hungry. The Coyote said he was hungry. The woman began to cook some meat for him, and when she had cooked it she gave it to him. While the Coyote was eating, this woman began to ask him some questions. She asked him if he had any children. The Coyote told the woman that he had a daughter about her age, who resembled her very much. The woman then asked the Coyote if he could spare his daughter and let her come and live with her, for she lived alone in the daytime, and at night her brothers came home from hunting. The Coyote said in reply: ˙ "Well, woman, when I get home, I will tell my daughter to come over and live with you, and you will find that I have a fine-looking daughter who resembles you. When your brothers come home they too will find that my daughter resembles

*Told by Ignorant-Woman (Man) (Towakoni).

you." After the Coyote had told the woman that he would send his daughter to live with her the woman gave him all the meat he could carry. Being strong, he took home plenty of meat in his pack. As the Coyote started the woman asked him to be sure and send over his daughter, and promised him that when his daughter was living with her she would give him all the meat he might want for his family and she would treat his daughter well. She also told the Coyote that when her brothers should come home they would stop a long way from the lodge and ask her what she had in the lodge that was decayed, for they were high-class people and not used to anyone coming around. These brothers could always tell by the scent of the place whenever anyone had been around. The Coyote went on home, having plenty of meat with him for his family.

On the following day the Coyote arrived home with his meat. As they were always hungry they ate the meat in a short time. The Coyote forgot what the woman had told him, for he had no daughter who was similar to her, nor had he one of the same age. Some time after this he thought again of the woman and resolved to go back. He left his home to go to her. When he came to the river he looked for the deepest place, and finally succeeded in finding such a place, and then stripped off all his clothing and went into the water. The water was about half-way up on his body. The Coyote then got ready to dive into the water, and said: "The time has arrived when I will turn into a woman." As soon as he had said this he dived, and when he came out he looked at himself, and saw that he was a woman, but not like a grown woman. He dived again, the second, the third, and the fourth times, then looked at himself again and saw that he was full grown. Then he looked into the water and found that he was similar to the woman he was going to visit. The Coyote having become a woman, he came out of the water to the land. He got his old quiver and his robe which he put around him after the manner of a woman. He then threw his quiver where he had his arrows. When the Coyote arrived at the woman's place he made a noise to attract her attention so as to make her come out. Of course, the woman came out and went in the direction the sound came from. But the Coyote, to be a little contrary, after he had made the noise, went from the woman, around the other way and dodged her. Failing to find anyone the woman thought she must have heard an echo in the lodge. The Coyote now went on the south side of the lodge and made the same kind of a noise as before, to make the woman come out again. And indeed, he did cause the woman to come out, and this time the Coyote had his head down, facing the wall of the grass-lodge. The woman then found the Coyote and asked him if his father had sent him down to live with her. The Coyote would not say a word, but shook his head for "Yes." The woman then told the Coyote to come into the grass-lodge. She was proud of her company. She asked the Coyote if he wanted something to eat, and he told her that he did, so the woman gave him something to eat. While the Coyote was eating the woman asked why his father had not come along, since he had promised to come with his daughter. The Coyote said that his father had turned off some other way and that he would come some other time. The woman then began to tell the Coyote woman about her brothers, who were away hunting, saying that they were away hunting and were to return late that evening, and that on their approach they would ask her to take out of the lodge whatever she might have there, as the smell of the Coyote would be like a stench to them.

Late that day they heard the brothers returning. As soon as they came near the grass-lodge the men began to ask their sister what she had in the lodge that smelled so badly. During the day she had fumigated the room by burning some kind of brown weeds. Still the men could smell what was in the lodge. The woman told her brothers that she had a woman in the lodge to live with her while they were away; that they had told of their love for her and promised her that she might do as she wished. The brothers then said to one another, "Well, let us go and see what she has in there, for we love our sister, and whatever she says will be all right." The men then walked into the lodge and they saw no one. The woman began to cook some food for her brothers. After everything was cooked she gave them the food, and when they began to eat, the woman pulled the robe from the Coyote woman and asked her to get up and eat with her. When the Coyote woman got up the men began to look at her, and this made her somewhat ashamed as she looked at her companion's brothers, and she was already enamored of them; and the next thing that came to the Coyote woman's mind was that she was bound to marry them. The woman then cut up the meat for the Coyote woman, but she ate only a little bit. The woman then told her brothers that this Coyote woman was a daughter of the man who had visited her sometime before; that she had asked him if he had any children and he had replied that he had a daughter about her age; and that they could now see that the woman was about her own age. The men saw that the two women were about the same age, and believed that the Coyote woman had been sent from her home to remain with their sister during their absence.

After eating they all went to bed. The two women slept together. The next morning the woman again cooked her brothers' food, and when they were through eating they went out again, the same as usual. The woman was no longer worried, for she had some one to stay with her and talk to her. They went off in the timber and cut wood and brought it home with them, and during that day both hauled about four or five loads, and the remainder of the day they stayed at home.

Time went on, and the woman began to ask the Coyote woman how people obtained children. She said she wished she might in some way have a child, for she was very fond of young children since she had heard about other people having children. The Coyote woman then said that a man and a woman had to marry in order to get a child, and that was the way her father and mother made her and the other children of the family. The Coyote woman then told her that her mother and father had told her all about these things, and how a child must be kept, and that was how she came to know so much about it. The woman then asked the Coyote woman if she could by marrying one of her brothers bring a child. The Coyote woman said she could, for her father and mother had told her if she could get hold of some good man for a husband she could have children the same as they had. So the woman offered her brothers to the Coyote woman to marry, for she knew that they were good enough for this woman to marry, and she knew that they would do whatever she might tell them to do. So they talked at home and things were now ready for the Coyote woman to marry the other woman's brothers. The next day, when the brothers returned from hunting, their sister began to tell them what she had thought of; that she had always wanted to know how a child was brought, and through the Coyote woman, who had been told all about it by her father and mother, she had learned that to get children a man and woman must marry. The woman then said to her brothers that she wanted them to marry the Coyote woman, as she wanted to see a child born to one of them. This was first directed to the oldest brother, who said that his next younger brother should have her. This brother refused her, and so on down, till it came to the youngest brother, who said he did not understand why the responsibility was laid upon him, since his sister had desired that they all should marry the Coyote woman. Said he: "I thought it was for us to do whatever our sister wants us to do, so I think it best that we should all have the woman between us." All agreed that this was right. The oldest of the seven brothers slept with the Coyote woman first. As they were ignorant, the Coyote woman had to show them what to do when married. As they went out on the next day the oldest brother began to tell the rest how he had been with a woman for the first time in his life, and promised them that they would be delighted when it came their turn. When they arrived the next day the Coyote woman did most of the work in feeding the men, for she was now their wife. At night the next oldest took his turn sleeping with the Coyote woman, and he was shown how to work at night. Thereafter the men took turns sleeping with the Coyote woman.

Some time afterwards the Coyote woman told her sister-in-law that she was pregnant, "for," said she, "my mother has told me that when a woman is in my condition she is pregnant and must not sleep with men any more. My mother and father no longer sleep together when a child is in my mother's womb. Moreover, before any brothers and sisters are born, my father cuts twenty-four dogwood sprouts to make a cradle, and other material that is used in making a cradle." The woman listened attentively to all that the Coyote woman had to say about the handling of a child after it was born, and it sounded strange to her. When the brothers came home she repeated all that she had heard; how they were not to sleep any more with the Coyote woman, and how they were to cut dogwood sprouts to make a cradle for the child. She told them they could sleep with the Coyote woman once more, but after that the two women would sleep together. Some time afterward the men were out cutting the twenty-four dogwood sticks to make a cradle with for the child, and other materials that had to be used were the things that they always had. So everything went on the same as it had always gone. While the two women were together the woman would feel around where the child was and wonder whether it was going to be a boy or a girl. Some time after, the Coyote woman told her sister-in-law that she was about to have a child, and she would after that remain at home and let the other woman do the work. Sometimes the woman would say: "I wonder why your father does not come to see us." The Coyote woman would say: "Perhaps he has all he can do and has no time to come around." Whatever the Coyote woman did she would relate what her father and mother told her, but she was the old man Coyote herself. Finally the Coyote woman became sick, and said she was going to have a child. So the child was born.

The woman, not knowing anything about having children, asked the Coyote woman what to do, and she told the woman to cut the navel off. After doing this the woman took the robe of one of her brothers and wrapped up the child in it. After the child was born the Coyote woman told the woman she had heard from her mother that bearing a child affected the legs, so that her mother always took a rope and went after wood and put a load on her back, which straightened her up. "So let me have a rope," said she, "and I will do the same as my mother does." The woman handed her a rope and she brought about three loads of wood on her back. After she had done this she was washed. "Now," said the Coyote woman, "my mother has told me that whenever a child is born it is the rule that men may not enter the lodge until four days have elapsed. So we must not allow the men to come in, but let them remain somewhere else until after four days." The woman kept watching for her brothers to come home, so she could tell them about the child, and tell them to remain somewhere until after four days should pass. Finally they came home, and there was the woman, waiting to tell them of the child's birth.

The woman stopped them before they came near the place and told them about the birth of the child. They asked her if the child was a boy or girl. She told them it was a boy and that they could not come in the lodge until the fifth day, for the Coyote woman had said that that was the rule. So the men, when returning from the hunt, stayed outside the lodge for four days. On the fifth day they were allowed to come in. They all saw their child, which was now in a cradle. The men were proud of the child, so they passed it around from one to another. After this the Coyote woman would remain at home with the child while the other woman did the work. This is the way they did things around the lodge. The child grew pretty fast.

After a time the Coyote woman began to think about leaving these folks to go to some other place to marry some chief of a tribe, for she knew nearly all the villages near there. One day while the woman was away she took the child and went up the creek a little way and sat down. When the woman returned to the lodge she went out to look for the Coyote woman and the child. She found them up along the creek bank sitting down. The woman then said to the Coyote woman that she was through with her work and that they would go home, so they went back. The next day the woman went out again to bring some wood, and this time the Coyote woman decided to leave them. As the woman went off the Coyote woman started off with her child, going toward the north. They were a good long way from home when the woman returned. But she had more wood to haul, and, knowing that the Coyote woman and the child were accustomed to go out and sit down for a while she did not pay much attention to their absence. She thought they had gone somewhere for a short time. When she came back she went direct to where she had found them before, but could not find them this time. So she went all around and failed to find them. She then went straight home. She was now sure that they had deserted, and she cried all that day.

The next day, when the brothers returned home, they heard something unusual and stopped to listen to learn what it was. One of the men said: "It is our sister crying." They then entered the lodge and asked what was the trouble. She told them that the woman had deserted with the child. The oldest of the seven brothers then said: "I have always known, sister, that you were fooled, but never mind, we will get that child, so stop crying and let us have something to eat." The woman began to cook food for her brothers. After eating supper all went to bed. The next morning, after breakfast, the oldest man asked his sister to bring in a pot of water. They then all stood in a group and poured the water on the fire, and as the smoke went up they went up too. When they had got up high they saw the Coyote woman and the boy, so they went after them. As they got so near that they were only one hill apart they got on their feet again, still running after the two. They soon overtook them, and the oldest brother said to the Coyote woman: "Before you go any further let us have our child." The child was taken away from the Coyote woman, and the brothers, their sister, and the child now went up into the sky and became the Stars known as the "Seven" (Kiowhits), the Dipper. The sister also became a Star, but she did not stay with her brothers. The oldest brother had the child with him.

Sometimes when we see the Seven Stars we notice the first one having a small star beside it; sometimes it is with the next one, and so on, just as it used to be when the child was first born.

After the brothers, sister, and child had ascended into the sky the Coyote woman jumped, and said: "I will be there again and take my child." But by this time the Coyote woman noticed that she was a coyote, having a long tail and a different shape from what he used to be. Now he thought of his old home and that he had better return there. So he went on and on until he got there. When he came to the place the only thing he could see was hair and bones, the remains of his family. Then he went off on the prairie and cried as the coyotes cry. So whenever a coyote howls or cries it means that he is still howling or crying for his wife and children.

11. OWNER-OF-BLACK-AND-WHITE-FLINT-KNIVES AND HIS SON.*

In olden times some of the people lived in villages and some out by themselves. There was a family, father, mother, and daughter, who lived out by themselves. The old man made his living by hunting game, buffalo, deer, turkey, etc. The woman hauled the wood and did the work which fell to the women to do. One time she went out in the timber after wood, and when she had tied the wood with buffalo rope and was all ready to go home, she sat down, and was about to rise on her feet when she saw an arrow in the ground in front of her. As she was about to pick it up she saw some one coming, who said that the arrow was his. He was a fine-looking young man. His name was Owner-of-Black-and-White-Flint-Knives (Dahaacutsnaatiah). He told her to give up the arrow, but she refused to give it up, and the young man started back toward the west, where he had come from. The young woman followed him, asking him to stop and get his arrow, but he kept on, and the woman followed him. They went a good way from where she was putting up the wood, when the man finally stopped and she gave him his arrow. Then she discovered that she could not turn back, the young man having charmed her. Finally darkness came, and they stopped for the night. They built a fire and ate some meat. When they retired the young man told the woman to lie down by herself, and he lay down by himself. Early the next morning, they started again, and traveled all that day, until darkness overtook them, and they camped again for the night. This time the woman thought that she was to sleep with the man. When bedtime came the man told the woman to lie down on one side of the fire. On the next day they started again, traveling until darkness overtook them. They stopped to rest for the night. By this time, the woman had given up all hope of ever sleeping with the man. They built a fire, ate supper and went to sleep, the woman sleeping in one place and the man sleeping in another. In the morning after breakfast, they started, and traveled all day, and finally arrived at the home of the man.

The woman now saw the young man's mother and four sisters. The young man asked for something to eat, and they gave him some meat. His sisters also ate the same kind of meat. When the woman's supper time came the old woman gave her some buffalo meat and some parched corn. The strange woman thought that she would sleep with the young man's mother. She went to bed with the old woman. Next morning all ate breakfast and the young woman noticed that they had

*Told by Ahahe (Waco).

food of their own, the man and his sisters having meat for themselves, the old woman meat for herself, which she shared with the young stranger. That morning they supposed that the young man was going out hunting, and his four sisters went out to swim, for they were fond of swimming, so the strange woman was left at home with the old woman. The old woman began to tell the young woman how mean her children were; that their food was human flesh; that her son went out hunting, not for any kind of game, but for human beings; that he had great powers to attack human beings; that when he killed anybody he would butcher him and bring home his flesh for himself and his sisters. She told the young woman a great deal about the young man and his four sisters. All that day the young man was out hunting and his four sisters were out swimming. The old woman told the young woman that this way her children passed their time. At sundown the four sisters came home, and after a while the young man came, and they were all hungry. The man made his sisters prepare their supper at once. The young man was feeling bad because he had not killed any game, and said he was going to try again the next day. The next morning, after all had eaten breakfast, the young man started on his hunting trip again. His sisters went out to the lake for their bath, and the old woman remained at home with the young woman until the brother and sisters came home. This happened every day. One day the old woman said to the young woman, "Let us get the young man to eat some food." They pounded some corn into meal and put it away until the young man returned. After the meal, all went to sleep, and the two women who had remained at home rose from their bed, and while the young man was asleep, put the corn meal into his mouth and made him eat it. The young man rose from the bed and said to them, "Now, since you have done this to me you have taken away from me my powers, and now I shall have to live like any other human being, and will always have less powers, for I had great powers before you did this to me." After he had eaten the meal he hunted all kinds of game, such as deer, turkey, and buffalo, for his meat from this time on. After that time the four women went out to the lake and ceased to return. The young man now called together all his neighbors, who were the wild animals and fowls of the air. They came to his place and asked why he had called them. He told them that his sisters had gone to the lake and had not returned home since the two women had done him the wrong, and he wanted his sisters to come home. He told them that his sisters had laid their clothes on the dry ground; that he wanted some one to go and get them; that whoever should get them and bring them home should have the four women for his wives. He cautioned them, saying that they must keep themselves concealed before reaching the place, and must run hard after taking the clothes, for, if overtaken, they would have to die. All agreed to accept the offer made by the young man. They were asked to make the trial one at a time. The Jack-Rabbit (Watsch) was the first one to try. He at once started for the lake, and had to sneak around in order not to be seen. He finally succeeded in getting the clothes, and at once began to run back to where he had started from. When the women found out what had happened to their clothes they started after the Rabbit. When about half-way to the young man's lodge they overtook him and killed him, and took their clothes back to the lake. These four women were Ducks (Sotshodes), and were fast runners and swimmers. Each man tried his luck, but every one failed to reach the home of the young man. There was a man known as a swift runner, whose name was Swift-Hawk (Gusseiŏs), who tried his luck. He kept himself pretty well concealed until he reached the place where the clothes were. Then he picked them up and bgan to run as fast as he could. When the four women found out that some one had taken away their clothes they started after him. They caught him near the young man's home, and killed him while running, took their clothes and returned to the lake. There was now but one man left of those who had entered the contest to get the young man's sisters for wives, and this was Small-Hawk (Kasiossekits). He started for the place where the clothes were. He kept himself pretty well hid, the same as the rest had done, so as not to be discovered. Finally he reached the lake, took the clothes, and commenced to run for the young man's home, but the sisters saw him and ran after him. Small-Hawk, being the fastest runner known, ran his best and kept running, and reached the door of the lodge nearly exhausted. He ran into the lodge with the clothes and just as he entered, the four women passed the door. Small-Hawk was now within the lodge with the clothing. The four sisters passed the lodge, and when they turned back they stopped at it, begging the people to give them their clothes. The brother of the four women asked them to come in, and said if they did not come in he would not let them have their clothes. They finally agreed to live in the house if he would give back their clothes. The brother told his sisters that Small-Hawk would be their husband thereafter, and they agreed to do anything that he should ask them to do. Small-Hawk was there, ready to become their husband. They were again all living together with Small-Hawk and their brother's wife, whom he had brought a long distance.

Once upon a time the brother took a notion to take his wife back to her home, when he learned that she was pregnant. It must be remembered that Owner-of-Black-and-White-Flint-Knives now had less powers, since the women had fed him what human beings ate; but there were still people who feared him. They started on their journey and traveled until about the middle of the afternoon, when they stopped for the night. The man told his wife to gather a big pile of wood; for some one would be around at night to fight him, and in order to have light they must have plenty of wood to keep the fire burning all night. He said he knew he was to lose his life, for he no longer had the same feeling or the same powers as he had had in his earlier life, when nothing could bother him, but now, having less powers, some sort of animal was going to carry him off. In order to prevent this for a time they must keep up a good fire and remain near it. He also told her that when the child should be born, she should call him Young-Flint-Knife (Tahaaniyer); that when it was about time for her to give birth she should be left alone in the lodge; that she must not allow the child to come out any other than the usual way for a child to come out; that she should keep talking to the child inside, for he would refuse to come out, but she must keep telling him to come out just where a child ought to come out; that when the child should be born she should give him one piece of black flint and one of white to eat, and the first time he should want to know what sort of things were for boys to play with, bow and arrows should be given him. That night, when they had the fire built, they heard some creature asking if he could come around. The man told him to come on; that he was ready for him. The creature came and they at once began to pull one another. Every time the creature pulled Owner-of-Black-and-White-Flint-Knives a little distance from the fire, he would begin to pull back, and would bring the animal to the fire. Thus they pulled back and forth to and away from the fire, the animal's intention being to carry off the man. They pulled each other back and forth all night, but as soon as it was daylight they parted. The foe was Double-Faced-Monster (Witschatska). The man and his wife began to travel again, going toward the east. About the middle of the afternoon they stopped and gathered a big pile of wood. About dark there came that same thing that had visited them the night before, which asked if it might come around, and the man told him to come around, and that he would meet him. They began to get hold of one another. The Double-Faced-Monster would try to carry the man far enough into the dark so that he could take him off, but about the time he would carry him far enough to get an advantage, the man would pull the Double-Faced-Monster back and would call his wife to make the fire burn and have plenty of wood on it, for he intended to throw the Double-Faced-Monster into the fire. They continued this pulling back and forth until morning, then parted. The husband and his wife began to travel again. About the middle of the afternoon they stopped to get plenty of wood, for they knew that the Double-Faced Monster would come again. At dark there came this same Double-Faced-Monster. They met and began to pull each other around, one pulling to the light, the other to the dark. The woman kept the fire burning all night, and whenever the wood began to burn out, the Double-Faced-Monster would begin to carry the husband a good distance from the fire. Then his wife would put some more wood on the fire, and when it commenced to burn they would come back to the light. They continued this until morning, then parted. Owner-of-Black-and-White-Flint-Knives was getting tired of this hard fighting, which had continued for three nights. Again they traveled, and there was two days' journey yet to go, and the husband knew by the way his strength had been reduced that he would be carried off the next night. While they were on the way he began to tell his wife that perhaps she would have to go to her home alone, for he knew that he would be carried off; that she should not tell her son who his father was until he should get big enough, and then if he wanted to know, she should tell him that something had taken him away; that when he should call for playthings she should give him his elk horn bow, and arrows. They traveled all day, and stopped the same time as usual and commenced to bring wood and pile it up, getting ready for the fight. About dark the Double-Faced-Monster called to the Owner-of-Black-and-White-Flint-Knives to get ready for the fight, for he was coming again to take him. They again began the fight and the woman kept up the fire. When he would be taken off for a distance he would call for his wife to build the fire, and then he would come back with the Double-Faced-Monster. About daylight she began to run out of wood, so that the Double-Faced-Monster gained a little greater distance into the darkness, and when they came back they did not approach as close to the fire as usual. The strength of Owner-of-Black-and-White-Flint-Knives was becoming less, the wood was burning out. When there was no more wood to make a fire Double-Faced-Monster took off the Owner-of-Black-and-White-Flint-Knives. His wife heard him calling to her to build up the fire; but there was no more wood, and then the daylight came and the woman was alone.

She continued her journey alone and arrived at her home about noon. The people were surprised to see her again, and greeted her with joy. She told her parents about her life among the strange people and how she was taken away; what sort of a man she had, and how he came to lose his life while on the way to her home. She then told her parents that she was pregnant, that when born the child should be called Young-Flint-Knife. Time soon passed and she began to prepare for her confinement. She told her parents to leave the place and allow her to stay alone until the child was born. When she was giving birth the child began to talk inside of her womb, asking to be allowed to come through her mouth, but the woman refused. She told him to come through the same place that all children came, but he said he did not want to. They kept arguing about this and finally she told him that by coming out of her mouth he might kill her; that he should hold his breath and come out. The child did, and there was born to the woman a boy, and it was named Young-Flint-Knife. When the child was born it did not need to be carried around like a young child, but sat down and called for something to eat. She gave him the black stone, then the white stone to eat, telling him that that was his food, and after he had eaten it she would nurse him. Day after day the child grew, and finally he began to hunt and shoot with his arrows, killing birds of all kinds, turkeys, and deer. He became a famous boy in every way. He had great powers, as his father had had, but he was not really like his father, for his food was like that of any other human being. When he grew older and of better mind, he began to ask who his father was, and what had become of him, and whether he was dead or living. As soon as his mother began to realize that he was fully grown, she told him that something had taken his father off while they were on the way to her home, and she told him where the place was where he had been carried away from her. Young-Flint-Knife then told his mother to grind enough meal for him to take along with him, and he would go and hunt for the being that had carried off his father. He started on the trip in search of his father. When he came to the place and found the trail of the Double-Faced-Monster he followed it. He kept traveling until he came to a deep canyon with steep sides. He looked down and saw that there was no way to get down. The sides of the canyon were smooth and perpendicular, so that it was impossible for any one to go down. He followed up the canyon, looking to see whether he could see anyone, until he came to where he could see but very little, and down there he saw a man getting water. From the description, he thought that the man was his father. He slid down the steep wall when he saw this man again, and called him, saying, "I am now here to get you, and am bound to take you back home to mother." He asked Owner-of-Black-and-White-Flint-Knives what the Double-Faced-Monsters were, when they were home, and what time they came home. His father said that it was dangerous for him to be around, for the older Double-Faced-Monsters were out somewhere, and he supposed that they already knew of Young-Flint-Knife's arrival. They at once went up to the place where the creatures were. They walked in the caves, and there they saw the young ones at home by themselves. The children came up to them and began to scratch their legs, and whatever blood was on their claws they would suck. Young-Flint-Knife noticed some things hanging inside the place, and he asked the young ones what these things were. They replied that they were their hearts; that they were hung there so that there would be no chance of anyone killing their father and mother. Young-Flint-Knife took his arrow and struck one of these, and down went one of the young ones. Young-Flint-Knife then asked whose were the other hearts; then he stuck his arrows into them, one after another, until he thought he must have killed all of them.

Young-Flint-Knife and his father walked out, and the Owner-of-Black-and-White-Flint-Knives was released from his troubles. They looked for the deepest place in the creek, and when they found it, Young-Flint-Knife asked his father to dive in. He dived, and when he came out of the water he was changed so that he bore the same appearance as before he was carried away from his wife. They then went on to Young-Flint-Knife's home. When they arrived the parents were glad to see them again, for they had known that Young-Flint-Knife was going to meet danger when he set out, and had not expected him to return; but Young-Flint-Knife, having great powers, knew how to get to the safest place, and knew when the Double-Faced-Monsters were at home, and when they were away. He was now much stronger than his father. They were at home but a little while, when Owner-of-Black-and-White-Flint-Knives told his son that he had less powers than formerly. He said that because he was old and had less power, he feared that the Double-Faced-Monster, or some other enemies might capture him, and make him suffer again all that he had so recently suffered. In order to prevent a recurrence of this, he wanted his son to leave with him and become something else. So the Owner-of-Black-and-White-Flint-Knives and his son, Young-Flint-Knife, waited until night, then went up in the sky and became Stars. They left their people behind, who exist on earth as human beings.

12. THE DEEDS OF AFTER-BIRTH-BOY.*

Once upon a time there were two villages. There were a good many people living there. The two villages were connected by a street-like way, though they were two different villages, each controlled by a chief. The space that divided the two villages was a place where all sorts of games were played every evening. There were a good many young men and young women who amused themselves here by playing these games. Once in a while there would be some one who would send out a war-party, and on its return there would be so much the more fun for the people living here, because every one danced all kinds of dances. Men and women both had their fun.

Each of the two chiefs had a child; the one on the north side had a girl, the one on the south side had a boy. The boy and the girl were unknown to each other, and the boy, when he had become a young man, refused to marry any one who wished to marry him. When women came around him he would drive them away, and this is the way he refused women. When the chief's daughter on the north side was grown to be a young woman, about the same as the chief's son on the south side, she rejected men, and remained single. Once upon a time the chief's son on the south side, after hearing many things about the young woman on the north side, and how she was rejecting men, thought to himself: "Now, suppose I were to go there. She it is whom I would want for my wife—but suppose she should reject me. I would like to see whether or not she would have me." The young man had this in mind. At the same time the chief's daughter got to thinking about the chief's son, of whom she had heard so much, and she wished for a way by which she might get to see him some time, for she thought that he would be her choice. She had heard of his rejecting women and thought that she also might be rejected. The notion once in her head, she could not get it out; it seemed to trouble her, and she was anxious to see the chief's son. One night the chief's daughter thought to herself: "Now, if I should stand over there some time to-night, after everybody has gone to sleep, I suppose I could get to see the chief's son all right." The chief's son was getting anxious to see the chief's daughter, and so on. The same night he took a notion to go and visit the chief's daughter. About the same time, the chief's daughter thought she had better go that night and see if she could find the chief's son. She arose from her bed and went toward his village. The two were on the way to each other's home, each to see the other and to ask the

*Told by Ahahe (Waco).

other's consent to marry. When the chief's son got to the edge of his father's village he saw some one coming out of the opposite village. The chief's daughter, at the same time, noticed some one coming out of the village opposite hers and wondered who it could be. They approached each other, each having in mind to visit the other, though they had never spoken together. They met in the middle of the space. They asked each other where they were going. The chief's daughter replied: "I have heard a good many things about a certain young man who is the son of the chief in your village, and I know him to have rejected every woman who has wished to marry him, and now I am going to see him." Then the young man said: "I was going over to see a certain young woman about whom I have heard many things. I have heard that she has rejected all who have wished to marry her." The young woman said that she was the chief's daughter. The young man replied that he was the chief's son. They said to one another: "Well, we are of the same mind. What shall we do? Shall we go to my home or to yours?" The chief's son replied, "Well, we will go over to your home." Then the chief's daughter told the chief's son that they had better go to his home instead of hers. After they had decided where to go they agreed to marry, whether their people liked it or not.

They went out to the young man's home to live, and on their arrival went to bed. Early on the next morning, when the people woke up, they expected the young man to come down the same as he had always done. It was customary for the old men to gather at the chief's lodge and pass the time by talking; so also, the old women came to see the chief's wife, if they belonged to the same family. It was the duty of the chief's wife to do the cooking for those who came around the tipi. Early the next morning there was no sign of the chief's daughter at her home, and her people were surprised that she was sleeping so late. Finally the girl's mother went up to the girl's bed, and there was no sign of her in the bed. They then supposed that some one had carried her off and killed her; for they knew that if any one asked her for connection she would refuse. This is what made them think some one had carried her off to kill her. Over at the young man's home the people waited and waited for him to get out of bed and go to the creek for a bath. They sent some one of the family to see why the young man was not getting up. When the person reached the place where the chief's son was lying he found that there was some one else in bed with him. The person returned and notified the people. They then thought the chief's son had been away to get married and had come home with some one. They again sent the person to tell the young man to come to breakfast, and, if it was a woman with him, to come at once and let them see who she might be. The chief's son and chief's daughter came into the lodge where the young man's parents were. When the people knew who she was they were angry, for both had always refused to marry outside of the chiefs' families. The two ate breakfast, and after this, the people told them that if they remained husband and wife they would have to leave the place and go somewhere else to live.

In the girl's village, the chief sent out men in search of his daughter, but she could not be found in the village. The Coyote, who was then servant for the chief, went through the village where they lived, then went to the other village, looking for the chief's daughter. He went from one grass-lodge to another, until he came to the chief's lodge, and there he found the chief's daughter with the chief's son. The Coyote returned to his own village and notified the chief there that his daughter was living with the other chief's son. When the chief heard this he was troubled, because his daughter had refused to marry any one in her own village. This chief then sent word by the Coyote to his daughter never to return to her home, since she had gone away with the chief's son. The young folks had no place to stay. They at once began to think of places wherein they could live and not trouble anyone. They decided to leave the village and live by themselves somewhere else, out where there was no one living.

One night, after all had gone to sleep, they prepared to leave their home permanently. They started on a long journey looking for a new home for themselves. The young man had all his weapons, so as to hunt for food, and the woman had all she could carry, having everything she needed. They traveled nearly all day, and when the woman grew tired they stopped for the night. The next day they ate and traveled again. That entire day they looked for a place to live, but no place suited them, and when darkness came, they made a camp and stayed all night. The next day they traveled all day until night, but still could not find a place to suit them, and stopped again for a night's rest. The next morning, after breakfast, they started on another day's journey. They traveled all the folowing day until night and stopped for a night's rest. They traveled the next day, and about evening they came to a place where there was plenty of timber, and a river by the timber. They selected this place for their home. They fixed up the place and the woman built a grass-lodge and a sort of drying arbor for corn and meat. From this time on the man went out hunting every day, and when he went out hunting he sometimes brought home buffalo meat, deer meat, or any other things that he could kill. Some time afterwards the woman told her husband that she was pregnant. Once upon a time when this man was going out hunting he told his wife to fix up a piece of meat to cook by the fire; that while he was gone some one would come and eat the meat. He told her not to look at him when the person should come in; that when she should hear him coming she should get into her bed and cover herself up; that she would have to do this every day while he went out hunting. That morning, after the woman had done as she had been told, her husband went out on a hunting trip. He would sometimes stay out late and come back at night, sometimes before night.

While the woman was staying at home by herself she heard some one talking and saw some one coming toward their place. She got into bed and covered herself with buffalo robes. The person came in and ate the meat that she had cooked, and after eating the meat up he went away. After the woman heard him go she got out of her bed. Late that evening her man returned from the hunt and asked his wife if the man had come and eaten up what she had cooked. She said the person had come and had eaten what she had cooked. Again her husband told her that she would have to do this every day, but that she must not look at the person and must not pay any attention to him while he ate. From that time on, every morning her husband went hunting, and she prepared the meat, so that it became a part of her work. Every afternoon she began to think of taking a look at the person, just to see what sort of looking man he was who came to visit her during her husband's absence. Time went on, and she still had in mind to try some way to take a look at him. One time, after her husband had left, she bored a hole in the robe and took a piece of hollow grass big enough to look through and put it in the hole, and before she heard the person coming, she lay down on her bed, which was on the west side of the room in the grass-lodge. Finally he came, and began to eat, and after he had eaten what beef was there by the fire he started away. As he was leaving, the woman peeped through the grass stem, and saw that the man was double headed and had a mouth on the back of his neck. Just then the man turned back, and said: "Oh, you have looked at me!" He came where she was lying, killed her, cut her open and took out the child that she had in her womb. After taking out the child, the man wrapped it up in a robe and put it away in some other place instead of putting it where its mother was lying. He then took the after-birth, thrust the fire-stick into it and threw it into the water; then he left the place.

That evening, when the man returned from the hunt, he found his wife dead, and thought that she must have disobeyed and looked at the man. He took his dead wife some distance away and laid her there for burial, but instead of burying her under the ground he laid her on top of the ground, and returned home. After he went home he heard the child crying somewhere, but could not find where the sound of the child's crying came from. He finally succeeded in finding the young one. He nursed the young child, which was a boy. The only way he could nurse it was to give it fresh beef and let it suck it, and in that way he reared it. When the time came that he had to go out hunting he had to take the young child along with him, and there were times when he had to stay at home on account of the young child. But the child grew rapidly, and finally he got so big that he began to crawl around, and after a while he began to walk. Still the man would take the child along hunting. At last the boy was big enough to play by himself. The man then made a bow and arrows for him to play with, also a shinny ball and stick. This ball was what we call "ball-for-young-boys" (kasints-wiks).

After a while the man when going out on a hunt left the boy at home, for he knew that he was old enough to take care of himself. After the boy's father left, while he was in the grass-lodge by himself, the boy heard some one coming around where he was. When the boy looked back at the door there he saw a boy about his own age, who was calling him to come and have an arrow game with him. The game is called "shooting-a-small-plaited-sinew-on-the-fly" (liakucks). The strange boy won all of the arrows from the boy of the lodge. After the strange boy had won all of the lodge boy's arrows he went off toward the river, and the lodge boy saw him going into the water. Before leaving, the strange boy told the lodge boy that they were brothers and that he should not tell their father regarding his coming around. After the strange boy had left, the lodge boy began to wonder who the strange boy was who claimed that his father was also the father of the other boy. When the father came back that day he asked his boy what he had done with his arrows. The boy told him what his brother had instructed him to say if asked this question by his father. He said he had lost all of the arrows that he had given him and could not find them. His father then asked him if they both might not go and look for the arrows, but the boy refused to do so, and said that he knew that the arrows were lost and could not be found. So that evening the man began to make some more arrows for his son, and when he had finished them, gave them to him and told him not to lose them as he had lost the rest of his arrows. When he should shoot he was to watch the arrow and see where it might go, for there was much trouble in making arrows. The next day the man went out on a hunting trip. After he had gone, the strange boy came again and asked his brother to come and have that same game with him again. They commenced to play, betting their arrows. All that day they played, until the strange boy won the game from his brother. The lodge boy was without arrows again. Before leaving, the strange boy said: "Do not tell your father that I have been here and won all of your arrows, but tell him that you lost them shooting birds." The strange boy then left again, going toward the river, and the lodge boy watched to see where he would go. He saw him going into the water again, instead of going on dry land and living there. In the evening the boy's father returned again from the hunt. When he arrived he asked his boy again what he had done with all his arrows. His boy repeated what he had been told to say, saying he had lost all of his arrows shooting birds. He said that he had been off a good long way, where he lost the arrows. The boy's father again asked if they could not go over there and see if they could find the arrows, but the boy said he thought he had lost them for good, and they could not be found. After the boy said this, his father had to believe him, and at once started to make just as many arrows as the boy had before.

The boy's father began to think there must be something wrong, for he did not understand how the boy could lose all his arrows in one day. On the next morning, after they had eaten their breakfast, the boy's father went out hunting. He left the lodge boy at home. Every time he went out he would cook some meat for his son to eat while he was away. As soon as the boy's father had gone the strange boy came around again and called the lodge boy out to play the arrow game with him, the same as they had always played. They again began to play their arrow game, and about noon the boy invited his brother to enter the lodge and have something to eat with him. They both went in and ate what the lodge boy had, and after they had eaten they commenced to play again, until the visiting boy had won all the arrows from the lodge boy. After winning the arrows he repeated the same words that he always had said about what he should tell his father regarding the loss of his arrows. The strange boy started off again, going toward the water. He went into the water. The lodge boy now began to wonder how the strange boy could live in the water. He then decided to tell his father, so that they might attack the strange boy and make him stay with them instead of living in the water. He also wanted to find out from his father why this strange boy called him brother. The boy's father arrived again, and when he asked the boy what he had done with all his arrows, the boy said to his father: "There is always some one around me, a boy about my age, who calls me 'brother.'" The lodge boy then described the strange boy to his father. He told him that the strange boy had a wonderful tail that looked like a stick used for a poker, and that this boy was the one who won all of his arrows; that when the strange boy left he always went toward the river and got into the water; that he always called him "brother." The boy's father asked him if he had learned the strange boy's name. He told his father that the strange boy called himself After-birth-Boy (Hawhiswiks). The boy's father then began to think how the strange boy could live in the water, and why he called his son "brother," and himself "father," the same as his son. He then found out who the boy was and told his son that the strange boy was surely his brother; that the boy's mother had been killed by some man; that he had left him (the lodge boy) in the lodge, and had taken the after-birth and perhaps thrown it in the water; that this, possibly, was the way the strange boy came to live in the water. The man then made some more arrows, and on the next day they arranged to attack the strange boy and make him stay at home. On the next day, the man remained at home instead of going out hunting. He then instructed the lodge-boy, saying: "Go ahead and play the arrow game, and when the strange boy wins all the arrows I will be somewhere about the lodge. You must invite After-birth-Boy to come in with you and eat. Then get him to look in your head for bugs, then get him to let you look in his head to see if there are any bugs; but let him look in your head first, so you can look in his head last. Then tie his hair up so that you can get a good hold when attacking him."

That morning After-birth-Boy came around again and called the lodge boy out to play with him. Their father then turned himself into a fire stick and lay down by the fireplace. The lodge boy went out and met After-birth-Boy, who called him "brother," and they began to play the arrow game. After they had been playing the game a while the lodge boy made out that he was tired, and told After-birth-Boy to go into the lodge and rest a while and have something to eat. So they went into the lodge. As soon as they had entered the grass-lodge After-birth-Boy went right back out, and said to the lodge boy: "The old man, our father, is in the lodge. He has turned himself into a stick used for a poker." After-birth-Boy then went out into the water and did not come back. Their father then appeared and told the lodge boy that After-birth-Boy was a wonderful boy and had great powers. That evening the man made some more arrows for his sons to play with the next day, that he might in some way capture After-birth-Boy. The next day he again put off his hunting trip. That morning After-birth-Boy came around and called his brother to come out to him and play the arrow game. The lodge boy went out to meet him and to have an arrow game, but before After-birth-Boy came their father hid himself behind the door, turning himself into a stem of grass. While they were playing, After-birth-Boy asked the lodge boy if their father had gone out on a hunt. The lodge boy said that he had. Again, at noon, the lodge boy began to beg After-birth-Boy to stop a while and rest and then eat before they played any more. After-birth-Boy was then wild, because they had tried to play a trick on him. He looked into the grass-lodge and found no one there. They entered and ate dinner. After dinner was over the lodge boy told After-birth-Boy that his head itched, and asked him to look into it and see if there were any lice there. After-birth-Boy then looked into the lodge boy's head for a long time. When he got tired the lodge boy asked him to allow him to look in his head. The lodge boy got hold of After-birth-Boy's head and looked into it, but instead of looking for lice, he began to tie his hair and tangle it up so that he might get a good hold when he called his father for help. When After-birth-Boy was tired he would ask the lodge boy what he was doing, for the lodge boy was hurting him. Finally, when the lodge boy had got a good hold, he called to his father to come and help him, saying that he had a good hold. Just then After-birth-Boy jumped up and began to run, dragging the lodge boy. Their father got to them and they had a hard time holding After-birth-Boy. The lodge boy would beg After-birth-Boy to stop, saying he had always called him brother and he wanted him to live with them instead of visiting him. But After-birth-Boy kept dragging them toward the river, and then their father began to beg the boy to stop. Before they reached the river After-birth-Boy told the two to loose him for a while; that he was willing to live with them thereafter. After-birth-Boy was released and jumped into the river, and when he came out of the water both of his arms were full of arrows that he had won from the lodge boy. So they all went toward their grass-lodge to live together thereafter.

The next day the boys' father made a shinny ball and two sticks and some more arrows and a netted ring. When making the ring he told the boys not to roll it toward the west. He then forbade them to go to several places: Spider-Woman (Itsezgarhenegits), Thunderbird-that-had-a-Nest (Geleassegits), Double-Faced-Monster (Witschatska),

Headless-Man (Chearppeschaux) ; and the place where they were told not to roll the ring. These were the places their father forbade them to go. The next day the father of the boys went out hunting and told the boys to remain at home, for they must not go out in the timber to shoot birds. Their father was out hunting that whole day. When he returned from his hunt he found his boys at home. The man then cooked for the boys some fresh meat that he had brought home with him. This was the second night that After-birth-Boy had been with his father and brother. The next day the man went out hunting again. After-birth-Boy asked his brother to go with him where their father had forbidden them to go, where the Spider-Woman was. So they started early, right after their father started out on the hunt. While on the way they shot a good many birds to take to the Spider-Woman. They finally reached the place where the woman was living. They went to a place where they saw smoke coming out from the ground. On entering they were received kindly by the Spider-Woman. The two boys gave her the birds they had shot for her to eat. The Spider-Woman then asked the boys to sit down in her lodge. This woman was pleased to see them, and asked where they had come from. She then told the boys that she loved to eat birds, and that they should bring the birds to her; that that was the best thing anyone had ever done for her. She then told the boys to bring a pail full of water. There was a pail, but no one knows where the pail came from, nor what it was made out of. The boys did what the old woman told them to do. While they were out after the water After-birth-Boy told his brother that after their return with the water the woman would boil the water, and as soon as it should begin to boil she would catch them and throw them into the boiling water. After-birth-Boy told his brother to get on the side where the water was not boiling; that he himself would be on the boiling side; that while in the bucket he should urinate and de-fecate in the boiling water, and when he (After-birth-Boy) should get ready, he would notify him to make a quick jerk, and in that way he would upset the bucket and pour the boiling water on the Spider-Woman and scald and kill her. When the boys took the pail of water into the lodge where this woman was she took it and put it on the fire to boil. As soon as the water got to boiling the woman crowded the boys away from the door, caught them and threw them into the boiling water. After-birth-Boy had great powers, and gave his brother power to live in the boiling water. He got on the side where the water was boiling the most, and both urinated. They could hear the Spider-Woman say that they were awfully fat, as was shown by the movement in the water. All at once, After-birth-Boy gave his brother a slight nudge and they both got ready to upset the bucket and pour the boiling water on the Spider-Woman. This they did, and scalded the Spider-Woman to death. After they found they had killed the woman where their father had told them not to go; they said to one another, "Let us go home and tell our father what we have done." They turned back to their home and on their arrival they found that their father had not come home. The next evening the boys' father came home from his hunting trip. The two boys were then old enough to do the cooking, so they did the cooking for their father. While they were eating supper they told their father what they had done. They told him that they had been to Spider-Woman's home, where he had forbidden them to go, and had killed her.

The father told the boys not to go where the Thunderbird had its nest. Some time after, After-birth-Boy took a notion to go and see the nest of the Thunderbird. When their father had left on his hunting trip the two boys started on their way to the nest. They had their arrows and bows along, and while on their way to the place they shot at birds for fun. They finally reached the place where the nest was. After-birth-Boy told his brother to watch him climb the tree. The tree was a high cottonwood, having hardly any limbs, only at the top, where the nest was. After-birth-Boy began to climb the tree, and when about half-way up there the Thunderbird came after him. When After-birth-Boy heard the Thunderbird coming, the bird made a sound like heavy wind, and left a streak of lightning which took off one of After-birth-Boy's limbs. But he kept going up the tree, and when he went up a little higher down came the Thunderbird, and this time it took off one of his arms. Whenever this bird took off a limb After-birth-Boy would ask his brother to bring his limb to the tree, so that he could get it again. He kept on going, for he wanted to see what was up in the nest. He continued to climb, and when he had got higher the Thunderbird came down again, and this time took off his left leg. He called his brother to get his leg and bring it where he was so that he could get it. After-birth-Boy first lost his right leg, then his left arm, then his left leg, until he had but one limb left. He was still going, and as he approached the nest down came the Thunderbird again and took off his right arm. This left him without any limbs, but he was right there at the nest. He looked in, and there he saw four young birds. He then bit one of the young ones on the wing and asked it what sort of a young bird it was. The young bird answered him, saying he was the child of Early-Morning-Weather-when-there-is-no-

Wind-the-Sun-rising-slowly-followed-by-clear-Weather.   He set the young bird back and told it that he was the kind of a child he wanted to see. He picked up the next one and asked what kind of a young bird it was. The young bird answered him, saying that he was a child of Hard-Windy-Weather-followed-by-hard-Rain-accompanied-by-Lightning-that-strikes. After-birth-Boy threw the young bird off, and told it that it was a bad young bird. He then picked up the next one and asked it what sort of a young bird it was. The young one answered that it was the child of Quiet-Foggy-Day-Weather-such-as-comes-in-early-Morning. He then set the bird back and told it that it was a good child. Then he picked up the last one and asked it what sort of a child it was. The young one answered him, saying that he was a child of Cyclone-Weather. He threw this bird off and told it that it was a child that he had no use for. After-birth-Boy now began to slide down; for he could not climb down. When he came down he told his brother to get his arms and legs, for he could not move to get them himself. He ordered his brother to put on him the right arm first. Then he told his brother to put on his left leg. He ordered his brother to put on his left arm. Then he ordered his brother to get the right leg and place it in the right place. The brother obeyed, and the boy had on all his limbs again. The boys then started to their home, and on their arrival they found their father already home. Their father asked the boys why they had been late in coming. The boys told him they had been to the Thunderbird's nest, where he had told them not to go. After-birth-Boy said he climbed the tree and had all his arms and legs pulled off by the Thunderbird, but that he reached the top, killed two of the young birds and saved two of them, as they were good young birds. Their father then began to think that he had a wonderful boy, and that he must have great powers, judging from what he had already done.

Some time after they had been to the nest they started out shooting birds, and while they were out they found a long stone lying on the ground, that was somewhat like the shape of a human being. After-birth-Boy told his brother that they must take this home, for their father to use in sharpening his knife. They carried it home. The boys reached home that day before their father came; the boys showed him what they had brought for him. Their father asked them where they had found the stone. The boys told where they had found it, and then the father told them to take it back where they got it, for it was their mother. After their father had laid her away the woman had turned into stone. That evening the boys took the stone back where they had got it.

The next day, after their father had gone out to hunt, After-birth-Boy asked his brother to come and go to the caves, where something that killed their mother was living, where their father had forbidden them to go. The boys started on to this place, and they traveled all around the rough places, and finally came to the caves. There they found some young Double-Faced-Monsters. Upon entering the place the young ones tried to scratch them. When they scratched After-birth-Boy these young ones broke off their claws. When they scratched the other boy they would leave some blood streaks and suck their claws. The boys then noticed some things hanging in the cave. They asked what these things were. The young Double-Faced-Monsters said that they were their lungs and that if anything attacked their father and mother they would come out safe, for there were no lungs in them. After-birth-Boy then took one of his arrows and stuck one of the lungs with the point of an arrow. These were the largest ones, and when he stuck one the other one began to move, and the young ones said that that was their father's lungs. Then he stuck another of the largest ones, and as soon as he had done so it stopped moving around. Then he commenced on the little ones, and whenever he stuck one, one of the young ones would fall to the ground. He kept on until he had killed every one of them but one, and this one they saved for their father for a pet. They returned to their home, and on their arrival found their father. They presented the young Double-Faced-Monster to him and told him that they had been where he had forbidden them to go; that they had visited the Double-Faced-Monsters, and had killed all of them but the one that they had saved for him to keep for a pet. Their father then told them to take it back where they got it and turn it loose, for he did not want it. The boys took this young one back and turned it loose and returned home at once.

It was several days before they took a notion to go off somewhere else, and when the time came they went out after their father had gone on a hunt. They took along their shinny ball, two sticks, bows and arrows, and at once started to where they were forbidden to go. On their way they saw some one standing a good way from them, who told them not to come near him, but the boys kept on until they came where he was. This man was the same man that their father had told about, the Headless-Man. This man had a shinny stick and ball. He told the boys that their lives would be taken, but first, they would have to play the shinny game, and if they should lose the game they would have to die. After-birth-Boy told the Headless-Man if he should lose his game he would have to die, too; and that at first they must use their ball instead of his. But the Headless-Man refused to do so, and said that they would have to use his, for his was the best. So After-birth-Boy told his brother to go toward the west as far as the ball would fly to him and to knock it back, for in that way they wanted to make the Headless-Man give out first, before they should make the ball go over the goal. The boy went as he was told to do. After-birth-Boy then asked the Headless-Man to let him see his ball, and see if it was the best. When After-birth-Boy got the ball he tossed it up and knocked it to pieces. The Headess-Man then told After-birth-Boy that since he had spoiled his (the Headless-Man's) ball they would have to use theirs. The Headless-Man then asked for the ball, expecting to do the same thing as After-birth-Boy had done when tossing up the Headless-Man's ball. When tossing it up After-birth-Boy hit the ball, and it went where the other boy was. While the ball was flying the Headless-Man was right after it. When it reached the lodge boy he knocked it back again toward After-birth-Boy, and the Headless-Man was right behind again, after the ball, to catch it before it could reach After-birth-Boy. This showed the boys what a fast runner the Headless-Man was. They kept knocking the ball back and forth, and the Headless-Man was always right behind it. Finally, when they found that the Headless-Man had nearly given out, After-birth-Boy knocked the ball once more, and it went over the lodge boy, over a small creek that the Headless-Man had chosen for a goal. The Headless-Man then stopped to take one long breath, and said: "This is the first time I ever had so hard a game as I had to-day." The Headless-Man then begged the boys to let him live and not to kill him, promising them the same kind of powers that he himself had. After-birth-Boy told him that he did not want any such powers. After-birth-Boy then took the string off from his bow, passed it four times through his hands, and killed the Headless-Man with it. The Headless-Man's ball was black, and his shinny stick was black. The two boys had a green ball and green sticks, green representing the spring of the year. Since that time the shinny game is played in the spring, under the power of After-birth-Boy. After they had killed the Headless-Man the boys returned to their home, where, upon their arrival, they found their father, who asked them where they had been. The boys told him that they had been where the Headless-Man was, where he had forbidden them to go, and that they had had a hard shinny game with him, but that he could not do anything with them and that they ran him down and killed him.

After that it was their custom to remain at home several days, and once in a while to go out and shoot birds, and sometimes to remain at home without going anywhere, for their father was doing the hunting.

One day while the boys were at home After-birth-Boy asked his brother to bring out the netted ring and roll it where they were forbidden to roll it. The boy went into their lodge and brought out the ring and rolled it toward the west, then they ran after it, but the ring kept on going, and they went after it with the expectation of catching up with it. The boys were running as hard as they could, but had no idea that they could not stop. Finally After-birth-Boy tried to stop, but could not. After-birth-Boy then told his brother to go on, and see where the ring was going, saying they would soon find out. They kept on until they saw a great lake, and the netted ring was going toward it. It kept going until it went into the water. The boys followed, and found themselves inside of some great water-monster. After-birth-Boy said to his brother that this was the first time anything had ever mastered them without his knowing it. There is no telling how long they stayed in there.

When their father reached home he found his boys gone, and thought they were in trouble, or were killed. He left the place, became a Star, and went up into the sky. The boys were still inside of the water-monster. After-birth-Boy took the string of his bow, passed it through his left hand four times and commenced to swing it around, and when he swung it hard up went the monster, and it fell somewhere. The monster fell on dry land, but they did not know where. They at once began to look for a place to get out. They went through the hind part of the monster. They then saw that it was a great, big fish. After they were out they started toward their home. They reached their home and found no trace of their father. The weeds had grown up and the vines had grown over their grass-lodge in places, and in places the lodge had turned to the bark of a tree. After-birth-Boy began to look around to find out what had become of their father. He found his track, but the track ended, and he could not find what his father had turned into. After-birth-Boy told his brother that there was one more thing he wanted to look into when darkness should come. They remained at their former home until night. When darkness came After-birth-Boy got on his father's trail again, and where his tracks stopped he looked up into the sky and found one star, and this he thought to be their father. He then told his brother that he was going to shoot at the star with an arrow, and if it was his father a drop of blood would fall. He took one of his arrows and shot it up in the sky, then waited a moment, and while they were standing a drop of blood fell on After-birth-Boy's hand. He told his brother that a drop of blood had come down, showing them that the star was their father. After-birth-Boy then called his brother to come where he was, and when the boy went where his brother was he shot up into the sky two arrows, by means of which they climbed up into the sky to be with their father. These two boys were great boys to do all sorts of things that were supernatural, but they were but young boys, especially After-birth-Boy, who was known to have been raised in the water. These boys were the ones who killed all the meanest things that lived in those times. After they had gone up into the sky the whole of the story of After-birth-Boy and his brother ends.

13. THE THUNDERBIRD AND THE WATER-MONSTER.*

There was once a village that had two chiefs. They had a sort of division line between them. On the east side, the Thunderbird (Kitihakuts) was chief, but no one remembers who was chief of the west side. The Thunderbird had a good character and everybody thought well of him, though there were a few people who wished to do him wrong and hated him in every way. In those times the people who had evil thoughts were called Evil-Spirited-Persons (Naaniawacadiki). In this place there were played all kinds of games, and they wagered the life of a person, the winner taking the life of the loser. In the Thunderbird's village there lived the Coyote (Ketox), who was nephew to the chief. Once in a while the Coyote would go and see the hand-game played by some of the people, and expected to beat them playing. The hand-game was the gambling game of the people of these times, and the wager was generally large, as they bet their lives and weapons. Whenever the Coyote went to see the game the chief would beg him to bring along his uncle the next time he came, and on his return the Coyote would ask his uncle to go along with him the next time he should go; but his uncle would refuse to do so, for he knew that it was a dangerous place to go, for the people in the place were seeking in some way to do him wrong.

The Thunderbird was a great hunter, and the things he hunted were the ones that hated him. The Coyote continued to go and see the hand-game played, and every time he went the chief would ask him why he had not brought his uncle along. So every time the Coyote came back from the hand-game he would tell his uncle what the people had said regarding him, but his uncle would say it was a place to lose one's life cheap. Once upon a time the Coyote asked his uncle again to go along with him to see the game. The Thunderbird said to his

*Told by Ahahe (Waco).

nephew: "All right, if you think the fun is more for your advantage than for mine, I will go along with you to see the game." The Coyote began to think that there must be some danger. He said to his uncle, "What do you mean?" The Thunderbird said: "You will see, and you will wish that you had never begged me to go along with you to the hand-game." They entered the place where the hand-game was going on. When they were seen the Coyote was in the lead, and felt proud because his uncle was there. In the lodges where they were having the hand-game, the door faced east, and upon entering the lodge the people were called to the wet part of the lodge, where they saw a sort of high hump, and it was covered up. The Thunderbird was asked to sit down, which he did, and the Coyote felt proud because he thought he and his uncle were being treated with distinction. The game went on, and was being played by some stranger who had come there and was asked to play. When the stranger lost the game the playing came to an end and the men began to leave the place, but the Thunderbird thought he had better wait until everybody had left the lodge before he should leave. So when everybody had left he started to rise, but failed, for he had been stuck to the hump in the presence of everybody. The thing began to move, and when it moved he found that it was some sort of a water-monster that was under him, and it moved toward a small lake that the people knew to be deep. It moved slowly, and the Coyote followed after to see what was going to become of his uncle. Wherever the Thunderbird went he always carried his bow and four arrows, his bow painted black, two of his arrows painted black and two blood color, and his bow had a sort of red tassel at the upper end. He told his nephew that as long as he should see the tassel he might know that his uncle was still alive, but when it was no longer in sight he might know that he was drowned. There were a great many of the people who followed the monster to the shore to see what it was going to do. The Coyote was right by the side of the monster, talking to his uncle, and saying: "You have great powers, why do you not free yourself from the monster? You can do it." But the Coyote was then told that it was all his fault that he had lost his uncle. The Coyote would then cry out fearfully for his uncle, but there were a great many people who mocked the Coyote and were glad to see his uncle die. The monster reached the lake and went into the water. He went to the bottom of the lake instead of swimming, and they kept going down and down, until only the top of the monster's head could be seen, then the water went over the Thunderbird's head. Then the bow began to sink until the tassel on the end of the bow could scarcely be seen, and finally the whole thing was gone. After this, everybody left the shore of the lake and went to their homes. Some were glad to see the Thunderbird drown, for they hated him, but there were some who regretted it and wept bitterly for the loss of their chief. There was the Coyote alone when his uncle had lost his life for his sake, the Coyote having begged him to go along to see the hand-game. On the next day most of the people left the village to go somewhere else to make their homes, and finally everybody left their former village and followed the rest of the people.

In this village were left an old man, old woman, and their grandchildren. For a long time these folks lived here alone. The boys would go around the village into other grass-lodges and look for things that had been left by the people who had left their homes, and would go around the lake and shoot birds, which was their way of having fun. Once upon a time, when these boys were around the lake they heard some one singing, but did not know for certain where the sound came from. They stood around to catch the sound and find out where the singing was. When they could not locate the sound, they left the lake and turned back to their home. They told their grandfather and grandmother about the singing they had heard, and the old man sat there, thinking what it could have been, till finally it came to him. He asked the boys where they had been. They told him that they were near the lake. Then he told them there was some one who was known to have lost his life in the lake; that the person was the Thunderbird, who had been a great chief and a man of good character; that he had been to a hand-game, was seated on something that was covered up, and when he came to try to get up he found that he was stuck to a water-monster so that he could not get off, while the monster moved off into the lake and he was drowned; that he must be the one who was doing the singing. So he told the boys that if there was still any flesh on that man there was life in him; that they should again go over to the lake and bring rocks to the shore and get plenty of them, too, and after so doing they should pile the rocks up and haul plenty of wood; that they should pile the wood on the bottom and some on the top, and after that should burn the wood; that when this was all burned up they should throw all the stones into the water. The boys went to the lake the next day, and there was by the lake a small hill, and from this place they carried stones all the following day, and after they thought they had stones enough they hauled plenty of wood to the shore where they had piled the stones. After they thought they had enough wood they spread it on the ground, piled the stones on top of it, and after they had put all the stones upon it they again piled wood on top of them and then everything was ready but the fire. One of the boys went back home to bring a burning stick and at once started back to the lake. On the boy's arrival he set the wood on fire and it began to burn. After the stones were heated red hot they took them and threw all of them into the water, then returned to their home and told the old man about it. On the next day the old man told the boys to go back to the lake and see what had been done there. The boys went on toward the lake, and on their arrival there they found the lake all dried up, and there they saw the water-monster. They again turned back to their home and reported to their grandfather regarding the water-monster. Then all went down to the lake and cut up the monster, and inside the monster they found the bones of the Thunderbird. They took all the bones, examined them, and found on the bones of the fingers a small piece of flesh. Then the old man told the boys that this must be the thing that was doing the singing, for there was still life in the hand. They then took the bones home. When they reached home the old man told his wife to build a small grass-lodge, big enough for the man to stand inside of it. The old woman at once began to work on this as the old man had requested her to do. Next day the old man took the bones of this man and put them all in their places, and after so doing set the lodge on fire. When the lodge commenced to burn the old man hallooed to the Thunderbird and told him to get out of the lodge, for it was on fire. Then he hallooed the second time, the third and fourth time, and at the fourth time there came out from the burning lodge the Thunderbird, his bow and arrow with him, and he was the same as he ever had been.

When the Thunderbird got out of the burning lodge the first thing he asked was, where the people had gone who used to live in the village. They told him that the whole village had left and that some had left the village happy, and some mourning for him. After this they all went into the lodge and the Thunderbird was given something to eat. After he had eaten he went out hunting, and the following day he killed a buffalo and brought it home with him, and it was as much as he could haul. He went on back to where he was staying, and late in the evening arrived at the place with the meat, and the people had plenty of meat to eat this time. The Thunderbird then told him that he had left some of the meat hanging in a tree, and that on the next day he should go hunting he wanted the boys to go with him and bring home the rest of the meat, while he should go on to hunt some more. So on the next day he and the boys went out to the place where he had left the meat, and on their arrival at the place they took the meat and brought it home, while the Thunderbird went on to hunt again. On the follow-ing day the Thunderbird again came in with the deer meat, and from this time on he went out hunting every day. The people had plenty of meat to eat, and the boys were growing rapidly. After a time the boys went out hunting with the Thunderbird, and the Thunderbird gave them power to become great hunters. In this place he stayed for a long while. Once in a while the boys would go out hunting by themselves and let the Thunderbird stay at home, because the boys began to like to hunt. The Thunderbird gave them powers to hunt and the boys never failed to bring in something when they came from the hunt.

Long afterward some of the people began to return home, and after several days came the Coyote with the crowd. On his return they told him that his uncle had been brought to life and was now in the village. The Coyote went straight to where his uncle was and saw him and met him at the old people's home, where he had been brought to life. The Coyote at once called his uncle, the Thunderbird, to his home, where he stayed for the rest of his time. The rest of the people never returned, for they knew they had lost one of the best men in the village, and they expected him never to live again. After this the people remained in the village for all time, for they had no one to do them harm. The Thunderbird remained as a chief at all times, and his nephew was the second chief for this village. Now there were changes in the village, but all remained as human beings, with the exception of the ones who went off and never returned.

14. THE DEEDS OF WETS-THE-BED.*

There was once a village that extended east and west, and in the village lived a chief whose name was Head-Chief (Esaraketskati). The chief used to paint himself under the chin with yellow paint, which extended clear across his chin below his nose. There was another man living near him who used to paint himself in black. There was a third chief who painted himself on his head and legs. These three chiefs lived in the village. No trouble or sickness had ever been known in the village. All enjoyed themselves. The people now often sent out war-parties against their neighbors, who were known as the Tricksters (Kinas). When they found the Tricksters they would fight them, kill them, and bring home their scalps to the village. Thus they would en-tertain themselves. In the north part of the village, in a small grass-

*Told by Towakoni Jim (Towakoni).

lodge, lived an old man and an old woman with their little grandson. The boy's name was Wets-the-Bed (Weksidahos). These people were very poor. Their food was scant. As the people went by they would amuse themselves by urinating on their lodge. The boys of the village beat the little boy for fun.

As Wets-the-Bed went around the village picking up things to eat he heard men saying that a war-party was to be sent out by one of the foremost leaders. He went back to his grandparents to tell them he wanted to go along with the war-party. His grandmother said: "You cannot go. You would give out, for they will go a long way, and there are some bad people that go with these war-parties. You know how badly they have treated you at home, and if they get you away from home they will kill you instead of killing the enemy. They will treat you worse away from home than they have at home." Still the boy said, "I must go." The time came for the war-party to start away, and Wets-the-Bed was determined to go. The day they set out they camped pretty early, and they waited for those who had fallen behind to come up with them. Late in the evening they looked back on their trail and saw some one coming. As the person came he appeared smaller and smaller, and finally proved to be Wets-the-Bed. The men said they would send him back, for he was too small to travel with them. There was a certain man in the party that was impetuous and had a quick temper. He got up, went toward Wets-the-Bed and told him he must go back home, saying: "We do not want you to go along, and if you do not go back I will kill you." The leader of the party told his men to let the boy alone and allow him to accompany them. The next morning, however, when they started out, the leader told Wets-the-Bed that he must go back, for they were going too far for him, and they were not yet very far from home. Wets-the-Bed remained there while the rest of the party started off. After they had gone on he followed after them. When they stopped to rest the boy would catch up. They had their spies out to look for the enemy. When the boy came up with the crowd he started on. The two spies came in and reported to the leader what they had seen. They said there was a village very close to them. They proceeded to come close enough to charge upon the enemy. They got ready, taking off their robes and leaving them with Wets-the-Bed, telling him to remain there while they were out after the enemy. All had painted themselves and had their weapons ready for use. When they were gone, Wets-the-Bed went and jumped into a creek near by, and when he came out he was changed to a man; then he followed on to the village. As he went along he was seen by the war-party. They wondered who he was. He went on and got ahead of them. He was the first in the village. He went on through. He entered first so as to frighten everybody in the village. The people in the village were awakened, and unable to get their weapons and fight because of their fear. So the war-party had an easy time fighting them. The only weapon the boy had was a war-club. He wore a war-bonnet that none of the war-party had ever seen. It was hair dyed red. When he got through the village he went back to the creek, dived in, and when he came out he was the same as before. He then placed himself in position to watch the robes. He saw the people coming bringing captives and scalps, and they were talking about the strange person, for no one in the crowd had such a dress as Wets-the-Bed wore. When the men got back they kept talking about the man they had seen in the lead, but they could not find out who he was. The next day when they arrived home dances were made. When the boy got home the old people had to get up and have a dance by themselves, since the boy had been in the party. The men in the village talked about the man who had led in the attack upon the enemy. They were not able to find out who he was.

Long after the war-party returned the same leader announced to his warriors that he was about to send out another war-party. The news came to Wets-the-Bed, who went home and told his grandparents that another war-party was going out and that he wanted to go with it. His grandfather and grandmother thought that they had better allow him to go, for he had been once, and if he had endured once, he might go again. A day was set to start. When the day came all started and the boy followed. When they camped late in the evening the boy was seen again. The men said nothing whatever about him this time. After dark the leader told his people to keep their eyes on the person that should be in the lead when they should make the attack on the enemy, for he knew that he himself was a pretty fast runner, and when he saw this young man go ahead he knew there surely must be some one who could run faster than he. On the next day, early in the morning, two spies were sent out. While on the road the spies found the enemy's camp and returned to report to the leader what they had seen, saying they had found the village of the enemy. They went near enough to the village to attack it. When they came to the place they dressed themselves and got ready to make the attack. They left behind them their robes and things that they did not need in care of Wets-the-Bed. When they started out, the boy turned around and went to the creek, dived into it, and came out changed. He went to attack the village. His people watched to see who he was. As he went along he was so fast that the party saw fire fly behind him, and the fire was of all colors. He entered the village in advance of the war-party. As he entered everybody was awakened and frightened, so that they were unable to protect themselves. They forgot to get their weapons. When Wets-the-Bed got through the village he went on around by another way and came to the creek, where he dived in the water and came out changed, and went back to the place where he was stationed and stayed until the war-party came back. When the men returned to the boy and their goods they went home, but the boy never got a scalp. It was the custom to take scalps to make presents when returning to the village. When the war-party got home they had their dances and the boy and his grandparents also danced.

Long after, the war-party went out again, and Wets-the-Bed again went along. This happened four times, always as before. At the end of the fourth time, when they arrived home the leader of the war-party began to think about the man who had always beat them to the village of the enemy. They wondered who it could be. The leader knew of no faster runner than himself.

Once upon a time the leader called all of his men together at his place in the night. When the people had gathered, Wets-the-Bed went there also to show himself. As he came around, the quick-tempered man came to him and said, "You do not need to come around, for you have no chance to get the chief's daughter for your wife." The boy went around to hear what the chief had to say. The chief then offered his girls to the man who could prove that he had arrived at the village before the rest of the warriors and had been in the strange dress and had run ahead of the war-party when they attacked the enemy. After he had announced this to the people every one was still. No one could prove that he was the man. Finally Wets-the-Bed rose to his feet and told the people that he was the man that was first in the attack upon the enemy. Then he sat down. The chief announced to the people again that he had always thought that Wets-the-Bed might have been the man. He said: "If that is true, I offer my girls to him if he can prove that he was the first to attack the enemy and return to the village." The oldest of the girls did not like Wets-the-Bed. She wished that some one else might have proved himself to be the man. She determined not to accept the boy. After Wets-the-Bed had proved he was first to attack the enemy the men began to return home.

It was now bedtime. Wets-the-Bed went to bed with the two wives. The oldest of the girls did not like him, so she kept away by herself and allowed the younger girl to lie with him. The people of the chief's village would now gather at the chief's lodge, sit up part of the night and talk about the past. While they were with the head chief sometimes they would whisper, and say, "I do not see what the chief's son-in-law is good for." Wets-the-Bed, while living with the chief's daughters, went home daily and came back at night. One day as he went back to his old home it happened that buffalo were seen on the north side of the village, and the men from the village gathered around the buffalo and killed them. It happened that Wets-the-Bed was at his home. When the men were butchering buffalo Wets-the-Bed said to his grandfather: "Go out there and get me some intestines. When you get there, help yourself and cut off the intestines. Bring them to me. I am hungry for them." The grandfather said: "I do not want to go. You know how we are treated. If I go there they will harm me." But the boy said: "Go on." The old man thought much of his grandson, and so he went to the place where they were butchering. He grabbed at the intestines and was about to help himself, when all at once one man came around and said to him: "What are you doing? This is not yours. Why do you help yourself? It is right that you should ask for what you want." The old man said nothing. They made the old man put down the intestines, and they bored a hole through his cheeks, cut off some hide and tied it through the hole and sent the old men home. When he returned home he was covered with blood. As he entered he said to the boy: "I told you they would do something to me." The boy said: "That is all I want to know." The boy went out and dived in the creek. When he came out he was the same as when with the war-party attacking the enemy. He went where the men were butchering. He attracted everybody's attention. All looked, and they asked one another if they knew the man. No one could tell who he was. Wets-the-Bed asked who it was that had cut his grandfather's cheeks. They pointed out the man. Wets-the-Bed took a knife and served the man as he had served his grandfather. He then commenced to talk to the people who were butchering, telling them that he had always thought that he was of some use to them; that he was doing them some good through his powers; that through him they had easier times in attacking the enemy; but that now, the more good he did them the worse they treated him; that they were treating his people worse than ever. He went back to the creek, jumped in and changed himself, then came back to his place.

The people began to talk about what they had seen, and many said: "I always thought that Wets-the-Bed must be the one who had done wonders." All at once the men took their loads of beef on their backs to Wets-the-Bed. The chief of the village called for the largest tipi to be found. When the tipi was found it was put up for the grandparents of Wets-the-Bed. After the tipi was put up Wets-the-Bed went back to his wives. As he entered his home he told some of them to sweep out the place. He then took his young wife to the east, and they finally reached the creek. He dived into the creek, and when he came out he was the same as when attacking the enemy. He then took his wife and threw her in the creek. Soon he saw her hair floating on the top of the water. As she came up she was changed and was very beautiful. They went toward the village. In the night everybody smelled a scent the two had on them, and they did not know what it was. They wondered who was passing. Wets-the-Bed and his wife arrived at their home, and he changed his bed so that it looked like new. The older girl would never eat with Wets-the-Bed, for she hated him and her sister, but when she saw that he was changed she did not know what to do. She had remained the same, and now she wished she looked as well as the man and her sister. She now wanted to sleep with Wets-the-Bed, but the young girl refused her. She now did all the cooking for the two, trying to gain their favor, so that she might share the husband. Still the young girl refused, and told her if she wanted to be near them she might lie down by the bed to make a step for them to step on. The older sister agreed. She was losing her flesh and her appetite longing to be with Wets-the-Bed.

When Wets-the-Bed and his wife were about sixteen years old the people of the chief's village gathered in the chief's lodge. When they entered the lodge they saw Wets-the-Bed and his wife. When they were told to sit down the chiefs of the village began to whisper, saying: "You made a mistake in saying that Wets-the-Bed was not a good son-in-law. You now see who this Wets-the-Bed is." Others said among themselves, "I always thought there was something to this poor boy." While Wets-the-Bed was living with the chief's daughter his sister-in-law was getting thin, but his wife told her that she had done wrong when she had refused her father's command to marry Wets-the-Bed.

Time went on, until finally the head chief called his servant, who was of dark complexion, was a very fast runner, and could move around very fast. He sent him around through the village to tell the men of the village to come to his place. Crowds began to gather. When it was thought they were all present they made it known to the chief. They asked why he had called them together. He said to the chiefs:

"Head warriors, and all you leaders, I tell you what I want done. Since I am getting old and am not able to remain always as your head chief, I will now appoint my son-in-law to be your head chief hereafter, and I will remain as a common man hereafter. My son-in-law is yet a young man and he will be a good head chief and a good leader in all things." This was all the head chief had to say. The other chiefs made their speeches regarding Wets-the-Bed's advancement, saying that he was the right kind of a man to be head chief. No objections were made. Wets-the-Bed was appointed as head chief, head warrior, and leader. When the people returned to their homes it was announced through the village by the different men that the chief had appointed his son-in-law to become the head chief in his place, and that hereafter they must recognize Wets-the-Bed as their head chief, head warrior, and leader. Wets-the-Bed took his seat as chief and the sub-chiefs of the village visited him the same as they had their former chief. They found that Wets-the-Bed was in every way just. Everybody was treated aright, and everything went along all right.

The first of the main chiefs of the village was a man who painted himself around the nose; the next painted himself black all over and then made white spots on his body; the third chief painted himself white on his head and on his legs. The first was the father of Wets-the-Bed. The leader of the war-parties which Wets-the-Bed had accompanied was painted with white clay from the corners of his eyes backward, and from the corners of his mouth backward. In the leader's band of warriors was a certain man who was always sent out to spy. He was of dark complexion and painted himself with black paint. Wets-the-Bed had a war-bonnet made of hair, dyed red and yellow. He also painted himself across his body with black and white bars. His bow was made out of a fire poker, and his arrows were made out of sticks used for roasting beef.

Long after Wets-the-Bed had begun to serve as head chief he was troubled because the older chief's daughter was wasting away in flesh, for her younger sister would not allow her to share her husband. Finally he called his people together to his lodge. When they had come together he announced that since his appointment as chief many things had gone all right, and that the people had done whatever he directed; therefore, since he had helped them in many ways he now wanted to go where he had come from and he wanted the people to do as they pleased about themselves. Said he: "If you wish, you can become something else, but I will go where I came from. Hereafter, when I am turned into something else, if any one does as I have done and carries out my powers as I used to perform in the warrior ceremonies, I shall help such persons, and in attacking their foes I shall show myself as I did while on the war-path." Wets-the-Bed turned around and spoke to his father-in-law, saying: "Since I have been living among your people, you see the fame I have won, my reputation as a great warrior, and since then you have appointed me as the head chief of the village, and gave me your daughter, for my wife, and gave up your place as chief, that I shall not keep. I shall not take your daughter along when I leave. I shall, however, beg that I may have the same kind of dress that you have." The chief said he could have it. Wets-the-Bed now called himself "Bird-having-War-bonnet-made-of-red-Haired-Scalps" (Itschidistariak), the Red-Start. He had received his powers from Shooting-Star (Hassedaawa), when a little boy, when the Star wanted him to rise as a great war chief and become a head chief. Now the leader of the war-party announced himself to the people. He told them that while living in their village, in sending out war-parties his powers should continue in the village, but he wanted to be something else. He promised to the people that should remain that if they did the same as he had done he would give them as easy a time to find the enemy as he had had. Then he turned into a Swift-Hawk (Gusseios).

Now the spy made his talk to the people, telling them that he would leave his powers to them, and the man who should do as he had done would have the same luck as he had had in finding the enemy. He told them that he was going where he had come from; that hereafter he would be with the buffalo instead of living in the village, so he turned into a Buffalo-Crow (Kawitor), or Raven.

The old chief of the village now told the people that he was going to do the same as the others had done and become something else; that in the next generation there would be a man called chief and head warrior; that hereafter he would be up in the air, and he was going to select the place he wanted for his home; that hereafter he should be known as Eagle (Kos).

The next two chiefs then said the same as the old chief had said, and the one that painted with black stripes and white spots said he was to be known as Black-Eagle (Kaseya), with a spotted tail. The chief that painted the face and legs white made the same talk, and said that he was going to change as the others had done; that thereafter he would be known as Bald-Eagle (Kaisiskos).

After the announcements were made the people began to collect in groups at the chief's place. They took a small bowl and filled it with water. They poured it on the fire, and when the smoke went up it sounded like thunder, as the people who had determined to change their nature flew up in the air. Those that wished to exist as animals went in different directions, some to the timber, some to the prairie, and some to the water. All but a few left the place, and they remained as human beings.

15. THE DEEDS OF WETS-THE-BED.*

There was a village where Wets-the-Bed (Weksidahos) lived with his grandparents. Wets-the-Bed was a small boy. His name signifies that he urinated in bed at night. They were living near the edge of the village. Many people abused them and especially the Coyote (Ketox), who would pull the grass out of their lodge and defecate on it. Young-Man-Chief (Tonekitsanias) was the only man in the village who liked Wets-the-Bed. This chief was a young man, but he was a chief of all the chiefs who lived in the village. In this village all the chiefs had signs before their homes to show that they were chiefs. The sign was the wooly forepart of a buffalo hide, which they hung to the outside of the doors of their homes. Wets-the-Bed made his living by going around the village where there were ash piles, looking for something to eat, such as parched corn. Another thing he did was to eat at the mortar where they ground corn. On this account he received another name, Corn-Meal-Boy (Weksiwistataa), so that he had two names. Everybody hated him, because he was an orphan and dirty, and his people were old and poor.

The men of the village were in the habit of going out on the war-path against their enemies the Tricksters (Kinas). There was a family consisting of an old man, his wife, boy, and four girls, living in the east part of the village. The boy was never of much account as a warrior. He would stay at home while all the other young men went on the war-path. His sisters were all beautiful. Once upon a time each of these four women went out to the woods to get a load of wood. Before they were ready to start back the oldest called to the rest to come where she was. They all went, and they asked what she had to say. She replied: "Let us all go home and ask father to let us go out with some war-party and leave our brother at home; or let us form a war-party to take us out, and put some one in the lead, when we get home." To this they all agreed. They hurried back home, and finding the old man in bed, asked him to get out of bed and listen to what they had to say. The old man got out of bed and asked what they wanted. They told

*Told by Ahahe (Waco).

him that they wanted to form a war-party to go out on the war-path against the Tricksters, and that they wanted him to show them what he used in his time when going on the war-path. The old man took down an old war bundle which was done up in an old robe, and unwrapped it. The women saw four more bundles that were tobacco pouches, and everything that went with tobacco. These pouches were made out of a small animal called Pole-cat (Darkiaha). In the first pouch were found soft, white feathers, nearly worn out, for the old man had them in the earlier days of his life, and the pouch was nearly empty. The next pouch was a little better, because he used it after he had used the first one; and the third bundle was much newer than the second and first pouches, as also were the feathers and other material that were used in going on the war-path. The fourth tobacco bundle was the one he used before arriving at old age. After these were shown to the women they took the first bundle and asked for directions in performing the work before going out and before going into battle. The old man filled their pipe full of tobacco. This pipe was made of stone. After they had their pipe filled up they formed in line and each took her robe along and started for the place of Young-Man-Chief. He was their choice among the men for a leader. On arriving at his place they requested him to stand up. When he stood up, each of the women spread her robe, one on top of another, and seated Young-Man-Chief upon the pile, putting the pipe in his hand and asking him to take it and go ahead and light it. (This was the way the people of those times put a man in the lead. They took a pipe full of tobacco and offered it to some one to smoke.) So they lighted the pipe and smoked it. Young-Man-Chief asked the women what time they wanted to start, and they replied, "Within four days." Corn-Meal-Boy heard about these young women putting Young-Man-Chief in the lead to go on the war-path. This was the very man who liked him, and he was the only friend Corn-Meal-Boy had in the village. So Corn-Meal-Boy went home and told what he had heard, and said that he wanted to go along when the women should start. The old folks refused to let him go, for some one would send him back. Young-Man-Chief was known as a great warrior and chief, who always had good luck with war-parties.

Before they made their attack on their enemies some one was always seen going in the lead, and this person, whoever he was, had a war-bonnet different from any one else. After the battle Young-Man-Chief asked his men if there was any one in the party who was always in the lead while making the attack. This man in the lead was noticed again and again. The four days finally passed. Before starting out the four sisters pledged themselves to be the wives of the one who should first see the enemies. This was what made Corn-Meal-Boy want to go. After all had started Corn-Meal-Boy followed. They all went a long way and camped for a night's rest. Of course, as was the custom, they sent out men to spy. Next morning before they started they looked in the direction whence they had come and saw some one coming. He appeared very small and as he came nearer, proved to be Corn-Meal-Boy. They waited until he came up with them. When he arrived at the place, the Coyote abused him and sent him back, then they started again, traveling until night, when they all stopped. When Young-Man-Chief announced this the Coyote appointed himself to go along with his friend, "Nawane."* This is what the Coyote called all of his friends. When they were resting Corn-Meal-Boy passed the war-party, going beyond it, in the east direction in which the party was moving. The next morning, before daylight, Young-Man-Chief and the Coyote started out. They went for some distance, and found Corn-Meal-Boy lying down asleep. They went up to him and told him to go right back where the others were. They continued their trip a long way, and when they looked back they saw Corn-Meal-Boy still coming. They stopped again, and the Coyote abused him, and told him to go right back. The two started again, but still saw Corn-Meal-Boy following. The Coyote grew angry, and turned him over and whipped him. Young-Man-Chief thought that he had better take Corn-Meal-Boy along. He got the poor boy on his back; for they were going pretty fast. Finally they stopped to rest and smoke. Then the chief wanted to turn back, for there was no one in sight. The place where they rested was a little hill. The boy went to the top, looked over the hill, turned right back, and came back stooping, on the run all the way. It attracted the chief's attention. He asked Corn-Meal-Boy what he had seen and the boy said he had seen smoke, and suspected some one to be living there. So Young-Man-Chief and Corn-Meal-Boy both went, and they saw a great village of the Tricksters, their enemies. When they came back the Coyote begged Young-Man-Chief to tell the young women that he had found the enemies, so he could get the four women for his wives. They at once started right back, and traveled pretty fast. They arrived at the camp at midnight, wakened the people and told what Young-Man-Chief had seen. So everybody came to build a big fire, and they all gathered around him and he began his story: "At the beginning of the

---

*A special term applied to a friend on a war expedition to whom has been presented a scalp by his companion.

journey we were delayed by Corn-Meal-Boy." When the chief would say anything the Coyote, expecting the chief to say that he (the Coyote) had found the camp of the enemy, would repeat everything the chief had said. "We had to wait for Corn-Meal-Boy, and on this account stopped a couple of times for a good while; but he finally got on my back, and we traveled a little faster. While we were traveling the Coyote got a stick, sharpened it, and hit Corn-Meal-Boy on the rump. When we had traveled all day we rested on the side of a hill before reaching the summit. Corn-Meal-Boy ran on up to the top of the hill and saw a smoke and suspected some one to be living there." At this point the Coyote gave up all hope of the chief's saying that he (the Coyote) had found the village of the Tricksters, and stopped repeating what the chief had said. "So we went to see what was there. We saw some of the enemies' homes." Then the women said to one another: "How do you suppose such a fellow as he could ever find anything like that; and, although they had pledged themselves as wives to the first one who should see the enemy, the three older ones would not accept Corn-Meal-Boy for their husband; but the youngest of the four said that in order to fulfill her pledge she would take the boy and be his wife. So Corn-Meal-Boy was married while on the war-path. When they started for the place of the Tricksters the girl took the boy on her back and carried him all the way. They arrived there before daylight, and early that morning they made their attack. When they had started Corn-Meal-Boy was seen going ahead of everybody, getting in the village first, and doing the first fighting. When they all turned back they had captured many of the Tricksters, taking them as prisoners. Young-Man-Chief captured one man on his return, and he called for the wife of Corn-Meal-Boy and gave the prisoner to her and her husband.

Then all set out for home. When they had reached the point called Place-where-returning-victorious-War-party-halted (Nasaquadowene), where the chief usually signaled his returned to the village, on his return from the war-path, the people of the village said, "Tesatias;" that is, Young-Man-Chief's turn. Everybody went home. The girl and her new husband went to the girl's home, taking their prisoner. The boy stayed at the girl's home for a while, until her sisters got tired of them. The boy urinated in bed so much that the rest of the girls wanted to get rid of him, but the girl stayed with him and moved to the place where Corn-Meal-Boy lived.

It was once the custom for people who saw buffalo to drive them near to the village, surround them, and kill them. When this happened,

Corn-Meal-Boy asked his grandfather to go to the place where they were killing buffalo and get him some tripe; but the old man cried, and said that some one might cut his hands. He still wanted his grandfather to go, and so he went over to where they were butchering, just as a tripe was cut open. So the old man got hold of it, and some one cut both of his hands, bored a hole in his cheek, and tied a string through it. The boy heard his grandfather coming, and when he arrived he saw that his grandfather was badly cut. Corn-Meal-Boy stepped out to the water, dived in, and came out of the water a fine-looking man, and he had on a war-bonnet and carried a club, called "short-club" (haksteeneka). He went toward the village, yelling and hooting, and going to every place where there were chiefs living, and as he came to each chief's home he used his club to pound on the door, saying that he had made all the powers for them to become chiefs; that he had been abused many times, but had never felt badly over it, but the time had come when he had to feel badly over the way his grandfather was treated. He went from one place to another, pounding on the doors of all the chiefs' homes; though he did not go where Young-Man-Chief lived, for he alone had always treated him well. When going through the village, Corn-Meal-Boy heard Young-Man-Chief talking, and saying to himself, "That is just what I always thought about Corn-Meal-Boy." After going all through the village he went on to where the buffalo were being killed. Everybody saw him coming with a club, and they were afraid of him. He spoke to the people, saying: "I have given the men powers to become chiefs. If it had not been for me they could never have been chiefs. On the warpath I would show up before attacking the enemy and give you men an easy time." Corn-Meal-Boy met the Coyote, who called him "friend," as he was accustomed to do with his friends, but he hit the Coyote in his ribs with the club, and took his knife and cut the man who had cut his grandfather, bored a hole in his cheek, and tied a string through it. He then returned to his home. The old folks told him that theirs was no place for a fine-looking man such as he to come to—not knowing that he was Corn-Meal-Boy. He went in, sat down, held his head down, and held his club in his hand. When the people and chiefs found this out, one after another of the chiefs came with pipe, expecting him to forgive them for what the man had done to his grandfather, but every one failed to get him to accept the pipe, and he emptied their pipes right in front of him. He wanted his friend, Young-Man-Chief, to come and offer him his pipe, which, when he did, he accepted. Then each of the chiefs went over to Young-Man-Chief with his tobacco and asked him to go over to Corn-Meal-Boy and offer to him their tobacco, for they knew he would accept it from Young-Man-Chief. Finally Young-Man-Chief accepted the pipe and went over to Corn-Meal-Boy and offered him a smoke, asking him to put away ill feelings, which he did, and he smoked the pipe. The chief at once called all the people and ordered them to build a new home for Corn-Meal-Boy's people. They at once began work on his new home, and when they had finished it the old people were taken to it. After they had moved, he and his wife both went to the water, and he had his wife get in the water. When she came out, her appearance was changed.

When the sisters heard about this they all went to see her. When they saw that Corn-Meal-Boy had changed in appearance they wanted their sister to allow him to be their husband, but she refused, because they had not wanted him for their husband in the first place. When they came around she would force them out. The sisters finally wanted Corn-Meal-Boy so badly that they would come to his home at night and stand around by his bed, and after they got tired standing they would lie down on the side of his bed until morning. Finally the women were so desirous of him that they could not eat very well. They would sometimes invite Corn-Meal-Boy to come to their home and eat with them. So by the time they began to eat, Corn-Meal-Boy's wife would come and ask her man to come out and go home with her. This made the sisters want the more to marry him. Corn-Meal-Boy got tired of his sisters-in-law and wanted them to let him alone. He, of course, then had the power to win the love of any girl. He fooled the people by being a little boy and having all kinds of names given him by the people. The only time he ever showed up was when they went on the war-path, when, on making an attack, he would be seen by the people, who now knew who he was; and the chief would ask all the men in the party if there was one with them who did the first fighting in making an attack. The Coyote would say that it was he, but it was thereafter known that it was Corn-Meal-Boy who was always ahead of every one in making an attack.

At the time when his name was Wets-the-Bed, he wore a little, old, dirty string around his neck, and had something wrapped up and tied to it. This little thing, after he had proved to be a famous man, he showed, and it was his war-bonnet, appearing as it was seen when making an attack on the enemy before he ever made his appearance. When he appeared a good many of the men came and visited him at night, sitting up and talking about the past or telling war stories; and he would once in a while visit his friend, Young-Man-Chief, and stay there until late in the night.

On one occasion they went out on the war-path, headed by Young-
Man-Chief and Corn-Meal-Boy, the noted warriors. When they left
their homes they went towards the east, traveling until night, and then
stopped to rest. They sent out men to spy and see if they could find
any of their enemies. Some of the men came in at midnight and reported that they had found the enemy. So they started at once, arriving at the enemies', the Tricksters', homes, just before daylight. About
sunrise they attacked them. Again they saw a man in the lead, but this
time they knew who he was. Every time they made an attack they
would see him going in the lead, and his war-bonnet shone like fire.
He, of course, stayed with the party this time. On their return they
had a good many people whom they had taken captive. They turned
back to their home and traveled faster than they had done in coming.
As they returned, the sign was given at the usual place, Place-where-
returning-victorious-War-party-halted (Nasaquadowene). On their
arrival they had all kinds of dancing. Corn-Meal-Boy lived with his
folks a little longer, and then, after he had shown many other supernatural powers, he gave powers to men to hand down to other generations. He finally left all his people and went up in the sky. He was
then called "First-seen-by-War-parties" (Hasiilaawa). Before he left
he promised that he would help his people on the war-path if they would
just think of him, but that he would not appear as he used to, and it
would be just as if he were there. We, the people of these times, when
anything happens in that way, still mention this First-seen-by-War-
party, and expect to see something occur and to have easy times in anything we may do.

16.   THE THUNDERBIRD-WOMAN.*

There were three people living together in a grass-lodge, in front
of the north door of which stood a large cottonwood tree. We know
that the grass-lodge generally has two doors. The doors of the grass-
lodge opened north and south. In this lodge lived the Thunderbird-
Woman (Geleazigits), Little-Big-Belly-Boy (Wekskuniwidiks), and
the Libertine (Skiwis). The Thunderbird-Woman did all the cooking
and hauling of wood. Little-Big-Belly-Boy did the water-carrying, and
the Libertine did all the hunting, for he was a strong man, and had
many powers. They lived here for a long while, and Little-Big-Belly-
Boy and the Libertine always had a good time, for the Libertine was
very strong, and would carry a whole buffalo whenever he killed one.

*Told by Ahahe (Waco).

Once upon a time as the Libertine was going out hunting, a small piece of grass fell on his back and he could not get up, for somehow or other he could not lift little things. This small grass was a heavy load for him, and so he called for Little-Big-Belly-Boy to help him, but Little-Big-Belly-Boy wished to have some fun with him, and so he let the grass stay on his back until he was so tired that he gave out. Then Little-Big-Belly-Boy took the grass off his back and he returned home instead of going hunting. In order to cure his soreness, the Libertine took out a cottonwood tree by the root and stood it on his back and got the boy to bring some more wood and place it all around the root, and set a fire on it until it got hot. Then he took it off of his back, and was pretty well healed. Next morning he went out hunting and did not come back until late in the night. On his return, he caught a buffalo and brought it to their home alive. Early next morning, when Little-Big-Belly-Boy got up and started to go out, he saw a buffalo standing at the door, mad as it could be. It drove Little-Big-Belly-Boy back into the grass-lodge. In order to tease the boy, the Libertine stayed in bed longer than usual, so that the boy could not go out of the lodge. The boy kept begging the Libertine to take the buffalo off to some other place. He asked him to kill the buffalo, take the hide and make a robe out of it for him. The Libertine stepped out and got the buffalo by the horns, shook it, and there was the robe for Little-Big-Belly-Boy.

Some time after, Little-Big-Belly-Boy, expecting to get even with the Libertine, caught a mouse, tied it by the neck, and put it by the door. Next morning, the Libertine got up early to step out, and there he saw something outside. He came right back and was afraid of it, and asked Little-Big-Belly-Boy to release the mouse, so that he could step out, but the boy remained in bed and laughed at the Libertine. Finally Little-Big-Belly-Boy got out of bed, and the Libertine asked him to do the same as he himself had done and make him a robe out of the mouse. So Little-Big-Belly-Boy stepped out, got hold of the mouse, shook it, and there was a robe for the Libertine. The next night the Libertine got into his bed, but could not put on his mouse robe, because it was too heavy for him. He had to get the boy to put the robe on for him. Later in the night he could not turn over, for the robe was so heavy, and he asked the boy to pull it off. The boy pulled off the robe, then the Libertine finally went to sleep. Some time after this, Little-Big-Belly-Boy got to feeling sad over something, and went without eating for a time, and he would not play the same as he had done before, so the Libertine asked him to tell him just what was the matter with him. Little-Big-Belly-Boy replied that it had been re-vealed to him that somebody would come and carry him off. The Liber-tine stepped out and showed Little-Big-Belly-Boy what he could do, taking his arrows and bow and shooting at the tree in front of the lodge. The arrow went clear through the tree; but the boy told the Libertine that that was not force enough, for this person who was coming to carry him off had greater powers than he. The Libertine comforted the boy, and told him that he would in some way protect him.

It happened that while the boy was out playing, he ran in, telling the Libertine that his enemy was coming. The Libertine stepped out, and saw it coming like a cloud, from the north; it was a large bird, called Sun-Buzzard* (Aitskadarwiya). It had wings, tail, and head, and small, sharp flint stones all over its body. Its bill was like a sharp stone, so that nothing would go through it. The Libertine stepped out and the bird lit on the tree and the Libertine with bow and arrows shot at it four times, but failed to send any of his arrows through it. After the shooting of all of his arrows the furious bird came down, put the Libertine on its back and took him in the direction it had come from. It went a long way, and the Libertine saw great water at the place where they were going to. They finally came to a small island, where the Sun-Buzzard had his nest on a high tree, into which it threw the Libertine. Then it passed on toward the east to some other place. The Libertine saw under the tree many human skulls and bones. This showed that the Sun-Buzzard had made a business of carrying off people and throwing them into its nest. When the Libertine was thrown into the nest the young ones kept picking at him. He at once took one of the young ones and asked it whose child it was, and the young bird said it was the child of Cold-Weather-followed-by-Blizzard (Kitshasiyarni hasanaaxqua), so he threw it down and killed it. He took up another and asked it whose child it was, and it answered that it was the child of Nice-clear-Weather (Otshasihiniton sakatsasasaca), and so he put it down, saying that it was a good child. He took up an-other and asked the same question, and the young child replied that he was the child of Hard-Rain-followed-by-Hard-Wind (Kitsasaa kossasaniwaa), and so the Libertine threw it down and killed it. He picked up the last one and asked it whose child it was, and it answered that it was the child of Foggy-Day (Hassquawe). This was the weather everybody liked, and so he set the young one back again. These were the names of the parents of the children: Cold-Weather-followed-by-Blizzard,   Nice-clear-Weather,   Hard-Rain-followed-by-

---

*Literally, a Buzzard who dwells in the intense heat in the darkness at the back of the sun.

hard-Wind, and Foggy-Day. These were the children of the Sun-Buzzard, two of which the Libertine had destroyed. After he had done this he came down from the tree. He had nothing but his bow, and so he took off his bow-string from the bow, stretched it as long as he could and made it long enough to put across the water. After he thought it to be long enough he took the string and raised it, swung it, brought it down and hit the water with it, and parted the water. When the water parted he ran fast through the dry place and got through before the water closed upon him. The Libertine went a long way and traveled pretty fast in order to get home before the Sun-Buzzard should get him again. Nobody knew how long it took him to get home, but he finally got there, and told Thunderbird-Woman and Little-Big-Belly-Boy what a hard time he had making his escape from the Sun-Buzzard.

They lived together for a long time, and when the Libertine told them that the Sun-Buzzard was coming again to get him they saw it coming, and it lit on the same tree as before. The three inmates of the lodge all stepped out, the Thunderbird-Woman leading the other two. They went toward the mountains near their home, and reaching them, the Thunderbird-Woman carried her two companions through them on her back. Of course, in going through the rocks they would close up behind her and thus make it harder for the Sun-Buzzard to follow. Finally they all sat down to rest, and they asked the Libertine to go and see if the Sun-Buzzard was still coming. He went and heard it still coming, and returned, reporting it to his friends. They all went to the place where they had come out, listened and heard it coming rather slowly. It came through and fell to one side, and the Libertine killed it. Then the three returned to the place where they had lived. When the Sun-Buzzard came out of the mountains its bill was broken off, and its wings were pretty well broken to pieces. The Libertine told his mates that he was afraid that the same thing that had happened to him might befall him again; and so he went to the woods, and said that he would be seen on the dead wood of the woods thereafter. The Libertine was then a Big-red-Water-Worm. (Kaatsiaquatskiwats). Thunderbird-Woman went off toward the north, and called herself Rain-Woman (Kihitskahhahikia). Little-Big-Belly-Boy went flying toward the prairies; he became Dry-Grass-Bird (Nineca, or, Achini-kats), a small bird that lives in the grass.

17.   HEALTHY-FLINT-STONE-MAN AND WOMAN-HAVING-POWERS-IN-THE-WATER.*

In the story of Healthy-Flint-Stone-Man (Tahadiidakotse), it is told that he was a powerful man and lived in a village and was a chief of the place. He was not a man of heavy build, but was slim. Often when a man is of this type of build he is called "Healthy-Flint-Stone-Man," after the man in the story. Healthy-Flint-Stone-Man had parents, but at this time he had no wife. Soon afterwards he married, and his wife was the prettiest woman that ever lived in the village. When she married Healthy-Flint-Stone-Man they lived at his home. She was liked by his parents, for she was a good worker and kind-hearted. As was their custom, the men of the village came at night to visit Healthy-Flint-Stone-Man, and his wife did the cooking to feed them, so that he liked her all the more, and was kind to her.

Early in the morning a strange woman by the name of Little-Old-Woman (Kahedikits) came to their place and asked the wife to go with her to get wood. Out of kindness to Little-Old-Woman she went with her, leaving her husband at home. Little-Old-Woman knew where all the dry wood was to be found. When they reached the place where she thought there was plenty of wood they did not stop. They went on past, although there was plenty of good dry wood. The wife began to cut wood for the old woman and some for herself. When she had cut enough for both she fixed it into two bundles, one for each. Little-Old-Woman knelt by her pile and waited for the wife to help her up. Little-Old-Woman then helped the wife in the same way, and they started toward their home. They talked on the way about their manner of life at home. Arrived at the village, the old woman went to her home. When the wife got home she began to do her work.

Again, the second time, the old woman came around and asked the wife to go with her to fetch wood. They started away together, and this time went farther than on the first time to get their wood, though they passed much good wood. The wife cut wood for both and arranged it in two piles, but this time she herself first knelt by her pile and asked the old woman to take hold of her hands and pull her up; then the wife helped the old woman with her load. They returned home, and on the way the old woman said to the wife, "If you will go with me to fetch wood for the fourth time I shall need no more help from you." They again went far beyond where any other women had gone to get wood. When they got to the village they parted. The wife wondered why the old woman came to her for help. She found the

*Told by Towakoni Jim (Towakoni).

men passing the time talking of the past as usual. She kept on doing her duty day after day.

The third time the old woman came for the wife to ask her to help her fetch wood, as she was all out of it again. Again they went out, and this time they went still further for the wood, and now they were getting a long way from the village. The wife cut wood and arranged it in two bundles, one for each of them to carry. This time it was the old woman's turn first to be helped up with the wood. They helped each other, and on the way home the old woman told the wife that they had only once more to go for wood, and the work would all be done. She always seemed thankful for the help she received. They reached the village and went to their homes. The wife found her men as usual, and commenced to do her work. After the men were through eating they went home, though some stayed late in the night.

Finally the old woman came the fourth time to ask the wife to go with her and help her fetch some wood. This time they went about twice as far as they had gone the third time from the village. When the old woman thought they were far enough they stopped, and the wife began cutting wood for both of them. When she had cut enough she arranged it in two bundles. Now it was the wife's turn to be helped up with the wood, but the old woman refused to do it as usual and told her to go ahead and kneel by the bundle of wood. The wife refused. Now, each tried to persuade the other to kneel first against the bundle of wood. The old woman finally prevailed, and the wife knelt against the wood, and as she put her robe around her neck the old woman seemed pleased to help her, but as the old woman was fixing the carrying ropes she tightened them, after slipping them around the wife's neck until the wife fell at full length, as though dying. The old woman sat down to rest, as she was tired from choking the wife. Soon she got up and untied the wife. Now, they were in the thick timber, and there was flowing water through it. After the old woman had killed the wife she blew into the top of her head and blew the skin from her, hair and all. This she did because she envied the wife her good looks, since the wife was the best looking woman in the village, and her husband was good-looking and well thought of by all the prominent men, and the old woman wanted to be treated as well as the wife had been treated. Then the old woman began to put on the wife's skin, but the wife was a little smaller than the old woman, though the old woman managed to stretch the skin and drew it over her, fitting herself to it. Then she smoothed down the skin until it fitted her nicely. She took the wife's body to the flowing water and threw it in, having found a place that was never visited by anyone, and that had no trail leading to it. She then went to her pile of wood and took it to her home. She found the men visiting the chief.

The chief did not discover that she was not his wife. The old woman knew all about the former wife's ways, for she had talked much with her when they were coming home with the wood, and she had asked the wife all sorts of questions about her husband. She understood how the men carried on at the chief's place. The wife had told the chief that the old woman had said that they were to go for wood four different times, and the last time being the fourth time, he supposed it was all over and his wife had got through with the old woman. So, as the old woman was doing his wife's duty, he thought her to be his wife until the time came when the skin began to decay and the hair to come off. Still there were big crowds of men around, and the old woman began to be fearful lest they would find her out. So she made as if she were sick. The chief tried to get a man to doctor her, but she refused to be doctored. Finally he hired a servant to doctor her. This was the man who always sat right by the entrance, ready to do errands or carry announcements to the people. His name was Buffalo-Crow-Man (Kawitathakiwaitsa). He had a dark complexion. The old woman began to rave at his medicine working. He began to tell who the old woman was, saying that there was no need of doctoring her; that she was a fraud and an evil spirit; and that she had become the wife of the chief through her bad deeds. The old woman told the chief not to believe the servant; that he himself was a fraud and was trying to get her to do something wrong. The servant then stood at the feet of the old woman and began to sing:

"Kaw-kaw
Ka-ko-hi-da-de-he
Ka-ko-hi-da-de-he
Ka-ko-hi-da-de-he
Ka-ko-hi-da-de-he
Ka-ko-hi-da-de-he
Kaw-kaw."

(Crow calling himself.)
Crow calling something over there.

Then over her body he went and jumped at her head. Then he commenced to sing again, first on her left side, then on her right. He sang the song four times, and while he was doing this the decayed hide came off from her. The servant told the men to take her out and take her life for what she had done to the chief's wife, telling how she had fooled the chief. They did as they were told. The servant told the men he had suspected the old woman when she had come around to get the wife to go after wood with her; that when going after wood they always went a long distance, so that no one could observe them, but that he had always flown very high over them, so they could not see him, and had watched them; that on the fourth time they went for wood he had seen the old woman choke the wife with the wife's rope; how the old woman had secured the whole skin of the wife and had thrown her body into the flowing water. He told the men where the place was, and directed them there the next day. The men went to their homes, feeling very sad for the wicked thing the old woman had done. On the next day the chief went as directed, and he came to a place where he found a pile of wood that belonged to his former wife. He went to the place where he supposed his wife to be. He sat down and commenced to weep. There he stayed all night and the next day. He returned to his home, but he could not forget the occurrence. So he went back again and stayed another night and again returned home. The chief was full of sorrow. He went back to the place the third time, and when he got there he sat down and commenced to weep. Again he stayed all night, and early next morning it was foggy and he could not see far. While he sat and wept he faced the east, and he was on the west side of the flowing waters, so that he also faced the flowing water wherein his wife's body was thrown. He heard some one singing, but he was unable to catch the sound so that he could locate the place where the sound came from. He finally discovered that it came from the flowing water. He went toward the place and listened, and indeed it was his wife's voice, and this is what she sang:

"Nats-kets-o-ta-ha-nek
Nats-kets-o-ta-ha-nek
Te-he-tots-a-ee
Te-e-he-tots-hak."

This song was sung four different times, but the same words were used each time. The meaning of the song is this:

> Woman-having-Powers-in-the-Water,
> Woman-having-Powers-in-the-Water,
> I am the one (you seek),
> I am here in the water.

As he went near the river he saw in the middle of the water his wife standing on the water. She told him to go back home and tell his parents to clean their grass-lodge and to purify the room by burning sage. She told her husband that he might then return and take her home; that he should tell his parents not to weep when she should return, but that they should rejoice at her return to life, and that after that he could take her home. So the man started to his home. After he arrived he told his mother to clean and purify the lodge; that he had found his wife and that he was going back again to get her. He told her that neither she nor any of their friends should weep at sight of the woman. While his mother was doing this cleaning he went back to the river and stayed one more night, and early in the morning he heard the woman singing again. He knew that he was to bring his wife back to his home. When he heard her sing he went straight to her. She came out of the water and he met her. She began to tell her husband about her troubles—how she met troubles and how he was deceived. That day they went to their home, and Flint-Stone-Man's parents were glad to see his wife back once more. They lived together until long afterward.

After a time Flint-Stone-Man said he was feeling badly for the way the old woman had deceived him in making him believe that she was his wife. So he said he would become something else. He had some one to announce in the village what he was going to do, and to tell them to do as they pleased—if they wished to become something else they might. After this the Flint-Stone-Man went toward the south. He told the people that in time if they should go far enough toward the south they would find some flint stone, for he was going in that direction. His wife became the Woman-having-Powers-in-the-Water, and went into the water. Many of the people in the village became something else, such as flint arrows and animals, while some remained as human beings.

18. THE HAWK AND HIS FOUR DOGS.*

There was once a village, and in this village there was a head chief. Near the village there lived a man, his wife, daughter, and son. The son had four Dogs; one was white, one black, one reddish color, and the other one was copper color. The white Dog was named White-Wolf (Wesakakuts); the black Dog, Fox (Watayar); the red Dog, Panther (Woks); the copper-colored Dog, Bear (Wedadadiyakista). No one could ever visit the people at this place on account of the dogs, though they always kept them tied up. The boy would go hunting, killing all kinds of game, such as deer, buffalo, turkey, etc. He told his father, mother, and sister that if these dogs ever looked as though they were getting uneasy about something that they should untie them, for their anxiety would indicate that the boy was in danger.

One day while going toward the north to hunt, the young man met two good-looking women. He noticed that their faces were tattooed like the faces of the women of our times. These women wore buffalo robes. The young man, being a hunter, killed all sorts of game, though all the game he hunted was hated by the women. When these women appeared before him they said, "We have come to see you; will you not go along with us?" The young man started to go along with them. They went toward the north. On their way the women asked the young man what he could do to make his escape without being killed if he was attacked by the enemy. He answered that he could command himself to turn into a small ant. They went on, going fast, and the women again asked what he could do to escape from the enemy. He said again that he could command himself to turn into a small bird and hide in the grass. They continued their journey, going as fast as the women could go. After a little while they asked the young man if there was anything else that he could do to escape if danger should come to him. He told them he had four arrows and a bow, two arrows painted black, and two painted red; that he could shoot them. They asked him if he could run fast, and he said that he could run pretty fast. They asked him what else he could do, and he told them that he could not do anything more. They went over a divide, and there he saw a great herd of buffalo, and he saw that he was about to meet danger. When they were almost up to the buffalo, the women became buffalo, and the young man disappeared. The Buffalo asked the women what the man had said he could do to get out of danger. The women told the Buffalo that they must stamp the ground all around the place where the young man had disappeared. The Buffalo

---

*Told by Towakoni Jim (Towakoni)

stamped the ground all around the place; but the young man had become an ant and had crawled away, then he got on his feet and ran for
his life. The Buffalo ran after him, and when they were nearly up
with him the young man commanded himself to become a small bird.
Again the Buffalo asked what they should do, and the woman-Buffalo
told them that they must tramp over the ground, for the young man
had turned into a small bird and was running through the grass.
While the Buffalo were asking these questions the young man crawled
a long way off and got on his feet and was making a hard run for his
life. The Buffalo ran after him until they were near him, then they
saw that he was using one of his arrows. These were powerful arrows,
and would carry him along with them every time he shot them. First,
he shot the black arrow and was carried a long way with it until
he lit on his feet again. He stayed on his feet until the Buffalo were
nearly up with him, then he used another arrow, which carried him for
a long way. Then he went on his feet again for a while, until the
Buffalo nearly caught up with him. Then he used another arrow, and
in this way he traveled fast and kept ahead of the Buffalo until he
used his last arrow. Then he climbed up an elm tree and the Buffalo
gathered all around the tree and hooked it.

At home the young man's Dogs grew so restless and nervous that
the young man's father cut the ropes from off their necks and they came
to his rescue. The tree was about to fall when the dogs arrived, and
just as the tree fell the Dogs came running, one behind the other, first
the white, then the black, then the reddish-colored Dog. The Dogs
saved the life of the young man, for they chased the Buffalo a long way
off out of sight. The young man turned and went home; but he never
saw his Dogs any more. Arriving at his home, he told the story of his
narrow escape and how his Dogs chased the herds of Buffalo. After a
time the young man said to his father, mother, and sister that some
further accident might happen to him if they stayed in that place any
longer, and so they left their village and became Swift-Hawks (Gusseiõs). Their old home was changed into a tree; and the meat they
had was changed to the bark of a tree.

19. THE STORY OF CHILD-OF-A-DOG.*

In these times some of the people lived in a village, and some by
themselves, as we do now. Among those who lived apart by themselves
were an old woman and a young girl. The girl was the granddaughter of
this old woman, and the girl had a small dog that was living with

*Told by Yellow-Tipi (Towakoni).

them. At this place there were no people to be seen, so that the girl did not know that other people existed besides them, nor did she know of any such being as a man. The girl soon was old enough to go out by herself and to go after wood, and her dog accompanied her everywhere she went. When at home the old woman would often talk to her about villages that existed out a long distance from them, and also about her some time meeting some man when out after wood, who would ask her to become his wife. The old woman told her that when she should be asked she must not refuse, for it would be a great help to them, and not only a help, but that she would some time soon have a young child who would either be a boy or a girl. The girl was glad to learn of this, and whenever she went out she would wish that she might meet some man. Sometimes when the girl was at home she asked many questions about these things.

Once upon a time her dog seemed as though she was pregnant, and the girl asked the old woman what was the matter with her dog. The old woman told the girl that her dog must have met with some other dog. The girl then asked again, "Now when my dog does bring a young one what will it be?" The old woman replied that it would be a dog like the mother dog, only it might be a male or a female. Finally this little dog was unable to go around as she used to, so the girl would leave her dog at home when going out for wood. The young woman soon afterward went to work and built a small grass-lodge for her dog to lie in while in travail. Then when the dog seemed about to bring forth her young the girl took her in the grass-lodge where she had made a place ready for her. The old woman then forbade the girl to go around where the dog was until after four days. She told her that then she could go to see the young one or bring it in the lodge that they were living in. The dog kept groaning and groaning, and finally quieted down. Without the old woman's consent, and in spite of her admonition, the girl peeped into the lodge where the dog was, and there she saw a young child instead of puppies. She then turned right back and told the old woman that her dog had brought forth a child instead of puppies. The old woman asked her if she had already gone there where she was forbidden to go. The girl said that she had. The old woman would not believe her, but the girl kept on telling her that it was a young child. They finally went over there, and the old woman saw that it was a young child, and so she picked it up and took it to the creek and washed it, while the girl was preparing a bed for her dog. This bed she made on the west side of the lodge. The boy was called Child-of-a-Dog and was brought into their lodge, and the girl had more to do with the young child than her dog did. The dog would only have the child to nurse, and at night the girl would keep the child and sleep with it. The child grew every day, and began to creep, and soon it began to walk.

The old woman then asked the girl to go out and cut some sticks to make some arrows for the young child, and one large enough for a bow. So the girl did as she was requested, and she was shown how to make the bow and arrows. When these were made they were given to the boy. The boy now was able to go around outside and shoot. Wherever the boy went the girl would go along. Once upon a time while they were out the little boy shot a bird, and the girl was proud of the boy for doing this. They went straight to their home, and she told her grandmother what the boy had done and how close they were when the boy shot the bird. Thereafter, whenever the boy went the girl and the dog went along. This was the beginning of his career as a hunter. Soon he began to kill larger birds, such as turkeys, and afterward, when he began to grow up to be a young man, he killed deer and buffalo. Then the girl and the dog remained at home instead of going out hunting with him.

Once upon a time, in the night, there came two women, who were strangers to them. These two women were ugly-looking, and they had great sores on their necks. These two women were asked why they came and they asked each other to answer. Finally one of the women said that they came for the purpose of asking to become engaged to their son. The young man rejected these two women. As soon as he had rejected them they turned around and passed out and went on straight to their homes. Soon after this the young man wished that he had not rejected the women. He then undertook to follow them, and go with them to their homes. He started after them, taking with him his bow and arrows. After following them he finally succeeded in catching up with them. These two women then turned back and said to one another: "Look at our husband coming." The three went on together until they came to a small creek, where they saw a squirrel sitting on a tree. One of these two women requested Child-of-a-Dog to shoot the squirrel, saying that it was the very thing they liked for food. Child-of-a-Dog shot at the squirrel and killed it, but it caught on a limb up in the tree, when the two women requested Child-of-a-Dog to get it down so that they could cook it while on the way to their home. Child-of-a-Dog then climbed up the tree and reached the place where the squirrel was, but when he reached for the squirrel his feet and hands were stuck fast to the tree. After this had happened to

Child-of-a-Dog the two women told him that he should remain up in the tree and die. Then these women started off and left him in the tree to starve to death. Soon he saw a man who called him "son." He did not know the man, and this was the very first time that he had ever heard that he had a father. This man who had called him "son" was Thinking-of-a-Place-and-at-once-being-there (Tsikidikikea), or the Wind. As soon as he knew that the man was his father he knew that he would be taken off from the tree. The Wind told him that he had followed him because he was in bad company, and that he knew that he was in danger. The Wind commanded the tree to lie down gently, and when he had commanded this the tree slowly came down to the ground and Child-of-a-Dog was taken off from the tree. When he was taken off he was requested not to follow the two women again, for they were leading him into trouble. Soon after this his father departed, and Child-of-a-Dog followed along the trail of the women. This young man having power to travel fast by the gift of his father, the Wind, finally overtook the two women again. Not knowing what else to do with him, the two women took him on to their home. Late that evening they arrived at their village. Having arrived at their home they told the young man that he could have their two other sisters for his wives. This made the young man feel sad, after having come a long way and then having to marry another two instead of the two women that he had followed from his home. These two women called him all kinds of names, saying that they would not have a man for a husband that was the offspring of a dog. Then he was requested to have the other two women for his wives, because the two women were of the same class of people to which he belonged. In the place where they lived was also living with them their brother. These two women then left him with their two other sisters and brother. The brother of these two women then began to tell him about these two women, and told him what sort of women they were. He said that each of these two women had two husbands; and these four men were all brothers; and that the sisters had taken him for their husbands to eat, for these four brothers were mean, and ate human beings; that when the sisters left their home they went to their husbands to tell them of his being there; and that about midnight he could see them come around their place eating human flesh, for that was what they lived on at all times; and that on the next day he should be challenged to run in a big footrace, and that he must have great power as a runner to win the race from these four brothers. That night Child-of-a-Dog went to bed with these two women. After going to bed with the two women he was told that he was going to meet something more dangerous than anything he had ever met before in his life. He was told to request aid of them and they would help him to come through all his troubles safe. He was told that when choosing a starting place they would come to a pole stuck into the ground, and that he must say that the place was not far enough for him yet; that he should again refuse at the second pole and the third, and that at the fourth he should make their starting place; and that that place would be further than anyone had ever gone when racing against the four brothers. He was also told that at the start, he (his brother-in-law) would first race against his four other brothers-in-law.

From the advice given by these two women he knew that they had taken pity on him and were going to help him to survive all his trouble. He was given certain things to use whenever he wanted to leave them behind. The things that were given him were, a comb, a gourd, clay, a cockle burr, a bow-string, a looking-glass, power to command the sun to shine, and a soft, white feather. After he had used the first seven of these things they would be nearer to the village, but not quite there. Then he was to use the white, soft feather, so that he would fall lightly. He was also told that before running with one of them he should tell the one he was running with to run his best and to hit him once on his back, and he was also to tell him to shut his eyes, for he himself, when running, had to shut his, in order to run his best; that after running the race he would not be seen by the crowd, but upon his arrival there would be one more thing for him to accomplish, which was that the other two women would try to get him to drink water out of their water gourds, and that that was as dangerous as the race against their husbands; but he must not drink out of their gourds, for they would help him until he should succeed in drinking the water from their own gourds; and that after drinking the water he should turn back where he had left his opponents and shoot them down; that even then he should have enemies who would try to do him harm in order to get even with him. This was the instruction and advice given him by these two other women who had been given him for his wives during the night. It was dark in the lodge, there being no fire, and while they were awake these two women came in with their four husbands. After coming, they started up a fire and began cooking. It was then long after midnight, and Child-of-a-Dog and his two wives were still awake, and saw the others eating and saw what sort of looking men the husbands were.

The next morning Child-of-a-Dog was called to come to see these men whose wives he had tried to obtain. He first went to the creek to take his early morning bath. He then went to the place where the race was to be. There were great crowds of people gathered around to see them start, and also to see what kind of a looking man Child-of-a-Dog was. In this crowd he saw the two women whom he had followed from his home, and also his wives. He had already given full instructions, and had the things that were given to him for his use. He met his opponents and started off due north to their starting point. Child-of-a-Dog was accompanied by his brother-in-law. When they came to the first starting point he refused to start from there, saying it was too close to start from. So the oldest of the four brothers said to his other brothers: "This is the first time that any one has ever said that. We are going to have the hardest race we have ever had." They started on to the next starting place. They had to travel fast in order to get to the starting place right. Finally they came to the second pole, and again Child-of-a-Dog told them that a man who was considered a racer ought not to call that a starting point, for it was yet too close for him. This same man, the oldest of the four brothers, again said to his brothers that he knew that they for the first time were to have a hard race. They again started for the next starting place. They had to travel fast in order to have the race at once. Finally they came to the third pole, and again Child-of-a-Dog told them that it was too close. The four men began to think that there must be something the matter, but they went on again, to the fourth place, and asked if it was far enough for him to start from. He said to his opponents that it was far enough, and there was where the big race was to begin.

They then started, Child-of-a-Dog's brother-in-law doing the first part of the race against his other brother-in-law. Child-of-a-Dog stayed back behind the others, waiting for his brothers-in-law to give out. Finally this man gave out and Child-of-a-Dog then asked to try his speed with these men. Child-of-a-Dog began his race against these four brothers, and in order to get ahead of them he dropped the comb and there was behind him thick burrs of some kind that stuck these four brothers on their feet, so it was impossible for them to travel very fast. While they were coming slowly, Child-of-a-Dog got far ahead of them. Finally the four men passed the place and in order to catch up with him they commanded the wind to blow from the south, and it howled so that it was impossible for Child-of-a-Dog to travel rapidly. These four men passed him and left him behind. Then he took his gourd and commanded the wind to get in the gourd. The wind obeyed and ceased to blow. Child-of-a-Dog began to gain on them again, and after overtaking them he threw the piece of clay in front of them, and it made a boggy place for the other men to travel over, and so he again passed them and left them a long way before they got out of the boggy place. They began to gain on him again, and when they overtook Child-of-a-Dog again they commanded it to snow, and the snow made it so cold for him that they passed him again. It was impossible for him to travel fast enough to get warm, but the other four men went on as if they were traveling on a nice cool day. He finally began to gain on them, and overtook them. Then he dropped the cockle burrs, and when these men saw the cockle burrs they said to one another: "Let us go in those cockle burrs and roll around in them, for that is the very thing that we have long been looking for." The four men went into the cockle burrs, and they rolled around and put on their robes, while the other man was getting away ahead of them. At this place they forgot about the race, but finally they all jumped up, and said to one another: "Say, we are having a race, let us go." So they went on, traveling fast, as the other man, Child-of-a-Dog, was away ahead of them. It did not take very long for them to overtake him again. When overtaking him these men commanded the prettiest birds to come around. There were plenty of birds of all kinds, and when Child-of-a-Dog saw this flock of birds he at once stopped and began to try to kill some of them. At this place he was detained for a while, trying to kill some of the pretty birds, and the other men were leaving him a long way behind, when he thought of his race, and finally traveled on and overtook them again. As he passed them he dropped the bow-string and extended one end toward the east and the other west, and then he went on and left these other men to get over a deep canyon which the bow-string made. The men went around to see if they could find a place to get over. Child-of-a-Dog was getting ahead of them, and leaving them far behind. Finally they found a way to get over and began again to gain on him. They overtook him and when passing him they did the same thing to him, leaving a deep canyon behind them, so that it was impossible for Child-of-a-Dog to get over. He stopped a moment and wondered how he was going to get over. When he was in great trouble he called for his father to come around and help him to get over. He finally succeeded in getting his father to help him. The Wind lay down, and had his son get on his back and then he went over the canyon. Child-of-a-Dog began to travel fast again in order to catch up with his opponents, and he finally succeeded in over-taking them, and when he overtook them he dropped the looking-glass behind him and went on. When these men came to this place they saw that it had snowed and rained and the ground was very smooth and that it was impossible for them to travel. Child-of-a-Dog kept on, the same as the others did whenever they succeeded in stopping him. After they had gone over this place they again overtook Child-of-a-Dog, and they made him go through the same thing. It commenced to snow and rain, and it was impossible for him to travel. The four brothers went on and left him behind. Finally he got over this place and then again he commenced to gain on them, and soon overtook them. When passing them he commanded the sun to shine and make it warm. This was done, and it was now so hot that it was impossible for these brothers to travel very fast. Finally they passed over this heated place where the sun was shining. Then the four men caused the sun to shine, and young Child-of-a-Dog, being barefooted, had to stand on one foot, then on the other, on account of the heat of the ground. Finally he passed the place and told these men that the final test would have to come and that he would race them, one at a time. He said that when running a race it was his habit to shut his eyes, and that they would have to do the same. At this time he used his soft white feather which was given him by his wives. When using it he stuck it on the back of his head.

The final race then came off between the oldest of the four brothers and the boy. At the beginning of the race Child-of-a-Dog patted the oldest on the back and told him to do the best running that he had ever done in his life, and told him to shut his eyes and said that he would do the same. When Child-of-a-Dog commenced to run the waving feather which he had in his head made him light in weight. While running he would pat the other man on the shoulder and request him to keep on, for he was a little ahead of him all the way. Thus this man had to pack Child-of-a-Dog on his back, and so he soon gave out entirely and could not go any further. Then the next to the oldest brother took his turn in running against this Child-of-a-Dog, and he did the same thing to him. So this other man ran as hard as he could, and Child-of-a-Dog kept patting him on his shoulder, telling him to keep on, for he was right at the side of him and a little ahead of him. This man finally gave out and could not go any further, and then the third of the four brothers took his turn and again the same thing happened to him. He gave out and stopped, nor could he move any further. Then the last of the four brothers took his turn to run, and this time Child-of-a-Dog told this last one that he would have to try his best, for they were near to the village. So, at the start, he patted this man on the back and requested him to try his best, and then lit on his back and began to pat him on the shoulders, and this man, of course, had to run his best, while Child-of-a-Dog was riding on his shoulders. Finally this fourth man gave out, and Child-of-a-Dog left him to remain there until he should return from the village.

So Child-of-a-Dog kept on until he was seen, and then he heard the yells by the people, who were glad to see these men lose their race. As he approached the crowd he saw his wives coming to meet him, and ahead of them were the two women who had brought him from his home, and he saw that they had water gourds, and had water in these for the winner to drink. His own wives were kept out of the way by these two other women, who expected him to drink out of their gourds instead of drinking out of his own wives' gourds. But, as he already had been instructed not to drink from them, he refused. His wives finally succeeded in giving him a drink, and then he turned back where he had left all his opponents. He arrived at the place where he had made the first one give out, and commanded that for generations they would not be human beings, but Buffalo, and that when people should get hungry for meat they would be killed and would be shot on the side, under the shoulder. Child-of-a-Dog shot the first one, and then the next one, and told him the same thing. Then he shot the third one and the fourth one, and told them the same thing again. Then he left them there and went on straight to the village.

Upon his arrival his wives and the other two women began to quarrel over him. They all undertook to haul wood to show this man, Child-of-a-Dog, who could do the fastest work. They went off and in a few moments the two women who had helped him out of his troubles arrived with plenty of wood, while the other two were still away. Finally the two others arrived, but the other two had already come in with their wood. Then the two defeated women made another challenge with the two other women, hoping to make this man, Child-of-a-Dog, think that they could do more than the two women who were offered to him as wives. They went to bring back water, but while they were gone, one of the other two women made a pond on the side of their lodge, and did not have to go after any water. When the other two came back, they found that the two others were bringing more water than they could bring. They sent them from their homes, and told them to remain away forever, never to return any more. One of the bad women became a Dog, and the other a Hawk, in order that they might have the man to themselves. But he had been requested never to have anything to do with them, for they once wanted to do him harm. His two other wives were gone. But his Dog, who had been one of his wives, was still in the village, but not living as a human being any more. while the other woman, who had turned into a Hawk, had left.

Once in a while the Dog would come around and tell Child-of-a-Dog not to let people from the village take him over to their home, for they were still after him and were planning to do him harm some day. So he remained at his former brother-in-law's. Once upon a time, late in the evening, the Dog (who was his former wife), came around and told him that he ought to go back home, for his mother had died because he never returned home. All the time these people kept after him to come to their homes to pay them a visit, and so one time he decided to accept an invitation to go where all the men went to pass their time in sitting up at night. He went on where he was invited to be present, and when entering the lodge he was requested to pass on to the west side of the lodge, where there was a robe spread out for him to sit down on, and when he sat down, he fell down into a hole. This was the scheme that they had to entrap Child-of-a-Dog. As soon as he fell into the hole the news began to spread, and with it a request for all people to bring all the hot ashes from their fires, and throw them into the pit, where their victim was. So as soon as he heard this, he began at once to dig a hole on the side of the wall of the pit, large enough for him to get in when they began to pour the hot ashes down. He was in a safe place when the people began to pour down the hot ashes. They nearly filled the pit with hot ashes and then he heard some man announcing to the people to remove their village and go on a hunting expedition. So all the people began at once to move away, and they left Child-of-a-Dog to die in the pit. There were some people who remained outside of the village in the timber, who had some children, who, after several days, decided to go and see if this man was still alive. These two boys went to the pit wherein this man was thrown and asked if he was still alive. Child-of-a-Dog told the boys that he was still alive. The boys then returned to their home, and begged their parents to come with them to get him out of the pit and save him. They started for the place to remove the ashes and to get him out of the place. On their arrival they commenced to move away the ashes. Finally they succeeded in getting him out of the pit, and found Child-of-a-Dog still alive, but badly scorched. After getting out of the pit, Child-of-a-Dog went straight to the creek and dived in. After doing this, Child-of-a-Dog was just as he always was. Then he went to the home of these people who had saved him from destruction.

On his arrival he at once began to hunt for them in order to do them some good in return for the good they had done for him. He remained for a while, and then was requested to return home, but instead of doing this he followed again after the people who had done him harm. After a few days, late one evening, he caught up with them. He then began to think what to do with these evil people. After dark he stopped outside of the village and whistled four times. When he whistled, there came to him the Dog, his former wife. He told her that he wanted to save her from destruction, for she once did him a great favor by getting him out of trouble. He then shot one arrow toward the south, and one toward the west, and another toward the north, and the last one where they were, and then fire began to come up from every direction. After doing this, Child-of-a-Dog requested this dog to go somewhere else to live. The dog then told Child-of-a-Dog that his mother and the old woman were both dead, and only the young woman was still alive, but that she would soon die, for there was some one who had found her and made her his wife, and that she was in danger, and if he did not get there in time, her man was planning to kill her and eat her. So Child-of-a-Dog at once departed from his former wife and went straight home.

When he arrived home he did not find the woman. Then he went due east, and there he saw a pond, and on the bank of the pond he saw this woman sitting, watching the ducks swimming. Without showing himself he took one of his arrows and shot at the ducks and struck one. While this woman was looking at the ducks she noticed that one was struck with an arrow which had belonged to her son, whom she had not seen, and so she wept, wishing that he would return once more to his home, as she was now living all alone, and as she knew that the following was to be the last day of her life. As she turned around, looking back towards the west, there she saw the young man who had returned. She then wept for joy at seeing him, for she knew that she would be saved. She had with her some kind of a pail, in which she was cooking acorn soup for her husband. Child-of-a-Dog requested her to accompany him to their home, and while on the way she told of her troubles with her husband, and that this man had already told her that when returning from hunting, if not having any meat with him, that she would be killed and be eaten up. But Child-of-a-Dog told her to never mind about that. When they were in the lodge, they heard this man's voice, calling for her to hurry with acorn soup, and the woman began to cry, for this man was coming towards the place. But Child-of-a-Dog requested the woman to step outside, and then come right in again, so that this would cause the man to enter the lodge. The man was then talking about the boy, saying that Child-of-a-Dog must be back, from the way they acted. As he approached the grass-lodge the woman walked in the lodge and was followed by the man.

After he entered, the woman following, there was no way for him to get away from them any more. Child-of-a-Dog then took his bow-string and with it cast the man down into the ground and commanded him always to live in the ground, and sometimes in a pile of dried weeds and bushes, and that he should always like acorns for his food, and never more to have the same powers he had when living like a human being. So this was the end of the woman's troubles with her husband. This man was Wood-Rat-Man (Likishsewatsquetsa). Child-of-a-Dog found that the woman had no more meat to eat and at once began to hunt, killing all sorts of game for them to live on.

Long after this, when this woman went after water, she saw six deer near her, and immediately she returned to the place and told Child-of-a-Dog all about the deer that she had seen and requested him to go and kill them. So Child-of-a-Dog followed the deer, trailing them, and finally saw them, after he was a long way from home. It so happened that these deer stopped a while, giving him time to shoot at them. After killing each one of the deer, he thought of cooking some meat before returning to his home. For this was always his custom before returning home. He started up a fire and commenced to cook some meat.

While cooking the meat he saw two women coming toward him. When these two arrived at the place where he was, he noticed that one of them was old and the other was much younger. These two women requested him to give them something to eat. He was then cooking liver, and while he was cooking this, before it was done, the older woman called for the liver to be taken out, for it was ready to be eaten. So Child-of-a-Dog took the liver from the fire and gave it to the women, for them to eat, and he noticed that the older woman did not give the other any of the liver, but ate it herself. The older woman then requested this man to put some more meat on the fire to cook for them, for they were hungry. By the time of doing this the sun went down and it began to get dark, but this woman kept on asking him to cook some more meat. The trouble was that this older woman would call for the meat before it was done. Finally they ate up one whole deer. But the older woman kept asking him to cook on, for they were pretty hungry. By about midnight, they had eaten one more whole deer.

Now, the oldest woman said that this young man should be her son-in-law, for she found him to be a good hunter, and knew that she would be well fed if this young man did the hunting for her. So she was going to take him home and let him marry her two girls. So she kept on asking him to cook some more meat for them. Finally they ate up another whole deer, but they did not yet seem satisfied. So the older woman said to the young man that she had to go out. When she went out the younger woman told the young man that she did not eat any meat, but that her sister ate everything for herself, and as for her selecting him for a son-in-law, it was a bad thing for him to go with her for this purpose, for she had two girls that were very dangerous, and by means of them she destroyed men's lives; these girls have teeth in their vaginas, with which they could cut off his manly member. Just then, after this woman had made known to him how dangerous they were, the old woman returned. As soon as she came back she again asked for some more meat. But the other woman had already told the young man to let the meat cook until it was done before he gave it to her, for this woman was preparing to take his life if the meat was eaten up before daylight. So the young man did not pay any attention to the old woman any more, whenever she called for the meat, but waited until it was done before giving them meat. Thus again they ate up the whole deer, and there were but two more. This young man then took his time cooking the meat after having learned what the woman's object was in trying to hurry him in cooking the meat. This was then the fifth whole deer that he began on, and at this time he took more time in cooking the meat for these two women. Before eating up the meat the daylight came. As soon as daylight came the old woman requested this young man, Child-of-a-Dog, to go with her to her new home to see his new wives. While on the way the other woman told him that on their arrival the old woman would request him to bring one whole log to burn; that the wood would burn all night, so that she would sleep good. She also told him that she would give him instructions, and that the two girls were pretty; that the younger was the prettier. So the young man thought to himself again of his being in another dangerous place because he had followed the deer, but he thought that he was safe, because the younger woman was aiding him. They soon arrived at the home of the old woman and there he saw the two young women and was taken to the place where they lived.

On the following day the old woman requested her son-in-law to bring for her one dead burnt log for her to keep burning while she was asleep. So the young man, Child-of-a-Dog, went to look for the log, and he went straight on where the other woman had told him to go. He found this woman's place. He was then given an ear of black corn and was told that when he would take this black corn it would turn into a log as soon as he got there, and in carrying it into the lodge he must not go in, but get out of the way quick and push it in instead of going in. This woman also warned him of the nature of the people he was now living with. "On the first night," she said, "when you have gone to bed, you must not lie with the girls, however much they try to persuade you. You will hear the grinding of their teeth in their vaginas. Moreover, you must not go to sleep during the night, because the old woman will come often to see if you have done anything. If you have not lain with the girls, she will ask them why you have not. Be on your guard, therefore; for if you should go to sleep, it will mean your death. The old woman, who indeed appears to sleep, never sleeps." This was the information given him by this other woman, for she did not want him to be killed, as had been already many other men, for thus were these people mean and took many men's lives through the old woman bringing them to her girls.

After he had received these instructions from this woman he returned to his wives with the log on his shoulder. Arriving at the place he opened the door with one end of the log and pushed it in, and the old woman attempted to strike him with a war-club, but she fell outside without even touching him, for he had already been warned how to get out of the way. The old woman then told Child-of-a-Dog that he had pushed the log too hard, and knocked her down, but he knew what had happened, after seeing the weapon she had as she fell. Of course, there was no danger afterward from this when this was all over. He then went into the lodge and placed the log upon the fireplace. It was sundown. Then the old woman ordered the young man to lie down on the bed between the two girls. When he did so the girls attempted to have intercourse with him, but the young man was unwilling. He could hear the old woman snoring as if she were in a deep sleep; he perceived, however, that she was only trying to deceive him. Throughout the whole night the old woman often got up from her bed to see if the girls had killed the young man yet. But whenever she came he moved. Then the old woman again ordered the girls to have intercourse with him. All this night Child-of-a-Dog stayed awake, for he knew that it was dangerous for him to go to sleep. Early the next morning he got out of bed and went out, and while he was outside he heard the old woman talking to the girls about this man and asking them why they did not kill him.

He stayed all the following day, and about evening again he was requested to bring two logs. He went out again and went straight to where this other woman lived. On his arrival he was asked how he got along with his wives. He told how the girls had acted during the night, and that he was this time sent to get two logs. Again two long and hard stones were given to him to use when he was sleeping with the two women. He was told that when he had chosen the girl whom he wanted for his wife, she could be made harmless if he would wear down, by grinding with the rock, the teeth in her vagina; and that he could kill the other girl if he would thrust the rock deep into her vagina; that after killing one of the girls he could escape with the other by going straight west, traveling fast to a high hill, where he would find a woman who had many children; but that she was slow to act, though when she decided, she could save him; but that he would have to beg her, and keep on begging her until she helped him out of his troubles; that after getting help from this woman she would require him to go on home. She also told him that the old woman at home would not sleep soon, but that when she did go to sleep she would sleep so hard that no one could wake her; and that this would be the first time she had ever gone to sleep, for she never slept a wink at night nor in the daytime.

The woman then took the two ears of black corn and put them upon the fire and told Child-of-a-Dog that that would make the old woman go to sleep and that she would not wake up until he was a long way off. Not only this, but he was also given one white, soft feather to use over the fire, that the feather might go up in the air, and that they would go out with it; and thus their trail would not be discovered so soon; and this time in taking the logs, instead of taking them in, he was to throw them down outside, but she told him that the old woman would try to coax him to take the logs in, but that he should tell her that her daughters could take them in just as well.

Child-of-a-Dog now returned with the two ears of black corn and entered the lodge, and the old woman complained about his not bringing the logs into the lodge. That day soon passed and then darkness came and he knew how to act. Finally the two girls brought in the logs that were lying outside and put them in the fire to burn all night, and then the old woman requested them all to go to bed. They all went to bed at the old woman's request, and while they were lying in the bed the old woman would once in a while come around to look at them, but the young man wanted her to go to sleep first, for he knew well that she would soon go to sleep for the first time in her life. Before any of the young people went to sleep, they heard the old woman snoring, and she was put to sleep by the influence of somebody that made her go to sleep. The young man immediately turned his attention to the younger girl, because he had been informed that she was more cruel than the other. And so he thrust the stone into her vagina, just as he had been instructed, and after a short time he heard her teeth gnawing at the stone. Moreover, when the teeth themselves had been swiftly worn down, he thrust the rest of the stone into the vagina so deeply that she could not catch hold of it with her fingers to take it out. And therefore the girl quickly died. Next he made the other girl harmless, as he had been instructed, and suitable for a man to have intercourse with.

After having this done, then he told the woman that she would be saved, for he did not intend to kill her, as he had chosen her to be his wife for all time. He now said: "We surely must leave this place, or else we will be killed." The young man then requested the girl to stand ready by the fire. Then Child-of-a-Dog took out his feather and when he had put the feather over the fire, the feather flew up, and they were with it when it went up in the air, and as it rose it flew toward the west, and they went with it. For a long time the feather flew toward the west and finally fell to the ground with them, and then they had to travel on foot. Still the old woman was sound asleep.

The other woman who had given power to Child-of-a-Dog now deserted her home, for she knew that she would be suspected by the old woman of having aided Child-of-a-Dog to overcome the girls and escape. She had already told Child-of-a-Dog that the girls were not the true daughters of the old woman, but had somewhere been captured when young girls, and had been kept in the condition they were in. Now, this woman, after she had learned that Child-of-a-Dog and his wife had escaped, went to the timber and climbed a tree. She jumped from one tree to another in order to cause the old woman to lose her trail. She had to do this in order to make her escape from the old woman, who had great powers, and who also was an evil-spirited woman.

The young man and the young woman kept on traveling. The man was told first to use his powers in order that they might travel faster. So Child-of-a-Dog took his arrow and shot it and they traveled with the arrow, and when the arrow stopped, they stopped also. But we must know that these arrows went a very long way wherever they were shot off for traveling. So the young man, having four arrows, shot four times, and every time he shot they would accompany the arrow. After having shot all the arrows his traveling power was exhausted, and they could travel fast no more. So now he depended on his wife, and at this time they could hear the old woman talking, and as far as they were away from her, they could hear her asking for them wherever she would meet any one. But some one had aided this young couple to get away. Of course, the old woman had power by which she could soon find their trail, and then go after them. Thus it was that these young people soon heard her talking, saying that she had found their trail and that they had no chance to make their escape.

So from this time on, the woman had to assist in their flight. This woman now used her double-balls, and when she would throw the double-balls, they would be on the balls. This was the way they continued to travel while trying to make their escape. But they soon again heard the old woman talking, for she was getting nearer all the time, and this being the last resort they had, they had to do the best they could in order to prevent the old woman from catching up with them, but they could hear her talking, and it sounded closer to them every time. This woman finally used up all her traveling power, having used the double-balls four times, accompanying the balls when pitched. They finally saw the place of their retreat, and at the same time they heard the old woman coming nearer and nearer. But they kept on traveling, and now they had to go afoot. The girl was frightened and began to weep, for she knew what was going to happen to them if caught by the old woman. For this old woman was hard to get away from. Her name was Little-Spider-Woman (Itsishkaheidikits).

Little-Spider-Woman now arrived where the woman had helped Child-of-a-Dog and his wife, and she requested the woman not to help these people again, for she was after them, and she told her that if she did not give them up she also would kill her with them. But as this woman was quiet and not having much to say at any time, she sat there for a long while before she would do anything. This woman was named Buzzard-Woman (Awiasquaatskaheka). The Buzzard-Woman again thought of helping this couple, and so she went up under the old woman before she could move, and flew up in the air with Little-Spider-Woman. She then kept flying higher and higher. The people waked up and saw them, and they could hear the Little-Spider-Woman begging the Buzzard-Woman to let her live, saying that she would give her the same kind of powers as she had, but the Buzzard-Woman would not listen, but kept going up higher and higher. Finally the people could not see them any more, they were up so high, and then they heard something falling; it was Little-Spider-Woman weeping, and finally they saw her coming down, and she was already dead before she fell to the ground. They then again saw the Buzzard-Woman coming down again, and when she lit upon the ground she told the people to go wherever they desired. So they thanked the Buzzard-Woman for helping them out, and they went back to Child-of-a-Dog's home. The woman at Child-of-a-Dog's home was worried again, as she was when Child-of-a-Dog first left, and she thought that for his sake the boy had perhaps gone off to some other place, never to return any more. But he was near to home, and when he, with his wife, arrived, the woman was glad to have him again, and also to see his wife.

So from this time, Child-of-a-Dog and his wife and the other woman lived together, and whenever Child-of-a-Dog would go out hunting the women would remain at home. When they were all at home the wife of Child-of-a-Dog told of the troubles she had had while she was living with Little-Spider-Woman. She told that Little-Spider-Woman was not her mother, but had captured her and also the other girl. She told that when but a young girl Little-Spider-Woman had carried her away from her parents, and that she used to live in the woods, where she belonged, her parents being the Striped-Animals (Kitiishtadau), Raccoons; and that the other girl who was living with them was also captured by this woman when but a young girl, and that she lived in the woods; that her parents were the Hump-Backs (Nikidets), Owls. She also said that the woman who had helped them to escape was also living in the woods, and that she was a Squirrel-Woman (Watsadakaheha).

So they lived together for a long while, and finally there was born a baby boy to them. The child grew fast. Once upon a time there came a woman who wished to take the child home for a while, and when she went out with the child, they sank into the ground right by the door of their lodge. The parents were at home all this day, for it happened that Child-of-a-Dog did not go out to hunt, so he knew what had happened, and he saw that this woman had not returned their child. So Child-of-a-Dog went off to search for his child all the following day, but he returned without finding it. He then called on his wife, saying: "My wife, you have great powers. Can you find our child? If you can, do so." His wife's eyes were all swollen from crying all that day, thinking that some one had been cruel enough to kidnap the child. So the child's mother then said to her husband: "Let us go off toward the west." So they went on wherever this woman wanted to go. Finally they saw where this woman had been, and then they trailed her, and at the end of the trail the woman called to her man, requesting him to take one of his arrows and take the feather part in his hand and draw it along on the ground, so as to leave a line on the ground. This was done by the man, and then they saw down in the ground the woman with the child. Child-of-a-Dog went down and got his child and he dragged the woman who had kidnaped his child out of the place. Child-of-a-Dog then told this woman that she was cruel for kidnaping his child, but he would not kill her, but that she would have less powers thereafter, and would always live under the ground. So she was cast down in the ground, to remain there always. This woman was a Mole (Iskutukethas). They then took their child back to their home. On their arrival, the other woman was glad to have the child back again. There-after, they kept a strict watch over the child at all times. This other woman was more like a mother to the child than its own mother, for she was always carrying the child on her back, even more than its own mother.

Once upon a time the child began to cry, and no one knew what the child was crying about. The father of the child tried everything he could to stop it from crying, but could not, and the other woman tried every way she could to stop the child from crying, but it would not stop. The child cried all that day. They wondered what was the matter with the child. The mother did not pay any attention to the child, but depended on the other woman and on her husband to stop the child from crying. Finally the man asked his wife to find out what was the matter with the child, saying: "You have great powers, and you can predict anything that is going to happen." Finally the mother turned to her husband and told him that the child was crying for his father to tell them all about his own life—from the beginning of his early days and of his manhood days, and what hard times he had been through. Child-of-a-Dog then called his boy to come to him, and to stop crying, for he was now ready to tell him all about his life, and about all the hard times that he had ever been through. The child then stopped crying, and sat down on his father's lap, and the father then commenced to tell about his mother's life and about the other old woman with whom they used to live, and of the child also who had long since lived with them; and he told him how he was born and what had made his mother preg-nant, and how he was taken away by two women to strange countries, and how he met his enemies there, and as to how he was aided by another two women, and how he had won the race over four brothers who were Buffalo, and how after having done this he was called to a feast, and how he was thrown into a pit to die, and also how he was saved by some people who had not gone off to the hunting expedition, which had been sent out by these people who had thrown him into the pit. He then told all about his life among the strange people that had done him wrong, and what sort of people these were who had saved his life. He told that these people who had saved his life were Quails (Kakia), who were living in the timber where the Quails always lived, and also how he followed up the crowd of people who went out on this expedition, and how he whistled to his former wife in order to save her when he got ready to destroy the people who had mistreated him while living with them. This was the story he was telling his son, and the boy sat on his father's lap listening to him. So the father continued and told all about his trouble among strange people, and how he destroyed all the people who had done him wrong, saving out only one person, who was once his wife, who helped him when first he had a footrace with the men who were brothers, and how he finally came to his old home, and how he found his aunt to be suffering hardships by having troubles with her husband when her son Child-of-a-Dog was gone from home, and after having arrived at home what trouble he also met when first seeing the mother of his baby boy. This was now the beginning of the tale of his father's and mother's life after becoming husband and wife, and what troubles they met before he was born. This story was mainly all about their trouble with Little-Spider-Woman and their escape from her, and of the time of his birth, and this was then ending the whole story of his life.

So after recounting so many troubles, they said to one another: "Let us become something else, for we have met so much trouble, and we are likely to meet more, and in order to prevent this we must leave our old home and be something else." So, as Child-of-a-Dog was the son of the Wind, he became the Wind and his boy child also became something. Sometimes, when the Wind blows and is blowing slowly, it is the child of Child-of-a-Dog, and sometimes, when it blows harder, it is Child-of-a-Dog. The mother then became a Raccoon. This is why the raccoons know so much, for it is said that raccoons are the smartest of living beasts.

Now the old woman was left at home by herself. She then thought that it would not do for her to live by herself and so she took a gourd of water and poured it on the fire, and as the smoke went up, she went up too, and became Black-Eagle (Kosetskawe).

20. THE OLD-AGE-DOG WHO RESCUED THE CHIEF'S SON.*

Young-Man-Chief (Toniketsanias) was a young man belonging to a chief's family; therefore he was considered a fine young man, and everybody admired him, because he was a kind-hearted young man; but he refused to marry and wanted to be single. The village where he lived was built on a wide, open place, with timber quite a good way off, on the north, east, south, and west. The people were rather fearful of their enemies, the Trickster-Spies (Kinas Kitikeahara), for they were troubled by them. In time of wood-hauling the women who hauled the wood were accompanied by men with weapons, who were always

---

*Told by Ahahe (Waco).

ready for battle with the Tricksters. Once upon a time the women went to the woods to haul wood on their backs, and they were accompanied by the men. Young-Man-Chief was in the crowd and all the men had their weapons along, for they were always ready for their enemies. The men folks hunted a little while the women gathered wood. When the women returned home Young-Man-Chief remained behind, and looking behind, he saw a woman with the wood on her back, ready to leave. The woman called Young-Man-Chief to her. Young-Man-Chief turned back to see what she wanted. Then the woman got hold of him and would not release him, and they were there for a long while, and Young-Man-Chief begged the woman to let go. It got to be late in the evening, and they were attacked by the Tricksters. They retreated toward their homes and fought their way, and finally Young-Man-Chief left the woman and she was captured by the Tricksters, and she was taken away from her people.

Young-Man-Chief went back to his home, feeling sorry for the captured woman. Arriving home, he was asked why he was still at large when everybody had returned home. He told how he and the woman had been attacked by the Tricksters, and how she had been captured for his sake. Young-Man-Chief regretted the loss of the woman, and he wandered about by himself for a long while, until he took a notion to go to the enemy's place to look for the woman. He told his mother to make a pair of moccasins for him and one pair for the woman, and a robe for her. Then he asked his mother to grind enough corn meal to take along, for he was going on a long journey, and was going to look for the lost woman; he was going to set out at once. When everything he asked for had been made ready he turned toward the southwest, where he thought the enemy were living. He, of course, took along all his weapons, bow, arrows, and shield. For a long while he wandered around, looking for the homes of the Tricksters. He finally succeeded in finding their homes; but as it was getting late in the evening he made up his mind that he would not go in the main village until night.

The next night he walked into the village and looked in every lodge he came to. He finally found one place where there were a great many people, and there he saw the woman sitting by a great, big man, whom he suspected to be her husband. He thought to himself: "Well, what must I do now in order to get her out?" The place was a tipi, and he had to look out for himself in order to escape notice; for he knew that he would be killed if discovered. He finally went around back of the tipi, took one of his arrows and punched a hole in the tipi. He took a long piece of grass and put it through the hole and punched the woman's back. Finally the woman walked out, and he met her. He told her that he had made a long trip to look for her, and that her folks were anxious for her to return home, and that this was her best chance to make her escape and to return home. The woman was rather contrary about it and asked him that she might go inside the tipi and get her moccasins and robe, but Young-Man-Chief told her that he already had a pair of moccasins for her and a robe, too. Still the woman wanted to return into the tipi again before leaving, and she promised that she would be out again in a little while. When the woman returned into the tipi she quietly told her husband, that some one was outside begging her to make her escape from him, and this man was the man who had left her when she was captured. So the woman sought revenge on Young-Man-Chief for leaving her behind and permitting her to be captured. The woman at once stepped out, having her husband behind her, and walked toward Young-Man-Chief, whom, when she reached him and was talking with him, her husband attacked, making a big yell and calling for help and saying that he had captured some one from another place; and being a chief he at once ordered his men to set a big fire. The men immediately brought in wood and made a big fire, and besides this the chief ordered the men to get a long pole and stick it by the fire so they might tie the man to it and dance around him while he was burning up. When they had built the fire they then stuck up a long pole by it and tied their victim to it. The people began to come in, and at once started a big victory dance. They were in the habit of dancing around their victims in their dances. The woman and her husband danced around Young-Man-Chief, saying he had once done her wrong and they were now going to have their revenge. While the dance was going on they scorched him until he was burned to death and the dance ended.

On the next day the Trickster people moved their homes to another place, their custom being to wander; but they left behind an old dog by the name of Old-Age-Dog (Waadihasa). The Old-Age-Dog wandered around and finally found the place where the body of Young-Man-Chief had been left. The Old-Age-Dog thought to himself: "Well, I might as well save this man that the Trickster people have put to death." So the old dog sat by the body and made a big howl, then stopped and looked at the body; again he howled, looked at the body, and there was no sign of its coming to life. The third time he howled and called out: "Young-Man-Chief, you have gone to sleep. Too bad! Get up!" Then the body began to move around a little. The fourth time the dog howled and called, and Young-Man-Chief arose from the dead, rubbed his eyes and said: "I have slept too hard." When Young-Man-Chief looked he saw an old dog sitting by him, and at once he rose on his feet, took hold of the dog and kissed him for raising him from the dead. Young-Man-Chief was pretty sore from the effect of the fire, and the dog insisted that Young-Man-Chief should go with him to the nearest stream. They at once started for the water, and when they arrived at it they looked for the deepest place, and the dog commanded Young-Man-Chief to dive four times. Young-Man-Chief dived four times, and when he came out of the water after the fourth time he was all healed. After doing all this they at once set out for Young-Man-Chief's home. When he was burned to death his bow and arrows and other things he had were taken away from him. When the dog commanded him to dive in the water he had his arrows back again. When they were on the way home (and they were on the way about four days, in a straight course), Young-Man-Chief hunted for some game to eat. He slept with the dog at night until they reached home.

When they reached home, Young-Man-Chief bade his father call all his men to listen to the story of his life while he was away. The chief at once called all the men together at his place, and when they had come they saw Young-Man-Chief and the Old-Age-Dog, In those times it was the custom of the people on the return of some one that they had not seen for a while, to hug the person who had been absent; so they hugged Young-Man-Chief, and after learning that the dog had saved his life they hugged the dog. Young-Man-Chief began to tell the story about his life while away. He said that he had wandered a long while looking for the homes of the Tricksters, and finally he discovered them; that he had to wait until darkness came on before he could do anything; that when darkness came he walked to the village and looked in every tipi seeking the lost woman; that finally he succeeded, finding her in the tipi where there were a great many people; how he had taken one of his arrows, punched a hole through the tipi, and with a long piece of grass through the hole punched the woman's back in order that she might know that some one wanted to see her outside; how he succeeded in getting her out to talk with her; how she made a fine talk in order to get back into the tipi; how she went into the tipi and brought back her man concealed, that he might attack him; how he was attacked by her man, who at once called for help, and ordered his men to build a big fire in order to have a big victory dance over the victim; how he was scorched; how the woman abused him by punching him with a burning stick; and how his life ended; how when he was dead the Trickster people left the camp and left their dog there; how the dog roused him from death; how the dog would be his brother, and what times they had while on the way home.

Young-Man-Chief then told his people that he wanted to send out a war-party against the people who had scorched him to death, for the Old-Age-Dog on their arrival home had told him to send out a war-party against these people. The following night they formed a big war-party to go on this expedition, and on the next morning they started out. When Young-Man-Chief was telling of his life while among the Tricksters, the father of the woman who had been killed was among the crowd and heard what Young-Man-Chief had said about his life, and about how Young-Man-Chief had been put to death. They set out on the journey to look for the Tricksters, and they were on the way about six or seven days, and the seventh day they all stopped. Then Young-Man-Chief made his offering of smoke and told his men that he and his brother, the Old-Age-Dog, would go out spying for the Tricksters, for they had already been spying. So they set out at once, and the dog dived in the water and came out of the water a young dog. They traveled faster, and finally succeeded in finding the camp of the Tricksters. The Old-Age-Dog told Young-Man-Chief that he would do all the work, for he was himself the chief of dogs. It was getting late in the evening. The Old-Age-Dog went on the top of a hill and howled as loud as he could, calling for all the dogs around, and when the dogs heard this they began to howl too, and they went to the old dog. When all the dogs had arrived where the Old-Age-Dog was they asked him why he had called them together. The Old-Age-Dog told them that the Trickster people were mean to them, and in order to make them suffer he wanted them to take away all the Trickster-Spies' weapons, chew off all their bow-strings and carry away all their war-clubs, for there was a big war-party that he was with that wanted to attack these people. All the dogs returned to the camp to destroy everything and carry off everything. Then the Old-Age-Dog returned where Young-Man-Chief was and told him what he had done, and they at once started back to where the other men were. They arrived at their camp about midnight, and the war-party started at once for the Trickster-Spies. They traveled all that night, until nearly daylight, arrived early the next morning and then made their attack. When they made their charge, Young-Man-Chief and Old-Age-Dog kept going among the Trickster-Spies and killing them and looking for the woman who had put Young-Man-Chief to death. They found her with her man. They overtook them and said to them: "You have put Young-

Man-Chief to death, and now we are going to put you to death." The dog jumped on the man and Young-Man-Chief killed the woman. Before they turned back Young-Man-Chief captured a fine-looking young woman, then they turned back from the battlefield with all their men. Young-Man-Chief's men captured many more, and scalped many people. So when they all met again Young-Man-Chief told his men that he had killed the woman and captured another woman to take her place with the father of the woman he had killed. They at once returned victorious to their homes.

According to custom, while a party was out on the war-path, there was some one on the watch to see if they were returning, and when the watch saw some indications of people returning he made a sign called "Degairneayars," which was the sign that the war-party was returning victorious. So the village people knew that the party was coming. When the war-party arrived at the village Young-Man-Chief went straight to where the father of the woman he had killed lived, and gave the Trickster young woman to him, and said that he had killed his daughter and this woman was to be his daughter in her place; and the man was satisfied. Of course, when they returned they had all kinds of dances over their victory. So, Young-Man-Chief and the Old-Age-Dog returned to their home.

Later on, Young-Man-Chief got married to a young woman. He had the habit of sleeping with his dog; so that when he was married they all slept together and ate together. The dog once told Young-Man-Chief that he was jealous. Later on, Young-Man-Chief sent out another war-party, leaving his dog at home in care of his wife. When the woman would go to bed the dog would lie down at the foot of her bed. It was not very long until they heard that the war-party was returning, and when it arrived they, of course, carried on dances. Though Young-Man-Chief left his dog at home the dog had such great powers that his master got through everything safely. They passed on until Young-Man-Chief took a notion to send out another war-party. He went out again, leaving his wife and the dog at home. On the night of the day that Young-Man-Chief left some man came to this woman's bed and lying down beside her, asked why she kept the dog at the foot of her bed. The dog barked, and the man told the woman to kick the dog off from the bed. The woman kicked the dog off from the bed. Early the next morning the man left, and when the folks got up the dog was lying off the bed; and they wondered why it was. The folks tried to feed the dog, but he would not eat. So they asked the woman what she had done to the dog, and she said that the dog was cross and got off the bed itself. On the next morning they found the dog outside the grass-lodge, and again tried to feed him, but he would not eat. On the next night the dog got up again and moved away, and the next morning they looked for the dog and found him a good way from their place. Again they tried to feed him, but the dog would not eat at all. On the next morning the dog moved outside the village. The next morning they again looked for the dog and found him outside of the village, lying down, and they tried to feed him, but he would not eat. On the next night the dog moved again, this time to the hill where the war-party had always made its appearance when returning. The next morning the folks looked for the dog again, and when they had found him, tried to feed him, but he would not eat. Here he remained until his master came back. When Young-Man-Chief returned with his war-party to this place he bade his men go on while he remained behind until he found out why his dog had come down so far from home. The men folks returned to the village and Young-Man-Chief asked the dog why he was there. The Dog replied: "You know that I told you I was jealous; some one came around our wife's bed, and the woman kicked me off." Young-Man-Chief told the dog he would remain there, and whatever the dog wanted to do he would do. On the next morning the folks brought food for Young-Man-Chief and the dog to eat, but they would not eat. The next day the people brought food again for them, but the other food was still there. The folks noticed that the two had both sat down, and underneath they were turning to stone. On the next day when the folks came back the stone had grown up above their legs; the next day they came around again and the stone had grown up below the neck; the next day they were turned into stones. When two stones stick up like these the people call them "Young-Man-Chief and his dog."

21. THE OLD-AGE-DOG WHO RESCUED THE CHIEF'S SON.*

Chief's-Son (Niasedia) once lived with his father in a village situated in an open place having but little timber, on the east side of a stream of water. On the west there was a large piece of timber, and in those days the country was pretty wild, and foes frequently attacked the people who lived in the village. Whenever the women went after wood they were accompanied by the men, who would take along all their weapons, that they might at any time be ready for an attack, never knowing what would happen.

*Told by Ignorant-Woman (Man) (Towakoni).

Once upon a time, early in the day, when the women went out to bring wood, Chief's-Son and other men went along to accompany them. By afternoon, having gathered enough wood, they began to return home. It happened that Chief's-Son went on further than anyone else. When he began to return he saw a woman, who, perhaps, had watched him and was waiting to go home with him. The woman called him to her, for he was a single man, and she thought she might induce him to have her for a wife. When Chief's-Son got to the woman she caught hold of him and would not let go. He wanted to go, but she would not let him. While she still had hold of Chief's-Son they were attacked by the Trickster-Spies (Kinas-Kitikearaha). Chief's-Son finally made his escape from the young woman and she was captured by the enemy. Chief's-Son having made his escape, went home and told of the woman being captured by the enemy. The missing woman belonged to a prominent family. Chief's-Son regretted the loss of the woman for his sake, nor could he get the affair out of his mind. He was so annoyed by it that he resolved to go and look for the woman and bring her home from captivity. He told his parents that he wanted to start for the enemy's country in search of the woman whom he had suffered to be captured. His mother made for him two pairs of moccasins. For the woman she made an extra pair of moccasins and a robe, and she prepared a little lunch to take along while out on the trip. Chief's-Son finally set out on his journey to bring the woman back home. The people, knowing that the Trickster-Spies were very fierce, thought that he was running a risk. For several days Chief's-Son was on the road, looking for the Trickster-Spies' villages. As the Trickster-Spies were constantly moving from place to place he finally succeeded in finding an old trail. This he. followed for a good while until it appeared to be only several days old. Chief's-Son, of course, traveled faster than the Trickster-Spies, since they moved along with their families. Finally he came to a place where the trail was only a day old, and he knew that he was about to overtake them. He went on, and the next day he had to travel in obscure places, so as not to be seen, for the Trickster-Spies were always on the lookout for their enemies. Later in the day he overtook them. He concealed himself. and after dark entered the village. He went from one tipi to another and peeped in every door he came to, looking for the woman. He finally came to the largest tipi of all, and peeped in, and there he saw the woman on the west side of the tipi. Now, that he had found her, he went outside of the village and secured a long stem of grass to use in attracting the woman's attention, for thus it would be easy to get her out of the tipi. He returned to the tipi, to the side where the woman sat, bored a hole in it, and putting the grass through the hole, punched the woman's back, and attracted her attention. She finally went outside, and there he met her, and said: "My woman, I am here looking for you, and your parents are wanting you to come home, and now I want you to go home with me without fail." The woman asked if he would permit her to go back into the tipi to get the things she needed, but this he refused. They talked for a good while about her going back into the tipi. The woman at length gained his consent and went back into the tipi, although he had the things she needed. Inside the tipi, she told her man that the man from whom she had been captured was outside. She told her man that she wanted him captured that she might be avenged for his having left her. She went out of the tipi with her man, both wrapped in the same robe. She went up to the man to talk, and her man jumped out and got hold of him, then called for help, calling out that he had seized an enemy trying to take away his wife. Then men ran from every direction to assist, and the man was overpowered and there was no way to escape. The people at once brought wood to burn while they should dance in celebration of the capture of an enemy. A long pole was secured to tie the man to. In a little while a fire was made in the middle of the village. They tied the victim to the pole and the big dance began. The woman and her man came close to the pole and danced around him, and the woman would say to him: "You suffered me to be captured. You are a coward. I do not like you. I am taking revenge upon you." After the people were through dancing they set fire to the wood around the pole and burned him. The great dance was ended by scorching the man to death.

The next morning the Trickster-Spies moved away again and left his remains at their old camping ground They also left a dog by the name of Old-Age-Dog (Waadihasa). This old dog was so old that he was unable to keep up with the camp, so he was left behind. Old-Age-Dog went around where the man was burned to death. He found the remains of the burned man and raised him up, restoring him to life. The man now saw where he had been lying upon the ground. The old dog asked him to rise and follow him. Chief's-Son then roused from his death bed, went along with Old-Age-Dog and followed him. They finally came to a creek, and Chief's-Son was told to dive in. He dived, and when he came out of the water he appeared the same as when he had started from home. Old-Age-Dog jumped in the creek, too, and when he came out he was a fine young dog. They turned back toward home. While on the way the dog began to tell Chief's-Son all about how the Trickster-Spies lived, and that he, the Chief's-Son, could at any time go back and search for the woman and kill her instead of bringing her home, for he was chief of all the dogs; and how he (Chief's-Son) might send out a war-party against the Trickster-Spies; how they would have no chance to do any fighting, for the reason that he could call up all the dogs in the village and could ask them to destroy all the bows and arrows and carry off the clubs, so that the enemy would have nothing to fight with. This is the talk that the dog was giving the Chief's-Son. He also told Chief's-Son that, having sent out the war-party against the Trickster tribe, and after taking the life of the woman and her man, whenever he might want to go on the war-path it would not take him long, and having been left at home he (the dog) would guide him through all time free from danger. Chief's-Son told the dog that he would have a good home to live in and that he would always be treated well for the good he had done him. They traveled four long days and arrived at the young man's home. While on the way Chief's-Son had no difficulty in killing game to eat. The dog he had was white, and it was now called White-Dog (Waaikots).

When Chief's-Son arrived home his people saw that he had a dog with him. Immediately on his arrival Chief's-Son called all the people together at his home. The crier was told to tell all the people of the village to assemble at the chief's place to meet Chief's-Son and hear what he had to tell about his journey among the Trickster-Spies. The people assembled at the chief's place, and the father of the captured woman was in the crowd. Chief's-Son began to tell all about his journey; how he was betrayed by the woman; how he had been captured; how she had abused him and danced around him with her man, the chief of the Trickster tribe; how he had been burned to death; how on the next day he had been restored to life by White-Dog, who was now before him; how he had resolved from this time on to call White-Dog his brother, and that they should look upon the dog as his own brother; that the dog was now to be the chief's son; how he was going out in search of the Trickster-Spies who had put him to death; that he was going to take his life and that of the woman; how he and his brother White-Dog were going to send out a war-party against the Trickster-Spies, with whom all who wanted to might go.

Chief's-Son was asked what time he wanted to start on the expedition. He appointed the third day for the start, so that the people could have plenty of time to get ready. At the end of two days the great war-party was sent out, starting toward the southwest, Chief's-Son being the leader. The party was on the road for about ten days before they were able to find any trail of the Trickster-Spies, though spies were sent on ahead every day. On the tenth day Chief's-Son and his dog went out alone to scout, leaving all the rest to remain at their camping place during their absence. They followed up the trail and at about midnight came to the enemy's village. Chief's-Son was asked to stay behind the dog. As they drew nearer to the village he was asked to stop and remain, the dog going on alone. By the place where the village was situated was a high hill, and on this hill White-Dog howled as dogs always do—not barking, but howling. After he had howled this way the dogs in the village all began to howl and they came to White-Dog, for he was calling them to him. In a little while all the dogs of the Trickster-Spies were assembled. White-Dog now asked all the dogs how they were being treated by their masters. All said they had not been treated right. · White-Dog then told them all to return to their village, carry off all the weapons and chew off the bow-strings, saying that he had a war-party that was ready to attack the Trickster-Spies, and that the party would be there at break of day. The dogs all went down the hill howling. White-Dog went back to Chief's-Son and told him that he had arranged everything so that the enemy would have no opportunity to do anything. Both now returned to the war-party and Chief's-Son told what had been done. All the men began to move toward the enemy's camp. About daylight they attacked the village, and when the enemy, seeing their village attacked, tried to find their weapons, they found their bow-strings gnawed in two, so that there was nothing left to do but to run for their lives. Chief's-Son and White-Dog went through the village, paying no attention to any one until they overtook the captive woman and her man. When they had overtaken them Chief's-Son called to the woman, and said: "Your life is mine. I am going to take your life." The woman turned back and begged not to be harmed, but the dog jumped on her and bit her right on her throat and killed her, and Chief's-Son went after her man. When they had killed the two they went through the rest of the people and killed others. Chief's-Son captured a young woman about the age of the woman they had killed to place her in the family from which she had been taken, as an adopted daughter for her father, who was in the crowd. The war-party began to return home, and soon completed their journey. Before they reached the village, according to custom, they set fire to the prairie, to show the people at home that they were victorious. Having shown the people at home that they were victorious they told them how they had made the people suffer. Of course, the father of the girl adopted the captured woman to live with him permanently.

When they arrived home the dog turned again into Old-Age-Dog. Thereafter, whenever war-parties returned from the war-path, they had all kinds of scalp dances, which continued whole nights.

After a time, Chief's-Son got married. Hitherto he had slept with the dog, but now that he was married the dog had to sleep at the foot of his bed. Chief's-Son forbade his wife to whip the dog, for he thought more of it than he did of her, and he said that if she should whip the dog she would have to leave the place.

Time passed, and the dog told Chief's-Son to go out on the war-path, while it would be his duty to stay and watch the woman constantly. Chief's-Son went out with a war-party and left the woman in care of the dog. Now the dog slept at the foot of the woman's bed. One night after Chief's-Son had been gone for several days there came a man to the woman's bed. The dog barked to warn the people that some one was in the woman's bed. The man said to the woman: "What is the use of your having the dog sleep at the foot of your bed?" He asked the woman to kick the dog off the bed. She complied, and the dog went and lay by the door. On the next day the chief's family saw the dog lying by the door. They knew what had happened and offered it some food to eat, but it would eat none of the food that was offered. Then they talked to the dog and asked what was the matter, but the dog would not answer them. They asked the woman what she had done to the dog, but she refused to tell what she had done, but said: "Perhaps the dog has just become contrary." The next day the dog lay by the door the entire day. The next day the people found the dog a long way to the south from his place, and again offered him food to eat, and again he refused to eat. He would allow no one to touch him, especially the woman who had kicked him off from the bed. The next day the dog moved on further south, and this time he was found in the outskirts of the village. The people offered him food and again he refused it. Here he remained till night, allowing no one to touch him, then he moved toward the south, where there was a high point, where victorious warriors always appeared on their way home from war. There he awaited the coming of his master. The next morning when the people looked for the dog they were unable to find him. But some one from the village happened to go around by the high point, and finding the dog lying on the ground facing the village, they notified the chief's people, who all went to the dog with food for it to eat, but the dog again refused to eat. They talked to the dog and begged him to go back with them and put away his sad feeling. They began to get uneasy about Chief's-Son on account of the way the dog was acting. They all mis-

trusted that he had lost his life, but the dog was grieving on account of
the actions of the master's wife. Several days elapsed before the return
of Chief's-Son, and in the meantime the people took food to the dog,
which he still refused. When Chief's-Son returned he was preceded by
a good many men. When they came to the high point all stopped.
They found the dog lying there. When Chief's-Son came to the high
point the men told him of the presence of the dog, supposing he was
feeling sad. Chief's-Son knew at once what was the matter, and sent
all his men on home, saying that he would remain with the dog and learn
what was the matter with him. The men all went home and told what
Chief's-Son had said. Chief's-Son then asked the dog what was
troubling him. Old-Age-Dog then told his master that while he was
gone, some man had come to the wife's bed and had asked her why
she kept the dog at the foot of the bed. The dog said: "I have always
told you that I was jealous of our wife. A certain man came to our
wife's bed, and I, of course, barked at him. For this reason the man
became angry at me and told our wife to kick me off from the bed,
which she did. This is why I am grieving." Chief's-Son then told
Old-Age-Dog to lead off; that wherever he wanted to go he would
follow. Old-Age-Dog then told his master that they would remain
where they were. Now all the prominent men came from the village
and asked them to return home. They brought things to eat, but the
two would eat nothing. They were resolved to cease to exist as human
beings. The men failed to persuade them to return home. They remained lying on the ground, facing the village. The people noticed
that the under side of them was turning to red sandstone, so they left
them where they were. Thereafter the people visited them every day
as they gradually turned to red sandstone. Now, when we see two red
sandstones like these lying together we know that they are the two who
once turned into red sandstone. Thus did Chief's-Son and his dog
leave their home on account of jealousy. The village still exists, nothing more happened, and all remained human beings.

22. YOUNG-BOY-CHIEF WHO BECAME AN OTTER.*

Once upon a time there were two villages, and in each village
there was a chief who controlled the village. These two chiefs each
had a child. One of the chiefs had a boy, and the other had a girl. The
chief having a son lived on the north side, and the chief having a girl

*Told by Killing-Enemy-Instantly (Towakoni).

lived on the south side of the village. During all the boy's life, the people, especially the old folks, would come to see him and would sing songs for him. During the singing great crowds would gather around the place where the singing was going on. The men were near to the singing, while the women stayed a long distance and were not allowed close to the singing. This is the way the chief's son enjoyed his boyhood days. In order to have this continue he had to remain single all his life, so there was no chance for women to stay around where the young man was and try to become his wife. The older men were the ones who were received at his home, for they were the ones who talked to him and told him all about things that a young man had to do in days to come, and sometimes they told him about wars that some of these men had been in. This is the way the young man spent his time. His name was Young-Boy-Chief (Waiksedia).

At the other chief's place the chief's daughter was kept at home and was watched closely, so that no man ever had a chance to come around. She remained single until she became a young woman. Her father had company every day. It was the girl's place to do the cooking for these men who came to visit her father. There were times at night when men came and sat up with her father. During these times she had to sit up, too, for her father would call on her to do the cooking for the men who came and sat up with him. This is the sort of life she led with her parents. At her home she had a high-elevated bed, set up on high poles. The place was higher than a man could reach, and whenever she wanted to go to bed she had to take a ladder, that was made of a tree trunk with notches cut in one side for steps. Young-Boy-Chief had the same kind of bed, so that there was no chance for young women to get to him. In those times young men and young women went around by night after one another.

Once upon a time Young-Boy-Chief got to thinking about going to see the chief's daughter, but he knew from what several other young men had said that she always refused whoever went over to see her, and there were times that she would kick one off the bed, and when one was kicked off he fell a long way to the ground. One night Young-Boy-Chief started to the place where the chief's daughter lived, with the expectation of seeing her that night and, if she should accept him, of telling her to keep everything secret, so that their parents might not know of their doings. He started for her place after everybody had gone to sleep, and on his arrival he called the chief's daughter, and kept calling her until she woke up. She looked down to see who it was. Young-Boy-Chief then told her that he was the chief's son from the other village. He asked her if he could come up where she was. The

chief's daughter had to study what to do, and finally told him to get
the ladder and get up where she was. The chief's son got the ladder,
leaned it against the bed and went up to bed with her. Toward morning the chief's son left the place, went home and went to bed. He slept
until morning. From this time on he would go over and visit the chief's
daughter at night, and no one knew anything about it, for the chief's
son had asked the chief's daughter not to let any one know of their meet-
ings. He also told her that, should she become pregnant, he could furnish her all the materials used for making a baby cradle; that he had
sticks already cut, ready for making the cradle, and had dyed hair to
cover the child's face when the child should go to sleep; a shell for the
baby's use in drinking water, to be worn about its neck; an otter skin
(used to tie the hair), that could be used for wrapping the baby to the
cradle; a pad (worn around the necks of men and women) for use under
the child's feet, to hold up the feet—it was matted and had weaving on
the breast, and the relic was made out of bones. These were the materials he promised the chief's daughter should she become pregnant;
but it would be some time before he would bring these things.

At the chief's son's home the men still visited him and sang for
him, for they thought the young man was what we call "wiasucks,"
a boy who had never had intercourse with women; but Young-Boy-
Chief was conscious that he was what we call "waitz," a man, or a
married man; for he kept visiting the chief's daughter by night.
Some time afterward the chief's daughter told the chief's son that she
was pregnant. The chief's son told her that he would bring something she could use for fixing up a cradle for the child. After this
the chief's son left the chief's daughter and did not return. Finally
the people found their daughter to be pregnant. They then asked her
to tell to whom the child belonged, but she would not tell, for Young-
Boy-Chief had told her not to betray him. Young-Boy-Chief remained at his home after the chief's daughter had told him she was
pregnant. At her home her parents tried to find out to whom her
child belonged, but she refused to tell. Long afterward, the child was
born, and the chief's daughter waited for her man to come back to her
and bring with him the things that he had promised to bring when he
should hear of the child's birth. She waited patiently for this young
man to do what he had agreed to do.

At the village the men continued singing for the young man.
Whenever they sang for him the men formed in a circle; a man was
placed in the center and the chief's son was placed on his lap while the
rest of the men did the singing. When the singing was over the men
would let the boy go. By so doing the men would get plenty of things

to eat that the chief gave them, and then there would be something presented to them for singing to Young-Boy-Chief. At the chief's daughter's home, after her child was born, her parents asked her many times to tell them to whom the child belonged. They told her that some one ought to come and see the child, if her husband was not living with her. As she refused every man who came to her, now that she had brought the child in this way, the child having no father, they told her that she must either leave the place or tell whose was the child. Still she would not tell. She still had hope that her man would come back to her some night with the promised things for the child. Every day her parents kept asking her about this. She got very tired of waiting, and determined that the very next time she heard about the men singing for the chief's son she would go and take the child to him and make the people think that he was the father. The next time she heard about the men singing for Young-Boy-Chief she started for his place. On her arrival there she saw large crowds of women on the edge of the crowd of men, and she saw that no woman could get near to where the singing was going on. She went through the crowd of women and was told not to go further, for the women were not allowed there, especially those having children. But still she kept going, until she came where the young man was; then she placed the child in the young man's arms and turned back by the way she had come, before the singing was over. The men, having found out that Young-Boy-Chief had a child by the strange woman, stopped singing. The child was left with Young-Boy-Chief. When the chief's daughter started off, the chief's son got up with the child in his arms and followed her. He thought that perhaps she would stop at her home, but he saw her pass her home; he followed her. Then the folks saw to whom the child belonged and followed the chief's son.

The chief's son thought that the chief's daughter would soon look back and stop to see her people, but she kept on going and did not look back. After they had gone a long way the child began to cry. The chief's son then called to the chief's daughter to stop and let the child nurse, saying that if she stopped he would live with her and the child. But she would not stop, and the child kept crying. Finally the chief's son began to cry, for it made him feel badly to hear the child cry and to see his mother leaving them. She kept going until Young-Boy-Chief saw a large lake. The chief's daughter was headed for it, and he began to think that after she should come to the lake perhaps she would stop for them, and that perhaps she wanted to take a bath before she should turn back to speak to him. Then he stopped crying, but the child did not. Finally the chief's daughter reached the edge of the water, took off her clothing and left it. Then Young-Boy-Chief saw her flying over the lake, and they could hear her whistling like an eagle.

The chief's daughter had turned into an Eagle, and on their arrival at the water where the clothing was Young-Boy-Chief found that the garments had turned into grapevines. Here he stopped with the child and expected his wife to come back. Both cried again, but still he could see nothing of his wife. While all alone they both went to sleep for a while, and while they were sleeping the woman came back with another man whom she had already married, and they were both Eagles. While Young-Boy-Chief was sleeping the Eagles took the child away from him. He then awoke, but did not find his child. Young-Boy-Chief looked around for the child, but could not find him. He finally looked up, and there they were, three of them, flying over him. They kept sailing around over him, and finally the woman Eagle began to sing to him, saying:

"Kit-e-he-ki-as-si-a-ka
Kit-e-he-ki-as-si-a-ka
Hos-ta-kes-o-ti-na-sĕ
Wa-ka-na-kuk.

"Kit-e-he-ki-as-si-a-ka
Kit-e-he-ki-as-si-a-ka
Ja-di-yak-o-ta-nas-ĕ
Wa-ka-sats-ka-dats.

"Kit-e-he-ki-as-si-a-ka
Kit-e-he-ki-as-si-a-ka
Ki-tish-o-ti-lak
Wa-ka-ka-ti-ŏs.

"Kit-e-he-ki-as-si-a-ka
Kit-e-he-ki-as-si-a-ka
Ki-ki-a-di-kits-a-ho-ti-das
Wa-ka-as-sa-ki-ats
Kit-e-he-ki-as-si-a-ka
Kit-e-he-ki-as-si-a-ka."

In repetitions the last four measures become:

[After a pause the same tune is sung in a lower key, and apparently to different words, as most of the sixteenth notes disappear.]

You have said there were dogwood sticks ready cut for use in making a cradle for the child.

You have said there was dyed hair to cover over the head, and beading for the cradle.

You have said there was a tanned otter skin for use to wrap the child on the cradle.

You have said there were long bone beads to put under the feet, to hold the feet of the child.

Then, before leaving him, she sang to him this song:

"I-ti-sesh-i-heĕ-he
I-ti-sesh-i-heĕ-he
Ne-ti-kit-i-hĕ
I-ti-sesh-i-heĕ-he.

"It-sezh-e-hĕ-he
It-sezh-e-hĕ-he
Hi-da-zesh-si-a-wĕ
It-sezh-e-hĕ-he.

"It-sezh-e-hĕ-he
It-sezh-e-hĕ-he
Hi-da-zesh-si-a-wĕ
It-sezh-e-hĕ-he."

Let me give a feather to my husband!
Give a feather to your wife's first husband!
Give a feather to your father!

Each time she sang this song there would come down a feather, and it would land on the ground. Each of the three Eagles gave three feathers to the young man, then they left him and went off, flying towards the east. Young-Boy-Chief took the feathers and went on home. When he arrived home he found everybody had left the village, and no trail of them was to be seen. Then he went to a river and turned into an Otter (Kitish). Before Young-Boy-Chief turned into an Otter he took the feathers and pitched them into some brush that arrows are made of, commanding that the feathers be used in the next generation, together with the brush that the arrows are made of. So this is the way Young-Boy-Chief was treated for not fulfilling his promise to his wife after she was pregnant, and this is the way the story of Young-Boy-Chief ends.

23. YOUNG-BOY-CHIEF WHO BECAME AN OTTER.*

Once upon a time there was a village which had two chiefs. The village was divided into two parts by a wide, street-like space which extended east and west. On the north side of the division was a man named Young-Boy-Chief (Niasedia), who was the son of the chief of that part of the village. Sometimes great crowds of people assembled at this chief's place, and the prominent men would sing for Young-Boy-Chief, who was considered as "wiasucks" (a boy who had never had intercourse with women), a name given to young men who have no thought of marrying. While the singing was going on only the men were allowed close to the singers, while just beyond them were the women of the village. This song ceremony was always carried on for Young-Boy-Chief. Now, there were several women who thought that Young-Boy-Chief was old enough to marry. They went by night to see him, but he rejected them, for he had no thought of ever living with a woman. His parents often talked to him regarding marriage, but he would not listen to them and continued with his boyish acts and had no thought of women. The chief of the south village had a daughter, whose ways were similar to those of Young-Boy-Chief. She had no thought of men. A great many of the young men of the village desired her for a wife, but she rejected them. She was not in the habit of going around like other women, but always stayed close at home. Only a very few people knew her, it being the custom for the chiefs to have company every night. The chief's daughter did most of the cooking for the visitors.

Once upon a time Young-Boy-Chief thought of the chief's daughter, who, at the same time, thought of him, each wondering how the other appeared. On a certain night each thought of going to see the other, but neither knew what the other was thinking about. Young-Boy-Chief got up from his bed at midnight and went straight toward the south village. At the same time, the chief's daughter got out of her bed and went toward the north village to see Young-Boy-Chief. Neither knew that the other was on the way. As they approached the dividing line between the two villages they saw each other. Young-Boy-Chief asked the chief's daughter where she was going. She replied: "I am going to see Young-Boy-Chief." The woman, seeing certainly that this was the man, asked where he was going, and he replied that he was going to see the chief's daughter who was living at the south village. Then said Young-Boy-Chief: "I am that same

*Told by Kadas (Wichita).

Young-Boy-Chief," and the woman said, "I am the chief's daughter." They came closer to one another and commenced to talk about whether they should go to his or her home. Finally they decided to go off in the distance, where they could live permanently by themselves. Young-Boy-Chief said he would go back to his home and get what things he needed, and he told the chief's daughter to do the same and to meet him again where they were. They departed to their homes to get what they needed, so as to be ready to leave the village. After a short time both returned. They started toward the south and traveled that night until nearly daylight, when they went to sleep for a while, and the next morning they started out again, traveling fast, for they knew that some one would be after her, and in order to get her clear out of sight they would have to travel fast. They traveled the whole day and stopped when it was dark. Two more days they traveled before finding a good place to live. At the end of the fourth day they found a place which just suited them. The woman commenced to fix up the place, making a grass-lodge, while the man hunted. Finally they had their home prepared.

The parents of the woman sent out men to look for her, but they failed to find her. Sometimes Young-Boy-Chief would say: "Whenever we get a child I will go home and get what things we need for a cradle. I have dogwood sticks ready for making the cradle, and I have an otter skin for wrapping around the child's cradle. I have some hair to cover the child's eyes while in the cradle. I have a small pipe bone, to be used under the child's heels when in the cradle. I also have another thing, a round, flat shell with two holes in the rim, that the child can have for a cup to drink out of." Long afterwards the woman became pregnant. A boy was born to them, of which they, of course, were very proud. Young-Boy-Chief would go out hunting while his woman and the boy remained at home. This is the way they lived. Some time afterward the young man thought of his home. He began to think about leaving his wife and child. One time when he was out hunting he took the trail to his old home. He left his wife and child far behind him. It took him but a short time to reach home. His parents were glad to see him, but he did not say anything about being married to the chief's daughter, nor about leaving her and the child far away from the village. He remained at home, and his wife wondered why he did not return. Young-Boy-Chief had now resumed his former life as if unmarried. Men came to sing for him while he was seated on the lap of one of the men. Still they thought him a young man without wife or child.

After several days had elapsed the chief's daughter got tired of living alone, far from the village. So she took her child and packed him on her back, determined to return to her home and see her husband. She started for home, and in four days she arrived at the village and went straight on to the home of Young-Boy-Chief. It was the very day that men had come to his home to sing for him, and an immense crowd of people were gathered at his home. On her arrival she went straight toward the place where he was seated on the lap of the main man, who was singing for him. The people tried to coax her not to go there, for women were not allowed where the singing was going on. But she went through the crowds, going direct to her husband. She took her child off from her back and put it on the lap of Young-Boy-Chief, walked back, and turned northward instead of going to her home. The men who were singing were surprised at the young man. Crowds of people began to move away, for they had learned that Young-Boy-Chief probably had a wife and child. Young-Boy-Chief took his child and followed his wife. As soon as they got outside of the village he called to her to stop, so that he might plan what was the best to be done. But the woman would pay no attention to him. She kept on going north. The child commenced to cry, so Young-Boy-Chief again called to his wife to stop, but she would not stop. As they went further the man and the child both began to cry. Otter-Man was feeling sad over the crying of the child. After they had gone a little way further the woman commenced to talk to Young-Boy-Chief, telling him that he had treated them meanly by leaving them so far from the village. Young-Boy-Chief then called to her to stop, and said: "I will stay with you hereafter if you will stop, and we will stay at home," but the woman would not stop, so they kept on going. The child kept on crying and Young-Boy-Chief cried, too, for it made him feel sorry that the child should cry and that the woman would not stop when he told her to stop. They kept on going north. The man then began to think that, perhaps, after a while she might stop. But the woman commenced to sing to him about the things he had promised for the child's use in the cradle:

"Kit-e-he-ki-as-si-a-ka
Kit-e-he-ki-as-si-a-ka
Hos-ta-kes-o-ti-na-sĕ
Wa-ka-na-kŭk.

"Kit-e-he-ki-as-si-a-ka
Kit-e-he-ki-as-si-a-ka
Ja-di-yak-o-ta-nas-ĕ
Wa-ka-sats-ka-dats.

"Kit-e-he-ki-as-si-a-ka
Kit-e-he-ki-as-si-a-ka
Ki-tish-o-ti-lak
Wa-ka-ka-ti-ŏs.

"Kit-e-he-ki-as-si-a-ka
Kit-e-he-ki-as-si-a-ka
Ki-ki-a-di-kits-a-ho-ti-das
Wa-ka-as-sa-ki-ats
Kit-e-he-ki-as-si-a-ka
Kit-e-he-ki-as-si-a-ka."

You have said there were dogwood sticks ready cut for use in making a cradle for the child.

You have said there was dyed hair to cover over the head, and beading for the cradle.

You have said there was a tanned otter skin for use to wrap the child on the cradle.

You have said there were long bone beads to put under the feet, to hold the feet of the child.

As the woman sang this song to the man, he would say: "Yes, I made those promises; and I have all of them ready, and if you will just stop a moment and let me tell you more, and if you will go back to my home, our child shall have all of those things." But the woman kept on going, while she was singing this song to him. When she was through singing they came in sight of a large body of water. Young-Boy-Chief thought that might be where they were going, and that perhaps his wife would stop and talk to him. So he did not speak to her any more about stopping. She was a long way ahead of him. When she reached the water she took off her robe, and away she went, flying over the lake, and she turned into an Eagle (Kos). When Young-Boy-Chief got to the place where the woman had left her robe there was no longer a robe, but a wild grapevine. Young-Boy-Chief sat down on the bank and the child commenced to cry, and he also cried, because the woman had left them. Finally Young-Boy-Chief saw two Eagles flying over him. The woman, having turned into an Eagle, had already married some one who was also an Eagle. The two Eagles flew around over them, and it happened that Young-Boy-Chief felt sleepy and went to sleep. Suddenly the Eagle woman came down and took the child away from him. This awakened him. There were three Eagles now flying around over him, the young one being with them this time. Young-Boy-Chief now cried to be taken up as the child had been taken up, but the woman began to sing again:

"I-ti-sesh-i-heĕ-he
I-ti-sesh-i-heĕ-he
Ne-ti-kit-i-hĕ
I-ti-sesh-i-heĕ-he.

"It-sezh-e-hĕ-he
It-sezh-e-hĕ-he
Hi-da-zesh-si-a-wĕ
It-sezh-e-hĕ-he.

"It-sezh-e-hĕ-he
It-sezh-e-hĕ-he
Hi-da-zesh-si-a-wĕ
It-sezh-e-hĕ-he."

Let me give a feather to my husband!
Give a feather to your wife's first husband!
Give a feather to your father!

Suddenly the Eagle woman shook herself, and there came down one feather, and the feather landed by Young-Boy-Chief's side and he picked it up and kept it. Again the Eagle woman sang, telling her Eagle man to give a feather to Young-Boy-Chief. He shook himself, and there came down another feather to Young-Boy-Chief. Again the Eagle woman sang, telling her young one to give its father a feather. The young one shook itself and there came down another feather to Young-Boy-Chief. Now the Eagles commenced to fly away from Young-Boy-Chief, and when he saw that they were leaving him he went back toward his home, still having the feathers.

Arriving at his home, Young-Boy-Chief found that everybody had moved away, and where the village had been there was nothing but tall weeds, which showed that the people had long since moved away to another place. Young-Boy-Chief stood around the place where he used to live, turned to each direction and wondered which way the people had gone. He concluded he would not follow the people, as he thought it would take so many days that it would be too much trouble to catch up with them. So he went south, and there was a river that he wanted to reach, and on whose banks there were large dogwood bushes. When he came to the place he pitched his feathers into the bushes and commanded that in generations to come, feathers should be used for feathering arrows, and this is the reason why people of the present time use feathers on their arrows. After Young-Boy-Chief had done this he went to the river and turned into an Otter (Kitish). So the young man became an Otter, while his wife belonged to the fowls of the air.

24. THE MAN WHO BECAME A FLAMINGO.*

Once upon a time there was a village, and in this village lived a chief who had five daughters. This village was situated by a river, and the people in the village carried their water from this river, and bathed there daily, morning and evening. The five daughters of the chief were all single, and always refused to marry. In this village also lived Man-having-greater-Powers-than-any-other-Man (Waitsaidiawaha). He lived on the edge of the village. Once upon a time Man-having-greater-Powers-than-any-other-Man thought he would play a trick on the oldest of the five sisters, the daughters of the chief. These women had a certain time to go to the river to bring water or to take a bath. One day Man-having-greater-Powers-than-any-other-Man found the trail of the women and put a small bone cylinder or pipe-bone, about two inches long, that is used for wearing around the neck, on the path for one of the women to pick up. It happened that the oldest of the five sisters found the relic on her way, and picked it up and put it in front of her under her blanket. After she had done this she did not think of it any more until she reached home, then she began to feel around to see if she could find the relic that she had picked up. She knew that it was pretty, and she wanted her sisters to see what she had found, but she failed to find it. After a time she became pregnant, but she did not know how she became pregnant. Everybody found out her condition, and people wondered. This worried the young woman, for she knew for certain that she had never been with any man. Her father asked her to whom the child belonged, but she said that she did not know. The child was born, and was a boy. The child began to grow rapidly. When he was old enough to creep, he began to cry, and cried all the day long. The chief ordered the men to make arrows and bows, and to come around about the chief's place and present their bows and arrows to the child. The chief said that whoever had his arrows accepted by the child was to become husband of the mother of the child. He told the men that when offering the bows and arrows to the child, they must say to it: "Son, come and accept my arrows and bow, for I have brought these for you." When all had their bows and arrows made they made known to the chief that they were ready. Then the chief called all the men into his lodge. There were large crowds of men, and in the crowd was the same man who put the relic on the trail for this young woman to find. When everybody was in the chief's lodge they began to pass around the child, and the men offered their

---

*Told by Towakoni Jim (Towakoni).

bows and arrows to the child, but he kept on crying. In the crowd of men was the Coyote (Ketox), who wished his turn would come, for he knew that he could stop the child from crying. The child was handed to every man, and was offered bows and arrows, and each man would call the boy "son." Finally, the Coyote's turn came, and he knew that when he could stop the child from crying he would become the chief's son-in-law. When the child was handed to the Coyote he called the child "son," and told him to come to him and get his arrows. He made all kinds of talk to the child, telling him that he had long been wanting to take him, and that he was his father. Just then the child stopped crying and played around for a while, and this made the old Coyote happy, for he would become the chief's son-in-law. The Coyote wanted to get rid of the crowd of men. He wished that every one would pass out, for now that he had stopped the child from crying there was nothing else that these men could do. Soon the child began to cry again. So he had to be passed on, and this made the Coyote mad, because the men had waited too long in passing out. The child was finally handed to Man-having-greater-Powers-than-any-other-Man. When the man's turn came he called the child "son," and told him to come to him, and he called the child's name, which was Child-sprung-from-Pipe-Bone (Kiadiya), the relic that he had put on a trail for the women to find, and he presented his bows and arrows to the child, and took him on his arm, wiped the child's tears, and said: "My son, I have long been wishing to take you, but your mother does not know how she came to have you." Just then the woman thought of the relic that she had found while she was going to the river for water. So Child-sprung-from-Pipe-Bone forgot all about crying, but commenced to play around with the bows and arrows that were presented to him by his father, Man-having-greater-Powers-than-any-other-Man. The Coyote was angry at this man, because he was the first man who stopped the child from crying. He called this man all the names he could think of—"Long-Neck," "Long-Legs," and "Long-Nose." So this Man-having-greater-Powers-than-any-other-Man became at once the chief's son-in-law, instead of Coyote.

The chief then announced to the men that he was satisfied that his grandchild had found his father, and that he wanted every one to pass out except this man, who would remain at his lodge hereafter. All of the men passed out, and there was one man who was selected by the chief to announce to the people that Man-having-greater-Powers-than-any-other-Man had become his son-in-law. After these men passed out, this was announced and was made known to all the village. On the

following day this man stayed at the chief's home, and late that evening he went back to where he lived and brought everything he had—
such things as war-bonnet and some other war materials that he had,
and went to his new home with the chief. He asked his new wife to
put all his things at the head of his bed. Early the next day he started
out to hunt and kill game for the whole family. It was a custom that
any man marrying a young woman should at once begin to support
the family by going hunting, or on the war-path to bring home a scalp
for the family. So this became Man-having-greater-Powers-than-any-
other-Man's duty, for he was a great warrior, and a great hunter.

Another time the chief called the people to assemble at his place,
and when the people came about the place he announced to the men
that he had made up his mind that his other daughter was old enough
to become some one's wife; that he (the chief) was wanting the men
to go out hunting; and that any one killing a red turkey and bringing
it to him should have his next daughter. Then the men all went about
their places to be ready for the next day, for they thought the chief's
daughter to be a great prize. On the next day all the men went out
hunting for the red turkey. After they had gone, Man-having-greater-
Powers-than-any-other-Man went out to hunt for the red turkey, and
the very first thing that he did was to scare up a big bunch of turkeys,
and in the midst of these turkeys was one red turkey. He took a shot
at the red one and killed it. After killing this turkey he returned
home. On his arrival he found that some one had already killed one.
This was done by the Coyote. When the Coyote had killed the turkey
he found that it was a white turkey, and he had painted it red so that
he could make the people believe that it was a red turkey. The Coyote
was hanging around the place, thinking that he had won the prize,
and that he would become the chief's son-in-law. When this Man-
having-greater-Powers-than-any-other-Man arrived with the red turkey, and was seen by everybody and proved that he had killed the real
red turkey, then the chief said that he would give the young woman to
him for his wife. The Coyote was angry at this man who had won
the chief's daughter away from him the second time. This young
woman became the second wife of Man-having-greater-Powers-than-
any-other-Man.

The chief had three more unmarried daughters. Some time afterward the chief called all his men to assemble again at his place. The
men came about the chief's place, then the chief was asked by the people
why he had called them to come to him. The chief told the men that
he had made up his mind that his third daughter should become a wife

to some one, and that late that evening he wanted all the men to hang up their war-bonnets, so that the woman could come and walk around to see who had the prettiest bonnet, and the one whose bonnet she thought was the prettiest was to have her. Then all the men passed out, awaiting the time to come. That evening they all hung out their war-bonnets. Man-having-greater-Powers-than-any-other-Man hung out his bonnet on one of the highest tipi poles, and everybody else had his hung up. The Coyote hung his bonnet, too, and as he looked out to see how everybody's else bonnet looked, he saw at the chief's place one hung up that looked as though it had a fire flying around it. The Coyote then called the chief, telling him that his place was on fire. The Coyote kept hallooing at the chief, telling him that his place was on fire. Just then the woman came out to look around at the bonnets, and to see who had the prettiest bonnet. The Coyote was then right close to the chief's place, and he began to tell the young woman that he had the prettiest bonnet, and asked her to come to his place to see his bonnet. After she had looked all around she looked up above her father's place and saw a bonnet hanging up there, and she thought that that was the prettiest bonnet of all, because it was different from any other bonnet, and so she called it the best one. This bonnet belonged to Man-having-greater-Powers-than-any-other-Man. The chief then told the men to take down their bonnets, for there was one already chosen to be the husband. This made the third one of the sisters a wife of Man-having-greater-Powers-than-any-other-Man. The Coyote went off discouraged, because he could not coax the woman to choose his bonnet.

Time went on, people doing the same old things, the men doing the hunting and also sending out war-parties, for this was their custom in those times. Long afterward, again the chief called the men to come to his place. Then the men all came about the place wherein the chief resided. When everybody had arrived the chief was asked why he had called them together. The chief then said that his daughters, the two youngest ones, were old enough to become some one's wives, and that he wanted them to choose their husbands. He said that all the men must dance that evening, so that his two daughters could see them, and that whosoever they might think to be the funniest dancer could have the two girls. It being early in the day the men went about their business and waited for evening to come. When the time came, the men built up several big fires, so that there would be light enough for the girls to see who was the funniest dancer. After this was done the dancing began. The men had all their best clothes on, for they all wanted to win.   The men were allowed to pass close to the women, so as to let them see who was the funniest dancer.   The chief intended that anyone at whom the girls would laugh would be the one to have them.   The Coyote would dance right close to them, and would make all kinds of faces, so as to make the girls laugh at him, and then he would say, "Laugh at me, girls, and you shall be my wives," and then it would be only a short time until the Coyote would come around to where the girls were again, telling the same things over and over again.   Every man passed by them, and after all there was a certain man who was seen by the two girls at whom they laughed when they saw him pass by.   This was a sort of light-complexioned man, but small.   This little man was Man-having-War-club (Waitskadaidaiyoks), Opossum.   The chief gave his daughters to this man, and now he had two sons-in-law.   The Opossum then had two wives, and it worried him to have two wives.   Therefore he split his member into two parts so that each wife might enjoy her own part.

After all the chief's daughters were married the village existed the same as ever, having no trouble whatever until later on.   One time the chief's first grandson disappeared some way.   This child was Child-sprung-from-Pipe-Bone, the son of Man-having-greater-Powers-than-any-other-Man.   The chief then called forth all of the men most noted for their great powers.   All the most famous men came about the place to find out why they were called.   Then, when they all arrived at the chief's place, they asked the chief why he had called them together.   In reply, the chief said: "My grandchild, Child-sprung-from-Pipe-Bone, has disappeared, and I want the help of the most famous men to help me to search for my grandchild.   Any one finding the child may become the chief of the whole village."   This was the reward he offered for his grandchild.   Then all the men prepared to hunt the child.   Some went one way and some another.

The man who was the father of this child, Child-sprung-from-Pipe-Bone, went off too, in search of his child, going from one place to another, and he stayed away for a number of days, until he found where the child was.   He found that his child was in the water, and he saw that Woman-having-Powers-in-the-Water (Otskahahakaitshoidiaa) had taken his child off into the water.   This Man-having-greater-Powers-than-any-other-Man remained where he had found his child for a long time, watching his child in the water.   Finally, some others found this man standing by the bank of the river.   He was then asked why he was standing on the bank.   In reply, he said that he had found his child in the water, and that he was standing there watching his child, and that he would remain by the bank for all time. He said that for generations after generations thereafter, when he should be seen standing by the banks of the water, it would be known that he was still watching his child under the water. So he never again returned to his former home. Man-having-greater-Powers-than-any-other-Man then became Stick-standing-on-the-Bank (Hakeikouwi), or the Flamingo.

The news was carried back to his wives. After the news had reached the home of the chief, then the chief called all the people of the village to assemble at his home to hear what he had to say. The crowd began to rush to the chief's lodge to hear the chief's talk. When everybody was present it was made known to the chief that all the people in the village had assembled. He then made his talk, telling them that all the people had lived happily during all the times, but now, since his troubles had come and he had lost his grandchild, he wanted to become something else. He told all his friends that they could do as they wished. Everybody went off; some became fowls of the air, and some wild animals, and some remained as human beings.

25. THE SPIDERS WHO RECOVERED THE CHIEF'S GRANDSON.*

There were once two villages that were separated by a street extending north and south; and in these villages were two chiefs, who had great multitudes of people. These chiefs, like the people, made their living by raising crops of corn and hunting for their meat, and were in the habit of sending out war-parties. The chief on the east side of the street had a full-grown son, while the chief on the west side had a daughter; and both the son and the daughter refused to marry among the young people of his or her own village. The young people in chiefs' families like these were in the habit of having a sleeping place outside of the main lodge of their parents; this was fixed up with four tall upright forked poles and two long poles laid across in their forks, with plaited willows across the horizontals to make the structure solid; then they had sewed together enough tanned buffalo hides to cover the place, and they entered by means of a high ladder. When the children had gone to bed the parents would remove the ladder, so as to keep anyone from getting up to the bed.

---

*Told by Ahahe (Waco).

One night the chief's son took a notion to go and see the daughter of the chief in the west village, expecting, if possible, to make her his wife; for he knew that she had refused many others. At the same time the chief's daughter in the west village resolved to go and see the chief's son in the east village, with the expectation of marrying the young man; for she had heard of the young man refusing to marry the women of his own village. It happened that both, on the same night, after everybody had gone to bed, started, each for the other's place. When the young man got outside of his father's village he saw some one coming from the other village; and this young woman when she was outside of her father's village, saw some one coming out of the village on the east. She went toward him, and they met. Each asked where the other was going. The young man said that he was going over to see the chief's daughter, in the west village; and the young woman said that she was going to see the chief's son, in the east village. The young man said that he was the chief's son; and the young woman, that she was the chief's daughter. They consulted as to whether or not they should go to the boy's home or to the girl's home. Finally they decided to live at the young man's home, so they at once started and arrived at his place and went to bed. The young people of those times were in the habit of getting up early in the morning and going to the nearest creek or river for an early morning bath. So the next day, at the young man's home and at the young woman's home, the parents noticed that their children were not getting up as early as usual. The young man's folks wondered why the boy did not get up as early as usual; and they sent the young man's mother to see what was the matter, and when she went up on the ladder she turned right back, for she saw some one in the bed with the boy. When she came down, she reported that there was some one there with the boy. She was told to return and tell her boy and his wife to come down at once and be like any other married couple, and have their breakfast.

In the west village they looked for the chief's daughter. They first looked for her in the west village and then in the east village. We might say that the Coyote (Ketox) was the principal one in the crowd of those who were looking for the chief's daughter; for he was always the chief's servant. Finally the Coyote came to the boy's village and came to the chief's home. There he found the girl, and on his return reported to the chief that his daughter had slipped away at night and had gone home to the chief's son. But the chief was satisfied, for his daughter had become the wife of the other chief's son. The new man and wife lived long at the young man's home, until there was a child born to them, which was a boy. The women folks used to take the child around to their lodges, according to custom, for he was the child of a father and mother, both of whom belonged to chief's families. When the time came for the child to nurse, they would bring him home and let him nurse. The women continued to take the child around, and as soon as one woman would return the child another one would come and take him, after he had nursed. When the child was kept a little too long, the Coyote would go around talking through the village, and asking who had the child, and would bring it home right away. Finally it happened that while the people were still asleep, a woman came early in the morning, and asked for the child, saying she was never sure of getting it during the daytime. The mother, still in bed, took the child out of the cradle and handed it to the woman. This old woman walked with a stick, which showed that she was old. The old woman took the child early that morning. The following morning the mother called for her child to be returned to nurse. The Coyote went around the village, talking and asking who had the child and giving word that it should be returned to nurse. Finally they called for the child again, but failed to have it returned. The chief ordered his men to go through both villages to see if they could find the child. Later in the morning all the men folks returned, having failed to find the child. The chief called on all of the prominent men and others who had great powers, to recover the child. The people began to come to the chief's place and ask the chief what he wanted. He ordered these men to look for the child, and he promised that any one who should find the young one should become a great chief among this child's grandfather's people. This included the wild beasts and fowls of the air, as they were called at this time. So it was a good while before the many men returned. They failed to recover the child, and finally all of them returned, not a single person having found the trail of the woman who was supposed to have carried off the child.

Finally there came a little old woman who asked that she might try her luck in recovering the stolen child, and she asked that she might begin to search at the same hour the little old woman had taken the child. Early the next morning she came around the chief's lodge, repeating the same words that the little old woman had said when she took the child, and acting the same as she acted when entering the lodge. She had a walking-stick like the old women use, and made as if she were going to get the child. She walked across the ground like the old woman had done, and when stepping out just at the door of the grass-lodge she found where the little old woman had sunk and gone under the ground with the child. This woman who tried to recover the child was called Spider-Woman (Aitsisohedikits). She was gone the entire day, trailing the little old woman with the child, who was traveling under ground. She found her trail, but lost it again, and so returned. This showed that some one had greater powers than she. It happened that after Spider-Woman had failed to recover the child the chief called all his men to his place. When they came to order he told his people that he wanted them to leave their homes for a little while and to go on a big hunting trip with him, so that he might forget some of the sad feeling he had in him on account of the loss of his grandchild. A few days after he told his people this the people began to move out, following their chief. When this was announced the Coyote spoke out, saying that he would remain at home, for he had a big family, and would move to the timber and live there for a while, until the people should return. When the people moved away the Coyote removed his family to the timber, near a creek. The Coyote hunted around and fished for his living. Besides his family, he was the only soul to be seen around the homes of the people.

Once upon a time the Coyote went along the creek, watching the fishes under the water, trying to shoot them with his arrow. While he was standing there watching the fishes some one came around behind him, telling him to go ahead and shoot the fish. This surprised the Coyote, and nearly scared the life out of him, and he said: "My friend, you surely scared me, for I knew I was the only man living around here, and did not expect to see anybody else here talking to me that way." The man who talked to the Coyote was Moving-Fire (Kiatsatoria), Spider-Man. He was dressed differently from any one the Coyote had ever seen or known, having a feather on his head, and wearing a robe that had an arrow for a button, on his breast, and besides this he had about four arrows. When the Coyote saw this man he admired his way of dressing; so he begged Spider-Man that he might dress like him and asked him where he lived. Spider-Man said he lived right close to the Coyote, and when going hunting he always thought he would come in and see him, as he always passed the Coyote's place. Spider-Man then took the Coyote and dumped him in the water, then called out, and when the Coyote came out of the water Spider-Man told him to look at himself in the water. The Coyote looked and saw that he was like Spider-Man. Spider-Man then asked the Coyote if he was hungry, and the Coyote said that he was. So they both went to Spider-Man's place, which was right close to the Coyote's place. When they had entered the Coyote looked around and saw by the fire a small piece of meat hung on a stick, roasting. The Spider-Man gave the Coyote this meat to eat, and he ate until it was nearly gone; then Spider-Man took the stick that had the piece of meat on it, and taking it on his hand, turned it, and there it was, a large piece of meat again. The Coyote continued eating the meat until he had enough. Spider-Man asked the Coyote if he was brave, and the Coyote said that he was. Spider-Man told him that that was all he wanted to know about him, for he wanted him to go after the chief's grandchild and wanted him to hasten in doing it, for power would be given him to enter where the child was. He told the Coyote to hurry, for the child had been scorched nearly to death.

The Coyote went back to his home, taking what meat was left to his family, and when his children began to eat the meat he showed his wife how to turn the stick once, so as to make the meat large again, when it was nearly all gone. Then he told her that he was going a long distance, looking for the lost child. The Coyote went to Spider-Man's place again, and Spider-Man told him to go back home to tell his wife that she was thereafter to be his sister instead of his wife, and he was to have a separate bed made where he was to sleep on his return. The Coyote went back to his home and told his wife that they would no longer be married, but be brother and sister; that he was to have a separate bed for himself, so that when he returned home he might sleep by himself. The Coyote then went right back to Spider-Man's place to get ready to start for the chief's grandchild. When the Coyote entered the place he was asked if he had done as he was ordered, and the Coyote replied that he had. Spider-Man then told the Coyote that he would have to go by four dangerous beings before reaching the place where the child was, but if he was a brave man these four dangerous men would not scare him. He then started the Coyote off on the trip.

The Coyote traveled fast until he came to some one standing, who told the Coyote not to come near him, for he would not be allowed to pass. Now, before the Coyote started he had been told what to do when he should meet these four men, who would talk to him in an abusive manner. He was also told that he would enter the place in the night, and that there he would find the child suffering from the heat of the fire; and there he would see a great multitude of people standing around and dancing over the child; that he would notice once in a while, people running to their homes, saying that Spider-Man had come, for they knew that Spider-Man was the only living being that could recover the child. The Coyote had also been told that when he got the child he should run hard, for something would explode, so that if he made any movement in dodging it he would be hit by the explosion of the thing that was hid under the pole that the child was hung on; that he should take his four arrows and shoot one toward the east, one toward the west, one toward the south, and the last one toward the north, so as to destroy the people by fire. When the Coyote came to the first dangerous man he noticed that it was a Headless-Man (Ohearppeschaux), who tried to chase him back; but the Coyote continued his journey, and when he reached the place where Headless-Man was he at once went around him, set his face to the north and stuck his feet to the ground. Headless-Man then said: "Spider-Man, you have made up your mind to go after the lost child, have you? You are on the right road now." So the Coyote continued his journey until he came to the next Headless-Man, who was the same as the one the Coyote had met before; but the Coyote kept on until he came up to him, and he said the same thing to him that the first one had said. The Coyote went around him once, faced him north, and stuck his feet tight to the ground, and he said: "Spider-Man, you have great powers, but you want to look out, for they will get you instead of your getting the child, if you do not." The Coyote went on until he came to another Headless-Man, and he faced him. The Headless-Man asked the Coyote why he had come to that place, for that was his land. When the Coyote approached him he threw up his hands, saying: "Spider-Man, this is you, and you have made up your mind to recover the lost child. The child was carried by here, and if you get him you will have to sneak around." The Coyote then went around the Head-less-Man, faced him toward the north, stuck his feet fast to the ground, then continued his journey, for he was told that he must get there before the child was scorched to death, so he had to go fast. The Coyote ran on to the last Headless-Man, and did with him as he had done with the others. The four Headless-Men were a sort of guard for the people who had the child, and since the little old woman had such guards, it was certain that she was famous. If anybody beside the Coyote had found her trail these four Headless-Men would have done the fighting before any one ever could have reached the place where the child was. When the Coyote came to the last Headless-Man he was abused with all sorts of talk in order that he might be turned back, but the Coyote had full power to go by, for he had already passed the other Headless-Men. Drawing near to him, he said to the Coyote: "Oh! That is Spider-Man. You surely are going to pass through here, are you?" Then the Coyote went around him once, faced him toward the north, stuck his feet tight to the ground and continued his journey.

The next place to which the Coyote came was the village where the child was. Going in an easterly direction he reached the west side of the village. In the center of the village was a great, big fire. The Coyote took one of his arrows, shot it toward the east, and when the arrow struck in the ground there was started a fire. He then shot one arrow toward the south side, and when the arrow struck the ground it started another fire there. He took another arrow, shot it toward the north, and there was started another fire. He then took another arrow and stuck it right where he was, and there made another fire. Then he made a quick dash, and on arriving at the place where the child was the people ran a little, saying that Spider-Man had come, and all scattered, going in all directions. This gave the Coyote a good chance to get the child. The people were scorching the child every night, and were making all sorts of fun. They believed that Spider-Man was the only man who had great powers; and if he should ever try to get the child he would be successful; and this is the reason why the people at the village would say: "Spider-Man has come," and run to their lodges. When his chance came the Coyote made a quick dash, and took the child down from the pole, saying: "Spider-Man has come!" He ran hard as he could back to the open space, in order to escape from the fire himself. The fire was about to cut him off, when he reached the place and passed through. Then something exploded, and he could hear thundering and something like a streak of lightning coming near him, but he still went on at full speed. This was the last thing to escape. The things that flew by him were small stones, that are said to strike things when we say "lightning has struck" anything.

The Coyote, having made his escape, stopped a moment, having the young child on his arm. He rested here for a while and then continued on his way back home. Spider-Man, of course, already knew that the Coyote was coming back with the child, for he had powers to foretell anything that was to happen. The Coyote left the village, burning up the evil ones who had stolen the child. On his way home the Coyote came to the last Headless-Man that he had met, and he made him carry the child on his back until he gave out, then took his bow and struck him on the head, killing him instantly. Then he started on home, came to the next headless-Man, made him carry the child on his back until he gave out, then killed him with his bow. He continued his journey, losing no time, for he was anxious to get home. He came to another Headless-Man, made him carry the child, traveling as hard as he could go until finally the Headless-Man gave out. As each one of these Headless-Men gave out he would beg to be released without harm. But the Coyote had been told not to mind anything they should say, so he killed them as he went along. He still kept on traveling, for he had power to travel a long distance without giving out.

On the way home the Coyote thought to himself: "Well, there are not two ways about my getting to be a great chief. I have recovered the lost child," and when he arrived he met Spider-Man. Spider-Man took the poor, suffering child, threw him in the water and called the child once, and up it came out of the water, floating. Spider-Man took him out of the water and told the Coyote to go and bring one of his children that was about the same age as the chief's child. The Coyote went up to his place, entered his home, called the old woman, saying: "Sister, I have returned from the hardest trip I have ever had in my life. I got the lost child and brought it home, and am now going to take one of our children to where Spider-Man is." So he took one of his children to where the chief's child was. Spider-Man took the Coyote's child and threw it into the water and called it again, and out it came. This made the Coyote's child like the chief's child, so that they could not be distinguished the one from the other. They went home, stopping at Spider-Man's place, where no one but the Coyote had ever been. The Coyote was given that same power, so that no one might see that he was living there. He was very proud of himself, for what he had done and what he was going to have when the rest of the people should arrive home. When he was given all these powers he was commanded not to have anything to do with women, for Spider-Man was a single man himself.

Time passed, and the people began to come back home from the hunt. The Coyote was told to go to the chief's place and to tell the chief that he had recovered his child, and that the child was living with his folks. He was also told that the chief was going to send for the child; that he (the Coyote) would be given a home by the chief's people, and would live well thereafter; that he was to remember that his own wife was not to be his wife any more, or any one's else. So, late in the evening, when the people arrived at their homes, the Coyote went toward the village, and there met some one whom he asked to show him the place where strangers went when visiting the place. He was told to go to the largest grass lodge in the middle of the village. He walked on until he reached the place, and entered. The chief and others were surprised to see such a wonderful man as this. When he reached the place he was told that there was sadness among the people, and it would not be pleasant for visitors to be around for a while; that there was a child that had been carried away before they went on the hunt, and that this was the reason why the people had left the place for a while. They asked him the object of his visit, and the Coyote requested the chief to call his people together, for he wanted to say something. The chief sent out a man to call all the people to come to his place, for there was a stranger in the village that wanted to say something to them. The people came to the chief's place and were told to come to order, so that they might listen to what the stranger had to say. The Coyote was then called upon to say whatever he had to say. The Coyote began by saying that he was the man whom they had known as the Coyote. Then he commenced to tell his story—how these chiefs had their villages divided by the street; how one of the chiefs had a son, the other a daughter; how they came to be man and wife; how the child was born to them; how it disappeared, some evil person having carried the child off for the sake of mischief; how it happened that the chief called all the prominent men to look around for the child; how every one had failed to recover the child; how Spider-Woman, after finding the trail of the little old woman, had failed; and how they were compelled to leave the village for a while. The Coyote then told how he remained at home and moved his family near the water in the timber; how he made his living by hunting and fishing; how some one had taken pity on him to make him such a famous man as he was. He told everything that took place while the people were gone, and how he was sent after the child. While he was telling the fore part of the story the people would say, "Yes," and "Yes." But finally the people would not say a word when he began the real story of getting the child. It was the custom, as a sign of attention when any one was talking, for the people all to say, "Yes," "Yes," "Yes." The Coyote then began the story of his life while on the way to the place where the child had been carried to, telling what a hard time he had in pursuing the directions he had been ordered to pursue; what narrow escapes he had had in getting the lost child; how he succeeded in reaching the place; how he had destroyed the evil village; how he returned with the child; and so he told the whole story of his life and that of the child's. He ended his story by saying that his wife was never to be his wife any more, but that she was to be his sister thereafter; that the child was over to his home, and the people would be allowed to go and get it, and another child of his own.

The chief at once sent forth men to bring the child. The Coyote told the people where he was living. When the people went out to get the child they failed to find the place. The Coyote knew that they would not find it, for he had been given power to conceal his lodge so that no one could ever know there was anybody living there. The Coyote rose from the ground and went forth himself with a crowd of men after the child. They took a large robe to carry the child and the Coyote's child. They arrived at the Coyote's place, and the men folks laughed a little at each other, saying to one another: "Why, we have been right here, and why is it that we could not find the place?" They took both children, and the men folks said to one another: "Which one of these children is the chief's grandson?" for they were both alike. When they arrived at the chief's place the Coyote asked the father and mother of the child which one of the children was theirs; and the people were astonished at the likeness of the two children. The chief's son and the chief's daughter were happy to see their child once more, and gave the Coyote high honors for recovering it. The chief at once ordered the people to commence a new home for the Coyote; for the Coyote was given full power to become a great chief. They at once went after his family when his new home was completed. The child's father and mother adopted the Coyote's child for their child, too, for the two children were alike. The Coyote moved into his new home that the chief had given him to live in, and he called often on Spider-Man, as he had been told to do. Here the Coyote lived for a long time, until the women began to admire him and tried to marry him; but the Coyote still remembered the orders that were given to him, and refused to marry every woman who came along at night, though the Coyote was a fine-looking man. But after a long time the Coyote took a notion that he would accept no one but Woman-who-wears-Shell-Rattles (Nekastarahars), who was fine-looking. He said to himself that if that woman ever came along he would accept her, and have her for his wife. So once upon a time he heard this woman coming, and she had on loud rattling shells, so that anybody might hear her a good way off. When she came the Coyote quickly allowed her to lie down. Spider-Man at once knew that the Coyote had forgotten his orders and took away his great powers that night, and the next morning when Woman-who-wears-Shell-Rattles woke she had a true coyote sleeping with her. The woman was scared nearly to death, and this caused the Coyote to wake up, and he, too, was scared. So the Coyote ran out of his place, going out in the wilderness as he is to-day. In this way, whenever the Coyote had powers given to him he would by misfortune lose them. As soon as the chief had heard this he called all his people together and told them that since some one had done him wrong, and he constantly felt that some other wrong might befall him, he would allow his people to go where they wanted to go, and become animals if they wished. So, some went in groups, according to families, turning into some other form; some went up in the air, becoming the fowls of the air; and some turned into wild animals. The chief remained as a human being, as also did his family, and the majority of them still were his people.

26. THE ORIGIN OF THE EAGLES.*

There was once a certain village in which there was a chief by the name of Young-Boy-Chief (Waiksedia). In those times the people were in the habit of wandering around on all kinds of expeditions. Whether they went hunting or on the war-path they were always led by Young-Boy-Chief. When starting on an expedition they would go south. After leaving the village they had to cross a deep river. In crossing this river Young-Boy-Chief would stay at the crossing until everybody had crossed.

At one time, when they went out on a hunt, they crossed the river and Young-Boy-Chief, as usual, waited until everybody had crossed, then he followed the people. It was his business to help everybody at any time help was needed. When they came to any place like a river he was the first one there and the last one to leave. During this trip they hunted, and sent a war-party against the Tricksters (Kinas), their enemies. The Tricksters were what are now called "eheehe" (prairie-chickens). They were great warriors. Although the people of those times had greater powers than we have, the Tricksters were also great warriors, and there were worlds full of these people, and they were famous in warfare. They were double acting people—right handed and left handed. When in battle, they shot their arrows with the right hand and with the left hand. They were great warriors to fight against. The other people carried on all kinds of wars against them. When they came to fight, sometimes they would break apart, having killed equal numbers in battle; and sometimes one side would get the better of the other.

This expedition that Young-Boy-Chief went out with was a hunting party, and they killed game of all kinds, such as deer, buffalo, and turkey. It was a long while before they returned home. On their return from the hunt Young-Boy-Chief did his duty in helping the people when help was needed. When they reached the river, on their return home, he would remain a little longer than the others. While waiting there at the river there came an old woman with an old

*Told by Ahahe (Waco.)

woman's walking stick. Young-Boy-Chief asked if he might help her across, and she said that he might. After entering the river the old woman asked Young-Boy-Chief to pack her up on his back, for she said that she was not able to wade the river. Young-Boy-Chief packed the old woman across on his back, and when they landed on the other side he asked her to get off, but the old woman refused to do so, and told him to let her down on the edge of the village. Young-Boy-Chief went on with the old woman on his back. When they reached the village it was getting dark, but he still had the old woman on his back, for she refused to get off. Young-Boy-Chief then asked her if she wanted him to pack her to the place where she lived, but she said: "No; you have refused to marry any one, and since you always refuse to marry I have made up my mind to be your wife." Young-Boy-Chief said to the woman: "If this is the case, now get off from my back and you shall be my wife, and I will live with you always." But the old woman said: "No, no! I am now on your back and I shall never get off; I am on to say." Young-Boy-Chief then thought to himself: "Well, if I am going to have this woman on my back, I might just as well go home."

Now, the men were in the habit of sitting up with the chief, Young-Boy-Chief's father; and they were waiting, wondering why he had not come home, for it was late. When Young-Boy-Chief got to the place he stopped outside and waited until some one should step out to bring in some wood to put upon the fire. Finally, some one stepped out, and when he returned said: "Young-Boy-Chief is outside standing with some one." The chief called to Young-Boy-Chief, saying: "If you have selected some one for your wife, bring her in." Young-Boy-Chief went in, went toward his bed and at once lay down. When Young-Boy-Chief had lain down the old woman spoke to his people, saying that she was their daughter-in-law. The people said to the woman: "If you will come off from the back of Young-Boy-Chief you may have some supper." But Young-Boy-Chief's wife did not come off to eat. Then men returned to their homes, and Young-Boy-Chief went to bed, thinking how he could get rid of the woman. On the next day he still had the old woman on his back, and he finally found that he could not get rid of her, for she was stuck to his back. Then the old woman on his back began to urinate and defecate. Young-Boy-Chief ate but twice a day, and felt pretty bad. His life was about to come to an end, because the old woman was such a nuisance to him, and his people were afraid he was going to die.

One time the Coyote paid the chief a visit, and said that he wanted all the chief's men called for the purpose of getting the woman off from Young-Boy-Chief's back. The chief called his men to his place and they asked him why he had called them. The Coyote then told them that he wanted them to help the chief's son to get rid of the woman who was on his back. He selected four of the strongest men in the crowd. He then told Young-Boy-Chief to take hold of a pole of the grass-lodge while the four men pulled the old woman. The pulling hurt Young-Boy-Chief so that they had to stop, and they failed to pull the old woman off. Every day the men were at the chief's place, watching Young-Boy-Chief, to see what was going to happen to him. One day there was a boy on the edge of the village shooting at birds. While he was shooting he shot at a bird, but missed it, and the arrow glanced some distance and lit near the place of an old man named Ears-Painted-red (Watatskatia), the Turtle. While there picking up his arrow, the boy heard the Turtle say: "I wonder how Young-Boy-Chief is getting on with the old woman on his back? It would be easy for me to get her off if they asked me to do it." The boy listened closely to the old man's remarks, then he ran to Young-Boy-Chief's home and entered. He was then about to say something, when they put him out of the place, and he returned to his play. One of the men finally spoke, saying: "Did not the boy say something about some one?" Another man spoke, saying: "I believe the boy had something to tell us." They at once sent for the boy to find out what he had to say. They finally succeeded in finding him, and brought him before the chief to say what he had tried to say when entering the lodge the first time. The boy began to tell what he had heard some one saying at a certain place. He said that while he was out shooting birds he shot at a bird and missed it, and his arrow glanced some distance and landed right behind a man's lodge. While there getting his arrow he heard a man saying that he wondered how Young-Boy-Chief was getting along with the old woman on his back, and that if they should ever call him he would very easily get the woman off. They at once sent the Coyote to bring the Turtle, that he might repeat what he had said. The Turtle said that he could take the old woman off the young man. As soon as he said this the old woman who was fastened to Young-Boy-Chief began to talk, saying that there was no one who could take her off, and she raged when the Turtle said he could unfasten her. The Turtle then ordered the chief to have four men go on a buffalo hunt and get the fat from the hump of the buffalo's back. The chief at once sent out four men, and the Turtle returned to his home. Before he returned he commanded the chief to get a full grown buffalo robe and have it spread on the ground and have Young-Boy-Chief seated there, facing north, so that when he returned everything would be ready. He promised that he would do the rest of the work himself. The following day the men returned from their hunt with the buffalo fat. When the Turtle returned home he made a small bow and four arrows, and got some kind of paint called "darequits." Early the next morning he sent word to the chief to have everything ready. Immense crowds of people began to gather around the place to see some wonderful performance, for the people knew that it was dangerous to do the work that the Turtle was doing. The following morning the Turtle began to sing, walking very slowly:

"Ah-he-nar-he-no-neer-ah.
Ah-he-nar-he-no-neer-ah-
hare-ne.
Ah-he-nar-he-no-neer-ah.
Ah-he-nar-he-no-neer-ah.
Ah-he-nar-he-no-neer-ah-
hare-ke."

[Seven repetitions. The singer gradually sharps so that the last time over is a full degree higher than the first.]

This is the song he used, putting in the words himself. He told about the life of Young-Boy-Chief—how he did his duty in helping along his people; how kind he was to his people; how he helped the old woman across the river; how she stuck to him; what she had told Young-Boy-Chief about his refusing to marry; how he was then suffering from the troubles he was having; how he was going to get rid of the old woman by having the Turtle to help him out; how the Turtle was coming, and was about to enter the place. He kept singing the song, putting in the whole story of the young man's life. He entered the place and kept on singing until he went near to where Young-Boy-Chief was, having his bow and arrows and some others that he intended to use after getting the woman off. While the Turtle was on the way to this place the old woman kept saying that a fellow like him could never get her off, for there was no man that could do it, and she meant to stay on Young-Boy-Chief's back for all time, until she should ruin him. The Turtle entered, and the old woman found that he was a powerful man, and that he was painted in accordance with the meaning of the name, which was Water-Monster-Turtle. The Turtle was painted on both sides of his head. Now the old woman began to keep quiet, and promised to give the Turtle all the powers she had if he would leave her alone, but the Turtle would not listen to her. When he entered the grass-lodge he came around to the south side of the room, then stepped behind Young-Boy-Chief. He commanded one of his arrows to land upon the back of the old woman's right hand. He took another arrow and commanded it to land upon the back of her left foot. Then he shot, and off came the woman's left foot. He took another arrow and commanded it to land upon the back of her left hand. He shot, and off came the woman's left hand. He took his last arrow and commanded it to land upon the back of the woman's right foot. He shot, and off came her right foot.

After the wicked woman was taken off of Young-Boy-Chief's back the Turtle gave the men permission to do with her as they pleased. Then the Coyote took a club and beat her to death. This woman was Something-that-will-stick-to-anything (Tatiniyarskaharts), a green tree frog, such as is often seen now-a-days. The Turtle then took the buffalo fat that the four men had got and rubbed it all over the sore places on Young-Boy-Chief. He then took the red plaint that he had ground up and put it over the sore places and the young man was healed and returned to his home at once. After this had happened, the chief feared that something else might occur, so he at once called all the people to his place, and when they had come he announced to them that they already knew what had happened to his son, Young-Boy-Chief; that he was afraid something else might occur; that he wanted his people to do as they pleased about leaving their homes the next morning. The people returned to their homes, and on the next morning they began to go out in groups, especially by families; some turning into fowls of the air, and some into beasts of the woods and plains. The chief's family took a gourd of water and poured the water into the fire, and when the smoke went up in the air they were in the midst of the smoke, and became Eagles (Kos). Some of the people remained in the village.

27. THE COYOTE AND THE BUFFALO.*

Once upon a time there was a chief called Wolf (Wasaka), who controlled a large village of hunters. These people lived chiefly by hunting buffalo, but there came a time when no one could ever see any more buffalo, and they did not know what had become of them. In this village there was one person who was considered the swiftest

*Told by Cheater (Wichita).

runner of all the people, and this was Black-Wolf, and was always sure to kill whatever he went after. One time the Coyote decided to go out a long way off to see if he could not find some trail of the buffalo, for the people at home were in need of food. He went toward the north, and traveled four long days, but still could not find any sign of buffalo. At the end of the fourth day he came to a lodge all by itself. He did not show himself, but kept his eye on the people who were living there. He saw there was one man with his family, and noticed that they had plenty of meat. He sneaked around to find where the man kept his meat, but he could not find out, and so he thought that he would try a trick. He turned himself into a little dog, and after dark crawled into the lodge. When the children saw him they petted him and played with him. The old man told them to let him alone, but the children were pleased to have a little puppy to play with and so they fed him and took him with them to bed. Early the next morning, before the old woman was up, the old man rose from the bed to go out hunting. As the old man fixed himself up to go out the Coyote crawled out the other way to follow him and see where he got his meat. As soon as he saw the man going over the hill toward the west he changed himself into his usual form and followed the man. Every hill the man went over he would follow, until he saw the man going toward the large hill, and there he saw a great, big stone lying on the side of the hill. When the man reached the place he went around to hear what he would say. He finally came to a place where he could not be seen, and there he commanded the stone to get to one side, and called to the fattest buffalo to come out. When he had said this the buffalo came out and the man shot him with an arrow and commenced to butcher him. After he had taken off all the lean meat he commanded the buffalo to rise and get back in the hole, and as the buffalo went in, the stone moved back to its place again. The man then packed up and cleaned the place where the buffalo had been lying. The man was Raven (Kawita), Crow-Buffalo. The Raven then started back to his home, and as he went over the hill the Coyote went to the place, and said to himself: "I wonder if that stone would obey my command?" He then commanded the stone to move to one side, and called to all the buffalo to get out. When the stone moved to one side there slowly came out a great herd of buffalo. Then he commanded the stone to move back again. He then chased the buffalo toward the place where he had come from. He traveled the same length of time that it took him to come. He reached his village at midnight, and called on the Wolves, and told what he had done, and said that his people need never go hungry any more, and that the children would cease to cry for food, for he had found the place where the buffalo were hid, and by whom they were taken away; that it was the Raven who had done it. He told what a hard time he had had traveling so long a distance to find where the buffalo were, and he said that on the next day the men could go out as they used to do, instead of having to go out so far, for the buffalo could be seen close to their village. He told the chief to have this announced to the people at once, so that everybody would know that he was to have something to eat the next day. The chief himself went out, passing from one lodge to another, singing:

De-gee-lar-ler-sger-air-ah-sch-gee-
Noe-ah-schgee-hee-he Wer-le-
gar-saits-ger-le-wek-eh-hee-he.
Noe-ah-schgee-hee-he-dahl.
De-dar-gee-dar-le-wa-wa-
Se-wa-lar-har-ha-
Wa-ar-har-ha, etc.

[There is no essential variation in the several repetitions. In measures 10-16, inclusive, the notes are sometimes transposed, the dotted half notes occurring on F, but in such instances the note in the sixteenth measure is always F. After a pause, the song is taken up four degrees higher and repeated literally at the new pitch.]

This night has come the Coyote.
He has said that the herds of buffalo are near.
He has said that the herds of buffalo are near.

Wa-ar-har-ha. (Barking of the wolf.)
Wa-ar-har-ha. (Barking of the wolf.)

When this announcement was made, everybody in the village woke up, saying: "If this is the case, we are sure that we are going to have meat hereafter." On the next day the herds of buffalo were seen, and the men went to kill them, and they found that the buffalo were not wild as they had been. From this time on the people had all the meat they wanted, for there was no one to cut off the buffalo from them any more. They knew afterward that it was Raven who had played the trick on them to starve them out, and that it was the Coyote who had recovered the buffalo from the place where they had been put. After all had eaten all that they wanted the chief Wolf announced to his people that because of the hard times they had had, and so that it might not happen again, he thought that they should remain what they were. So they did, and they remained in the earth-lodges, and they were Wolves, Coyotes, and Black-Wolves. All these belonged to the same class of animals. Here all these animals lived in their earth-lodges, and they still live in that way.

28. HALF-A-BOY, WHO OVERCAME THE GAMBLER.*

Half-a-Boy (Weksnikataiwa) lived in a village where there were a great many people. This boy was small in height, for he had a hard time in his early life, and that kept him from growing. The place where this boy lived was a lively place, and the young people played all kinds of games, such as shinny, women's double-ball game, arrow games, etc. These games were played every evening by the young people. This boy Half-a-Boy played his games with the boys of his size. In this village there was nothing that could harm any one, but there was another village north of this village where there was a bad man, who never let any one escape from his village without being killed. Once upon a time this boy Half-a-Boy decided to pay this village a visit. He often heard of a man who could play the wheel game pretty well, and so he took along with him plenty of things to bet when playing with this man. The wheel game was different from other wheel games played in the village where Half-a-Boy was from, and the rules of the game were harder than theirs, so that when any man from another village was defeated he never again returned to his own village, because he had either to lose his life or win the cruel man's life.

Half-a-Boy started to the village, and it took two days to get there. The village where the boy was going was due north. It was late in the evening, and he noticed that the village extended east and west, and had in the middle an open place, and in this place he saw a great many people playing some kind of a game. He waited until sundown before entering the place. The place where he waited was a small hill, and at the bottom was the village, and north of the village was flowing water. Upon entering the place that evening he asked the person he met if he could tell him where he could find a place for shelter. Half-a-Boy was directed to go straight to the north side of the village, where he would find the largest tipi, and there he could stay all night. The

---

*Told by Man-who-harms-while-Jesting (Waco).

boy was told that that was a public stopping place for visitors. On his arrival at the place he entered the largest tipi, and he found that that was the home of the chief of that part of the village. Half-a-Boy was requested to pass on where all visitors generally were directed, on the north side of the lodge. Then the chief began to tell him what trouble there was in the village, and how all his visitors suffered when they came to visit him. The trouble was, that any one who visited in the village lost his life, and that there was no way for any one to escape from death on account of the cruel man who lived there. This chief also told the boy that, perhaps, the servant of the cruel man had already seen him and had carried the news of his arrival, and that early next morning he would be called to come to the ground where this man played his wheel games. He told the boy that he would not only have to play his wheel games, but also would have to bet whatever he had, and when he had lost all he would have to bet his life. After telling Half-a-Boy all this he was given something to eat. At this time some of this chief's friends came around to visit, and later that night they went to their homes. Then Half-a-Boy went to sleep.

Early the next morning he was called to go to the grounds to meet his opponent. Before going there, he first went to some flowing water for his early morning bath. On his return from the bath he went back to the chief's lodge to get his things that he had brought along to bet. When going to the grounds he was accompanied by the chief and his friends. Upon their arrival they commenced to play the game. In the game that they played they used two long sticks and a wheel. First, they threw the wheel a long way, then ran to it and pitched the sticks into the ring. When they started off the boy lost, and he kept losing until late that day, and finally lost all of the things he had brought along to wager. When he told his opponent that he had lost all of his things and there was nothing else for him to bet, the man told him that he had to bet his life, for his life was just as good as the things that he had already won from him. The boy was told that his body was equal to three bets, the right side of his body, the left, and his backbone. At this time the sun began to get lower and lower. The boy made the first bet and lost, and when they turned back the boy lost again, and at this time the sun went down, and it began to get dark. The boy then asked his opponent if the third part of his body could be left until the next day, but the man said he had never had any man whom he would play with on the second day, and so he would have to kill him without winning the part. They talked for a good while before the boy could persuade him to have his life spared until the next day.

At last they agreed that he would remain at the grounds and sleep there, so that the next morning the man could come back again and win the other part of his body. This man then called the boy Half-a-Boy, because he had lost part of his body by gambling, and so this was when he first got his name Half-a-Boy.

Everybody left the grounds, and Half-a-Boy remained there where he had agreed to stay all that night. Half-a-Boy then did not know what to do after this, and so stayed awake until he saw that everybody had gone to sleep. After everybody had gone to sleep he heard two women coming toward him where he was lying, and calling his name, "Half-a-Boy," and saying to one another: "Go ahead and speak to him." The boy heard everything they said, and finally both of the women came to where he was and called to him to rise, for they were coming after him. The boy arose from his sleeping place and went with the two women. While on the way they told him that they had taken pity on him, and they asked him if he could run fast enough to keep up with them. The boy told them that he was a fast runner. The two women then told him to come, and the boy found out that the women were Buffalo cows. They all then began to travel faster, so that the boy could have plenty of time to come back. They traveled part of that night, and while traveling he saw a light a good long way from them. Then the two Buffalo cows told him that where he had seen light was where they were going, and that the light was their grandfather and grandmother taking a smoke. They then finally reached the place, and he saw an old man and an old woman sitting down smoking. These two young women then requested the old people to make haste and give him powers, so that he could get out of his trouble. Then the boy was told to go behind the bull and, as soon as he had seized his member, to demand a "black stick"; then having seized the member again to demand a "red stick." Accordingly he did these things. Then he was told to go up to a cow, seize her vulva, and demand a ring. After he did this the boy now had two sticks and a ring. Then the boy was requested by the old man to place the black stick where it belonged. This black stick belonged in the ring, representing the old man and the old woman. Then he was given instructions. He was requested to let the black stick remain in the ring, where it belonged, and to give the red stick to his opponent. He was instructed not to allow any one to get the black stick out of the ring. The first thing he was to do on arriving at the village was to go to the chief's house and place the sticks and wheel where he had his other things, on the wall between the tipi and the poles, and to let the black stick remain in the ring, and then go to where he had agreed to stay. He was told, in the beginning of their playing, when using his opponent's sticks, to pass the stick through from the left hand four times, and when he hurled the stick, to hit the other man's stick and break it, so that he would not have any to use; that after so doing, his opponent would call for his stick, just as a joke, knowing that he had already won his sticks; and when he should say this the boy should tell the chief quietly to go after his stick, not failing to tell him to let the black stick remain in the ring, and telling him also to carry the black stick with the ring on his right and the red one on the left, and also telling him to offer the red one to his opponent; that when bringing in his sticks to the grounds his opponent would try hard to get to use his stick, but that he should not let him use it. He was also told that every time he won, he should double his bets, and finally should bet his body against the body of the man; that when he had won part of the man's body he should not listen to his promises, but should keep on playing for the last part of his body; that then he should step out of the way and let them (the Buffalo) take his life. This was the instruction given by these two Buffalo.

The boy immediately turned back to the village. He soon arrived, and went straight to the chief's place, and placed his sticks as he had been requested to do. Then he went to bed for a while, until nearly daylight. Then he went straight to the place where he had agreed to stay all that night. Early that morning there came his opponent, ready to win the part of the boy's body. At that time, crowds from both sides of the village began to gather around the scene of the play ground. The chief whom this boy was visiting came around to see the last of the visiting boy. The boy then asked his opponent to let him see his stick that he was using, but this man refused to let him lay his hands on his stick. The boy kept begging to be allowed to see his stick, so that finally the stick was handed to him, and he was told if that would do him any good to go ahead and look at it. So the boy took the stick in his right hand and passed it through his left hand four times and then gave it back. Then they commenced to play the game. On the first trial, when pitching the sticks, the boy hit the man's stick and broke it in two. The man was angry, and was about to kill him. Finally he asked the boy in jest to go after his own sticks, if he had any, so that they might finish the game. The boy called the chief and asked him to go after his sticks. He told the chief to let the black stick remain in the wheel and leave it on the right hand, and the other on the left, and to be sure in handling the sticks to hand the red one to the other man, and the black one to him. The chief went off toward his home slowly, wondering if this poor boy had any sticks. When the chief arrived at the place he saw the sticks and took them, as he was requested to do. When he came to the grounds he handed the red one to the man, but he refused to accept the red one, saying that he expected to use the black one. The boy took his black stick and the man then had to use the red stick. The man asked to be allowed to lay his hands on the black stick, and so he was given the black stick, expecting to do the same thing that was done to him. Then the boy said that the wheel had to be thrown a long way in the grass before pitching the sticks.

Then the big game began. When first pitching the sticks the wheel always had to be thrown in the grass and the black stick would never fail to find the wheel, because the stick really belonged there. Night or day, the black stick would find the wheel. When they first pitched the stick the man tried to break Half-a-Boy's stick, but failed. The boy won the first time, and won back one third of his body. Half-a-Boy had already announced that he wanted to double his bet at all times. He won right along, without allowing his opponent to win a single point. Half-a-Boy finally won everything that the people in his opponent's village had, until the people began to carry out everything that they had, for they were glad to see some one win things from the cruel man. Before noon, Half-a-Boy won everything that was in the village. This man whom he was playing with was a shadow, and his name was Shadow-of-the-Sun (Ihakaatskada). He began to cry out, "This is the first time I ever had any one who could play so well! I wonder where he got such powers!" He told the boy that he had won all that he had, but the boy told him to bet his people off; that there were a good many of his people yet. In doubling the bets it did not take him very long to win all the cruel man's people. When the boy had won all the people, Shadow-of-the-Sun told the boy that he had won everything that he had at the present time, and that he wanted to stop. But the boy told him that he had to bet his life, as he himself had done, and that he would bet his own life against the man's life, in one bet. Finally Shadow-of-the-Sun said that his rule in betting human beings was always to bet three bets. He also asked the boy if his life could be spared, and told him that if he would spare his life he could have the same powers that he had, and could be a great chief among his people. But the boy told him that he did not have any use for his powers, and that he did not have any people for him to be chief of. They commenced to play again, and the boy won the first third of Shadow-of-the-

Sun's body, then the second, then the third part of Shadow-of-the-Sun's body. When he pitched the last stick he jumped out of the way, and when the stick entered the wheel there arose two great, big Buffalo. who set after Shadow-of-the-Sun and hooked him until they tore him in pieces. Wherever there was left a large piece of his body it would still run, and the Buffalo would take after it again. The boy then requested the people to gather wood to burn the body. While the people were getting the wood these Buffalo left the village and went toward the north. Then, when the people gathered enough wood, they piled it up and began to burn the body of Shadow-of-the-Sun. Half-a-Boy also had the people gather all the human bones that were lying around about the village, and these they threw into the fire. As soon as the fire began to die down, Half-a-Boy began to poke the fire, and one at a time, the men who had been killed by Shadow-of-the-Sun jumped out of the fire. When the fire went out there was a great crowd of men around there who were saved by this poor boy, Half-a-Boy. Before burning Shadow-of-the-Sun's body, Half-a-Boy told him that he would have less powers if he should ever live again.

Half-a-Boy then ordered the people to go to their homes. The chief told the boy that he could be the head chief of his village. Half-a-Boy refused to become a chief. He told the people that he had done them some good, but that he could not any longer be with them, for he was going to the people who had saved his life. He told the people that they could see him when they found the Buffalo. Half-a-Boy then turned into a Blackbird and flew off toward the north, where the two Buffalo had gone.

29. YOUNG-BOY-CHIEF, WHO MARRIED A BUFFALO.*

Young-Boy-Chief (Waiksedia) lived in a large village which was divided into two parts; and each part was governed by a chief. The village extended east and west and there was a broad street or wide space which was the dividing line. In this street the young people played games. Young-Boy-Chief was the son of the chief of the north village. In the south village there was a chief who had a daughter. These two children, who belonged to chiefs' families, had never seen one another and did not know one another, because they did not participate in the games with the others. The only thing that the boy could do was to watch the other boys play, and in this way Young-Boy-Chief passed all his time. The daughter of the other chief remained

*Told by Man-who-harms-while-Jesting (Waco.)

always at home, and did not go to see the others play. Whenever Young-Boy-Chief had a place to himself to take his early morning and evening bath, he allowed no other person to go to this place. Once upon a time, this young man began to think of the daughter of the other chief, and he wondered what she looked like. He thought that by watching the young women he might see her, and that perhaps he might come to know her.

From another country came a young woman who took a notion to visit this village where the young man and young woman lived. This woman was Young-Buffalo-Woman (Tarnatskēhakia). When Young-Buffalo-Woman arrived at the village she turned into a young woman, and looked like any other young woman of the village, but still she was different from the women in this village. Before she entered the village she decided that she would get on the south side of the village and would perhaps stop with some people who lived near the outskirts of the village. She went on the east side of the two villages, and while on the way she found a piece of dry grass, similar to a white, soft feather. This she took along to use for some purpose, whenever she might need it. It was in the afternoon, when the young people were gathered around the play ground to play their games. Being new, and already famous, she had a stick to play the double-ball game with the other women. When she was on the way to the grounds she was overtaken by another woman, who asked her if she would join her and she told her that she would. The woman who asked her to join her found that she was dressed entirely different from any young woman she had ever known. Not only was she different in dress, but she was also tattooed on her face. This woman then thought that the other woman must be from some other place. They arrived at the grounds, and the woman who had come from a long way saw this Young-Boy-Chief sitting in front of his home. It was at this time that Young-Boy-Chief was on the lookout for the chief's daughter from the opposite village, and when he saw this woman he thought from the way she was dressed that she was the chief's daughter. The young woman dropped the piece of dry grass, and the wind, being from the south, began to roll it toward the young man. Several more of the young women from each side of the village began to come around to play, and this young woman looked strange to every one of the other women. She was asked toward which direction she wanted to play, east or west. So she said that she would for a while play toward the east. The double-ball game was commenced. The woman attracted everybody's attention, for she wore a finely painted buffalo robe. In the center of the robe was painted a fine design that no one had ever seen painted on a robe before. Soon the people found that she was always ahead of all the other women in the game, and that she played the game out before any one could catch up with her. While the game was going on among the young women, the young men played their shinny game, and other games, such as arrow games, etc. The dry grass that the young woman had turned loose had rolled up in between the legs of Young-Boy-Chief. Young-Boy-Chief would throw away the dry grass, but it would come around again and crawl up between his legs. Young-Boy-Chief was anxious to see the games end, so that he could see where this woman would go, so that he could follow her. But the dry grass kept crawling in between his legs, and he was worried about this. He took the dry grass and went into the lodge, where he lived, and placed it in the wall of the grass-lodge, over his bed, and then he lay down. He wished that this had not happened to him, for he was bothered by the dry grass, but he did not know this was connected with a plot of the woman to win his love.

After Young-Boy-Chief went into the lodge, discouraged, the sun going down, and the game ended, the woman went back by the way she had come, accompanied by the same woman who had come with her. She left this young woman where she had found her. She then went to the creek and took a bath. After her bath, she began to study where to go during her stay at the village. She went into the first tipi she came to, and there she was requested to be seated on the south side of the tipi. She noticed that there was but a man and a woman and child in there. She also noticed that they had no provisions, for they did not offer her anything to eat. She then told them that she wanted to stay with them for a while, and they told her that she could do so. It then happened that she went out to urinate, and she heard the man telling his wife that she was a stranger, and had come from a long way, perhaps, and that she was a famous woman. When the man had finished talking about her she went into the tipi again. Young-Buffalo-Woman asked the people if they wanted something to eat. They told her that they did, and she reached around with her right hand to her left side and brought out a kidney and a piece of corn bread. She told them to save the fat of it, and then she gave it to them to eat. They began to eat the kidney and bread. After getting enough they gave the fat to the woman again, and she put it back where she had taken the kidney from. She then reached around again, this time with her left hand to her right side, and took for herself the same things that she had given the others to eat. She began to eat, too, and when she had eaten all she wanted she put it back again, where she had taken her food from.

About this time, Young-Boy-Chief began to examine every lodge in the village, looking for this young woman, for he could not keep from going out to look for her. After having gone through the whole village, looking in the doors of every lodge, he thought the young woman had left the place. He thought that he would look into the last lodge, and see if he could find her. Young-Boy-Chief then peeped in, and there he saw this woman whom he was looking for. Young-Boy-Chief, without stopping, walked right in, and was asked why he had come, for he had never been seen around by night before. He told them that he had come around to see the woman who was living with them. He was then asked to be seated by the woman. Finally all retired, and Young-Boy-Chief and the young woman went to bed. They did not have a good bed to sleep on, but they had to get along the best they could. After they had gone to bed, Young-Boy-Chief asked the woman if she was not a chief's daughter, and she told him that she was a chief's daughter, from a strange country, and that she was just visiting the village. Young-Boy-Chief replied that he had made a mistake, and had taken her for the daughter of the chief of the south village. He said that he was going to live with her any way, and that night they began to live as man and wife. Early the next morning, before daylight, Young-Boy-Chief told his wife that he had to keep his marriage a secret, but whenever she had a child by him they could move to his home and live there all the time. Every day, during her stay in this village, she would go to play the double-ball game with the other women, and at this time every young man in the village was seeking her. But she would reject them all, for she already had a husband who was better than the other young men, for he belonged to a chief's family. When night came, Young-Boy-Chief would go to the place where she was staying, and every time the women began to play their game Young-Boy-Chief would sit outside of his lodge and watch his wife play, for he knew that he had the best wife of all. So they lived together for a long while, until she became pregnant. As soon as she told Young-Boy-Chief this he ceased to come to see her at night. After a time the child was born. She still lived in this same lodge, and supplied the people with food, and waited patiently for her man to return to see his child. The child got so that it could walk and talk. He began to ask who his father was, but his mother would not tell him who his father was, because she was waiting for him to come and see his child some time. But the child got so anxious to know who his father was that the woman undertook to go over to her husband's home.

When they arrived at Young-Boy-Chief's home they entered the grass-lodge, and there they saw a good many of the older men sitting around with Young-Boy-Chief. The men noticed that the child called him father. Young-Boy-Chief wanted to remain a boy, and so he called to the men to remove this woman and child. So they were thrust out of the place. The woman then took the child and packed him on her back. She started toward the north, whence she had come, and when they got out from the village they turned into what they were—Buffalo, the woman being a female and the child being a young Buffalo calf.

Young-Boy-Chief then decided to go after them, but they were already a long way ahead of him. He kept on, thinking that he could catch up with them. Late that evening the child came to his father and told him that he would have to keep on, for the woman was not going to stop unless they had to stop for a night's rest. Then the boy went on ahead of his father, and caught up with his mother. Late that day the woman stopped, to await her man. When they stopped, this woman got a kind of bush that the buffalo like to eat, and used it for firewood. She then asked her husband if he wanted something to eat. The man told her that he did want something to eat, for he had come from a long distance. He was given a piece of kidney and a piece of corn bread to eat, for his supper. He was then told what troubles he would have to endure when he arrived at the woman's home; that he would have to meet his wife's husbands; that she had four husbands, all of whom were brothers. She also told him that she had a sister, younger and prettier than herself, and that she was near; that she would try to get him and would offer herself to him for a wife, but he must not accept that offer, but keep it to himself; that upon their arrival he would see a large herd of Buffalo and that in the middle of the herd he would see dust flying, for her men knew of his marrying their wife; that on the morning after their first night he would be called to meet them all, for he was taking their wife away from them, and in order that he might keep this woman for himself he must be able to find his wife from the midst of all the female Buffalo; and again, if he should be able to tell his wife from the other female Buffalo, he would be required to find from among the male Buffalo his wife's uncle; that every time they should ask him such a question all these would be lined up, and all of them would look alike; and if he should be able to determine which one of the four was his wife's uncle, then the next thing that he would have to do would be to be able to tell them which one of the older Buffalo calves was his child. In so doing, when he should look for

his wife, she was to have a piece of dry grass stuck up in her nose, so
that he would be able to tell the difference between her and the others;
that when he came to find her uncle, the male Buffalo would be lined
up, and he would have to start from one end of the line, and he would
be able to distinguish him by a mark over his tail. In looking for his
father-in-law he was to examine closely the heads of the males, and the
one having a cockle burr under his ear was to be the one to be pointed
out. He was then told that his sister-in-law would come around and
try to persuade him not to mind his wife in going through so many ceremonies, telling him that he could marry her without doing so many
things; that he must not listen to his wife, but attend to his own business, for if he did as his wife directed he would be killed anyhow for
not going through these things. The next thing, when he should be
asked to find among the old female Buffalo, his mother-in-law, he was
told that upon making a close examination of their feet he would notice
a large piece of dry mud between the claws of his mother-in-law's
right hind foot. When he should be asked to look through all the
young calves, to find his child, he was to notice their eyes, for the
young calf would cast his eyes to the right, without looking right at
him, and in this way he would be able to tell his child from the other
young calves. These were the instructions given him by his wife during the night when stopping for the first night's rest. Early on the
next morning he was again given something to eat, and then they
started toward the north on their way to the woman's home. Of course,
the woman was to travel faster than the man could, because she and her
child had become Buffalo, and thus they could travel faster than the
man. But Young-Boy-Chief kept on traveling after he had fallen
behind them. They traveled all that day, and about noon the boy was
sent back to his father to ask him if he was hungry. He told his son
that he was, and then the young calf caught up with his mother and
told her that his father was hungry. The calf was given one kidney
and a piece of corn bread for Young-Boy-Chief to eat. Then the
young calf stopped and waited for his father to come along, and then
he gave him the food and again went on. While the man was on the
way he ate his dinner. He traveled the rest of the day, until late that
evening, when they again stopped for the night for rest. This time,
when they stopped, the woman used tall, rank mustard weed for the
fire. Young-Boy-Chief was told that on the afternoon of the following
day they would arrive at home; that his wife would go on and leave
him, and the boy and he were to follow on; that the boy was to tell
him where their home was, then to enter the place. The next day,

after eating breakfast, they again began to travel, and at noon the young calf was asked to stay back until his father should come along, then ask him again whether he was hungry. The calf stayed back, awaiting his father. When his father came along he asked him if he was hungry. His father told him that he was, and then the calf went on to catch up with his mother, to tell her that his father was hungry, and when he caught up with his mother and told her that his father was hungry, he was given the same things for the man to eat as before. Then he waited until his father came along, then gave to him the food for him to eat. But he would not stay with his father, but continued on after his mother. Young-Boy-Chief then went on, and while on the way, he ate his dinner. After he had eaten all he had, there came in sight a high hill, and the woman went over it. Then he saw his son stop to wait for him to come along. He traveled until he came to the high hill. The boy then told him that his mother's home was over the hill. As he looked at the summit of the hill he saw a great herd of Buffalo. After seeing the herd of Buffalo, without knowing what had happened to his eyes, this herd became a large village. In the middle of the village he saw a large tipi, and this the boy told him was his mother's home. So they went to his wife's lodge. On entering he saw his wife, her brothers, uncles, sisters, father, and mother. The woman was asked if that was her husband, and she said in reply that it was her man, and that he was a chief's son. They began to ask Young-Boy-Chief if he would not have their sister for a wife instead of the woman he had, for there was going to be trouble between him and some other men who were brothers. But Young-Boy-Chief did not pay any attention to this request, for he knew that he was coming out of these troubles without great difficulty. After Young-Boy-Chief had entered the lodge his father-in-law told him that he would be called early the next morning to the place where the four brothers were, for they were already informed of his arrival. On the following day and night he remained with his wife's parents, and it seemed to him like living with any other human beings.

On the next morning Young-Boy-Chief was notified that he was to go and meet his brothers and prove whether he could meet all their requirements. When he got to the place he saw great herds of female Buffalo, all of them about the same age. They were all lined up, and facing north. Young-Boy-Chief then began at the east end and looked for his wife. He was accompanied by the men, who were trying to cause him to make a mistake while trying to find his wife. They believed that on account of the great number of these female Buffalo that he could not fail to make a mistake in picking out his wife. As he went on he came to one he thought to be his wife. He called her out, and indeed it was his wife. Next, Young-Boy-Chief was asked to find his wife's uncles from amongst all the middle-aged Buffalo, and this he did. Now, Young-Boy-Chief had to point out his father-in-law, and this he did. Then he was asked to pick out from the old female Buffalo his mother-in-law. This, too, he succeeded in doing. Now, the last thing he was to accomplish was to find his own child from among all the other young calves. Of course, all the young calves were alike, except for a slight difference in age. So Young-Boy-Chief went along at the calves' heads, and examined them carefully, until he came to one that was casting its eyes to one side, and then he was able to point out his son. After Young-Boy-Chief had done all that was required of him, all the Buffalo began to move back to their homes. Thus Young-Boy-Chief had more fun while among these families of Buffalo than while among his own people, and for some reason, the people here were better looking than those of his own village, especially were they dressed better, and their tattooing was better. So Young-Boy-Chief liked his new home better than his old one. After he had got used to these people he went among the female Buffalo the same as any of the Buffalo that were of his age.

A long time after this, the chief of the Buffalo undertook to go and visit the other people, and to trade with them. Whenever the Buffalo went on this kind of a journey it meant that whenever the people should find the Buffalo these people would put on their best dress when they should go to killing off the Buffalo. After killing the Buffalo, sometimes the people used to take nothing but the meat, leaving the hide on it, which signified that the Buffalo were to live again, if only their flesh was taken. And on the other hand, the best dresses that were worn by the people became the property of the Buffalo. The Buffalo made the visit to Young-Boy-Chief's home, but Young-Boy-Chief caused it to be understood that since living with the Buffalo he had to do as the Buffalo did. So when the Buffalo made their appearance to the people they were killed. But when killed this Young-Boy-Chief knew that he was to live again, and that he was always to stay with his wife's people. At this time he had a great many children by this Buffalo wife. So he always lived with the Buffalo after this, instead of going back to his people. Since this it has been known that whenever the Buffalo come to the people, their object in presenting themselves is to show their desire to trade.

30. THE SWIFT-HAWKS AND SHADOW-OF-THE-SUN.*

Once upon a time there was a village which was divided by a street running through its center from north to south. Each part of the village was ruled over by a chief. The chief who ruled the west part of the village was a good man. The chief who ruled the east side was a bad man. One time a boy, who lived with his father, mother, and three younger brothers in another place, decided that he would make a visit to this village. He took all of his bows, arrows, and other weapons, and started on his journey. On the evening of the fourth day after he had left his home, he came to the village. He stopped outside the village upon a high place, from where he could look down into the village. He noticed that the bad chief's part of the village was more lively than the other part. After viewing it all, he started to go down. Before reaching the village he came to a person standing and facing him. He kindly asked this person where he might find a good place to sleep all night. The person told him to go to the highest tipi that he had seen; so he went on to the place, as he was told.

On entering, he was requested to go to a bed in the west end of the tipi. In these times the people had tipis made out of buffalo hides, grass-lodges, and earth-lodges. The boy was requested to pass on to the west end of the tipi, because the tipis generally faced toward the east, and at the entrance there were always two beds, one on the south side and the other on the north side, one or two more at the southwest part of the tipi, and another at the northwest. When the boy entered, he passed on to the bed on the northwest side and sat down. This was the chief's place, and the chief told the boy that it was a rather bad place for visitors. On making his appearance, the boy found that word had already been sent to the other chief. These two chiefs each had a servant. The chief said to the boy that he thought some one had already notified the other chief of his arrival. The boy was told that early the next morning he would be called to enter a foot-race. They finally went to bed and slept until the boy was called by the other chief to the foot-race. The chief himself was Shadow-of-the-Sun (Ihakaatskada), and had a dark complexion. When the boy was called he and the other chief both went out to the nearest bathing place and took an early morning bath. Then they went on to the scene of the foot-race. Great crowds of people were present to watch the foot-race, and they saw that the young man was fine-looking. The young man and the chief came to the place where they were to start from. The foot-race began, both chiefs running first. Shadow-of-the-Sun outran the other chief.

*Told by Ahahe (Waco.)

Then the Coyote (Ketox), who was a racer, finally gave out, and then the young man raced. They then went for a long way, then disappeared, and then again they went for a long way, and finally came to a place where Shadow-of-the-Sun did his hardest racing, and here was a deep canyon. Shadow-of-the-Sun, of course, was used to this place, and when he came to it, passed it safely, but the young man could not pass it, and so was beaten. Shadow-of-the-Sun took his club and killed the young man. The reason why one side of the village seemed to the young man to be more lively than the other was that whenever Shadow-of-the-Sun had won in a foot-race, and had killed his opponent, he would carry off a lot of the other chief's people, and this would make the village more lively. Whenever there was a foot-race and Shadow-of-the-Sun came out the winner, the other chief would offer his life to Shadow-of-the-Sun for those of his people, but Shadow-of-the-Sun would refuse, and would say that if it had not been for him (the other chief) there would not have been any fun. Shadow-of-the-Sun won many foot-races, and killed many defeated opponents.

Now, another of the four brothers put on all his weapons and set out to make a visit. He traveled four days. On arriving at the high point by the village of the two chiefs he looked all over the village, and it was late in the evening. He went down toward the village and met some one, asking him where he might find a place to stay all night, and he was told to go to the place where he had seen the highest tipi. He went to the place, and on entering, was requested to pass on to the bed at the northwest part of the tipi. While passing, the chief remembered the young man's brother, and thought this must be the same man who had been killed, for the young man resembled his dead brother very much, though he was much younger. The chief told the young man the same thing that he had told visitors who came to his tipi; that there was danger at his place, and any one visiting him was not safe; for there was always some one looking out for such men as he. The chief supposed that some one had already sent word to Shadow-of-the-Sun that some one was visiting him, and so after giving the young man his supper he told him what were the troubles he would have to meet. He said that he wished he himself might be killed, instead of having to see his visitors killed. Early the next morning the young man was called to a foot-race. He, the chief, and the Coyote, all started to the nearest bathing place for their early morning bath. Now, they all went north, in the direction they saw the people going. They finally reached the place where the foot-race generally started. The chief and Shadow-of-the-Sun raced first, then the Coyote, then the young man. After Shadow-of-the-Sun and the young man had run a long way the young man gave out a little, and slowed up a little to get breath. Then he made another dash to win, but failed to outrun Shadow-of-the-Sun. When they got to the deep canyon where Shadow-of-the-Sun generally did the hardest racing, the young man failed to pass it. Shadow-of-the-Sun killed the young man. In this way he killed many who came to visit their village. The other chief would offer his own life in place of the visitors, but Shadow-of-the-Sun would never accept it. He would say: "That is where I get all my fun. If it were not for you I would never get any fun." Thus through his visitor's losing of the race the other chief would lose many of his people.

Another of the four brothers now started out to visit the village of the two chiefs, stopping at the same places his brothers had stopped. Four days he traveled, and he came to the high point by the village of the two chiefs, where he stopped for a while, and saw all kinds of games played by the young men and the young women. Late in the evening he went down toward the village, and met somebody there. When he met the man he asked him to tell him where he might stop over night. He was requested to go to the highest tipi that he had seen. When he entered the tipi the chief thought that he was the identical person who had once been killed. The chief requested him to pass on to the bed in the northwest part of the tipi. The young man sat down, noticing that the chief looked as though he felt sad, and he wondered what troubled him. The chief raised his head and said to the young man: "There is some one in the next village that always takes the life of my visitors, and you are in danger, for there is always some one spying around to carry back news of some visitor's arrival to Shadow-of-the-Sun. To-morrow morning you will be called upon to run a foot-race." He, the chief, and the Coyote, went to the water to take their early morning bath before the race; then they went on their way to the starting place. The foot-race began, the chief running first, and giving out; then the Coyote; then the young man raced with Shadow-of-the Sun. They ran a way, then slowed up, and the young man came out behind. They ran again till they came to the deep canyon, and the young man could not go over it. So Shadow-of-the-Sun turned around and killed the young man with his club. When the chief arrived, knowing that he was to lose some of his people, he offered his life to Shadow-of-the-Sun, but he would not accept the offer.

At the home of the four brothers there was now only one left, and this last one set out to look for his brothers. He traveled all day, and at dark came to a place where there had been a fire, and grass fixed like a bed. He had come to the place where his other brothers had stopped for a night's rest. He started again the next day, and traveled until night, when he came to another camping place. Every time he stopped he found traces of a camp. He traveled until he came to the place where strangers stopped. Here he stayed until later in the evening, then went down toward the village and met some one, and asked him where he might go for a night's lodging, and was told to go to the highest tipi he had seen. On entering this place the chief told the young man to pass on to the bed in the northwest of the tipi. The chief always felt sad to see any one coming to visit him, knowing that they would have to be killed. The chief told the young man that his place was dangerous to visit, for there were some that always were ready to kill any one who visited him, and there was no way to escape, once having arrived at this place; that early in the morning he would be called to a race, for Shadow-of-the-Sun always had spies to bring him news when there was a visitor present in the village. They went to bed, and early next morning the young man heard some hooting and yelling, and some one saying that he had heard of some one visiting, and that he was to come and have a foot-race before living in the village. The young man, the chief, and the Coyote went to the nearest bathing place and took their morning bath, then went to the foot-race. Shadow-of-the-Sun always started first to a certain place he had to start from. Crowds of men came and stood by to see the race. Shadow-of-the-Sun raced with the chief first, then with the Coyote, and finally with the young man. Shadow-of-the-Sun, in making the course, had fixed it over a deep canyon, so then it would be impossible for any one but himself to get over it. When it came the turn of the young man to race, they came to this place, and Shadow-of-the-Sun said to the young man: "This is the place where I always do my hardest racing." When they came to the canyon the young man failed to get over it, and was beaten and killed by Shadow-of-the-Sun. The other chief offered his life to Shadow-of-the-Sun, but he refused it, and after the race, carried off a lot of the chief's people.

Now, the father of the four boys had it in mind to visit the village of the two chiefs. He said to his wife: "My boys may think they are old enough to do what I can do, but they certainly are mistaken." Already the old man knew what had happened to his boys; so before starting, he asked his wife to get him a shell. He then took some water and some white clay and colored the water, making it white. He commanded his wife to look at this once in a while during his absence, and if the water in some part of the shell should turn into blood it would indicate that he was dead, and that she should leave the place; if it did not turn to blood, it would be a sign that he was still alive. He then set out, and traveled four days, just as his boys had traveled. At the end of the fourth day's traveling he came to the village of the two chiefs, and stopped at the point where strangers always stopped. He waited here until late in the evening, then went toward the village, and met a man whom he asked to direct him to the place where strangers generally stopped. He was told to go to the highest tipi he had seen, as there a chief was living. When he came to the place he entered, and was asked to pass on to the same place where visitors always were seated. The chief felt sad at seeing his visitor, for he knew that he would have to meet danger, and so he told the father that he would be called upon early next morning to run a foot-race. The man rested that night, looking for danger. Next morning the father was called by Shadow-of-the-Sun, who said that it had come to his mind that some one had arrived at the village. The father got up, and accompanied by the chief, and the Coyote, went to the creek for a bath before going to the race. The old man dived into the water, and when he came up, he had changed to a young man, and looked just exactly like the four young men who had been killed. They started to the scene of the foot-race. As soon as they got there the race began. The chief raced first, then the Coyote, and then the old man. The old man started the race with Shadow-of-the-Sun, getting on the right side of him, then on the left, and so on. He finally got up on his right shoulder, and the cruel chief saw that the man was giving him a close race. Then the man got down on the ground and climbed on Shadow-of-the-Sun's left shoulder. As the chief saw the father he would run harder, expecting to leave him behind. When they came to the place where Shadow-of-the-Sun always did his hardest racing he said to the old man: "This is the place where I do my best racing." The old man being on his shoulder, kicked him on the breast and in the back, and then went on and left him behind.

During this race the old man had his bow and arrows with him, and when he had won the race with Shadow-of-the-Sun, he took his bow-string off his bow, taking it with his right hand and pulling it through his left hand four times, then hitting the cruel chief and killing him with the string. He then got the people to bring wood to burn up the body. They brought wood and piled it up on the ground and placed the body on the wood and burnt it. While the chief was burning, the old man called his boys to come out, for their tipi was

burning. Finally, one at a time, they jumped out, until they were all
out. Men after men were jumping out of the fire. These were the
men whom Shadow-of-the-Sun had destroyed. After the burning was
done they all went to the chief's place and stayed one night before they
went back home. Next day the old man and his boys disappeared from
this place. They went back home to the old woman, who, not seeing
any blood in the shell of water, expected her man to return to her alive.
After they reached home the old man insisted that his family should
leave the place, because the same thing that had happened might happen
again. So they left the place, which now turned into a timbered
country, and they flew around and became Swift-Hawks (Gusseiŏs).

31. THE SWIFT-HAWKS AND SHADOW-OF-THE-SUN.*

Once upon a time there lived a man, his wife, and his three sons.
The oldest son was named Small-Hawk (Garseyasikits) ; the name of
the second was Striped-Tail-Hawk; and the name of the third was
Tears-in-the-Eyes (Wetskidikheya), Swallow-Hawk, which name he
bore because of the black streaks about his eyes. They, by themselves,
lived away from the village. The oldest boy went to visit the north part
of the village. He took with him his weapons—his shield, quiver with
bow and arrows, and all the things that he could carry. Having
traveled four long days he arrived at the edge of the village, late in
the evening. He waited at a high point at the south of the village.
He saw that many games were being played by the people living near
the village, such as shinny, the double-ball game, etc. When he arrived
he met a certain person of whom he asked where visitors were entertained. The person directed him to a certain place in the middle of
the village, where a large tipi was to be seen, and there he would find
accommodation, for the tipi was that of the chief. He went as directed.
When he reached the tipi he entered. He was told to go to the bed on
the northwest side. When he sat down on the bed he noticed that the
chief was grieving. After he had sat a while the chief rested his head
and commenced to talk to the boy. He said: "There is only one bad
thing about this place. You will be called early in the morning, for
in the south side of the village live evil-spirited people, and the chief
of these people, whose name is Shadow-of-the-Sun (Ihakaatskada),
will challenge you to a foot-race. As soon as you came in, perhaps,

*Told by Towakoni Jim (Towakoni).

some one from his village came to spy on you." After telling him these things the young man was given something to eat. The men in the tipi sat up until about midnight, then retired to their homes.

Early the next morning the chief of the village of the evil spirited men called the young man to a foot-race, with a loud voice, telling him that he had heard of his arrival, and that no one ever came to the village without being challenged by him. It was the custom that after a person had been challenged by Shadow-of-the-Sun the one who was challenged would always go to the nearest flowing water and take a bath, to prepare for the race. After the boy had gone down to the water, and had taken his bath, and was ready to go and race, the chief he was visiting was ready to go with him. The people from both sides of the village crowded around the ground when the young man and the chiefs arrived. They started to the west, away from the village. As they went along the young man saw that he was to have a close race, for he knew that Shadow-of-the-Sun was a fast runner. Finally they came to a place where the race was to commence. It was the custom of the chief to accompany, as far as he could go, the visitor in the race. Now began the race with Shadow-of-the-Sun. The boy raced with the chief until the chief gave out; then he began to race with Shadow-of-the-Sun. The boy's custom when racing was, first to get on the right side of his opponent, then, after giving out on that side he would get on his left side, and so on. Then, should he be beaten, he was to forfeit his life. This is how Shadow-of-the-Sun overcame his victims. They were going very fast toward the village. When they were near the village the boy gave out. Then Shadow-of-the-Sun took his club and struck him on the head. Whenever the visited chief's visitors lost a race this chief would lose some of his people, which he forfeited to Shadow-of-the-Sun. After the boy had been clubbed the good chief would offer his life to Shadow-of-the-Sun, because so many men had lost they lives through paying him a visit. But Shadow-of-the-Sun would refuse to take his life, saying it was through his visitors that he got all his fun. The trouble was always started by the evil spirited people.

At the boy's home, his parents were wondering what had become of him, and no one but his father knew, and he was disposed to let his boys go wherever they pleased. So at another time the second boy resolved to go and look for his brother. He told his mother to prepare some corn meal for him, that he might have it to eat on his journey to the village where his brother had gone. Four days he journeyed, and on the evening of the fourth day he arrived at the edge of the village. He sat down at the same place where his brother had sat, watching the people playing their games and amusing themselves. After the sun had gone down he went toward the village. As he entered he saw a certain person of whom he inquired where visitors were accommodated. The person told him to go to the middle of the village, to the largest tipi, and there he would find the chief, who always received visitors. The boy went on toward the chief's tipi. When he got there he entered. He saw a crowd of men about the chief's place. He was told to pass on to the bed on the northwest. As he passed on he noticed some things that looked familiar to him. He recognized that they had belonged to his brother. He hung his own things in the same place. He was told that Shadow-of-the-Sun might call for him the next morning to have a foot-race with him. The men in the tipi noticed that this young man looked just like the man who had recently visited him. They thought that he was the same man, but that he was much younger. Having been told these things the boy was given something to eat. He sat up a part of the night talking with some of the men who were visiting the chief. Finally all the men went to their homes. The boy now rested, for he had come a long way. The next morning when he woke he heard some one calling him to come to a race. He went to the flowing water, took his early morning bath and went back to the chief's tipi. The two chiefs went with him to the race course. When they got there they started off toward the west, and went about the same distance as the boy's brother had gone, and there they started the race. The good chief started. When he gave out the young man continued the race. He was defeated, as his brother had been, having made a great effort four different times and having failed to win the race. Now his life was taken. When the good chief had arrived he saw that the evil-spirited people had carried off some of his people. So he felt sad that the young man had lost his life through paying him a visit.

Again the parents of this boy at his home were wondering what had become of him, whether he was alive or dead. Soon after, the youngest of the three brothers decided to go out in search of his two brothers. He asked his mother to make him a pair of moccasins and prepare some corn meal to take with him. When these things were ready he set out. He journeyed four days, until he came to the village his brothers had visited. In the evening he sat down at the same place where his brothers had rested. He watched the people playing in the village. He asked a certain person, after the sun had gone down, where visitors were received. He was told to go to the middle of

the village, to the largest tipi that he should see. There he went.
When he reached the tipi he entered. He was told to go to the bed on
the northwest side. When he sat down he noticed many men gathered
around the chief's tipi. The chief commenced to tell him what he would
have to do; that the next morning some one from the evil spirited men's
village would call out with a whoop for him to come to a foot-race.
Now he was given something to eat. The chief's visitors, having sat
up talking until late at night, now left, and the boy went to bed. The
next morning he heard some one shouting for him, telling him to come
to the foot-race. He got up, went to the flowing water and took his
early morning bath, then returned to the chief's tipi. He then set out
with the chiefs to the course. They went the same distance from the
village as his brothers had gone with the chiefs. Now they started for
the race. The good chief was beaten. Shadow-of-the-Sun was next to
race with the boy. The boy would race a part of the way on the chief's
right side, and as soon as he saw that he was not gaining he would
go on his left side, then on his right and again on his left. Finally
he was beaten by Shadow-of-the-Sun, who then killed him. The good
chief's part of the village was again in trouble. The visited chief
grieved over the loss of his people, for some of his people were always
killed when his visitor lost the race. Then the visited chief would beg
the evil spirited chief to take his life instead, but he would say that it
was better to save him, for he was always having visitors.

Now, at the boys' home there was left the father and mother. The
old man knew that something had happened to his children. He resolved to go in search of his boys. He took a small wooden bowl in
which he put water. He then colored the water with white clay. He
told his wife to watch the bowl during his absence, and that if anything should happen to him, and he should be killed, she would see
blood in the water, which would be a sign that he was dead, but if
the water remained clear it would indicate that he was still alive.
After doing this he had his wife make a pair of moccasins and prepare some corn meal to take along for his food. He started out. He
traveled the entire day. Late in the evening he came to a fireplace.
Here he knew each of his boys had stayed over night. He took his bow
and arrow and shot toward the timber. He shot a deer for his food.
Now he had some meat to eat. The next morning he started out again
and traveled all day, until late in the evening, when he found another
fireplace where each of his boys had stayed for a night's rest. He knew
his boys had stayed there over night. Again he took his bow and arrow
and shot toward the timber and killed a deer. Now he had something

to eat. The next morning he started out and traveled all day until late in the evening, when he again found a fireplace where each of his boys had stopped over night. He knew his boys had stayed here over night. He took his bow and arrow and shot toward the timber and killed another deer, which he had for his meat. On the fourth day he started again, and traveled all day until he arrived at a high hill at the edge of the village. Here visitors were always expected to stop before entering the village. He noticed the young folks playing all sorts of games in the village. Later on, he went down toward the village and noticed a certain man of whom he asked where visitors were accommodated. He was told to go to the middle of the village, to the highest tipi he could see. There he went. When he found the place he entered the tipi, and was told to go to the northwest bed, which was for visitors. The chief saw that this was an old man that had come to visit him. He told him that there was one thing that always happened to his visitors; that there was a certain man, Shadow-of-the-Sun, who was always watching for his visitors, and that, perhaps, some one had already noticed his arrival, so as to carry the news back to him. As he hung up his weapons the old man noticed the weapons and things of his boys hanging up beside his bed. Now, he began to think that there was danger in the village, and that his boys had probably been killed, but he always had considered that he had as great powers as anybody else. He was given something to eat. The rest of the night he sat up with the men talking about things of the past. After midnight all the visitors returned to their homes. The old man went to bed and to sleep, for he had traveled a long way from home. On the next morning he was called to race. He went down to the flowing water, jumped in, and when he came out of the water he was changed to a young man, and he returned to the chief's tipi. Now the chief went with him to the race course, and the old man and the two chiefs went the same distance from the village as the boys had gone, to start, but when they had reached the starting place the old man refused to start the race at this point, for he said he had never raced from a place so close to the village. It was the custom to go out a distance from the village and race back. Shadow-of-the-Sun gave a whoop, and said it would be the first time he had ever had a hard race. Again they went on, till they had doubled the distance, and the evil spirited chief said this was another starting place, but the old man refused to stop. Shadow-of-the-Sun gave another whoop, and said he was going to have a hard race. Again they went a distance equal to the last, where Shadow-of-the-Sun said there was another starting place, but the old man refused to stop. Shadow-of-the-Sun gave a whoop and they went on, measuring off a fourth equal distance. Here they started the race. The visited chief started the first part of the race. He fell behind. Then the old man commenced to race with Shadow-of-the-Sun. As they went along Shadow-of-the-Sun saw that he was having a pretty close race, for the old man was with him all the way down, until the old man slacked up and went on his left. Again they had another race, and they were even all the time. Now the old man went around the chief again on his right side. Then he went back to his left. At the fifth time the old man turned into a Swift-Hawk (Gusseios), and lighted on the back of Shadow-of-the-Sun's shoulder. The chief would now turn his head to see where the old man was, but he was even with him all the time, but the old man said: "Go on! Go on! You have been looking for a hard race." He kept patting the chief on the back. Finally they saw the village. Shadow-of-the-Sun was still doing the racing, not knowing that the old man was on his shoulder. Before entering the village the old man kicked the chief on the breast, so that the old man entered the village first. Thus Shadow-of-the-Sun lost the race. The old man rested. Shadow-of-the-Sun came up to him and begged him to spare his life. He offered the old man his powers, but the old man refused to have any such powers as he had, for he knew that he was the man that had killed off his boys. He knew that many people had lost their lives by him. Finally the good chief arrived, and he was happy, for the old man had won the race. He knew that Shadow-of-the-Sun would have to die, and with him all of his people. The old man then rested for a long time, but Shadow-of-the-Sun kept begging him to spare his life. The old man refused, and everybody thought he ought to refuse, on account of the way Shadow-of-the-Sun had treated every one. Since he could not get anything out of the old man he went up into the sky, saying to the old man: "If you are going to kill me I shall go somewhere else, where I shall be safe." As he started to go up in the sky, the people thought the old man should hasten to kill Shadow-of-the-Sun. Finally, the old man got up on his feet, and asked the people where Shadow-of-the-Sun stayed when he went up in the sky. The place was shown him wherein he stood. Now his bow and arrows were brought to him. He shot up toward the sky and told the people to watch for results. So they watched for Shadow-of-the-Sun to come down. Finally they saw something coming down in the shape of a shadow. It came down and fell to the ground. The old man had shot him behind.

Now, the old man commanded all the good chief's people to bring all the wood they could find, and all the human bones they could find, skulls and small bones. When they had done this they placed the body of Shadow-of-the-Sun on the pile of wood with all the other bones. When they had placed all the bones upon the wood they started the fire. When the wood began to burn and to settle down, they stirred it up to make it burn better. Now, they called those who had been killed by Shadow-of-the-Sun, and as they called them they jumped out of the fire, one after another. When the fire went down, there was a lot of men. After this was done the old man returned to the chief's place, having destroyed the evil spirited people.

On the next day the people in the village were called together at the chief's place. When they had gathered around his place they asked the chief why he had called them there. The old chief told of the good things the old man had done for them; what hard times they had had while living with the evil spirited people, and said they had better not exist any longer as human beings, for they had had hard enough times; that by and by, by turning to other beings they might enjoy better times; that those who wished to live as human beings could do so. After this was announced the people began to return to their places, some going out and flying away from the village, some going into the timber and some into the prairies. The good chief became an Eagle (Kos).

After the people had moved away the old father took his boys back home. While they were gone the woman had known that the old man was still alive, for she had seen no sign of any blood, the sign for death, in the bowl of white mixture. So they lived for a good while. The old man thought perhaps some other evil things might befall him, the same as had happened to his boys. He thought they had better become something else, so they turned into Swift-Hawks (Gusseiōs).

32. YOUNG-BOY-CHIEF AND HIS SISTER.*

Young-Boy-Chief (Waiksedia) and his sister were living by themselves, and they had a dog which they called Little-Dog (Kiithar). Young-Boy-Chief was a great hunter. He hunted deer mostly. He had a bow and four arrows. Two of the arrows were painted red, and the other two were painted black. These weapons he used for hunting. They had plenty of dried and fresh meats. Once on a time, early in the morning, as Young-Boy-Chief's sister went to a creek, near by their place, to bring water, she saw a Deer sitting down. She turned toward their place and called Young-Boy-Chief to come out and shoot the Deer, but Young-Boy-Chief did not come. She called

*Told by Careful-Doer (Woman) (Wichita).

him four times before he came, and while he was getting ready she went to one side, got water and took it to their home. When Young-Boy-Chief went he shot at the Deer, but his arrow came off and broke to pieces. He shot again, and again, and again, until he had used up all his arrows, and all his arrows were broken to pieces. Then the Deer raised itself, and Young-Boy-Chief stood right still, not moving a step. So the Deer tossed him upon its antlers and carried him off. This was the beginning of Young-Boy-Chief's troubles. This deer was Big-Hail-Deer (Taahaitschidl).

After Big-Hail-Deer had carried off Young-Boy-Chief, Young-Boy-Chief's sister came to where Big-Hail-Deer had been, to find out why her brother had not come home. When she arrived at the place, she saw the broken arrows, gathered them up, and carried them home. After a long while she resolved to look for her brother. She and Little-Dog were alone at home. She mourned for her brother when she came to find out that it was Big-Hail-Deer that had been shot at by Young-Boy-Chief, and that he had carried him off. She resolved finally to go and look for her brother. She commenced to grind some parched corn into meal, enough to last until her return. As she started, she told Little-Dog to remain at home, saying perhaps she would be gone for a good while, but that she might return in a little while. She also told him to get lots of meat for her to eat. She left her gourd full of water for Little-Dog to drink when he should get thirsty. Thus she got ready to look for her brother.

While on the journey she would sing, then weep, and these were the words of her song:

Ki-di-wa-a-ta-ka-ki-da-e-da-ka
Ki-di-wa-a-ta-ka-ki-da-e-da-ka
Si-sa-aits-te-e-da-ta-ti-a-kak-wi-duk
Si-sa-aits-te-e-da-ta-ti-a-kak-wi-duk
A-quava-ta-haits-si-a-ki-a-kia.

It was my mistake in the first place!
It was my mistake in the first place,
        to call the boy to shoot the deer.
It was not the Deer; it was the Elk.

As she continued her journey she would sing again, then weep.

Finally she came to a place where some one was standing on top of a hill. When the person saw her he commenced to talk to her, using cross language to her and making as if he were going to keep her from passing the place. He said that he did not allow any one to come around his place. On her arrival where this man was she poured out some corn meal that she had brought along with her. When she had given him this, the man commenced to tell her about her brother's being taken by there some time before; that it was certainly a dangerous animal that had him; that he did not know for a certainty whether Young-Boy-Chief was still alive or not, but by going to the next place she would find another man who had still greater powers than he had. This first man that she had met was the Mountain-Lion (Wokis), a heavy set man, looking pretty strong.

She continued her journey, for she was told to make haste about getting to this place. Of course, like other women of those times, she had a double-ball and a stick to travel on. She traveled with this double-ball and stick, and would once in a while sing, then weep, using the same words as before. She finally came to another man standing on the top of a hill. When he saw the woman coming he did as the first man she had met did, using abusive language to her, but she kept going, and instead of looking at him she kept her head down. When she went near to him he tried to force her to turn back, but she had made up her mind not to be afraid of anything while she was on the way in search of her brother. When she came to this man she again poured out some of her meal. The man finally spoke to her in the most kind words a man could use, saying: "Oh, this is the woman that is in search of her brother." He told her that her brother had been carried there when first attacked; that she must remember that this animal that had her brother was dangerous to attack. He then told her to go on to the next man for further information, for the next man had greater powers than he had. This man was Headless-Man (Chearp-peschaux).

She continued her journey, doing the same thing she had done before, using her double-ball and the stick to travel on, and once in a while singing the song she had sung before, then weeping. Drawing near to the next man, she saw that he was like the other men she had met. He did not allow any one to come where he was, and tried to force her to turn back, but she was brave and kept her head down, instead of looking at him, and when she got near to him she poured out some meal for him. The man became good-humored and asked her if she was the woman in search of her brother. The woman said that she was. The man told her that he heard her brother sing when he was first attacked, but they hardly ever heard him since, so that he must be nearly dead, for Big-Hail-Deer had hardly ever had time to stop, unless it was for water. This man that she was talking to was Bear-having-great-Powers (Widadadiakisda). He told her to go to the next man, who had greater powers than he had, and she would get aid from him; that on reaching his place she would see a little boy playing around outside; that she must take the boy and pack him on her back, then walk in; that this was the child the father thought most of; that in doing this she must beg the old man to help her get her brother away from Big-Hail-Deer; that this man would not agree to get her brother for her for a good while, but she must keep telling him to do it for her until he began to help her; and she must give the corn meal to this child.

She again started on her way, doing the same as usual, singing, then weeping, and using the double-ball and stick to travel with. She came to a small hill, where this man lived in a sort of dug-out, and there she saw a little boy standing outside, playing. She went right straight to where the child was, took him in her arms, then put him on her back, and walked into the lodge that was under the hill. Without saying a word she sat down by the fireplace, then put the young child on her lap and gave the child the corn meal she had. Then she told the old man, whose name was Old-Scabby-Bull, that she wanted to get aid from him to recover her brother, Young-Boy-Chief; but the old man would not say a word to the woman. She kept on asking him to do this for her, until he agreed to do it. He told her that it was a hard matter to attack Big-Hail-Deer; that when they should attack it she must not weep at sight of her brother, though he was a sad spectacle; that if she should weep both himself and she would have to die. The attack was put off until the next day. He told her that she would hear the noise when Big-Hail-Deer should come.

That day Big-Hail-Deer came, and she saw him with her own eyes, and heard him coming. When he came there was something like a fire or a storm, and she heard her brother singing:

> "Ja-a-he-schats-as-ta-ki-di-a.
> Ja-a-he-schats-as-ta-ki-di-a.
> Tcas-ta-ki-tsi-d'-waika-i-ta-ti-a.
> Na-ki-di-wa, Na-ki-di-wa."
>
> The Elk is carrying me on his antlers.
> The Elk is carrying me on his antlers.
> I am still living.
> I am still living.

Then he moaned, for he was nearly dead, not having had anything to eat since he had been captured. He was getting poorer every day. Having put off the attack till the next day, the old man had made a small bow and one arrow. The woman stayed all night at his place, and she did all the work that had to be done, for she was anxious to get aid from the old man. Early the next day the old man told her to go with him and meet Big-Hail-Deer. They started. The old man told the woman to get the best hiding place she could find, and that she must keep herself hid there; that he himself was going to find a hiding place. So the old man now turned himself into a Snowbird (Natchkiwisdal), having the bow and small arrow with him. Finally, Big-Hail-Deer came. The wind began to blow while he was running, and when he came near he began to slow up, as if he had found out something. As Big-Hail-Deer approached, the old man hid himself behind a small bunch of grass, which was near the road. While passing, the old man shot him between the fork of the front feet, and down went Big-Hail-Deer. They at once jumped up, and the old man took his bow-string from off his bow and, passing it through his left hand four times, clubbed Big-Hail-Deer with it. The old man then helped Young-Boy-Chief off his antlers, and at once commenced to get wood to pile up over Big-Hail-Deer. He set it on fire and left it burning. Just as soon as they had left they could hear something exploding, making a noise like thunder, but they continued to this man's home. When they came to a creek the old man made Young-Boy-Chief dive in the water, then called him four times, saying: "Young-Boy-Chief, come out of the water! Your sister is here after you." Young-Boy-Chief finally came out of the water, and they saw him with his four arrows and bow. They went on to the man's home, and when they arrived Young-Boy-Chief remained with the people for a while. Young-Boy-Chief began to hunt for the people until they were furnished with much meat. Then the old man told him and his sister that they could go on to their home, for he had received all the meat he wanted from Young-Boy-Chief in return for the kindness he had done the woman.

On their return they traveled fast, the young woman using the double-ball and the stick to travel on, and Young-Boy-Chief using his arrows to travel with. They passed the other men that the woman had passed before, saying to them that she had recovered her brother. Now they came to a group of Turkeys (Naa), that were dancing and laughing. Young-Boy-Chief asked them what was making them so happy. The turkeys said they were happy to know that their enemy, Young-Boy-Chief, was dead. Young-Boy-Chief took a handful of ashes and threw them on their heads, and made their heads the color of ashes, commanding that they should always be that way. He told them that he himself was Young-Boy-Chief. Again they started on their way to their home, and they finally came to a woman up in a tree crying. Young-Boy-Chief asked the woman what she was crying about. She said that when Young-Boy-Chief was living she had had all she wanted to eat. Young-Boy-Chief replied to her, saying he was Young-Boy-Chief. He commanded the tree to bear fruit (wild grapes). This woman was Red-Bird (Itschidisaskatsa). As they commenced to journey again they traveled as fast as usual, until they came to a bunch of Deer. Young-Boy-Chief asked the Deer what was making them so happy. They answered that they were glad to hear of Young-Boy-Chief's death. Young-Boy-Chief made every one of them stand still, and he pulled their ears out long, then scared them and made their eyes open wide. He then commanded that they should always be that way, and in the next generation they were always to be killed for meat. Then again they journeyed. Finally they ran across another man by a tree. They noticed this man was weeping. Young-Boy-Chief asked why he was weeping. He replied that he could not help but weep, for Young-Boy-Chief had died; that when Young-Boy-Chief was living he could get all he wanted to eat. Young-Boy-Chief told this man he had been rescued, and was again living, and was on the way to his home. Then the man, wiping his tears away, walked up toward Young-Boy-Chief and hugged him, for he was the man who had always supplied him with food. Young-Boy-Chief commanded the tree to bear fruit, and there was the tree bearing fruit (persimmons). This man was the Opossum (Kadaiok). The Opossum then climbed the tree and had all he wanted to eat. Again they journeyed until they reached home. The weeds had grown up around their place. When they entered their grass-lodge they saw no sign of Little-Dog. Little-Dog had starved to death, and all there was left of him was a pile of hair. This young woman took the hair and bones, went to the creek, and threw them in the water. Then she called Little-Dog, saying she had brought their brother home; that he should come out of the water. So Little-Dog came out of the water, happy as he could be. They, of course, had plenty of meat. Little-Dog had never eaten any meat nor drank any water. Young-Boy-Chief and his sister lived in their home together again. Young-Boy-Chief hunted the same as he used to do, and they had all the meat they wanted. Young-Boy-Chief now told his sister, that since he had had so much trouble, and she had had a hard time to get him, and since he feared something else would occur to him, he wanted to be something else. They told Little-Dog to remain at home, and that in the next generation he (Little-Dog) would still exist among people as he was when living with them. So they got a gourd full of water, poured it into the fire, and went up with the smoke in the air, and became Eagles (Kos). Their dwelling place turned into grapevines and trees.

33. THE STORY OF NOT-KNOW-WHO-YOU-ARE.*

Once upon a time there was a large village, and in this village there lived a man by the name of Not-know-who-you-are (Kakiaasadad). The people in this village were very fond of sending out war-parties. Their occupation was to go out on the war-path at all times. When these people would come home from the war-path they would bring home many scalps and captives. At night the celebration would begin, there being victory and scalp dances. Once upon a time, when the dances had begun and it was about midnight, Not-know-who-you-are, instead of hearing the noise of dancing, heard crying. He wondered what had happened to the people. The next time they went out on the war-path, after they had been out a long time, they came back victorious, with many scalps and captives. They were to have their fun in dancing scalp dances and victory dances, but at about midnight, Not-know-who-you-are instead of hearing the noise of dancing, heard crying. He wondered what could be the matter. He learned that after having gone to dancing somebody was carried off by some kind of an animal. He wondered what it could be that was carrying off the people. He thought to himself: "Well, I have great powers, and perhaps if I send out a war-party, when I come home and get up a dance and watch pretty close, I can kill the animal."

On the next day, Not-know-who-you-are got up a war-party and went out on the war-path. They killed many people and took many scalps. When they got home they had-dances, because he was in the crowd when they came home from the war-path. While he danced he kept watching for the strange being, but could see nothing. All at once he heard the people crying again, saying that somebody was carried off. He did not understand about this. He thought to himself: "He has tricked me as he has other leaders, but by moving to another village I can do better." He got together his parents (he was a single man) and his sister, and they moved into another village. The

---
*Told by Ahahe (Waco).

first thing he did he got up a war-party to go on the war-path. After he had been gone for a while he came back the same as usual, with plenty of scalps, expecting to have a celebration over them. In this way he showed the people who he was. The people had their dance, and they knew nothing of what took place in the other village when they had their dances. About midnight, as the people were dancing, they heard some one who was being carried off, screaming. Not-know-who-you-are thought he would go and look for the being.

Once upon a time he went out and cut two long poles. He peeled the bark from them and marked them with a burnt stick, which he burned around them. Thus he marked the poles up toward the top. He stuck them up by his place. He, himself, was a fine-looking man, and being single the women in the village wished that they could have him for a husband. After doing this, he made up his mind to go and look for the strange being; that after killing it he would cut off its front feet and tie them on the ends of the poles which he was to set up in front of his place. Before doing this, however, he would have a guessing contest. Now, he told the people to tell the women that she who would guess correctly what the poles were for, and why he had come to the village, should become his wife. The women gathered around his place. Many young women were there awaiting their turn to guess, but most of them failed.

On the south side of the village lived a family called Horned-Owls (Nikitetswakasa). In this family were father and mother and four girls. In the morning the three oldest girls went out to make their guess, but persuaded their young sister to remain at home, for they told her they were sure she would be unable to guess correctly. The youngest girl remained at home. She was very ugly, and this was one reason the girls did not want her to guess, for, they said, such an ugly girl could not make a guess, and if she should guess aright the man would not have her. When the girls had started out, their father asked the youngest one if she wanted to go and make a guess. The girl said she would. The father then told her to say: "When Not-know-who-you-are lived at his former village his people went out on the war-path and returned home with scalps and captives, and would have their scalp dances and victory dances, but instead of having singing and dancing all night, they would be interrupted by some wild animal that would carry off the people; that Not-know-who-you-are had made up his mind to send out a war-party, so that perhaps he might find a way to protect the people from being carried off during dances; that when he had gone out on the war-path and had returned with scalps and captives, he had it in mind during the dance that followed, to watch for the wild animal and protect his people, but as the dance was going on some one was carried away; that he had made up his mind to move into this village where he was, that he might send out a war-party and somehow protect the people from being carried off; that he thought this thing should never occur again, but on his return from the war-path, bringing scalps and captives, and the dance beginning on the night after his arrival, he was present in the dance and some one was carried off again, the same as in the former village; that he had made up his mind that he would go and look for the wild animal; that he had cut the two poles, marked them with a burnt stick, and was going to make the women and beast guess, when he should capture it, what the poles were for; that the woman who should guess correctly should have him for her husband; that if the beast should fail to guess aright he would kill it, cut off its front feet and hang them at the top of the poles." The girl then went to the guessing place. When her sisters saw her coming they attempted to keep her away, for they were sure she could not guess what the poles were for. But the girl went into the crowd and waited her turn. The three girls failed to guess aright. They then tried to coax their sister to return home with them. Finally, the girl's turn came. As she went up to the guessing place she found Not-know-who-you-are lying on his bed. She called the man's name, Not-know-who-you-are, and said: "As you are here and have put up your poles before the women that they may make their guesses as to the meaning of the poles, and as the one who shall guess correctly their meaning shall become your wife, I have come to guess. The marks on these poles have nothing to do with the poles. When you were in your former village the people sent out war-parties that returned home with scalps and captives; they had dances late at night, and while they were singing and dancing they were interrupted by crying, for some animal carried some one off. Finally, you thought by going on the war-path yourself and returning with scalps and captives and having dances, you might do better than the others had done, but when you had your dances the animal carried a person off the same as before. You then thought that you might find out about the animal by moving to this village. You moved to this village, sent out a war-party, which returned with many scalps and captives; had scalp dances and victory dances; but while the dances were going on late at night your dancing was interrupted the same as before. You then determined to follow up the tracks of the beast. You cut two poles, marked them at the end with a burnt stick. You decided to have the beast guess the meaning of the poles and the black marks. You thought that after the animal had failed to guess aright you would kill him and cut off his feet and tie them to the upper end of the poles." While the girl was telling this, everybody's attention was attracted, for they thought that perhaps the girl was making a correct guess. After this guess, Not-know-who-you-are arose from his bed and told the people to move away, for there was the one woman that guessed aright about the poles. The crowds of people began to move to their homes, and the three sisters of the girl who had guessed correctly began to make fun of the girl, for she was so very ugly, and many good-looking girls had failed to guess correctly. After the people were all gone the girl was taken into Not-know-who-you-are's lodge. When darkness came they went to the creek and the girl was told to jump in the creek. When she came out of the water she was changed to a good-looking girl.

Now, Not-know-who-you-are went out to trail the beast. As he went out he found the trail of the beast, but it seemed to him that the tracks were pretty old. He followed them up for many days, until he came to fresh tracks. As he went along he kept himself well hidden, in order that the animal might not see him first. When the tracks became fresh he saw on the ground and in the grass where the animal's tail had passed, and the ground and the grass had been burnt by it. Finally, as he was going up the hill he crept close to the ground to prevent the animal from seeing him first. He finally came to the animal when it was not expecting any one. Not-know-who-you-are showed himself to the animal. When it saw him it came to him, angry as it could be. Not-know-who-you-are told the animal to make a guess as to what the poles were for. But the animal said: "I do not care anything about the poles, but I know what you have come here for. You are looking for me, that you may kill me. While you were in your former village and the people sent out war-parties which returned with scalps and captives and had their dances at night, and while the dances were going on, you heard some one crying, instead of dancing and singing, and you wanted to know what could have happened. After you had heard why the people cried you thought that if you would go on the war-path, on your return you could protect your people from me, but when you had your dances and expected the people to have a good time and continue your dances all night, I interrupted the dances at midnight, and carried off one of your people. You decided that you would move from your former village into the village you are now living in. You thought that by sending out a war-party you could, on your return, look out for your people better than you did when I first carried off some of your people. Since you did this you sent out a war-party and returned victorious, with scalps and captives; then had scalp dances and victory dances, and then I interrupted you again by carrying off some of your number." The animal, now thinking he had guessed correctly, said: "I am now going to kill you." Not-know-who-you-are then told the animal that he had not guessed correctly about the poles, and he said: "You must make the guess as to the poles, then you can kill me; but if you do not guess rightly about them I will kill you." The animal said the poles had nothing to do with Not-know-who-you-are's intention. The animal said to Not-know-who-you-are that nothing more should be required, as he had heard all the answers that were demanded. Not-know-who-you-are said: "Allow me to tell you what the poles are for." The animal permitted. When Not-know-who-you-are told the meaning of the poles the animal drew back, and said: "I forgot about that." When the animal had failed to answer all, Not-know-who-you-are took his bow-string from his bow and used the string to kill the animal with. He then cut off the hoofs of the animal and put them on the poles as he had intended. The name of the animal was Mountain-Lion (Woxis), or Spike-Tail. Not-know-who-you-are returned home.

Before leaving his home, Not-know-who-you-are had told his wife to watch in the west for him and the sticks, and if she should see the sticks showing up with the hoofs on the ends of them it would indicate that he had killed the beast. When he returned home he held the poles in both hands up in front of him. For many days he traveled, until he came to a place just over the hill from his village. The sticks were seen by the people, and they saw the hoofs on the ends of them. They thought that Not-know-who-you-are had killed the beast.

When Not-know-who-you-are arrived home he stuck the poles up by his lodge and told his people to gather around his lodge and have a big dance; that he thought no other misfortune could befall the people, for he had killed the beast that had carried off their people. The people at once began to dance, and continued to dance night after night, and everything went on well after that.

War-parties were now sent out, and when the people returned victorious, bringing many scalps and captives, they would continue their dances by night, having good times, without interruption. This is the way Not-know-who-you-are delivered the people from their troubles. The people in the village remained without further molestation.

34. EARLY-MORNING-DEER-SLAYER, WHO OVERCAME THE ELK.*

At one time there were five villages all in a line towards the west, and in the last of these villages, toward the east, there lived with his mother and sister a chief by the name of Early-Morning-Deer-Slayer. He was what we know as Mountain-Lion (Woxis). He was a great warrior and hunter and killed all kinds of game, especially deer. He also had great powers and was a famous man. He was liked by everybody in his village, and parties of men visited him to talk about things that happened in those days. During the daytime he went out killing game; and once in a while he went out on an expedition against enemies, and on his return to the village people would gather around his place with all kinds of victory songs and would rejoice over his heroic acts. One time he found out that something was going to take his life. This troubled him so that he stayed in bed all the time, and when men came to spend a part of the night with him he would not get up. This caused great excitement among his people, and they wondered why he was acting this way. Every night men would visit his place, but they would have to spend their time with his father, then retire without seeing Early-Morning-Deer-Slayer, so that they ceased to come. His sister asked him the reason for his actions. In reply he said that it had come to his mind that some one was going to carry him off and kill him.

One day, in one of the villages toward the west, was seen a powerful animal going toward the east. The animal entered one of the villages, and the people shot at him with arrows. After hitting this animal, the arrows dropped off, and the animal went on to the next place. The people shot at the animal with their arrows as the people did in the first village, but the animal went through without being hurt. The animal went on to the third village without being hurt, then on to the fourth village, passing unharmed, until he was seen entering at the last village. At this time, Early-Morning-Deer-Slayer got up and took his bow and arrows. He always had four arrows, two painted red, and the other two painted black. He went out and met his enemy, and shot him with one of his black arrows. Failing to send his arrow through the animal, he took the other black one, but this one also failed to harm the animal. He then used the red painted arrows, but these too failed to injure the animal. This animal was an Elk, and was above all the deers. Because Early-Morning-Deer-Slayer was a great hand to kill game, such as deer, he was attacked by this animal. After losing his

*Told by Ahahe (Waco).

last arrow, Early-Morning-Deer-Slayer still had his bow. The animal dropped his head toward Early-Morning-Deer-Slayer, put him on his horns and turned back to where he came from.

In going through the next village, there was a certain man who asked that he might go along, to see the last days of Early-Morning-Deer-Slayer. So he followed the animal that was carrying Early-Morning-Deer-Slayer. In going through the next village, the people saw that the man was being carried off, and another man ran along to see where this man would be taken to. They went on to the next village, and another man followed to see what would be done with this man. On they went to the last village, and from here another man followed, to see what was to happen. The animal continued his journey, carrying Early-Morning-Deer-Slayer, the four men from the four villages following. Once in a while the Elk would go fast and would leave the four men far behind, then he would slacken up again and the four men would gain on him, and so on, for a long way. Once in a while the four men would ask Early-Morning-Deer-Slayer to perform some of his great powers and make his escape. Then the animal would go fast, and while he was under full speed Early-Morning-Deer Slayer would stand up, take his bow and bend it around his head, for he was going so fast that where he was it would thunder. This would cause the animal to go slower, and then the four men would catch up again. The four men still asked Early-Morning-Deer-Slayer to do the same thing again and try to make his escape. In reply, Early-Morning-Deer-Slayer would sing this song:

> Ja-a-he-schats-as-ta-ki-di-a.
> Ja-a-he-schats-as-ta-ki-di-a.
> Tcas-ta-ki-tsi-d'-waika-i-ta-ti-a.
> Na-ki-di-wa, Na-ki-di-wa.

Etc.   [From this point a repetition of the melody a whole degree lower; and at the next repetition the same melody occurs another degree lower. This song is a remarkable example of changing tonality.]

> The Elk is carrying me on his antlers.
> The Elk is carrying me on his antlers.
> I am still living.
> I am still living.

While on the way, this animal spoke out, saying that he had been away a good while, and that he expected his children would be pretty hungry; then he would increase his speed and leave the four men away behind; then he would stop, and the four men would catch up again. Now Early-Morning-Deer-Slayer saw a high point in the direction they were going, and the four men following also saw it. When the animal got pretty near to the high place he made one run, saying that his children must be pretty hungry. When the animal and Early-Morning-Deer-Slayer reached the high place the four men could hardly. see them. There, in a great, big cave, lived Early-Morning-Deer-Slayer with his children, the Buzzards. Arriving at this place, the Elk stooped down to dump Early-Morning-Deer-Slayer off, when Early-Morning Deer-Slayer kicked the animal in the back of the head, and down they both went. There is no telling how deep this cave was, but on his way down the animal's children would eat a person up before he came to the bottom. As they went down the cave, the Elk was first, and Early-Morning-Deer-Slayer was behind, so that the Elk was eaten by the children. When Early-Morning-Deer-Slayer was about half way down he got hold of the root of a tree, and there he held fast. When the four other men arrived at the cave they all looked down, and there was Early-Morning-Deer-Slayer, hanging onto the root. They said to him: "You have powers to do anything, so make haste and save yourself!" Early-Morning-Deer-Slayer told the men to dig a hole where they were, big enough for them to lie in. When they had dug the hole, Early-Morning-Deer-Slayer took his bow-string and swung it over his head and caused the wind to blow from the north. When the wind blew, it threw him nearly out of the place. Again he swung his bow-string over his head and the wind blew harder, until it finally blew him out of the place; then it stopped blowing. The men got out of their places and looked down in the cave to see whether Early-Morning-Deer-Slayer was still there, but he was gone. The four men started on the trail of the wind, and here they found Early-Morning-Deer-Slayer.

When they had gathered around him they asked if he was tired, and he answered that he was not tired, but that he would return to the place he was brought from. He asked the man from the first village if he wanted to go back, but the man answered that it was too far to go back. So Early-Morning-Deer-Slayer took him up, and threw him in a way which caused the man to fly, and he became a small Sparrow (Ichinekats). Then Early-Morning-Deer-Slayer asked the man from the second village if he wanted to go back, and the man said he did not, and that it was too far. Early-Morning-Deer-Slayer took him and threw him as he had thrown the first man, and he turned into a Yellow-hammer (Hatsok). Early-Morning-Deer-Slayer then asked the third man if he wanted to go back to his home, and he answered the same as the first two men. So Early-Morning-Deer-Slayer threw him, and he became a Towhee (Itchitihakao). Now, the man from the fourth village was asked about going home, and he said the same as the others had said. So Early-Morning-Deer-Slayer took him up and threw him, and he became a Red-Bird (Itschidisaskatsa). If the yellowhammer be closely examined, it will be found that the feathers on its back are of different color from those on the other parts of its body. This is because when the Yellowhammer dug his hole by the cave, he made it too shallow. When the wind blew, his back being very near the surface, the skin was blown off, so that now, the coloring of the feathers on the yellowhammer's back signify that he once had a scar on his back.

Now Early-Morning-Deer-Slayer set out to return to his village. On his way home, he came to a place where the people were having a big dance. He stopped there for a while, and asked the people what their dance meant. They answered him, saying that they were dancing because their enemy had been carried off and killed, and now they could all live on, without any one killing any of their number. The Early-Morning-Deer-Slayer took some ashes from the fire and threw them on the heads of the people and commanded that their heads should always look that way. The people after that looked as though some one had thrown ashes on their heads. Early-Morning-Deer-Slayer went out again, and when darkness came, he stopped to rest. At this place he killed a deer, for after he had got out of the cave he had great powers, and he had commanded his arrows to come to him and they came, so that when he stopped to rest at night he killed a deer the same as usual for his meat. While Early-Morning-Deer-Slayer was at this place some men came around, whispering to each other, saying: "That is surely Early-Morning-Deer-Slayer." They went to him, and asked him if he was not the same Early-Morning-Deer-Slayer that they had known. He answered that he had got away from the monster, and invited the men to eat with him. One of the two men was his friend. They ate with him, and left him with joy and started for the woods, where they are always seen. They were Opossums (Kadaiok).

Early-Morning-Deer-Slayer continued his journey home; and when he arrived there he found that all the people had moved away. He fol-lowed their trail, until one day as he went over the hill he saw some one still going. He stopped for a while and wondered who it could be, and finally discovered that it was his sister. He took one of his arrows and shot it over her, so that she might find the arrow. While she was still going she came to the place where the arrow had stuck up, and looked around to see if her brother had returned, for, of course, she knew her brother's arrows. Early-Morning-Deer-Slayer finally overtook his sister, and noticed that she was packing something on her back, and he asked what it was. She told him that it was the Coyote's (Ketox's) children; that after he had been carried off everybody believed him to be dead; that their father and mother had both died because they believed their son had been killed, so she was all alone; and that the Coyote had taken her up and abused her and made her pack his children for him. Early-Morning-Deer-Slayer took the Coyotes and destroyed them. He asked his sister how she had been treated by everybody, and she told him that no one liked her, and that while packing the Coyote's children in the evening, the Coyote would come and meet her and whip her. Now they started to the place where the people had gone, and they saw the Coyote coming. Early-Morning-Deer-Slayer hid himself so that the Coyote would not see him. The Coyote met the woman and said that Early-Morning-Deer-Slayer must have been with her. The Coyote always abused her in this way, because he thought Early-Morning-Deer-Slayer would never return. Early-Morning-Deer-Slayer now appeared, and took the straps his sister had used to pack the Coyote's children, and a piece of his bow-string. He tied the straps together, and his sister got inside of them, and he set the Coyote to carrying his sister. He took the string part and put it on the Coyote's head, which began to work into his head and finally split it in two. After they had killed the Coyote they went on again, until they got near to where the people stopped, coming from the west. He told his sister that there was no use of their living there again, and so Early-Morning-Deer-Slayer took one of his black arrows and shot toward the north. He shot another arrow toward the east, another to the south, and another to where they were. These arrows he commanded to be used by other generations. When Early-Morning-Deer-Slayer shot the arrows to the four points, each stuck near the edge of the village, which caused a fire to start in each of the four directions. In this way he destroyed his village by fire. The other villages still existed. Early-Morning-Deer-Slayer and his sister went to the woods.

This is the reason mountain-lion can kill a deer so easily. In those times, when Early-Morning-Deer-Slayer was living as a human being, the deer was prey. So these two, Early-Morning-Deer-Slayer and his sister, were Mountain-Lions.

35. TROUBLE AMONG THE CHIEF'S CHILDREN.*

Once upon a time there was a village, and in the village lived a chief who was the head of his tribe. The chief had a son and daughter, both of whom had always refused to marry, this being the way that children in chiefs' families did. It was customary for chiefs always to have company every night and every day. The older men were always sitting up at night, talking about times in their early days. The young woman, of course, had to do the cooking for these men. These were times when young men would ask the chief's son if he could let them marry his sister. But when the young woman was asked she always refused, and she was single for a long time.

It happened that Man-fond-of-Deer-Meat (Taaniksiats) came to her. She thought to herself that he was the man she had been waiting to see for a long time, and so she accepted him. The next morning, her people noticed that she was not getting up as early as usual. They sent her brother to see what was the matter. When he reached the place where she was he noticed some one was with her in bed. He asked them to get out of the bed and come down and get their breakfast. After he had told them this he went to the main lodge and told his parents that there was some one in bed with his sister. He and his parents were very proud of this, and they were anxious to see who this man was who had married the girl. Finally the woman and her man entered the lodge, and they saw the young man. They knew him as soon as they saw him. When they were eating breakfast, the girl's father told her that she must either leave and go somewhere else and live with this man, or have him sent away, for Man-fond-of-Deer-Meat was known to be of no account for anything but hunting. They thought she should have some one who was man enough to go out on any kind of an expedition, especially on the war-path; that it was extraordinary among the people of those times if a woman such as she should marry a man who was of no account as a warrior and could not make the family more prominent by bringing them scalps. But the woman thought to herself that it was right for her to have her home and live all to herself and her man, so they could have everything to themselves, and have no one to say anything to them.

The following day, the woman got together her things that she thought she would need to build their new home with. After having everything ready, that same night they started on their way to some far distant place. They traveled all night and about daybreak rested and

*Told by Istor (Woman) (Towakoni).

went to sleep for a while, until plain daylight, when they started again, going toward the south until darkness overtook them. They again stopped for a night's rest, instead of traveling at night. They had something along to eat, and it was easy for Man-fond-of-Deer-Meat to kill any game that he wanted. When they stopped he went out a short distance and shot a deer, so that they had meat for their supper. The next morning, they ate their breakfast and journeyed again, traveling all that day until darkness came down on them. They stopped for a night's rest. Man-fond-of-Deer-Meat, being such a great hunter, did the same as he had done before, killing a deer and getting enough meat for supper and two other meals. When he arrived where his wife was they cooked their supper, ate, and went to sleep. The next day, after eating their breakfast they started, still going in the same direction. The following day they traveled until sundown, and again rested. The young man did the same thing over again, killing a deer and having deer meat for their meals. They slept again, and on the next day, after eating their breakfast, they traveled in the same course all day till darkness overtook them, when they stopped again. The man would do the same thing over again, killing a deer for their meat. So they again ate their supper and slept. The next day they journeyed, and this time Man-fond-of-Deer-Meat thought that they were far enough away from everybody. That afternoon they looked for a place fit to live in, and finally succeeded in finding one. Man-fond-of-Deer-Meat said to his wife that this was the place for them to live and make their home.

Here they lived, the woman fixing up the place, building their grass-lodge and sheds to dry meat, Man-fond-of-Deer-Meat doing all the hunting. The woman remained at home by herself, for there was no sign of any people living near them. She sometimes thought that hers was the kind of a man she wanted, one who would make a living, so that she would never be hungry, instead of having a man going out on the war-path and becoming a famous woman, the wife of a warrior. They lived here a good long while, the woman remaining at home, the man going out hunting every day. They always had plenty of meat, and the woman raised corn, so that they had plenty to eat. After they had lived a long while at this place Man-fond-of-Deer-Meat went out hunting with his four arrows and bow to kill deer, his most important meat, as is signified by his name. He saw a deer sitting down. He shot at the deer and missed it. Quickly he thought to himself, "Well, what can be the matter with me that I have missed a deer so close!" When he had shot at the deer it jumped up and ran. He stopped at this place looking for his arrow. It was early in the day and therefore he looked for his arrow. Finally he had to give it up and went straight on home, instead of looking for more deer. Arriving home he quickly ordered something to eat; told his wife about missing a deer when shooting at it, and that on the next day he would again go out looking for his arrow. This was the beginning of unfortunate times.

Early on the next day he started off again in search of his arrow instead of going hunting. Arriving at the place where he had shot the deer he looked all around again, and would once in a while turn back where he was when shooting the deer and aim straight to where the deer had been. Then he would go and look for his arrow. He was all day looking for it, until late. Then he went back to his home, calling for something to eat. While eating he told his wife that some way or other he could not find his lost arrow. This was the commencement of his misfortune. Instead of hunting again he would hunt for his arrow. Every day he went out looking for it, and for some reason he was greedy and came home later than usual. Every day he went out he got worse. He ceased to ask his wife to give him something to eat, but would help himself. All he would ask would be if the fire was still burning, then he would go ahead and cook for himself. His wife finally noticed that their provisions were running short, for her husband was eating up everything they had. Finally the time came when they had eaten everything. The man got to eating dry hides and everything else. Still he would go out hunting his arrow, instead of hunting game. After he had eaten everything his wife put out the fire, so it would give out but a dim light, and he asked her to go to bed. His wife did as he told her. She then heard him grunting, and she noticed him cutting flesh off from his legs and cooking it after he had again built a fire, and eating it. This time, instead of getting in bed with his wife, he remained where he was and went to sleep. This he continued to do until he was nearly nothing but bones.

One day a person come along who told the woman how foolish she had been to marry such a man as Man-Fond-of-Deer-Meat; that some one else influenced her, and that there was some one preparing to take his life, and when she had taken this notion she was clearing the way for his and her ruin; that he would never find his arrow; that being a hunter of deer, Big-Hail-Deer (Taahaitschidl) had taken a notion to ruin him, first by causing him to lose his arrow at Where-two-cardinal-points-met (Jadatsikádaannidi), the northwest, where the man's arrow could not be found; that there was no use of her telling her man, but that she should make her escape, for it was her day to die. He meant that on his return, Man-fond-of-Deer-Meat would kill her and eat her. This was early in the day, and it was the Sparrow (Ichinekats) who told her this. He gave her a stick and a double-ball, a handful of deer hair, bark from a dogwood tree and a bundle of reddish-colored pieces of fine stones for paint. She was first to use the double-ball to travel on when she would be pursued; then she was to throw the deer hair down, with which her man might busy himself by chasing deers to kill them, and so forget about chasing her, when she would get far ahead of him. Next she was to use the bark in the same way, and then use the red stones last. Finally she was to use her stick, dragging it behind her across her path once, when there would be a deep canyon. She was told to go ahead, make her escape and return home. The woman went out. She tossed up in the air the double-ball, toward the north, and was on it. This was to prevent Man-fond-of-Deer-Meat from knowing which way she was starting. She kept on going, using the double-ball all the time. Before starting she was told that she would hear her man talking, after he should find that she was gone, and that he would have to find her trail before he could start after her. She traveled all that day until late in the evening, when she heard her man talking and asking where she had gone, saying: "Who could have come around to tell her to make her escape, for the time has come that I thought I was going to get all I wanted to eat?" When she had escaped, she was without any blanket around her legs, for her man had eaten everything. He finally found her trail and commenced to pursue her. It was night and she was traveling, so that it was not very long until she was nearly overtaken. She used the deer hairs first, throwing them on the ground. She kept on going. When her man got to this place he said to himself: "Well, here are lots of deer. I could kill many deer here, instead of looking for my arrow." He at once commenced to chase the deer around with the expectation of killing one. By this time his wife had gone on a long distance, when he thought of the chase he had been making. He started after her again. She had heard every word he had said while he was chasing deer. Finally she heard him coming closer and closer. Now she took the bark of dogwood and threw it on the ground, and left the place with big bushes of dogwood. Thus she got a good way ahead of him. When Man-fond-of-Deer-Meat arrived at the place he commenced to cut down some bushes, saying to himself that he could come along again and find the place, when he would get all the dogwood bushes he wanted for arrow making. He sat down, cut some sticks and commenced to remove the bark and straighten them. Here he stayed longer, and almost forgot the chase he was making. He finally thought of the chase again, and began talking to himself. The woman heard every word he said, for she had been given power to hear him at a long distance. She was going fast, but still her man was a much faster traveler than she.

It was now day, and she heard him coming again. She emptied the bundle of fine red-colored stones for painting. Then she left behind her much of her red-colored paint. She went on, still using the double-ball to travel on. When her man came to this place he stopped, for he found just what he had been wanting for a long time. He said to himself that he had been a long time wanting to get such paint and finally he had found it, and he was going to get all he wanted. He remained here for a while, gathering up stones. Finally he was reminded of his chase for his wife, and he said: "Never mind, I will get you. You will never get away from me." Then he started after her again. This time, his wife found that she was getting nearer home. It was not very long until she heard her man coming. She used the stick, which was the last resort she had. She struck the ground, making a deep canyon. She continued her journey, using the double-ball. Now she was near her home, when some way or other Man-fond-of-Deer-Meat got over the canyon. She could now barely see the hill next to the village where she was going. She kept on going until she reached the top of the hill. When she looked back she saw her man coming right after her. It was now late in the evening. She saw young women of her age playing the double-ball. She kept on going toward her home. She frightened every woman who was out playing, and the women said among themselves that there must be something after her. She went right into the grass-lodge of her father and went straight to him.

There were a good many men inside of this place. When it grew dark they could hear Man-fond-of-Deer-Meat talking outside of the lodge, asking that she might be turned out and saying that he wanted her. The woman's father said to her, "Let me tell you a story." He then commenced to tell her the story about a chief having a daughter who married and left home for the sake of keeping her husband, when the old folks did not want her to keep her man. The chief told her the whole tale of her life while out by herself and with her man; how her man lost his arrow; how they soon ate up everything; how greedy her man became after losing his arrow; how some one came to notify her that her life was threatened; that in a short time on that day she should be killed by her husband; how she was compelled to make her escape by various means, in order to prevent her man from catching up with her; how she traveled fast, and what hard times she had had. It was now about daylight, when the chief was still telling the story, and everybody in the lodge with the chief heard him. But Man-fond-of-Deer-Meat was still calling for his wife when the chief ended his story. He ended the story about his daughter's life, telling her what time she arrived at the village; that she was without her blanket; how she ran for her life to her father's grass-lodge and what a crowd of men there were. It was daylight when he completed the story. At the same time, Man-fond-of-Deer-Meat fell dead, just outside of the lodge, so that the village had no further trouble. This is the beginning of times when children of chief's families were misled and had much trouble. The village remained here ever after.

36. THE TURTLE'S WAR-PARTY.*

There was once a village, and in this village lived the Turtle (Gegeezseyar). In the village there was a chief who had a daughter. She was a single woman and had refused to marry many men who wanted to marry her. But she offered herself to any man who could bring to her a scalp that had red hair. There were a good many men who went out on the war-path to look for a red-haired scalp, but every one failed to find any one of the enemy that had red hair. One man after another led out war-parties, but they all returned without the scalp.

Once upon a time the Turtle called on his mother to make some corn meal for him to take along, saying that he wanted to go out on the war-path by himself and secure that scalp for the chief's daughter and get her for a wife. His mother said to him: "You can not kill anything. You can not go very far in the way you always travel." But the Turtle kept on coaxing his mother to do this for him. She finally ground some corn for him and he at once started off on the war-path. He went toward the south and was on the way for several days, when he met a person. He asked the person where he was going, saying that he himself was going out on the war-path. The person then asked to join him, and so the Turtle allowed him to go along. This person was the Rat (Nikisiwatsa). On the way the Turtle told the Rat what he was going on the war-path for, saying that there was a chief's daughter who wanted to marry some man who could secure for her a red-haired scalp. The Rat told the Turtle that that was easy to be done.

*Told by Saved-another-in-the-Water-from-the-Enemy (Towakoni).

They went on and on for several days, and finally met another man. This man then asked the two where they were going. They told him that they were going out on the war-path, and they told him why they were going. The man asked to join them. The two allowed him to go along with them, for they knew that he was brave. This person was the Horned-Beetle (Oskanaats). They traveled on, and on, until they met another person, who asked them where they were going. They told him where they were going, and the person asked if he could join them. This person was the Locust (Koskatoch). They accepted him, for they all knew he was a brave warrior. While on their way they began to tell him what they were going out for. The Locust told them that it was easy to secure such a scalp. They then went on toward the south and met another person, who laughed at them and asked where they were going. They told him they were going out on the war-path. This person then asked if he could join them, but they refused to accept him, for they knew that he was a coward. When they refused to allow him to go along with them, this person said he was going along with them whether they wanted him to or not. They told him that they knew he was a coward and that if the enemy got after them he would leave them behind instead of fighting for their lives. This person was the Coyote (Ketox). The Coyote told them that if they would let him go he would do the spying, for he was a fast traveler, and so they consented and the Coyote joined the Turtle's command.

They went on traveling. As soon as the Turtle knew that he was pretty near to the enemy's village he sent the Coyote out spying. That evening the Coyote came back, bringing news about a village. They asked the Turtle what he thought of that. The Turtle told the men that he wanted to attack the whole village, but the Coyote told the Turtle that it was a large village and that they were too few in numbers to attack it. But the Turtle said that he wanted to get right in the middle of the village before he could do anything. The Coyote began to get scared at what these men were going to do. They told him they knew in the first place that he was too big a coward to be in their war-party. They were close to the village that evening, and when night came they kept on going closer and closer, and when most of the people had gone to sleep they entered the village. They went from one tipi to another, looking for a man with red hair. Meanwhile the Coyote grew more frightened, for it was unsafe to be doing that. They finally succeeded in finding a place where there was a large tipi. One of the men looked in there and saw some one who had red hair like they wanted. In this large tipi all of the great men were sitting up to pass the time. When everybody had gone to sleep, all the warriors thought that they would go to the tipi, but the Coyote told the men that he would remain outside, to look out for them. When everybody was asleep these men entered the place where they had located the enemy with the red hair. The Turtle went right straight to the place where this man was sleeping, cut his throat, and neck, too, and took his scalp. The Turtle then called his partners, who were going from one bed to another. They went out, and the Coyote joined them again. He had been scared nearly to death when they were inside the tipi. They started home, but before they were outside of the village the Turtle began to sing victory songs, and he woke everybody up. The people began to find out that there had been enemies in the village. All of the people in the village then woke up and found that enemies had killed one of their chiefs. They commenced to pursue the war-party, and overtook them just a little outside of the village. Four of the war-party hid themselves in the grass, while these enemies pursued the Coyote. They overtook the Coyote and killed him, but could not find any of his partners, so that the enemy returned to their home. The war-party then began to call one another and finally came together again. They went on until they came to a hill and there they found the Coyote lying dead, where the enemy had overtaken him and killed him. They found the Coyote full of arrow wounds, and badly cut up. The Turtle put the Coyote on his feet and called to him to rise, saying that he had slept too soundly. The Coyote arose, rubbed his eyes and said to these men that he had been sound asleep. The Turtle then told the Coyote he knew that he was a coward and could not stand it to be with such warriors and brave men as they were.

It was a good many days before he arrived home with the scalp and delivered it to the chief. The Turtle was bound to get the chief's daughter, because he had the scalp that she called for. The chief's daughter was then given the scalp that the Turtle had obtained, and the Turtle was given this woman for his wife. This was a surprise to every able-bodied man who could travel faster than the Turtle but who could not get the scalp required. The Turtle had not lived with this woman very long when the chief called forth all the men and women, and the children to his tipi, to hear what the Turtle had to say. When everybody was present the Turtle told the people that all he wanted to show them was where such a scalp could be taken; that it was pretty hard for a man to get; that had it not been for him a good many men would still be sending out war-parties to secure the scalp he had taken, which might cost some of them their lives; that for their sake he had saved every one from doing this dangerous thing; that because he had done this for them he wanted to leave the village, never to live as a human being again; that every one could do as he pleased, remain as human being always, or be something else. The Turtle then went to the prairie and turned into a Prairie-Turtle (Kikeskatoshkeyosh), and many of the people went off the same way, turning into something else. Some remained in the village.

37. THE TURTLE'S WAR-PARTY.*

There was once in a certain village, where the Turtle lived, a chief who offered his daughter to the one who should get for him a red-haired scalp. These red-haired people were the Wasps, and as they had White-Geese for their spies it was not possible for any one to reach their place without their knowing it. When people had tried to go there the Geese notified the Wasps that the people were coming. Many warriors failed in their attempt to get such a scalp. Once upon a time the Turtle asked his mother to make him a pair of moccasins and prepare him some corn meal to take along with him. His mother asked him where he was going. The Turtle said he was going after a red-haired scalp; but his mother would not allow him, for it was not safe for him to go, for those who had tried to get such scalps lost their lives. For this reason the mother thought it was not safe for the Turtle to make the attempt, but the Turtle thought he could succeed where others had failed. Finally his mother made him a pair of moccasins and prepared the meal for him, and he set out. He started to the west, where the red-haired people were known to live. As he went along he came to a high point where he saw smoke coming out. The Turtle was curious to know who lived there and if the man would be good enough to allow him to remain there for a time. As he approached the place he was allowed to enter. There he found the Mole (Iskuhukehhas). The Turtle was permitted to sit down at the south side of the Mole. The Turtle was told that it was through him (the Mole) that he had been induced to come to the red-haired people, and that he now would aid him to secure the red-haired scalp, in order that the Turtle might get the chief's daughter. The Turtle thought that was a very good plan, to have somebody else help him to get the scalp. The Turtle was permitted to stay there. The Mole said he would go and locate all the reddest haired men. When the Mole went to the red-haired people's place,

*Told by Ahahe (Waco).

instead of going on top of the ground he went under the ground, so he could not be seen by the Geese who spied for the red-haired people. When the Mole had entered the village of the red-haired people he looked around and located all the people. He turned back to his home to notify the Turtle what he had seen and how he had located all of the red-haired people. Then both turned back to the red-haired people's homes. They went by the same way the Mole had gone, under the ground, the Mole in the lead. They arrived at night. They waited until all had gone to bed. When every one had gone to bed the Mole spied around to locate some chief who had red hair, and after he had found one he turned back to get the Turtle. Now they went back to the place where he had found the red-haired chief. Both went direct to the red-haired chief, and the Turtle cut off his head. Now they started back, underground. They traveled all that night, back to the Mole's place, and when they arrived it was daylight. On the next day the Turtle was permitted to go back to his home and show his red-haired scalp, which he had got where everybody else had failed.

When he got to his village, instead of going to his home he went to the chief's home. He showed the scalp to the chief. He told the chief that the scalp was for him; that he had got it when everybody else had failed. The chief told the Turtle he might live there with him ever after, and have his daughter for his wife. The news spread in the village from one place to another about the Turtle bringing the scalp that all else had failed to get. When the Turtle was living with the chief's family there were great crowds of men who came around the place at night and sat up part of the night passing the time by telling stories. On one occasion the Turtle was asked how he got to the red-haired people's place without being seen. He told how it came about and the people were surprised when they heard. The Turtle lived with the chief's daughter thereafter.

38. LITTLE-CROW WHO BECAME A SPARROW-HAWK.*

There was once a village where lived four brothers and their mother. The brothers were not chiefs, but were prominent men, noted as warriors. There was a chief who had the control of this village. In these times the chief's home could be distinguished by the signs the chiefs had in front of their lodges—a tanned buffalo hide erected in front of the lodge, which was the emblem of a chief's lodge. Little-

*Told by Ahahe (Waco).

Crow (Kiisskawiharikitsi), who was one of the four brothers, would always go out on the war-path against their enemies, the Trickster-Spies (Kinas-Kitikĕahara). On their return they would bring scalps or some captives; this was their way of living. All the people of the village knew them as great warriors, as they were always out on the war-path. On one occasion, when the brothers were all at home, the oldest said to the others: "From this time on, since our mother has to do all the work by herself, let us make this arrangement: If ever we have to meet the enemy and anyone fails to be on hand, let us make that one wear clothes like a woman. Let us make him stay at home thereafter and help our mother to do the cooking."

Early next morning, Little-Crow went to the creek to take a bath. He, of course, had a certain place to bathe where no one else took a bath. While in the water, when he looked up on the bank where his things were he saw a woman standing there, looking at him, and he did not know what to do. He remained in the water, waiting for the woman to go away, but the woman remained standing there for a long while. She finally asked Little-Crow why he was not going to the scene of the battle that was going on that morning. She told him that it was of course known that it could not be anybody else but his brothers who were doing the fighting. Little-Crow came out of the water, took his things and went to the place, having in mind the agreement the brothers had made regarding the one who should fail to be on hand at the time of battle. He ran as fast as he could so as to be present at the battle. While he was on the way, he met a man coming home from the battle who told him that it was useless for him to go further, for he thought that the enemy had all been killed. Little-Crow kept on running, thinking that there might still be left some one for him to fight. After a while he met one of his brothers coming back, who told him that it was useless for him to go further, for there was but one enemy left, though that one was brave; but that the rest of his brothers had done most of the killing and were still after this one who was so brave. Little-Crow went on, in the hope of killing the last one or die, so as to escape having to wear clothes like a woman. He went on and met his brothers and they told him to go back, that he must always stay at home thereafter, to help their mother do the cooking, for there was only one of the enemy left to go on and tell of their defeat, and that he was a hard one to fight with. He went on to meet this enemy.

When the enemy found that Little-Crow was after him, he turned around, ran towards him, and shot at him with his right and left hand. "Sure enough," thought Little-Crow, "this man is dangerous." He then dodged away from him again, with the intention of using his war-club on him. He failed the second time. He tried again, and again, but the foe always escaped without injury. "Well!" thought Little-Crow, "I must try once more, to see whether I shall kill him or he shall kill me." This was his last chance. He then went up to the enemy in the same way as he had always approached enemies, and when his foe had missed him several times he finally got hold of him and began to wrestle with him. They kept rolling around, now one on top, then the other, the one at the top always trying to get an arrow so that he could stick the one on the bottom with the point of it. Finally Little-Crow got on top, pulled the enemy over to where one of the arrows was lying, picked it up between his toes and finally landed the point of it on the enemy's side and killed him. Little-Crow then sat down to rest, and he thought to himself: "If I take this man's scalp and behead him my brothers may not believe that I have killed him. They may say that I took the scalp from an enemy they have killed." Then he thought about what he must do to make his brothers believe that he had killed the enemy whom neither one of them could kill. Finally he decided to carry the whole body on his back to his brothers, so that they would have to believe him. It was then getting late in the day. He took the body, put it on his back and carried it some distance, then rested for a while to get breath. He kept on carrying it until he reached home.

When he got home he stood outside, still carrying the body on his back. When he was standing he heard his brothers talking about him, and they were wondering why Little-Crow had not yet come home. They said that when he met the foe he must have died, for they knew that this enemy was dangerous. They blamed their oldest brother for the whole thing, saying he was the sole cause of his brother's death, if he were dead, for he had proposed the agreement that the one who failed to be present during battle should wear woman's clothes; and because Little-Crow did not want to do woman's work he had died. Little-Crow, of course, heard every word that his brothers said. They sat up all night, talking about him, while he stood there listening, the dead body on his back. The brothers kept on talking about the matter, until a certain time came, when Little-Crow began to sing to them about his early life; how he grew to be a man and became a noted warrior; how he had been treated by his brothers; sent out with them on the war-path; what they had done on the war-path; what his oldest brother had commanded to be done if one should happen to be absent from a battle; how he went down to the water for a bath, and how a woman found him; how he was ashamed to leave the water till she told him of the battle being fought outside the village; how he quickly left the water, going to the scene of battle; how he went and got his weapons, met the men who said his brothers had performed most of the fighting; how he managed to be present at the scene of the fighting; how he met one of his brothers and was told that it was useless that he should go further, for his brothers had quite likely killed the last one in the battle; how he met his other brothers, and they told him there was one who was dangerous still alive; how he met this dangerous man and found him dangerous as his brothers told him. Thus he told in song the story, telling all of it in words. Then he told in song how he killed the enemy; failed the first time, and the second, then the third time and the fourth; how they wrestled all around there, rolling on top of one another; how he finally succeeded in getting an arrow while on top; how he landed an arrow point in the man's side and killed him; how he thought to show his brothers he had killed the same one that neither one of them could kill; how he carried home the body; how he rested when he gave out; how he finally succeeded in reaching home; and how now he stood outside, listening to his brothers talking. When he had ended the song he called his brothers, telling them to come out and see if he had not killed the same identical person whom they had failed to kill; then he threw the body on the ground. It was then daylight and everybody in the village was awake, when they heard him singing. He had waited until morning, thinking that his brothers might not believe him in the darkness; that they might think he had picked up some other dead body and brought it home. All his brothers came out and everybody else came, to see the body, and all said that it was the same man whom every brave had failed to kill. This was the song:

"Hi-na-ni-i-rai,
Hi-na-ni-i-rai,
Hi-na-ni-i-rai.
Ah-he-na-hi-na-ni-i-rai.
Hi-na-ni-i-rai,
Hi-na-ni-i-rai,
Hi-na-ni-i-rai.
Ah-he-na-hi-na-ni-i-rai.
Hi-na-ni-i-rai-

And so on

This is the tune of his song of his early life and his life on the war-path, in times when he did not want to do any home work, as his oldest brother had decreed for him who should fail to be present in battle.

Little-Crow having done this heroic deed the people gathered around their home, giving him a victory dance and praising him. After the dance was over in the daytime they again danced at night, continuing the dance until morning. This was the beginning of victory dances. It was now a good time when they lived with the people. Then they quickly called the people together, and when the people came, they announced to them that they wanted to leave their old home and to live hereafter somewhere else. So they commenced to teach their powers to the human beings for the next generation, and when they took pity on any one they gave him powers so that some one could do the same things they had done when they existed on the earth as human beings. After they had taught the people their powers they went into their lodge, threw a gourd full of water upon the fire, and as the steam arose the four brothers went up with it and became Sparrow-Hawks.

39. THE LITTLE BROWN HAWKS.*

There was once a family living all by themselves. This family consisted of father, mother, and four boys. Their name was Swift-Hawk (Gusseiõs). The old man talked to his boys and taught them to go out on the war-path and hunting. The four brothers resembled each other so much that the only way people could tell them apart was by their ages. The old man forbade the boys to go to the village called Fire-Light-like-Prairie-Fire (Hasaitsiaidadiwa), north of their homes. Once upon a time the oldest boy took a notion to visit the place. It took him four days to go, and when he got there he asked where there was a place for visitors to stay all night. He was told to go to the largest tipi that he could see, where he would find one of the leading men of the village and that he would be allowed to stay all night. He went on as directed and entered the place. The man whom he was visiting told the Swift-Hawk that there was danger at the place; that in this place was living Boy-setting-Grass-on-Fire-by-his-Footsteps (Weksnaquadniahaits), who was a dangerous man, and had the Coyote (Ketox) for his servant. While the man was telling how dangerous

*Told by Man-who-killed-three-blind-in-the-left-Eye-Osage (Wichita).

the place was the Coyote walked in, then stepped out again and carried the news back to his master that there was a visitor at the place. The next morning Swift-Hawk woke early and went to the nearest water to take an early morning bath. He was then called to a shinny ball game, where the loser of the game was to forfeit his life. They commenced to play. Swift-Hawk was a pretty good runner, but he could not equal Boy-setting-Grass-on-Fire-by-his-Footsteps, and he lost the game and was clubbed to death with a shinny club. When first starting from home he had all his war materials, such things as arrows, bow and quiver and shield, which he had left in the lodge where he visited over night. Soon after this, one of Swift-Hawk's brothers decided to set out and look for him. This second Swift-Hawk started. It took him four days to reach the village, which was the same his dead brother had gone to. He, as his brother had done, asked where visitors were received. He was told to go to the largest tipi that he could see and there he would find a place to stay over night. He walked in and was told to pass on to the west side of the tipi. There he noticed his brother's things hanging up. He then thought to himself that there must be some danger. He was told there was a dangerous man at the place who had a servant who would soon be in to carry the news of his presence back to his master. So Swift-Hawk hung his things with those of his dead brother. It was thought by the people that he was the same identical man whom they had killed. The next day he was called for; but before he went to the place he went to the creek for a bath, and then dressed himself. He put a white feather on his head, which made him resemble his dead brother. He was called to the shinny game. They commenced to play. When they ran, his opponent left the grass burning in his tracks. Swift-Hawk lost the game and it cost him his life. It was the agreement that he who lost should forfeit his life.

In these times everything seemed long, and everything seemed short. It seemed a long time since the Swift-Hawks left home. Another Swift-Hawk decided to go out in search of his brothers. It took him four days. He found the fireplaces of those who had gone before him, where they had built a fire, as darkness had overtaken them. He finally reached the village and asked where a visitor might find a place to stop over night. He was told to go straight to the highest tipi that he could see, where he would be allowed to stay all night. He went on as directed, came to the place and entered. The man living there knew when he saw him coming that he must belong to the same family as the two who had been killed. He was told to sit down in the visitor's seat.

Before he sat down he noticed the weapons that belonged to his older brothers. He sat down, and just then the old Coyote entered and went out again, carrying the message that he was present back to his master. He reported that there was another visitor that seemed to be of the same family as the two previously killed. The Swift-Hawk was given something to eat and a bed to sleep on. The next morning he rose before daylight, went straight to the creek and took an early morning bath. When he went back he was called to the play ground at the edge of the village. He went to the shinny ball grounds. He dressed like his brothers, and he was painted like them, and had some kind of a feather on his head. They then commenced to play the shinny game. The play ground extended north and south and it was a long way from goal to goal. The Swift-Hawk lost the game and forfeited his life, for his opponent was the fastest runner in the village. When running, he would set the grass on fire in his tracks.

Another Swift-Hawk now took a notion to go and look for his brothers. It will be remembered that this was the last of the four brothers. He also was four days on the way to the village. All traveled at about the same pace and camped for each night at the same places. The Swift-Hawk arrived at the village at sundown and asked where he could stop for the night. He was told to go to the largest and highest tipi that he could see, where he would find a man who would allow him to stay all night. So he went on as told, entered the place, and when the young man living at the place saw him he knew him to be of the same family as the three brothers who had been killed. The Swift-Hawk was asked to pass on to the place where visitors sat and slept. Here he noticed his dead brothers' things hanging up. He was told that his brothers had died, having lost their shinny games, and that there was a man in the village who had the power to win the shinny game; that early in the morning he would be called to the shinny game to play. He then was given something to eat and a bed to sleep on. Early the next morning he got up and went to the creek for a bath. When he had taken a bath he dressed himself and put on the same kind of clothes his brothers had worn. He was now called to the shinny grounds to play. When he was seen, it was thought that he was the same man who had been killed there before. They tossed the ball and commenced the game. It consisted of tossing the ball and one hitting it, the first running in the direction they were headed, the other following after him. They played for a while, until the Swift-Hawk played out and lost the game. He was then clubbed with the shinny club.

At the Swift-Hawks' home there were now left the old woman and the old man. The old man said to his wife: "I know well enough that they have gone where I always told them not to go, and they have disobeyed me. Suppose I try my turn and look for my children." He at once set out to look for his children. It took him four days to reach the place. He followed the trail of his sons, and stopped to rest at night where they had stopped. The old man finally came to the village late in the evening on the fourth day. He asked where he might be allowed to stay at night. They told him to go to the largest and tallest tipi that he saw; that visitors were received there. He went on as he was told. When entering the tipi he was told to pass to the bed for guests and to be seated. Then he saw some of his children's weapons. He began to think that his boys must have met death. He was given supper and was told that some one in the village had power to play the shinny game and no one else had power to win a game from him; that the first thing in the morning he would be called forth to the grounds to play a game of shinny. Early in the morning he went to the creek to take a bath. In those times this is the way they changed their feathers. Then he was called to the shinny game. When he was seen he was much younger than was expected. He wore the same kind of dress that the boys had worn, and was painted red. He went to the grounds to meet his foe. They tossed the ball and the game commenced. The old man saw how his boys had had a hard time playing with this man. Being old, he soon gave out and lost the game also. He was clubbed with a shinny club. The people were mean. The mean ones would dance over any one's death; so the people danced and had all kinds of sports.

At home, the old woman was alone. She remained at home by herself. Once on a time she went out to the creek and took a bath. When bathing, she heard some noise from the water. It was something like waves; but without further notice she went out of the water and went on home. It was not long until she found out that she was pregnant, old as she was. It was but a little while till a child was born to her, who was a boy. The boy grew rapidly every day, until he became a young man. He asked the old woman why they were living alone. She told him that the rest of the family had left their home and had gone to the village of Fire-Light-like-Prairie-Fire, and she supposed that they had met death there. He told the old woman that he must in some way get over there and recover them. He made the journey, and it took him four days. When he arrived at the village he asked where he could stay for a night's rest. He was then ordered to go to the largest and highest tipi, where he might stay all night with the young man living there. He went as directed and walked in. He was ordered to go on where visitors were always seated, and there he sat down, and near him he saw his supposed brothers' weapons. He was told that he, like the others, had to meet danger. He was then given supper. He ate and went to bed. Early next morning he went to the creek and took a bath, and on his return he was called to the shinny ground. He went over, having a shinny club of his own and a ball of his own. When both were at the grounds the boy that was visiting asked to have his ball used first, but they could not agree at all. His opponent asked that his own ball be used. Then the boy asked that his club be used. They could not agree. Finally they agreed to use the ball that belonged to the visiting boy. He tossed the ball up and they both looked up to see where the ball fell. When the ball was tossed up, hail began to fall instead of the ball coming down. All of the hail came down on Boy-setting-Grass-on-Fire-by-his-Footsteps and commenced to pelt him. It came on him alone and on no one else, and it killed him. After his death the young man commanded the hail to stop. They then took up the body of Boy-setting-Grass-on-Fire-by-his-Footsteps and brought wood to burn it up. In those days, when a man of this nature was burned, those whom he had killed would come to life while he was burning. So when they burned his body there were a good many men who came to life, coming out of the fire. Finally the four brothers and the old man came out. As the fire went out the young man who had killed his opponent commanded everybody who had come to life to return to wherever they were from. So the Swift-Hawks, with their father, went straight to where they had left their weapons and shields and went on home. It took them four days again to get home. When they reached home the old woman was glad to see them. They lived here a little longer. The old man told his sons that the things that had happened to them he feared might happen again. So he told them not to live longer as they were, but to go up in the air. They took a gourd full of water and poured it on the fire, and as the smoke went up they went up with it, and turned into Little-Brown-Hawks.

40. THE COYOTE WHO LOST HIS POWERS.*

At the time when the Coyote (Ketox) saved the lives of many people there were two villages, on in the east and the other in the west, situated some distance apart. The people of both villages were in the habit of going on the war-path, but on the return of their war-parties the conduct of the people in the east village was very different from that of the people in the west village. On the return of the war-parties from the east village the people had good times; but when a war-party returned to the west village there was crying, which, when it was heard at the east village, excited wonder, for the people in the east village knew that both villages were accustomed to sending out the same kind of parties. They thought it must be that the enemy met the war-parties of the west village and killed off all their men.

Once upon a time the Coyote resolved to visit this village, stay there until a war-party should go out, and find out why the people cried. He went to the village. A war-party was sent out, and the Coyote went along with them, to see what would happen to the men, so that he might find out why the people cried on the return of the war-party. They traveled all that day, and late in the evening the men stopped, and, there being so many of them, they gathered plenty of wood in a very short time. The Coyote noticed that the men cut some dogwood. He wondered, and, to be like the rest, he began to cut some dogwood himself, though he did not cut as much as did the others. The sun having set, the men made a fire. Then some one was heard to ask from a distance in the north, which was the way to the fire. So the man was directed the way to the fire. The Coyote wondered why the man should ask which way he should come. The Coyote was anxious to learn who the man was and why he had come. The man came up to the fire, and as soon as the Coyote saw him he was afraid of him, for he was dressed entirely different from any man that the Coyote had ever seen. His bonnet was red and hung down his back to the ground. Fringes of human hair hung from the sides of his legs and arms. Each of his legs was marked in front with four black dots like the eyes of a human being. In his right hand he held a war-club. His name was Sign-that-the-Enemy-would-be-weakened (Hossednawa), a Shooting-Star. But when living as a human being he had great powers, some good and some bad. He was a sort of evil-spirited man. The dress which he wore was made of tanned hides and was finished with hair of a human being. When he walked it sounded like thunder and the

---
*Told by Ignorant-Woman (Man) (Towakoni).

groaning of human beings. On his moccasins were to be seen human eyes, which were looking at the warriors. As he stood by the fire it was seen that he had plenty of dogwood with him, the same as the other men. The Coyote wondered what they were going to do with the dogwood sticks. Then, one at a time, the men began to use the sticks to count how many times they had killed their enemies, and each stick counted one enemy. The number of sticks used by a man showed how many men he had killed. But the stranger could count beyond any of the others. Then the trouble began with the Coyote's party. Whenever a man had told all his war-tales the stranger would kill him. This continued throughout the entire night. The Coyote wanted to be the last to enter into the contest. There were a good many in the war-party, but none of them could recount so many enemies killed as did the stranger. The men became fewer and fewer. The Coyote was watching for daylight to come, for he had an idea that if daylight should come before it was his turn he would have a chance to escape the danger. There were a good many men lying dead around the camp-fire. The Coyote was beginning to learn why the people at the west village cried. The men became very few about daylight, but they kept on telling war-stories. Finally it was daylight, and the Coyote asked to be excused for a little while. As soon as he had got out he began to travel very fast, in order that he might report at the west village what was happening to the war-party. As he went further he met a man by the name of Little-Man (Ihasikitse), one that existed in those times and are supposed to exist to-day, whom he asked to save him. Little-Man told the Coyote that he would receive him, and for him not to be troubled, for he himself had great powers and was not afraid of the strange man, although the strange man had blinded him so that he could not find his trail; that he was completely out of patience with his meanness; that he was going to give the Coyote power to kill the strange man. Little-Man gave the Coyote a bow and some arrows and told him that when he got to the west village he should ask for a dress to be made after the same fashion as that worn by the strange man, though buffalo hair might be used in imitation of the human hair; and that his moccasins should have eyes like those of the strange man's. Little-Man also told the Coyote that when he should get ahead of the strange man in telling war stories, he (the Coyote) should tell him that he was going to kill him right there; that the strange man would then say: "Well, you have beaten me in this, but we are yet to contest in a foot-race;" that when he should be asked by the strange man whether he preferred to race under the ground or above the ground he should reply unmistakably that he wanted to go on top of the ground; that by running on top of the ground he would beat the strange man to the goal; that when he should have beaten him he would be asked to spare his life in return for his powers, but that he (the Coyote) should kill the strange man, and not accept his powers. Little-Man also enjoined the Coyote that when he should have accomplished all he should not marry, lest by marrying he should lose his powers. Little-Man then said that when he should have killed the strange man he should gather into one pile the bodies and bones of those who had been killed of the men of his war-party; that he should then gather plenty of wood and place it over the bodies and bones, then burn the wood; that when the wood should get to burning he should call to the men to come out of the fire; and that all the men who had been killed would come out right there. These were the instructions given to the Coyote. The Coyote told Little-Man he knew he could perform all this without making a mistake, for he was too old to make any bad mistake. The Coyote then went on straight to the west of the village. When he arrived there he went direct to the chief's place and got the chief to call the people together at his place, for he had something to tell. The chief ordered a crier to tell the people to come to his place. Finally there was a great crowd of people at the chief's place, and when everybody was present the Coyote was invited to tell what he had to say. The Coyote said that he had come to their village to learn why the people of the village cried so often; that for this reason he had joined himself to the war-party that the people had sent out; that as the war-party had come to the end of their journey they had met with trouble and had been killed; that he was the only man to escape; that he wanted the people to get him buckskin or any other tanned hide which was good enough for leggings, shirt, and moccasins, and to make them for him; that he was going back to the place where the warriors had been killed and try to kill the man who had killed them, and, if possible, restore them to life and bring them home. Thus did the Coyote talk to the people, and the talk sounded good to them. Immediately the things for which he asked were brought, for the people were anxious to see the Coyote save all the men whom they had lost. Not only did they make the desired clothes, but they made the proper bonnet. So the things were made as the Coyote directed. After everything was finished, Little-Man gave to the clothing the real appearance of that of the strange man. The Coyote now told the people that he was going to the unsafe place where dire things happened when it was visited. He then journeyed to the place where everybody dies, to see if he too would be killed. He traveled a good deal faster than he had traveled the first time, for the first time he knew not where the place was. At length he reached the place and mimicked the men of the war-party in getting plenty of wood to last all night and in getting dogwood sticks to count with. Of course he had come to the place early enough to have time to get plenty of wood. All being ready, it began to get dark. The Coyote heard the evil spirited man coming to visit his camp-fire. The Coyote told him to come straight to the place where he always came when anybody camped there. When the strange man came up, there sat his opponent, the Coyote, whose dress closely resembled his own. He was surprised to note this close resemblance. The Coyote sat on the east side of the fire and the strange man sat on the west side. They commenced to tell their war tales, and at first they came out even at the end of every round. All night they continued, till finally the strange man began to fall behind. The Coyote told more tales than did the strange man. The strange man told true stories, but the Coyote being known to tell what was not true, could tell more tales than any other man; his stories were not half true. At about daylight he had not told half of his war-stories, but his opponent then had to search a long time in recalling his war tales, and the Coyote would hurry him, and he said that he himself had not come there to meet any one whom it took so long to recall tales. Finally it got so that the strange man had to search a long time for his tales. The Coyote would add more tales, so that it was impossible for the strange man to catch up with him. Daylight came and the strange man had told all of his war tales. The Coyote rose, took his weapon and was ready to take the strange man's life, when he told the Coyote that there was one more thing to be done before he could take his life, which was to run a race. He told the Coyote he might choose whether he would run on the top of the ground or under ground. The Coyote decided to race on top of the ground. At the south of them there was a high hill which was to be the goal. They commenced to run for the high point. It was agreed that whoever should get there first should be the winner. The strange man went under the ground and the Coyote went on top of the ground. The Coyote ran much faster than he had ever ran before, receiving his power from Little-Man. He ran very fast, and behind him he could hear the strange man coming under the ground. The Coyote finally succeeded in reaching the point first, and he noticed that the strange man had not yet arrived. So the Coyote got ready to take his life as soon as he should come out of the ground. Finally the strange man arrived at the place, and there was the Coyote, ready to meet him.

The strange man begged the Coyote to spare his life and offered him his powers. The Coyote refused, and killed the strange man with his bow and arrows.

The Coyote now dragged the strange man to his camp-fire and began to gather all the human bones that were lying around the place. He placed them in one big pile. He then brought wood enough to burn them. All being ready he set fire to the wood, and there was a great fire. He began to call out all the names of the men who had been killed right at that place, and there came out men from the fire, one at a time, until the fire went out, and all the men had been restored to life.

The Coyote was then with a crowd of men. He told the men to go to their homes, and those who were from his village he told to follow him. All started off, and the men wondered who this famous man might be that possessed powers greater than those of the strange man whom they knew to be famous and a dangerous man to attack; and who had killed the strange man. Finally, through the intervention of the Coyote, the men reached their homes. The chief of the village was surprised to see the return of those men whom he knew to have been killed, now restored to life. The chief ordered the servant to call the people together. The people came to the chief's place, and some of the leading men asked him why he had called the people together. The chief replied that since some one had favored the people by restoring the lives of their warriors and had killed their enemy, he wanted to appoint that one head chief over him; that he wanted them to build for that one a new dwelling place; that it was only right that some of the men who had been at the dangerous place should offer their sister to the man who had restored their lives. The Coyote thought that to be a pretty good announcement, and it was just what he wanted. Little-Man had forbidden him to entertain the foolish idea of getting a wife and becoming a chief; nevertheless, the Coyote having killed the strange man, thought it safe to disregard the admonition of Little-Man. The chief made the announcement and the people thought it only right that they should do the Coyote the favor and let him remain with them at their village. The people began at once to build the Coyote a home, but they did not know that it was for the Coyote. The Coyote stayed with the chief while his home was being built. Little-Man saw that the Coyote was disobeying his orders by accepting these offers. Soon the people had completed the lodge for the Coyote, and the Coyote had wives. He moved into his new home that the people had given him in return for his good work. After he had moved into his new home the most prominent men came around his place to entertain him during the day and night, just as they used to entertain the chief. The old chief would come around to visit him, and so there was a great crowd of men around every day. The Coyote had enough wives to do the cooking for his visitors. The Coyote's wives some became pregnant. His powers began to leave him, and one night Little-Man sent a whirlwind to the Coyote's place to take away all of the Coyote's powers and leave him the same as he was at first, because he had disobeyed his orders. After the Coyote and his wives had gone to sleep the whirlwind entered his lodge and took away everything that he had, and his powers, too. This was a punishment to the Coyote for not obeying the man who had given him powers. Early the next morning when the Coyote's wives woke up they saw a coyote sleeping with them in the place of a human being. They screamed and woke the Coyote, and when the Coyote saw that he was no longer a human being he ran out and left the village forever. When he was out away from the village he cried because he had lost his powers. So, often when we hear the coyote crying, it means that he is regretting his foolish disobedience which lost for him his powers.

The village still existed, and finally the news that the Coyote had lost his powers and that he had left the village began to spread. The people began to learn that this famous man who had brought them to life was the Coyote. After the departure of the Coyote his wives began to have children, and the children were all coyotes. The brothers of the wives then had all the people take one each to their home for pets. The village still existed there, and every one lived happy after the Coyote had killed their enemy.

41. THE BOY WHO LED WAR-PARTIES AND BECAME A HAWK.*

There was once a village, and in the village was a chief who had two boys. One of them was named Bad-Boy (Weksnakok), and he was the older one. The chief had great powers, like any prominent man of his day. He was a powerful warrior. Bad-Boy would not listen to his father's instructions regarding his powers, and the younger son was too young to be given instruction regarding them. The father would set out on the war-path accompanied by many men who thought him to be a brave warrior, and that it was safe for them to be with him in time of war. When at home, the father would try to get Bad-Boy to remain at home, so that he could give him his powers; but Bad-Boy instead of

---
*Told by Cheater (Wichita).

staying at home, would go around to other places and about ash heaps and pick up what parched corn had been left after the corn had been parched and the ashes taken out, and he would eat it. When darkness came he would remain where he pleased, and sleep on the bare ground where there was no one living. Of course, Bad-Boy had a good home, but being a bad boy, he thought himself all right staying away from home. Whenever he saw his younger brother he would abuse him, and hurt his feelings, and the poor boy would return home crying.

Finally the chief became tired of Bad-Boy's doings and sent out word for everyone to come to his lodge. After his criers had made the announcement the people began to come around the chief's lodge. When all were present, they asked the chief why he had called them. The chief announced to the people that if any one should see Bad-Boy among their lodges they should kill him or whip him, for he had done all kinds of mischief. All the men went to their homes. A man was selected to announce what the chief had requested them to do, and he went through the outskirts of the village, talking and telling what the chief had said in regard to Bad-Boy. The following night Bad-Boy heard the news that his father had given orders that his life should be taken, or that he should be whipped if he should be seen lying around anywhere. About midnight Bad-Boy went to his home to sleep on his bed, for he was afraid that they would surely take his life. The next morning, when the old folks were up, they noticed Bad-Boy in his bed. The following day Bad-Boy was rather quiet. He asked his father to instruct him regarding the war bundle that he had always offered to give him. The old chief took down the bundle, with everything in it, shield, quiver, bow and arrows, tobacco-pouch and war-club, the whole bundle being called War-secrets-Bundle (Narwitstanaseh). Everything was spread before Bad-Boy. The thing that was spread before him was a shield, and in this shield was a stuffed hawk, in each of whose feet was a scalp; one white soft feather, and tobacco-pouch with black stone pipe in it, this pouch being a stained skunk hide. The chief then told Bad-Boy that if he wanted to set out at any time on the war-path, or if he wanted to attack his enemy in their village, he should use the scalp in the left foot of the stuffed hawk; and if he wanted to attack them out in the wilderness he should use the scalp that was in the right foot of the stuffed hawk; that before going out on any expedition he must first go to some man whom he wanted to go along as Second-leading-warrior, having his pipe filled with tobacco; before entering, he must ask if the man whom he wanted was present in the lodge, and if present he should ask him to come out; then he should take off his robe and ask the man to stand, then spread the robe on the ground and ask the man to be seated, then offer the pipe to the man and ask him to smoke, then he should tell him the object of his visit, saying that he was willing to serve under the man; that after all this the man whom Bad-Boy had selected for Second-leading-warrior would ask him about what time he wanted to start, and if he wanted to leave within a few days he must leave the order with him to select another Second-leading-warrior, who should serve with him under the leader. The Second-leading-warrior who should be selected first should be on the right side of the leader, the other on his left. After leaving home he must, while camping for the night, have the wood for the fire arranged east and west, and he should face the south toward the open space, having his two men, one on his right, the other on his left, and his other men all in a circle, on his right and at his left.

When all this should be arranged, he must open his war bundle, having his things lying before him; must have his tobacco-pouch open, when the Second-leading-warrior would fill his pipe with tobacco and hand it to him; the same man should then rise and have with him a piece of dry wood, small in size, and light the pipe with it. Pains must be taken in these performances, when after the pipe should be lighted, he was to make his offering to the star-gods. After doing this he should hand the pipe back to the same man that had made the smoke for him, and after having the pipe, he must rise, leaving his seat and going toward the south, then around the fire, and offer it to the one on the left side. The leader then must pass it on to all the men and have them smoke. After the tobacco should be gone, his man should empty the ashes out of the pipe before him, which is called "dahanenornehuanadissaeh," the pipe being emptied with the pipe stick, the mouth of the pipe facing him. After this should be done, if there should be anything to eat, he must have one of these men get a bunch of grass, lay it before him for the food, and there must be a separate fire made on the south side of the main fire for cooking. After the food should be cooked, no one should be allowed to eat until he should have made his offering. After making the offering, he himself must eat the food first, and if there should be anything left it was to be passed on by the man on the right side, the same as should have been done by the man on the left side with the tobacco. Then they must all begin to eat, and cook some extra food, until they should get what they required. If he should want to smoke again, he should have the man on his left perform the same as the first one, and after making his offering this time, must have the man rise and pass to the one on the right and offer him the smoke, then go around in the opposite direction instead of passing it around like the first one did—north, east, south, and west—but this time he should go from north to the west, south and east. After the smoking should be over, he must have his man empty the pipe the same as before. He must send out his two men before daylight, to see if they were near to some enemy; he must have his choice whether to attack the enemy in the village or in the open; and if his men should come back, having seen the enemy, they must come back running, having painted their backs with burnt grass, and bring the news to him. Then he should ask the two spies to tell him all about what they had seen; and after they should tell it, it would be his place to command his men to fix themselves up and be ready for war. In dressing himself he must wear the white soft feather on his head and take his war-club, shield, bow and arrows. He was told how he must be painted with white clay, and that it should always be his luck to find the enemy without being seen. These were the instructions that Bad-Boy received from his father, when he asked his father to give him the powers that he had before offered him.

Bad-Boy kept all the things to himself, and therefore on the next morning he was asked to go to the creek and take a bath, then paint himself up, before he should try to get some one to serve under him. He was told that whenever he did this he must choose a foggy day— the kind of a day chosen by a man of great powers before sending out a war-party. Bad-Boy took a notion to send out a war-party one foggy day. He took his pipe, filled it with tobacco, and went on his way to select a man whom he wanted to serve under him. Arriving at a certain man's lodge, he called and asked if the man was there. Then Bad-Boy entered the lodge and requested the man to rise, which he did. Bad-Boy spread his robe on the ground and asked the man to sit on it. Bad-Boy then took his pipe and offered it. When the man took the pipe Bad-Boy lighted it and asked the man to smoke, saying: "I want you to serve under me on the war-path." The man accepted the pipe and asked Bad-Boy when he wanted to start. Bay-Boy told him that he wanted to wait a few days before starting. Bad-Boy then returned to his home. All that day he was quiet. On that night he took a notion to go somewhere else. Bad-Boy, bad boy as he was, thought that he had better be somewhere else, and show his powers. On the following day he left his home without telling his parents and his man who was to go along with him on the war-path. He traveled all that night and the next day until late in the evening, when he saw a village. He saw also, a cave-like pass, in which he left his things. Then he went into the village, where he saw a good many young people playing the game of shinny. When the boys saw him they began to call him, "Bad-Boy, where did you come from?" He went into the first tipi he came to and there he found an old man, old woman, and a small boy. He was asked to go to a better place, but he refused to leave, and soon he began to do the same things that he had done when he was in his father's village, going around the village and picking up parched corn that had been thrown away. Sometimes some people would invite him to eat with them; and whenever he ate he would save some for the folks with whom he was living. They all knew him to be the chief's son, and a bad boy; so that there were times that the boys of the village played a good many jokes on him, and had much fun with him.

It being their habit to wander around, the time came when all moved from their village, going out on a big hunt. They all traveled on foot and carried their provisions along. The people whom Bad-Boy lived with all went on this long journey with the people. Bad-Boy went along until they were a long way from the village, when he thought of his war things, and commenced to think whether or not to turn back and go after them. Finally he thought he had better turn back and go after them. He turned right around, went back to the village, and to the place where he had left his war things. When he got his things he dressed himself and went on, following the people on the hunt. He traveled on and on until he overtook them. Bad-Boy then went on the south of the people, where he met a group of young women, who began to call to him and ask what he had and where he got his things. He followed the young women, having a club. They laughed at him and made fun of him; so that he pretended to be angry, and told them that if any one of them should make fun of him again he would have to club her. He kept driving them on, until he had driven them away from the hunting party. Then he said to them: "Let us set out on the war-path." The young women were willing. They made a camp, and Bad-Boy shot a deer before night, so that they had deer meat for supper. He got the women to tan the deer hide so that he could make a quiver for one of the young women. He finished it that night. He followed the instructions that his father had given him, but, instead of having men, he had women to perform for him; but, that it might not be known how ignorant he was, he had to instruct the two women. The next day they started out and continued to travel for fourteen or fifteen days, and every evening they camped. Bad-Boy killed deer and made quivers out of the hides, besides making bows and arrows for the young women to equip them for war. Every time they camped the two women, Second-leading-warriors, had to go through the tobacco rite. It was rather hard for women to do such things, but they did it the best they could. Bad-Boy did not know much about it himself, except what he was told by his father, but he went through the rites properly.

The time came when Bad-Boy told the women warriors that he was going out spying, and he predicted that they should fight out in the open. Bad-Boy was always a good runner, and so he traveled fast, until he came to a small hill, and as he went slowly he saw some one coming toward him. He turned back to carry the news to his warriors. He had told them that if they should see him come on the run they would know that he had spied the enemy, and that they were to form in a circle and have an open place for him to enter, so that he might take his place and sit down. When he was seen by the women they formed in a circle and left an open space for him to enter. He came nearer and nearer, gave a whoop, and said: "I have seen it!" When he came where the women were, all seated themselves on the ground and he sat down and whispered to the one on the right side, and asked her to ask him how he traveled and how he had found the enemy. Then he turned to the one on his left and asked her to question him as to what sort of luck he had had while out spying, and asked them to ask him for the full story of his spying. (It is a rule that when a man goes out for such a purpose he has to tell everything he has seen.) Bad-Boy told all about his journey, and how he had seen the enemy. He then whispered to both, and asked them to ask him what he thought of it all, and the women asked him what he thought of it. He told his women warriors that it was his intention to go to this enemy he had seen. They at once rose and went on their way in the direction in which Bad-Boy had seen the enemy coming. They had to conceal themselves so as not to allow their enemy to see them first. They finally found the enemy. They saw him coming down a creek, and they awaited him under a little high place. Bad-Boy then ordered his warriors to follow him just as soon as he should start to run after this man. Bad-Boy made a quick dash and went to meet the enemy, the Trickster, and his women warriors were right behind. The Trickster came to meet them, and fought them, for it was better to fight than to run. Bad-Boy's intention was to club him on the head with the club he had, instead of shooting, but the enemy fought them by shooting arrow after arrow, until Bad-Boy got near enough to club him; then he clubbed him and took off his scalp. Then they all turned back, traveling faster and faster, in order to go a good way off when the other enemy should start after them.

Once on the way to the village it did not take them long to get home. In the meantime the rest of the hunting party had returned to the village. The war-party traveled fast every day, going straight, and they soon got to the place called Place-where-returning-victorious-War-party-halted (Nasaquatowene). When the people returned from victories the signal of victory was given to the people of the village at this place, by turning back twice, so that when some one was seen at this place the people said to themselves: "Who can that be? It is some of our people." The men went out to meet them, and there was Bad-Boy's female war-party.

Bad-Boy then entered the village, and the people praised this war-party. When night came, the people danced all night in honor of Bad-Boy. The prominent men of the village considered him a good boy, and the rest of the people admired him. Then the people whom he was living with received highest compliments for having kept him, and the people carried food to them and made their lodge more comfortable. Bad-Boy sent out many more war-parties, but of men instead of women; and he lived with these people until he grew old. Bad-Boy remained single all his life. When an old man, he called forth all the people, and when they had come they asked him what he had to say to them. He said to the people that he had been living a long time with them, known as Bad-Boy, a warrior, and now as one of their chiefs; and now, on account of his age, and having been a warrior for a long time, he was going to leave them and become something else. He asked them if they also felt like doing the same thing. He also said that some time during the next generation he was going to take pity on some one and give him his great powers. While Bad-Boy was before a great multitude of people he flew away as a Hawk.

42. THE COYOTE AND THE WARRIOR.*

The Coyote (Ketox) lived in a village, but wandered from one place to another. One day he went toward the east, and when he was far away from home he saw a man. He asked the man where he was going, and he told the Coyote that he was going out on the war-path. The Coyote asked if he could go along. The man told him that he could go if he was brave. The Coyote said: "Man, you do not know me. I am the bravest man you have ever seen. You will learn what sort of man I am when we meet some of our enemies." The man remembered that he had often heard that the Coyote was a big coward,

*Told by Ignorant-Woman (Man) (Towakoni).

but told the Coyote he was the kind of a man he wanted to have with him. They went on, and late in the evening the man told the Coyote that they were going to stop for a night's rest at a place called Where-Scalped-Man-sits-by-the-Fire (Tesahitatsak). The man noticed how frightened the Coyote was when he heard about sleeping at such a place. Before camping they killed a buffalo for food. The Coyote was so greedy that he made the man do all the cooking so that he could eat first. After eating the most of the meat they rested a little, then the Coyote cooked some meat for himself. He took the heart and cut off some pieces from the largest part, then he leaned backward and found himself lying down. Taking the largest part of the heart he found that it fitted his knee. So he took the heart and put it over his knee. Then he felt like sleeping a little, and so he went to sleep. When he awoke he thought he saw a Scalped-Man (Tesakiwetsa) sitting right before him. Without rising he took his club to strike the Scalped-Man on the head. He drew back the club to strike, and when he struck he found that he had hit his own knee. He got up, grunted, and rolled around for a while, and the man learned what the Coyote had done to himself. "Surely," said the Coyote, "I thought there was a Scalped-Man sitting by me." The Coyote's knee pained him very much, and that night it swelled up.

The next day when they started on, the man told the Coyote the place where they would next camp all night was at a place called Where-cooked-Meat-flies-around (Adusadiaqua). The man asked the Coyote how his knee was. He replied that it was feeling better and was not quite so sore. The next day they traveled until night, when they came to Where-cooked-Meat-flies-around. When the sun had set and darkness was coming on, something began to fly around. The Coyote knew he could catch some of the things. When they had caught all they wanted the meat stopped flying around. They sat up for a while and the man told the Coyote that the next place they would stay all night was called Where-Arrows-fly-around (Niquatsnahidias). The Coyote, perceiving that the place was full of danger, began to complain of his sore leg hurting him. The next morning they started for this place, and the Coyote said that his knee was hurting him pretty badly. He lagged along behind the man and began to make excuses so that he would not have to go to the dangerous place. Toward evening the Coyote's knee became worse and they stopped to rest. They built their campfire, and as soon as it was dark the arrows began to fly around them, some of which the man caught. The Coyote kept dodging for fear of being shot, and on this account the arrows began to come closer to him, but he kept dodging. He dodged so much that he was finally hit in the arms, and he thought that he was killed. The man kicked his feet and told him to get up. The Coyote rubbed his eyes and said: "I have been sleeping too hard." The arrows ceased to fly around. They ate supper and the man asked the Coyote how his knee was. The Coyote said that it was sore from the long journey. While they were eating the man told the Coyote that the next place they were to stop was called Where-Women-visit-the-Men (Niyahadnawas). The Coyote then said: "I am getting a little better; I wish we were at that place now. What time do you think we will get there?" The Coyote wished the next day might come quickly, and he lay awake most of the night wishing that he were already there. The next morning the Coyote did all the cooking and said that his knee did not hurt him. Again they went on, with the Coyote in the lead, who asked the man why he could not keep up with him. They traveled all that day until evening, then they camped for the night. The Coyote kept waiting for the women to come around. Finally two women came, one to the Coyote and one to the man. The Coyote thought that by cooking some tripe and eating it with the woman he would find out whether she were young or old. He cooked the tripe and gave it to the woman, and she ate it. He discovered from the noise she made that she was not a young woman, and so he told her to leave him as she was too old. The woman arose and took her apparel, which rattled like that of a young woman, and the Coyote saw he had made a mistake and that she was a young woman. She got up and walked off, and the Coyote followed her and asked if she was going out for a moment, but the woman did not pay any attention to him. She left, not to return, but the Coyote thought there would be some more women coming around. The man knew that the Coyote had committed some evil deed by sending away the girl, and he kept the woman who had come to him throughout the whole night. Now Coyote regretted his stupidity in sending away the woman, and thought about the pleasures he had lost. He was not sleeping but was carefully watching the man, hoping that he would be asked to sleep with his woman. The man, however, did not ask him. Coyote waited with longing for the woman until daylight. It was in vain; for she had now gone away. After breakfast the man said the next place they would stop for the night was called Where-War-clubs-fly-around (Hakstihidihaukstinahidias). Learning of the dangers of this place, the Coyote's leg began to pain him again, and he lagged behind. The man told him to hurry on and walk with him, but the Coyote's leg hurt him pretty badly. They traveled on the entire day, until late in the evening, when they again camped. When they were eating supper they began to hear war-clubs flying around. They became thicker and thicker, and the Coyote began to dodge them, although the man had told him not to dodge, for if he did he would get struck. The Coyote kept dodging the clubs, and finally one of them hit him on the head. The man kept on the lookout for the best ones. He got hold of one that he thought was a good club, and another he got for the Coyote, but the Coyote was lying on the ground, dead. Having secured two clubs the other clubs began to cease to fly around. The man kicked the Coyote's feet and told him to get up. The Coyote got up, rubbed his eyes, and said he had been sleeping too hard. The man now reminded the Coyote that he had told him there was no danger of being hit with the clubs if he did not dodge, and that the weapons were for their assistance when they should reach the enemy. While they were sitting there, the man informed Coyote that their next station would be Jatsnahidios, that is, the place of the flying vulvas. Again they set out. Now Coyote was able to make the journey painlessly, because he was eager to arrive at this place. Coyote asked the man what kind of vulvas these were, and if they were of various sizes. The man responded that they were of various sizes. Coyote asked whether they could fly about without women. The man responded that they could. The Coyote slept little and watched for daylight to come, so that they could start for the place. In the morning the man asked the Coyote about his knee, and the Coyote said that it was feeling all right. They started on and the Coyote was in good condition to walk, and left the man behind. They traveled until late in the evening, then camped. They cooked supper and then began to eat. While they were eating, certain things began to fly about. These were so numerous that they often struck Coyote's face; and tears appeared. Coyote, however, was unable to catch a single one of them. And so, his quiver emptied, he tried to catch them. In the meantime he saw that they were of different sizes. Finally with difficulty he seized one. Although he attempted to pierce the one which he had caught with his manly member, he was unable to do so. The man kept laughing at the Coyote. Now they sat by the fire. The man told the Coyote that they were coming to the real place the next time they camped, for they were coming to a place Where-Enemies-attack-their-Foes (Hidiokidiodes). Now they started again, and the Coyote's knee began to pain him, for he knew they were coming to the last place, and he thought it would be no fun when the enemy should get after him. The Coyote's knee hurt him worse than ever. He stayed behind his partner, but they kept on traveling. When the man got ahead of the Coyote he stopped and waited until he came up, and then they started again. They traveled till late in the evening and again camped for the night. The Coyote's knee hurt him pretty badly, and it pained him all that night, for he knew they were to be attacked the next morning. The next morning when they started off they found themselves surrounded by the enemy and they were attacked by them. The Coyote tried to run, but the enemy ran after him and killed him. Before starting, the man had told the Coyote not to run, that they had as much courage as had the enemy, but the Coyote was so much of a coward that he forgot all about this and ran away from his partner and was killed. After the fight the man went to see where the Coyote was. He found him lying on the ground, dead, and scalped by the enemy. The man again kicked the Coyote on the feet and told him to get up. Then he came to life and got up and ran again, and this time he ran away from the man and never met him again. The Coyote was so scared by the attack of the enemy that it made him wild. The man returned to his home. This man was a Chicken-Hawk (Ikataskiiyes).

43. THE END OF THE TRICKSTER-CHEATER.*

There were once people living in a village ruled by an old man. The old man had a wife, daughter, and four sons. The old man and his wife became blind, and in this way the boys came to be at the head of the village, and this was their home, and the people were their people. They would sometimes go on the war-path against their enemies, the Tricksters (Kinos), and would come home victorious with many captured people and would hold their captives as prisoners; and this was their business. Sometimes they would go hunting, wandering around over the country, and came back with plenty of meat. They always made their hunting trips in the fall.

Once upon a time the four brothers, the chiefs of the village, called their people to meet at their place, and when the people had gathered around the place they announced that they wanted to go out on a hunting trip for a while, and that the people should be ready in four days. The people waited for four days to pass. Before the fourth day came, the father of these four chiefs told them that it was useless for him, his wife, and daughter to go along, and that they wished to be moved into a safe place near to water and timber; and so the chiefs had them moved to a place where the old man intended to stay until the return of the hunters.

When four days had passed, the people began to move out; and, of course, in those times the people traveled on foot on any expedition. All of the people left the village, so there was nothing left but grass-lodges and tipis. When all had left, the enemies came about and went all through the village, but found no one. Among the enemy, who

*Told by Ahahe (Waco).

were called Trickster-Spies (Kinas-Kitikeahara), was one who went to
the outskirts of the village, found the old folks and their daughter
living in the timber, and noticed that both of the old folks were blind,
and that they had a good-looking girl. He thought to himself: "What
must I do? If I should call the rest of the men they might kill the old
folks and take the girl." He concluded to keep his discovery a secret,
so he went back to the rest of the warriors, and when he got there
they all left the place and returned to their homes. When they had gone
a good way off, the Trickster-Spy left the crowd and returned to where
he saw the old people and their daughter, with the expectation of marrying the girl. While on the way he killed a buffalo and took the meat
to where the folks were living. When he arrived at the place he stopped
by a tree, and when the girl stepped out, he made a motion for her to
come to him and pointed to the place where the meat lay. But the girl
went back into the tipi, telling her father that she had seen some one outside near by, making motions for her to come to him and pointing to
the ground. The old man asked the girl what kind of a looking man he
was, and she described the man just the way he looked to her. She
said that the man was large, with dark complexion and had his hair
tied behind. The old man repeated the words of the girl and said:
"Surely we are found by our enemies and are in danger." The Trickster-Spy kept making motions to the girl to come to him. She again
told her father that the man was still making motions for her to come
to him, and pointing to the ground. The girl noticed something on the
ground. She told her father again, and said she saw something in front
of the man. Her father finally told her to go over and see what he
wanted, saying: "It may be that he wants to make up some kind of
friendship." She went over, and when she had got there she saw a
pile of fresh meat lying on the ground, and the man asked her to take
the meat to where her folks lived. But on account of it being too heavy
for her to carry the man took the meat, put it on his back again and
made motions for her to go back to her folks' tipi, and when she started
he followed her with the meat. They both entered the tipi and the
Trickster-Spy delivered the beef to the folks. After entering the tipi,
the old man told his wife and daughter to do whatever the Trickster-
Spy should ask. The Trickster-Spy having great powers, knew what
the old man was talking about, and so he made up his mind to remain
there and marry the girl. So the Trickster-Spy and the girl became
man and wife. When the old man's daughter became the wife of the
Trickster-Spy he had to communicate with signs. The old man told
his son-in-law that he had four sons and that they were out hunting

with his people, and that they were chiefs, and the Trickster-Spy was asked to look out for them at any time. In the meantime he would go around hunting for game, and having great powers he always brought home meat. When out somewhere, if he should happen to see some of his enemies about to see him he would turn into something else, such as a deer or coyote, and this is the way he wandered around. Once in a great while he would look over the hill to see if his brothers-in-law were coming. One day as he went over the hill to see if he could see any one, he saw four men coming, and a large crowd of people following them. When he saw this he turned right back to where he was living and told his wife that he had seen a great many people coming. Then he lay down on the bed, covering his head with a robe. The Trickster-Spy's wife told her father and mother that their boys were coming home; that they would be in before night. Not very long afterward the people were heard coming into their homes, and the boys, the four chiefs, returned to their home.

On their arrival they saw some one else at their home lying in their sister's bed. After they had all arrived the old man told his sons that they had a stranger living with them and that he was their brother-in-law, and that he had kept them alive by hunting and had been good to them, and for this reason they would have to allow him to live with them. The chiefs were satisfied with their brother-in-law, because he had taken care of their people, and so the Trickster-Spy lived with these people for a long time. The time came when the wife of the Trickster-Spy had a boy, whom they called Son-of-the-Trickster-Spy. After this child was born Trickster-Spy would always take him along hunting. Once upon a time as the Trickster-Spy was out hunting, he noticed that the boy was pretty heavy, for he had been growing rapidly. So the Trickster-Spy came to a large tree, climbed up in it and left his child there; but before he left, he took the child and painted him with white clay from the shoulders to the top of his head; then he started on. It happened that some of his own people, the Trickster-Spies, came along and knew his ways, and besides, ever since he had lived with his new wife he had sent out war-parties against his own people; so when they came to this tree they saw something up in it, and found that it was a child. They knew that it was some of the Trickster-Spy's work, and therefore took the child down and at once started back home. It was early in the day when they found the child. Late that afternoon the Trickster-Spy came back to where the child had been and found that some of his own people had taken it. He at once started to trail the people; having great powers, he could travel as fast as he wanted to. At night he overtook them. He went ahead of them, and when he came to a small hollow he stepped to one side, and when the Trickster-Spies came along with the boy he joined the party. The people did not know that he was among them, and passed the boy from one to another, as they in turn became tired. The Trickster-Spy did most of the talking about passing around the child. Finally his time came to carry the child on his back. When his turn came he went but a short distance with the crowd and stepped to one side, letting them go on. He then turned back at once, traveling fast, so as not to be overtaken. He was a good way off when the people found out that he had already been with them and they began to ask one of another: "Who has got the child?" When they found that no one present had the child they began to say: "Surely the Trickster-Spy must have been in the crowd and must have his child, and perhaps he has carried it back to his home." That night he was a long way from the Trickster-Spies, so that they did not follow him, and on the next day he reached home.

The Trickster-Spy's child grew rapidly, but his father still continued to take him on his hunting trips, and when he got old enough the child had as great powers as his father. The Trickster-Spy trained his child by carrying him along on his hunting trips, giving him some powers as he had them. He finally had to leave the boy at home, for he was too heavy to carry, but the Trickster-Spy continued to go out on his hunting trips against his own people. He lived with the four chiefs for a long while, until he made trouble by beating his wife, when he escaped and fled to his own people, leaving his wife and boy. This made Son-of-the-Trickster-Spy angry at his father, and he looked for him that he might kill him. The boy, having the same kind of powers as his father, fooled a good many people, working all kinds of schemes. There were times that some of the enemies would see him, but he would turn into something else, such as a deer, coyote or any other living animal. The people finally sent out a war-party against the Trickster-Spies. When they were on the way, Son-of-the-Trickster-Spy went out to spy; but in the meantime, the Trickster-Spies had sent out a war-party against their enemies, so the Trickster-Spy and Son-of-the-Trickster-Spy were spying against each other's people; and when both saw each other they went in opposite directions, going but a short distance and around the hills, and there they met again. The son turned into a deer, as also did the father, but each was somewhat afraid to meet the other, so they left each other for their parties. Son-of-the-Trickster-Spy told his people that while he was out spying he met some one whom he thought was his father. When he told his story he said:

"When I was on the lookout for foes I turned into a deer, but I met another deer, and when I met this deer I was afraid. Then I found that it was my father who was trying to fool me, because I am always looking out for him to kill him, and he knows that I am going to take his life, as he is after my life. The war-party withdrew and returned to their home. Son-of-the-Trickster-Spy continued looking for his father to kill him. It happened that while on a hunting trip he accidentally saw some one who had killed some game, but when he saw this man he had to keep himself pretty well concealed, so that the man would not see him. At the point where the man was there was a small hollow. When the Son-of-the-Trickster-Spy went into this place he found there his enemy and decided to attack him, and he already knew that it was his father. Right by the side of Son-of-the-Trickster-Spy were some small bushes, from which he jumped, having turned into a big buck deer. He ran into the woods, then turned back into a small hollow, and followed it up until he came to where his father was. His father, when he found him again, was still looking in the direction the buck had gone, facing the other way. So he at once went for his father, and before his father knew what was to happen to him his son attacked him and killed him.

Son-of-the-Trickster-Spy, after killing his father, took his scalp and returned to his home with all the war material that his father had had. When he got home he turned over to his people the scalp and other things, telling them he had killed his father, and that was all he wanted to do. When this scalp was turned over to the people they had all kinds of dances, for joy, on account of the killing of one of their main enemies; for the Trickster-Spy was the meanest enemy they had, and they had never been able to kill him. This ends the story of one of the most noted men of the Trickster-Spies.

44. THE COYOTE, PRAIRIE-TURTLE, AND SQUIRREL.*

Once on a time the Prairie-Turtle (Kikeskatoshkeyosh) went to a creek, and the creek was swollen, so that he could not get across. He wished that some one would take him across. There were some Buffalo crossing the creek, and the Prairie-Turtle sat there waiting for one of the Buffalo to ask him if he wanted to be taken across. Finally there came one Buffalo and asked him what he was saying.

The Prairie-Turtle said: "O, nothing. I just wanted some one to be kind enough to take me across this deep water." The Buffalo

*Told by Dragging-Enemies-from-the-River-Bank (Towakoni),

said: "I will take you across if you will get between my hoofs." The Prairie-Turtle said that the Buffalo might step on him. The Buffalo said: "Well, get on my back and we will cross the creek." But the Prairie-Turtle said: "O, no, you might shake yourself in the middle of the water and throw me off and drown me." The Buffalo then asked him to ride between his horns, but still the Prairie-Turtle would not ride, but said that the Buffalo might shake his head and knock him off. The Buffalo finally decided to let the Prairie-Turtle ride over in his anus. "Well," said the Buffalo, "you could get into my anus if you would behave yourself while in there." The Prairie-Turtle said to the Buffalo that it would be more safe for him to get in there than any place else, so the Buffalo backed up against a high bank where the Prairie-Turtle was sitting, and the Prairie-Turtle crawled into the Buffalo's anus. While they were on the way over the water the Prairie-Turtle began to eat a part of the intestines of the Buffalo, and the Buffalo asked him what he was eating. The Prairie-Turtle told him that he was eating something that he had brought along with him. Just as soon as the Buffalo got across and went a little way he fell to the ground dead. The Prairie-Turtle began to wonder how he could get out, now that the Buffalo was dead. Finally he ate through the flank of the Buffalo, and in that way he got out. He said aloud: "I wish I had a knife so that I could butcher my Buffalo that I have killed."

The Coyote (Ketox) heard this, although he was a long way from where the Buffalo was lying. After a little while the Prairie-Turtle saw the Coyote coming down the hill, running to find where the sound had come from when some one had called for a knife. The Coyote then said: "Well, my friend, were you not calling for a knife to butcher a Buffalo?" The Prairie-Turtle said: "No, I was not calling for a knife to butcher a Buffalo, but I was calling for a knife to cut arrows." But the Coyote had already seen the Buffalo, and asked the Prairie-Turtle what that was lying down on the ground. The Prairie-Turtle told him that it was his robe. The Coyote asked the Prairie-Turtle why his robe had horns. The Prairie-Turtle then asked the Coyote if he had never had a robe that had horns. The Coyote then asked why his robe had hoofs on it. "Well," said the Prairie-Turtle, "did not you ever have a robe that had hoofs on it?" The Coyote again said that the robe had a tail on it. "Well," said the Prairie-Turtle, "did you never have a robe that had a tail?" The Coyote kept asking a lot of questions, and finally the Prairie-Turtle said that he had killed the Buffalo; that he wished that some one would come around with a knife. The Coyote was the very man the Prairie-Turtle was looking for. "Well," said the Coyote to the Prairie-Turtle, "let us butcher the beef, and I will take half, for the work I do, and give you the remainder." "All right," said the Prairie-Turtle, so they commenced to butcher the Buffalo. When they were through butchering, the Coyote said to the Prairie-Turtle: "Partner, let us have a foot-race, and let the loser of the race go without meat, and eat the blood that is left on the ground." The Coyote told the Prairie-Turtle that if he would not race that he would take the meat anyhow, so that the only way to have a little more fun out of this was to have a foot-race. The poor Prairie-Turtle had to run the race or lose everything. The Coyote told the Prairie-Turtle that he would give him the start. Their goal was to be where they had the meat, and the first one to jump over the meat was to have it all. They ran the race, and the poor Prairie-Turtle, of course, lost. The Coyote said to the Prairie-Turtle: "Well, partner, you can stay here and watch my meat while I go after my wife and children, and when I come back I shall give you some of the meat anyway." The Prairie-Turtle agreed to remain there until the Coyote came back.

As soon as the Coyote started off, there came a Squirrel (Watsada), who asked the Prairie-Turtle if they might not play a trick on the Coyote, and take all the meat up in a tree where the Squirrel was living. The Prairie-Turtle agreed to do it, and they at once commenced to take the meat away to a tree that was standing by a creek. The tree spread out over the creek. After they had taken all the meat to the tree the Squirrel began to haul it up in the tree, and when the Squirrel had taken all the meat up, the Prairie-Turtle still remained to be taken up in the tree. When the Coyote returned he found that his meat was gone. He followed the trail to the creek, and when he looked in the creek he saw the Prairie-Turtle and the Squirrel in the water. When he saw them in the water they looked at him and smiled. The Coyote then said to them: "I will get even with you." The tree spread out over the water, so that it was only the reflection of the Prairie-Turtle and the Squirrel in the water. The Coyote said: "Never mind, fellows, I will get you." He dived in the water and could not reach them. When the Coyote came out he looked in the water again, and there they were, smiling at him. He tried every way to get to them and kill them and to take away the beef from them. The Coyote said to his children: "Get me a stone so that I can go down deep and get to where these fellows are." The Coyote thought that they were in a place under the water and that by going deeper he could get them. The children got him a stone to tie around his neck. Before going into the water he told his children that when they should see some excrement floating they should call for some intestines. When the children got him the stone, the Coyote tied it around his neck and dived in, expecting to get to the Prairie-Turtle and the Squirrel. After he had dived, some excrement floated around that came out from the bottom of the water. Then the children began to call for intestines. After a while the Prairie-Turtle and the Squirrel began to howl at the Coyotes, telling them that they had drowned their father. The young Coyotes and their mother saw the two up in the tree instead of seeing them in the water. They sat up there and mocked the Coyotes, saying that the old woman had drowned her man, and the young ones had drowned their father.

The Prairie-Turtle and the Squirrel had some boiling meat and ate it up, and there was nothing but the soup left. The Squirrel called all the young Coyotes around the tree and told them that he would pour down some of the soup to them to drink. So the young ones came under the tree and the Squirrel poured the soup on them. The soup was boiling hot, and made them run in different directions. After the Squirrel had scalded the Coyotes he brought the Prairie-Turtle down to the ground and the two parted. Had it not been for the Squirrel all of the Coyotes would have stayed in droves all the time, but because the Squirrel scattered them they do not go together any more. Even the young ones, after they are old enough, separate, and no longer stay together.

45. THE COYOTE, THE RABBIT, AND THE SCALPED-MAN.*

The Coyote (Ketox) and the Rabbit (Kokish) once met to plan how to get something from some one else. They finally agreed to take a calumet pipe to the Scalped-Man (Tesakiwetsa), who never had been known to take his bonnet from his head. They made plans to get his bonnet, not knowing what sort of a headdress he had. So the Coyote said to the Rabbit: "We will go to him and sing songs to him, and in this way we can get nearly everything he has. We will get this bonnet of his, too. After he has given us the other things he will not be very stingy of his bonnet." So they started off at once for the Scalped-Man's place. When they arrived there they told the Scalped-Man that they had come to give him a dance. The Scalped-Man accepted their offer. They commenced their dance, one singing while the other danced. When one got tired of singing the other sang. After they had begun to dance and sing the Scalped-Man came with gifts of moccasins, clothing, and the like, for them to wear. Before giving these things away he, of course, had to tell a war-story. They continued for a

*Told by Kadas (Wichita).

long time, for the Scalped-Man had a good many things to give away. Finally his things were all gone, and he told the Coyote and the Rabbit that they had everything he had, and that he had nothing more to give. Not yet satisfied, the Coyote and the Rabbit called on him for his bonnet, but this the Scalped-Man refused, for he could not take it off, as it was for his own use and for no one else. But they kept asking him for it and told him that they had been wanting it for a long time. They said they would not stop their dancing unless he should give them his bonnet. It was customary before giving anything, for the giver to go off, then come back, then tell a war-story and then give away whatever he had to give. The Coyote and the Rabbit kept on asking for the bonnet, but the Scalped-Man refused. He told them that he had given away all he could. This made them feel like dancing and singing, and it was their intention not to stop singing and dancing until they had induced the Scalped-Man to give them the bonnet. Finally they prevailed upon the Scalped-Man, and when he came running toward them with his bonnet off they saw that he was a Scalped-Man. Both were afraid of him and they commenced to run, for they were scared at the appearance of his head. The Scalped-Man followed them until he overtook the Rabbit, whom he got by the feet. Now he started after the Coyote. When he overtook him he threw the Rabbit at him and hit him in the face, then gave up the chase. When the Rabbit got up the Coyote was gone. He trailed him and whistled to him to find where he was. Finally the Coyote heard the Rabbit whistling to him and answered, and they met again. They talked about the man's head. The Coyote said: "If I had known what was the matter with the man's head I would never have asked for his bonnet; but truly, that is the worst thing I ever saw. Were you not afraid of his head?" The Rabbit said: "I was truly scared when I saw him coming." The Coyote then told the Rabbit that when overtaking him the Scalped-Man must have wet his moccasin and hit him in the face with it. The Rabbit then commenced to laugh, saying: "Si! Si! Si! That was I. He got hold of my feet and threw me at you and hit you in the face, and he threw me so hard that when I landed in your face I urinated, so you thought you were hit with a wet moccasin. That was I." Thus they talked for a good while about their things that they still had at the Scalped-Man's place, but they were both afraid to go to the Scalped-Man's place after them. The Rabbit told the Coyote how foolish they were to try to get the man's bonnet when he refused it so persistently. So they had to laugh over their troubles. But they were both astonished at the head of the Scalped-Man. They parted.

46. THE COYOTE AND THE SKUNK, WHO INAUGURATED THE FEAST.*

The Coyote (Ketox) lived by himself with his family. He generally had a hard time, for he was sometimes lucky in killing game, and sometimes he was unlucky, for he was a notorious coward. Once upon a time while he was out hunting for something to eat he found the Skunk (Niwechia), and was about to kill him, for he was what he was looking for. The Coyote said to the Skunk: "My enemy, I have to kill you, for I am hunting for such animals as you. I was about to give up, but now I have found you and I must kill you, for my children and wife are hungry." The Skunk begged the Coyote to let him live, saying that he would give him power to kill other animals with more flesh, if he would only let him live. The Coyote then asked the Skunk where he could find these other animals. The Skunk told the Coyote that the Beavers (Gidisgardahits) were having a medicine-dance near by, and that by his sending for these men one at a time he and the Skunk could kill a whole lot of them. The Coyote then agreed to this proposition and was instructed what to do. He was told to go, and while they were dancing to point out the fattest one in the crowd and beg to have him come and doctor the Skunk, saying that he was very sick. The coyote went to where he was told to go and there he found the Beavers having the medicine-dance. When he arrived at the place the Coyote was asked what he wanted. In reply he said that his partner was sick and that he wished one of the men who was dancing would come over there to doctor him. The Coyote was requested to take his choice of the men, for they were all medicine-men. The Coyote looked at them, and he selected the fattest man that he could see in the crowd. After selecting him he and the medicine-man went out to where the sick partner was. When they arrived where the sick partner was the Coyote was asked what part of the man's body was hurting him. The Coyote told his partner to turn over and let the medicine-man see where the pain was. When the skunk laid on his back, Coyote lifted up his tail and showed his anus. Then the medicine man inspected the place where the pain had been said to be, and while he was holding his face near the anus, the skunk defecated into his eyes, so that he was blinded for a little while. Then the Coyote took a club and hit the medicine-man on the head and killed him. Then he went back to where his partner was. He cleaned the blood from the ground and told his partner that was a pretty good trick that they had done.

---

*Told by Towakoni Jim (Towakoni).

The Coyote was told to go and try again, and this time to tell them that the first medicine-man had failed to cure his partner and that the medicine-man had gone to look for some medicine different from the one he had. The Coyote went back to where the medicine-men's dance was, and on his arrival he told that the first medicine-man had failed to cure the sick man, but had gone out to look for some more medicine, different from what he had, and that he would soon come back. He said that he wished that he could have another medicine-man while this other one was out looking for his medicine, for his partner was nearly dead. He was then allowed to select another man. The Coyote then selected the fattest man in the crowd to doctor his partner. After selecting another man he and the medicine-man both went to where his sick partner was lying on his dying bed. When they arrived the Skunk pretended that he was dying and rolled from one side to the other. The Coyote told the medicine-man to make haste in doctoring his partner, for he was afraid that he would die. The medicine-man then asked where it was hurting him the most. The Coyote turned over the sick partner of his and raised his tail up and said that that was the most important place where the pain was. Then the medicine-man commenced to doctor him. While he was examining the place where the pain was the Skunk did as before, and again the Coyote took the club, and hit him on the head and killed him. The Coyote then again took this Beaver to one side, where he had laid the other Beaver, and then cleaned up the place again. They again played this same trick on another one and killed him, and then another one, until they had killed four in all, and then they quit. The Coyote thanked the Skunk for helping him to get something to eat. They parted. The Coyote went home loaded with the Beavers he had killed.

When the Coyote arrived home he requested his wife to do some cooking for him, so that he could call his friends to the feast. He told his wife that while he was out he had met a good many of his friends and that he had promised to invite them to come to his place and eat with him. The Coyote then asked his wife and children to leave the place for a while, when his friends should come, for there were some of the men who would not be looked at by women or children. The Coyote's wife began at once to cook for his best friends. The Coyote also asked his family not to eat anything first, before these friends of his had eaten. His family was hungry, but they all obeyed the old man's orders. When the cooking was done, the Coyote ordered his family to leave for a while until the feast was all over. Near their place was a little creek where he ordered his family to stay, and he told his wife not to allow any of the children to look toward their place. When the Coyote's family left the place the Coyote then rapped on the door and pretended that some one was coming in, and then he talked to himself and pretended that he was seating his friends in the room. The Coyote's intention was to eat all the meat by himself. The Coyote then commenced to eat from one of the places where the food was spread out. He went from one place to another until he had enough. At the place where he first started to eat while he was hungry he ate the most, at the next place less, and so on. After he had enough he again pretended that all of the men were passing, and he talked to himself as if he were telling his friends that he was glad they had come to eat with him. Then he closed the door, and after a while he called his family to come in.

When his family arrived he told them that his friends had eaten and that some were pretty hungry. The wife and children saw that there were places where some were seated that were hungry, and some that were not very hungry. The Coyote's family ate the rest of the meat, while the Coyote was sitting there, full as he could be. After the children and wife had eaten, he commanded his family to move away and be coyotes. He also commanded that in after generations there would be such things as making a feast for friends.

47. THE COYOTE WHO BECAME A BUFFALO.*

The Coyote (Ketox) once went to look around for something to eat. While he was looking he saw a very large Buffalo (Taah) grazing. The Coyote watched him eating and wished that he might get his food in the same way as the Buffalo did. Wherever the Buffalo went the Coyote would follow. Now, the Coyote decided to beg the big Buffalo for powers that he had, especially to live like the Buffalo lived, not having to look around for food. The Buffalo kept grazing, the Coyote following him. Finally the Coyote called to the Buffalo, and said: "Luiwah (a word of address generally used by the Coyote when meeting any one), I surely would like to have the great power you have and be as large as you are. Can you give these powers to me, so that I can graze around as you are doing now? I am sure you can take pity on your friend when he needs help." The Buffalo stood for a long time without saying anything to the Coyote. Finally the Buffalo asked the Coyote if he were brave, for it took brave men to become

*Told by Careful-Doer (Woman) (Wichita).

Buffalo. The Coyote told the Buffalo that he was the bravest man that was ever known; that he knew there was no braver man than himself. The Buffalo then said to the Coyote: "If you can tell me that you are brave that is all that is required for you to become a Buffalo." The Coyote said that he was a brave man. Then the Buffalo said to the Coyote: "Well, come on, go a certain distance and let me run against you once; you will get up, a great big Buffalo bull; then you can go out among the herds of Buffalo and live as I live, and you may associate with the female Buffalo." This pleased the Coyote, who went off a certain distance. The Buffalo told him to face him, saying that he would be run right square over, then he would be a Buffalo. The Buffalo ran as hard as he could toward the Coyote, and the Coyote looked right at the Buffalo bull, and he noticed that he had his eyes shut. The Coyote quickly stepped out of the way. The Buffalo turned around and said to the Coyote: "I thought you were a brave man and desired greatly to become a Buffalo." The Coyote then was given another trial. The Buffalo told the Coyote that he would have but four trials; that if he failed to be run over there was no other way for him to become a Buffalo. They tried the second time, and the Coyote failed to be run again this time, for he knew that if the Buffalo was trying to hurt him he would kill him. Without saying anything further the Buffalo again asked the Coyote to stand up where he was, and not to step out of the way again. The Coyote stood up again to let the Buffalo run over him. The Buffalo ran again toward the Coyote, and when he was near to him the Coyote stepped out of the way again. The Buffalo turned around and said to the Coyote: "Well, I will give you one more chance, and if I fail to run over you I shall let you go the way you are." So the Coyote was given one more trial. This time he closed his eyes and was going to let the Buffalo run over him, whether it should kill him or not. The Buffalo started on a run again towards the Coyote, and there stood the Coyote with his eyes shut, brave enough to let the Buffalo run over him, and over the Coyote went, and when he stood up he was a very large Buffalo bull.

The Buffalo then told the Coyote that he could go wherever he wanted to, but he must not hurt any one. They parted, and the Coyote-Buffalo went his way. He grazed around eating grass. When he came to a creek he went into the water to drink, and to see what sort of a looking Buffalo he was. He drank the water like any other Buffalo. After he had drank as much as he wanted he crossed the creek and went on an open prairie. While he was going he saw some one coming from across the prairie. He noticed that it was another Coyote.

He spoke to the Coyote, and asked him how he liked the way he was grazing. The Coyote told him that it was all right. The Coyote-Buffalo then told the Coyote if he wished to be like himself, power could be given him to do so. The Coyote asked how the power could be given. The Coyote-Buffalo told him that by running over him once he could be changed to a very large Buffalo bull and live as he himself was living, not having to live on any other food than grass, and could be among Buffalo and be with the female Buffalo. The Coyote accepted the offer, and stood off as far as the Coyote-Buffalo had stood from the Buffalo when he had been made into a Buffalo. The Coyote-Buffalo then ran as hard as he could, to run against the Coyote. Of course the Coyote-Buffalo asked the Coyote the same questions he had been asked when he first met the Buffalo. The Coyote said he was the bravest man he knew of. When he started to run over the Coyote, the Coyote jumped out of the way. He gave the Coyote four trials—the first, second and third time, and the fourth time the Coyote made up his mind to allow the Coyote-Buffalo to run over him. When the fourth time came, the Coyote-Buffalo ran over the Coyote, and when he fell over they both cried, the way the coyotes cry. They were both Coyotes again, instead of Buffalo. The Coyote-Buffalo was changed back to what he was first. The two Coyotes parted, one going one way and one the other. The Coyote who was a Buffalo never got into any herds of Buffalo, because he tried to make another Coyote into a Buffalo. This is the way the Coyote did when he got any kind of power from other animals. He would always do something wrong and let the power escape from him.

48. THE COYOTE AND THE ARTICHOKE.*

The Coyote (Ketox) was out hunting something for his family. He wandered from place to place. Once upon a time, as he went out to hunt, he went toward the north, and as he went further he met a good many people. The Coyote then asked these people where they were going. The people told him that they were going to dig some artichokes. The Coyote asked the people if he could go along. The people told him that he could. The Coyote then joined the party. As they went further, they came to a place where the artichokes were. and then the people began to dig for them. The Coyote began to dig, too. He noticed that some of these people were eating the artichokes as they went along digging. Then he commenced eating. Some one

*Told by Ignorant Woman (Man) (Towakoni).

at his side told him that he must save a piece always, so that it would grow again. This piece that he was told to save was near the rings. Every time he would eat one, this artichoke would say: "This is where you will have to save me." Then the Coyote would throw away that part. The Coyote then forgot all about digging and saving to take home, but kept on eating. Finally the rest of the people began to depart and he was left alone at this place. The Coyote then thought that he had better stay where he was, living on something good. He kept on eating the raw artichokes, and finally forgot about saving the part he had been told not to eat. The artichokes would remind him of it, but this time he would eat up every bit of it, so as not to let them grow any more and so that the people, whenever they should come back, would not find any more of the artichokes. So he kept on eating the artichokes, without saving a piece. When Coyote had stuffed himself so much that he began to pass gas, he wondered what evil had befallen him. He persisted in passing gas continually to his distress. Whenever he passed gas, it happened that he was hurled into the air, and little by little he was carried into the woods. Finally he fell into a half-burned tree and hollow trunk, and clung there, and he did not pass gas anymore.

But the Coyote was unable to get out, and he could do nothing but remain there until some one should come along. The Coyote remained in this hollow stump several days, and he was getting pretty poor. Once in a while he would halloo, and say: "I am a fat coon, and I am in this hollow tree!" Some time afterward the people came back, and when the Coyote heard them coming, he called out: "I am a fat coon in the hollow tree!" The people listened and tried to see where that sound came from. They finally caught the sound, and came to this burnt stump and began to cut the tree down, and when they had cut the tree down, there they found the Coyote, just as poor as he could be; he was unable to walk. So he was taken out, and his life was saved. The Coyote did not stay to see these people dig any more of the artichokes, but he went straight to his home, and when he got home he found that his family had starved to death. So he went off howling, and when he was howling he was crying over his family.

49. THE COYOTE AND THE WILD-CAT.*

Once upon a time the Coyote (Ketox) went on a journey, and after a while he got rather hungry, for he had gone a long way. He found on his way some dry bones. He picked up a rib bone and went on

*Told by Keechi (Woman) (Wichita).

until he came to some timber, and there he made a fire. After making a fire he thought that he would sleep for a while. He went to sleep, and when he woke he looked at the bone, and there was the whole rib of a buffalo and he had plenty of meat and fat. He cut a stick to hang the meat on, that he might cook it by the fire. After he had set the meat to roast he thought he would go to sleep again, for he was tired from traveling that day. While he was sleeping the Wild-cat (Waixsiits) came along and found the Coyote asleep. He saw the meat, took the Coyote's knife, commenced to cut down the meat and ate all of it. After eating, the Wild-cat took a little meat and filled the Coyote's teeth with it, rubbed fat on the Coyote's mouth, greased the Coyote's hands, and put all the bones before him, then greased his knife. The Wild-cat then went off some distance, and he, too, went to sleep.

Finally the Coyote woke up, and there were all the bones before him. He looked at his hands and felt that his mouth was greasy and that he had meat between his teeth. There was his knife before him all greasy. He could not imagine what he had done; for he was as hungry as he could be. The Coyote thought that he must surely have eaten, from the way he was all greased up; but he was still hungry. While he was still wondering whether he had already eaten the meat that he had cooked, he found the tracks of the Wild-cat and trailed him. The Coyote then said to himself: "I thought that I did not eat that meat, for I am still hungry; but never mind. I will get even with him." He found the Wild-cat sound asleep. He took the Wild-cat up on his back, and packed him to the nearest creek, put him on a high bluff and turned his back to the bluff, so as to make him fall off when he should wake up; for he knew that the Wild-cat when waking generally rolls over before getting up. The Coyote left him, and went off a good way, not expecting the Wild-cat to come back again. After the Coyote had got away he found another dry bone, and expected the bone to be the same as the first bone he had found, and so he went to sleep again. When the Wild-cat woke up, he rolled around a little and over he went into the creek. When he came out of the water he wondered how he came to be where he was and how he could have fallen into the water. The Wild-cat then found the Coyote's tracks. He said: "All right, Coyote, I will get even with you." He followed up the Coyote's trail and finally succeeded in finding him. There the Coyote was, again sound asleep. When the Wild-cat found the Coyote he put him on his back, carried him to the creek and laid him by the creek. He stretched his face and pulled his mouth further back, and made his teeth long.

He fixed the Coyote up in every way, to spoil his looks. (Before they met these animals were human beings.) After doing all this to the Coyote, the Wild-cat started off and went to sleep again. When the Coyote woke up he felt different from what he had felt before going to sleep. He went to the bank of the creek to look at himself. He found that he had hair on his body, and a long tail and a long face. He saw that his mouth was split far back, and when he smiled he saw what long teeth he had, and what long ears. He thought to himself: "How came I to be in this condition?" He then thought of the Wild-cat, and commenced to think that he had changed his appearance. The Coyote found the trail of the Wild-cat, and followed him until he found him, fast asleep. The Coyote then put both of his hands on the Wild-cat's face, one on the top of his head and one over his mouth, and pressed his hands together. This made the Wild-cat's face round. The Coyote changed him as much as the Wild-cat had changed himself. He cut off the tail of the Wild-cat and made it short. He made his back higher at the tail end of his body than at the fore part. Then he packed him to the creek and laid him down, so that he might find out what sort of a looking fellow he was when he woke up. The Coyote left the Wild-cat there and went off again. This time the Coyote thought: "When the Wild-cat comes back to me again I will play a trick on him and make out that I am asleep." After the Coyote had gone a long way off he lay down, and soon he was as sound asleep as ever. The Wild-cat now woke up, and he felt different from what he did when he went to sleep, and every part of his body felt different. So he looked into the water to see himself, and he saw that he had been changed, and that he had an ugly-looking face. Here he sat for a while, for he did not know who did this. He found out that the Coyote had been around again, and he commenced to trace him. When he found him he was sound asleep. This time the Wild-cat thought that he would make it uncomfortable for the Coyote, so he took the Coyote up in an old burnt tree and placed him in the hole. The Coyote was left up in the tree to suffer before he could get down. This time, the Wild-cat left him entirely. When the Coyote woke up he found himself up in the tree, and there was no way for him to get down, and it was too high to jump down. He called for every bird that he saw flying by the tree. He called for those that had the largest axe. Some fled by, and said that there was some one else coming behind that had a large axe. Finally the Wood-pecker (Korekitaha) came, and to him the Coyote called: "Friend! Help me out. I am in trouble."

The Wood-pecker commenced to work from the bottom, up, and finally succeeded in reaching the Coyote, and he got him out. The Coyote thanked the Wood-pecker for helping him out, and he told him that he had the sharpest axe that he had ever seen. The Wood-pecker's axe was its nose. Here the Coyote's troubles ended. He went off to roam over the prairie, but he always had hard times to get something to eat.

50. THE COYOTE, THE OPOSSUM, AND THE CROW.*

Once upon a time the Coyote (Ketox); Opossum (Waitskada-daiyox), or Gray-Man; and the Crow (Waitscowwi), met. When they met they asked one another what their names meant. The Coyote first asked the Opossum what his name meant. Opossum gave the definition of his name. Then the Crow said: "Yes, let us know what your name means." So the Opossum said that the name he went by meant Man-Having-a-War-club (Waitskadaidaiyoks). "This club that I have," said he, "I use in killing my enemies." The two others then said to the Opossum: "Is that what your name means?" Next, the Crow was asked the meaning of his name. He replied that whenever he attacked his enemies, after killing some of them, he always was ready to get into the home he lived in. The Coyote was then asked what his name meant. He had four names—Wetsikitox, Atatsyatskak, Hiquideskunniwai, and Kesawah. The Coyote replied that Wetsikitox meant that when anything happened he always wanted to go ahead before any one else was ready; or, sometimes in attacking the enemies, that he always went on and killed all the enemies first, before anybody did anything. He was then asked what the name Atatsya-tskuk meant. The Coyote said: "It is nothing for me to tell the meaning of my names. That means that I defecated on roads made by war-parties and nowhere else." Then he was asked the meaning of Hiquides-kunniwai. He replied that this was greater than either of the first two; that it meant that while out on the war-path, whenever he went out spying, that he defecated on a bunch of grass, and not on the ground, for the enemies might see that some one was after them. Then again the Coyote was asked the meaning of Kesawah. He replied that it meant that whenever he was out on the war-path and was wounded, some parts of his bones were fractured. In that way some of his bones remained in his stomach, and when carried home by his followers and when defecating, his excrement was mixed with bones.

*Told by Ignorant-Woman (Man) (Towakoni).

The Coyote then told the others that their names signified nothing compared to his names; that his names were all connected with war. So they told him that he had pretty good names. The Coyote said: "My names all mean something, for I will not bear a name that indicates fun. My names are great." They all put the word "Wets" with their names, which means "man," or "bold." So they all added this name to their names. Then, having learned what their names meant, they all departed.

51. THE COYOTE AND THE FISH-HAWK.*

Once upon a time there lived a Coyote (Ketox) and his family. He wandered around from one place to another, hunting, trying to support his family. He would sometimes find something easily, and other times with difficulty.

Once upon a time he was going along down the stream of a creek, and as he went along he saw a man sitting by a bank, and he supposed that the man was fishing. Once in a while he would hear the man say, "let some of you larger ones bite," and whenever he would say that, the Coyote would see the man draw back his head, and out would come a fish. The Coyote noticed that this man had a long string-like thing on his head that he used for a fishline. The Coyote then came up and was seen by the man. The Coyote was given some fish to take home with him for his family. He then said to the man: "My friend, I am captivated by your way of making a living. Can you give me the power so that I can fish and have all I want for my family?" The man then told the Coyote that it would be a hard thing to do, for he would have to follow his instructions, and if he did not, he would get into trouble, and besides that, he would have to go and look for a place just exactly like the place they were at. The Coyote said: "Well, I do not think I can make any mistake after you tell me what to do. I am too old to make any mistakes. I have long been looking for such things, and you are the man I have long been looking for." (The Coyote never had seen this man, nor had he heard about him.) So the Coyote was instructed to look for a place like the one they were at, and the thing was put on his head to be used for a line. The man said to the Coyote: "Now, my friend, you must never call for the largest fish in the water." The Coyote said that he would not, for he was too old to forget that. The man said that any other size he wanted he could get, and could get as many as he might want.

*Told by Ignorant-Woman (Man) (Towakoni).

So the Coyote left this man, telling him that that was the best secret he had ever learned, and that never after that should his family go hungry. He went on to look for a place that was like the place they were at. The place he had to look for was a bank, which projected out into the water. So the Coyote finally succeeded in finding such a place. He then commenced to fish. He caught all the fish that he wanted, and as many as he could pack on his back, and went on home. On his arrival he said to his wife: "Old woman, I have found some power, so you need never go hungry any more. You shall always have something to eat, and it is not hard to get, either." So the Coyote's family had all the fish they wanted to eat.

Thereafter the Coyote followed this way of living, and they had all that they wanted, but somehow or other the food would not last very long. He kept on fishing all the time, and sometimes he would catch so many fish that he would have to make three journeys to carry them home, and they would eat them in no time. But he kept on fishing. Sometimes he would take along his whole family to fish, and he would get as many as they could pack, and yet they would eat them in a short time. Once upon a time the Coyote wanted to catch the largest fish that was in the water, so that it would last longer. He said to himself: "Maybe my friend was just fooling me, and it may be that he wanted to keep the largest ones for himself, but now I will play a trick on him, and fool him this time." So, as he went down to fish he went alone, and when he got there he called for the largest fish that was in the water, the chief of all fishes. This fish bit his bait and he was unable to pull it out. The fish was about to draw him into the water, and the Coyote then commenced to beg it to let go the bait, for he said he had only been joking. But the fish kept pulling on his line, and finally took off the whole scalp of his head.

The Coyote then cried and ran home. On his arrival his family was afraid of him, since he had no hair on his head. But he called for them, telling them that he was the Coyote, the head of the family, but they all ran from him. Finally he gave up chasing his family, and then he died, through his own foolishness. The man that gave the Coyote the power was Having-Eye-directed-on-the-Water (Kitikowi), or the Fish-Hawk.

52. THE COYOTE AND THE BEAR.*

Once upon a time there lived the Coyote (Ketox) with his family. He wandered around from place to place hunting for food or working up some kind of a scheme on some others. Once upon a time he got up before daylight and went towards the north. He kept on going further and further. After daylight he came to a place where he heard a Bear (Widaw) coming, whooping at him and asking him why he should come to a place where he himself wandered, for he did not allow anyone to come to this place without killing him. The Coyote was frightened, and did not know what to do when he saw the Bear coming toward him. Just then some foolish idea came to his mind, and he thought that he had better play a trick on the Bear. As soon as the Bear approached the Coyote ordered him to stop, and not to kill him until his father looked at him. This Bear then stopped for a moment and wondered who his father was. Finally, the Coyote saw that everything was in his favor, and so he rushed forth toward the Bear, and just then the Sun rose. The Coyote then requested the Bear to go ahead and kill him or else he would kill the Bear. The Bear began to back, and the Coyote went forth toward him, and ran over him, and again asked him to make haste in killing him, saying that his father was now looking at him, and that that was the finest time for him to die. The Bear began to back up and give up all hopes of ever living again, because he thought that he had tried to kill the son of the Sun. The Bear thought to himself: "Well, now I have powers from the Sun myself, and if this man is the son of the Sun, he surely must have greater powers than I have." The Coyote kept pushing him around, asking him to hurry and kill him while his father was looking at him. He said that then he would find out what his father could do for him, and that if he attempted to make his escape it did not make any difference where he went; that he could be found and killed just the same, and that there was no chance for him to get away. The Bear finally begged the Coyote to allow him to live, and offered to let him have some of his powers; but the Coyote said to the Bear: "The powers you have do not equal mine, so I have no use for them."

The Coyote kept pushing the Bear back, telling him that he had made a mistake by trying to bulldoze him. The Bear again begged him not to kill him, and promised to go to his home with him and do all his work for him, and do the hunting for him and to feed his children. The Coyote then said to the Bear: "Now, you have made a good promise to me, and I am going to let you live. I was going to kill

---

*Told by Towakoni Jim (Towakoni).

you, for you did me wrong in the first place." The Bear begged the Coyote's pardon, and the Coyote then rode on the Bear's back toward his home. Before arriving home he ordered the Bear to go out hunting, saying that he must not try to make his escape, for he could easily get him back, no matter what kind of a good talk he put up. The Bear then went on to hunt for the Coyote, saying to himself: "I surely made a mistake by trying to kill him. If I had not put up such a good talk he surely would have killed me." The Bear went on until he came to a deer. He killed him, then he turned toward the Coyote's place with the meat. On his arrival he heard the Coyote telling his wife that he had captured a very large Bear, and that he would have killed him if he had not made a good promise; that from that time on he would live with them and do all the work for them, and hunt for them, too, and so he did not kill the Bear. Just then the Bear came in, bringing the deer meat, and the Coyote ordered his wife not to have anything to do with the cooking, but to let the Bear do all the work. The Bear sat down to rest, and the Coyote jumped up and took a burning stick and burned him and ordered him to make haste to do the cooking, for his wife and children were hungry. He told the Bear he was slow in hunting; that it did not take him that long to hunt. The Bear then commenced to roast the meat for them, and after cooking the meat he gave it to the Coyote's family to eat. This is the way the Bear's life began in living with the Coyote's family. His work was to support this family for a long while. The young ones treated him as their father had done. If he did not do his work in a hurry they scorched him. The children would ride him around whenever he was not doing anything.

Once upon a time when the Bear went out hunting he met somebody who told him that he was a big fool for living with the Coyote and supporting his family, for the Coyote was not a child of the Sun, and had no powers. The Bear was told that he was just following a hard life by living with them, and that when he arrived at the place he should kill off all the young ones, and the old ones too, for they could not do him any harm. The Bear returned without anything, and upon his arrival the young ones tried to do to him the same as they had always done, but the great Bear rushed forth and killed the whole family. After killing them he went back to his home.

53. THE COYOTE AND THE SMALLEST SNAKE.*

Once upon a time there went out the Coyote (Ketox) on the prairie, and as he was going along he found a little Snake (Hissquawasedikis; Never-grows-larger). The Coyote said to this Snake: "What a thing you are. I would not be so small as you are. You ought to be like me. I am a big man." The Coyote then said to the Snake: "Let me see your teeth." The Snake opened its mouth and showed the Coyote his teeth. The Coyote then opened his mouth and said to the Snake: "You see my mouth. What if we were to bite one another. You could not hurt me very much. My teeth are so big that I would just bite you in two." The Coyote bit the Snake, and then the Snake bit the Coyote. The Coyote said: "Now I will go over here a little way, and we will call to one another." The Coyote thought that by calling to one another he could tell if the Snake should die, for he thought it would die from the bite he had given it. The Snake went a little way off and lay down and the Coyote went the other way. The Coyote called to the Snake and the Snake answered weakly. Finally, the Coyote called and he answered pretty low. They then kept calling one another, and the Snake would answer pretty low, and the Coyote would say to himself: "I knew that I would kill that Snake." But the Coyote began to swell up where the Snake had bitten him, and it began to hurt the Coyote pretty badly, because his whole body began to swell. But they kept calling one another. It got so that when the Coyote was called he would answer very faintly, for his whole body was swelling up, and when the Snake was called he would answer very loud. Finally the Snake called the Coyote and the Coyote did not answer. So the Snake got up and went to where the Coyote was lying, and there he found him dead. So the Coyote died of the Snake bite, because he acted so smart and bragged of his large teeth. The Snake then left the Coyote after he had killed him. This Snake, it is known, was the smallest of all snakes.

54. THE COYOTE AND THE TURKEY.†

One time when the Coyote (Ketox) was hunting for something for his children to eat, he sneaked around back of a place and attacked a Turkey (Naa). The Coyote pulled all the feathers off the Turkey, put them around the Turkey's neck, and asked the Turkey if he was honest. The Turkey told the Coyote that he was honest. The Coyote

---
*Told by Ignorant Woman (Man) (Towakoni).
†Told by Dragging-Enemies-from-River-Banks (Towakoni).

told the Turkey to go to his place and to tell his wife to cook him and to save him (the Coyote) the wing. The Turkey agreed to do so. The Coyote then said: "Turkey, do as I have told you to do." The Turkey then went to Coyote's house, and told his wife that Coyote had sent him to have intercourse with her. The old woman ordered the children to leave while she obeyed her husband's orders. After the children had gone out, the Coyote's wife was treated as she had never been before, for the Turkey bit her on the back of the head and stamped her back with his feet. After that the Turkey told the Coyote's wife that his friend, the Coyote, had told him to tell her to cook the sinew and to break the arrow-sticks and to cook the sinew with them. The Coyote's wife did as she was told. Then the Turkey left the place and went off laughing at the Coyote's wife for the trick he had played on her.

When the Coyote returned home, before entering he commenced to call for the wing that he had asked the Turkey to have his wife save for him. The old woman said to the Coyote: "The wing? What do you mean? You have sent some one here, and he has got ahead of you." Then the old woman gave the cooked sinew to the Coyote to eat, and said: "You sent him here to tell me to cook the sinew, and to break the arrow-sticks to cook with it." The Coyote commenced to eat the sinew, and said: "I will kill that Turkey the next time I see him." He went out again to search for the Turkey, but when he found him the Turkey was up in a tree, and still had all of his feathers around his neck. The Coyote tried to coax the Turkey down, saying that he had something to tell him, but the Turkey knew that he was going to kill him if he got him down. The Coyote never did get the Turkey down. He went back, but when he got home, he had been so long on the journey after the Turkey, that his children and wife had starved to death. He found his children and wife dead, so he went off and cried. Whenever a Coyote cries or howls it is still said that he is crying over the death of his wife and children.

55. THE DELUGE AND THE REPEOPLING OF THE EARTH.*

In the times of this story there were many villages and many people, some good and some bad. There were also many wild animals. Some of the people thought that they had wonderful powers. They thought they were the only great people in existence and that they were the most powerful of all. They became famous. They showed many

---

*Told by Towakoni Jim (Towakoni).

supernatural powers. Things were going wrong, for there was no such thing as death. All the people who were old stayed old, and those who were young remained young.

In a certain village there was a chief whose wife became pregnant. Time passed very rapidly. In a very little while after the woman had become pregnant she brought forth four little monsters. They grew every day. Most of the powerful men of the village came around and visited the chief's place, saying among themselves that the monsters were a very dangerous sort of children. They said it would be better to carry them off and kill them, but the mother said that she thought that they would be good children. She thought the children might turn out well, and did not want them killed. There was in the village a man who was a prophet, and he could foretell things. He said that of all the animals existing there were none like these monsters; that their birth was a sign that something dreadful was going to happen. The monsters grew every day, and finally they began to go around. They had four feet, and they went around with the other children. The chief announced to the people that they should not harm the monsters. The monsters played with the other children. Sometimes they would run over them, but since the chief had forbidden that the monsters should be harmed the children could not say very much against them. As the monsters grew older they began to do much damage. They would eat buffalo robes, upturn tipis, eat rawhide ropes, etc. The chief's wife did not say anything more in the defence of the monsters, for she knew that they were dangerous. When the monsters were plundering the villages the people would try to harm them, but could not. Finally the monsters began to run over the children and to eat them, and they did more and more mischief. The prophet told the people that something fearful was about to happen. After the monsters began to eat people the chief of the tribe told the people to go ahead and do as they pleased with the monsters. They tried to kill them, but could not harm them. They kept on growing. Finally the monsters went to the middle of the village and stood together, one facing east, one facing south, one facing west, and one facing north. In that way they all grew together. As they grew higher they could not stoop down to their feet to get the people, but the ones who were far away they could reach. The monsters continued to grow. The taller they grew the better it was for the people near their feet, but whenever they saw a person coming from far away they would stretch their necks in that direction. They would bend down their heads and grab the person. The monsters continued to grow. The people looked up, and it seemed that they would soon reach the sky. They grew higher and higher.

The prophet was told by a voice from above that he had a work that was soon to begin, for everything was going wrong; that he was to begin a work; that things were getting worse. The prophet was told to get a tall cane, and place in between the joints all kinds of seeds, grass, corn, etc., using joint after joint of the cane. Then he was told to select in pairs those animals he thought best should be saved. He was to save all the good ones and leave out all the bad ones. The voice said it would attend to the bad ones. He also told the prophet to tell him when he had everything ready; he should set up the pole in the ground, crawl into it himself and then let him know that everything was ready. He was then told to go to the north where he would see some one standing; that he should tell him that he had everything ready, and beg him to go ahead with his work and do the rest. After the prophet had put everything in the cane he went to the man in the north and told him that everything he wished to save was in the cane, and he asked him to go ahead with the work and finish it. The man at the north replied that he would soon send some one back to the village of the prophet; that when the time should come there would be a sign indicating that dire things were going to happen; that the fowls and animals would be seen coming from the north and going to the south. On a certain day the fowls of the air appeared in the north, like a cloud, and they flew toward the south. The prophet crawled into the cane. The people wondered what was the reason for this. Finally the animals came, and the people began to find out what was about to happen. They began to cry and to run for the mountains and for other places, but it did them no good. After the birds and the animals had passed there came a flood, and the water was all over, and it got deeper and deeper. The bad people were drowned and everything else that was not in the cane.

While the flood was going on the monsters stood straight up. The thing that the man in the north was about to send from the north he sent, and it got under the feet of the monsters. After the monsters had stood a long time on the same ground they began to tire out. The thing that the man from the north had sent was a water-monster, the Turtle, and the Turtle was sent to destroy the monsters. The Turtle got under the feet of the monsters, that were still facing the four different directions. The cane stood up by the monsters, and it stood until after the water had gone down. When the flood was flowing swiftly the cane would roar like thunder. Finally one of the monsters said to his brothers: "How are your legs? Can you stand?" The other three said their legs were giving out; that it was getting slippery, for a large Turtle was under them and they were about to be destroyed.

Finally, the monster in the north said to his brothers: "My legs are giving out, and I will have to fall, and the direction in which I fall shall be called North" (Itarakadara—North-Room). So there were three monsters left. Finally, another monster said to his brothers: "How are you getting along? My legs are giving out, and I shall have to fall." He fell over towards the east, and when he fell there was a roaring toward the east, where the sun comes up, and the direction was called East (Naasakaskidi—Where-the-Sun-rises). There were now two monsters left. Finally, the third monster said to his brother: "My legs are giving out, and I shall have to fall; I can not stand longer; I shall have to fall toward the South" (Idikuts—Changing-Weather). He fell right over. The fourth monster had no one to talk to, but he said that he was giving out and that he would have to fall, and the direction he should fall should be called West (Nesakisudi—Where-the-Sun-goes).

After the monsters were destroyed the water began to go down. It wholly disappeared, so that the land could be seen, especially one high point. To this point the prophet and his wife were sent. Both were naked and they had nothing to eat, and they had nothing to live with.

When the man and the woman were placed on the high point and the water had gone down, they noticed foam where the high points of land had been, as far as they could see. While they were up on the mountains the prophet thought he had better go down to the bottom and see how the land was, whether it had got dry or was still soft. When he got down to the foot of the mountain he noticed that the ground was getting harder, because the wind blew hard. A long time after this the prophet was told that the ground had dried up and they must go down from the mountain. As they went down he found a small cedar tree. He noticed some other small trees, like dogwood and evergreen trees. He also found remedies. He found soapweed and a tree with brown berries with black and yellow seeds. All of these things were for his use. The dogwood was for his arrows, the brown berry wood being for his bow. The soap weed was for bow-strings; the medicine was to use in case of sickness, as also was the cedar. The prophet was told that the things were coming out from the cane; that he need not go back there to get them; that he would see them go from one place to another. About this time the grass was coming up. All the animals that he had saved in the cane began to come around him. When the prophet came back his woman had gone to sleep. When they awoke the next morning they found beside them a stalk of corn that had already grown. A voice said to them that this was Mother-Corn; that they should use it again; that all the things they had seen would be in use. The tree for the bow was also to be used for shinny clubs, etc., for it was hard; the cedar tree was for their lodges; the soap weed they were to use for grass-lodges, etc. From the time when the promises were made to them it was promised further on that they would have their grass-lodge built and would be given plenty of things to use, and there would be corn planted by the lodge, which they were to eat.

This went on until finally one morning they woke and found they were in a grass-lodge, and outside of this place they found four corn stalks, each having on it an ear of corn. They observed that the promises that had been made to them were being fulfilled. They had been promised a grass-lodge with a cedar frame; that in the future the people were to use cedar for their grass-lodge frames. These grass-lodges were to stand for a while without being torn down, and they could endure hard winds. After they had settled down in the place where they woke up they were told to go ahead with their work with the materials they already had. The man was told that it was time for the animals to generate, and it was his duty to hunt for his meat, for the weapons and game were for that purpose. The woman was told to teach others to plant the corn. Generation after generation the corn was to be used, and if the time should come that they planted corn and something else than corn came up, it would be a sign that the end of the world was at hand.

56. THE DELUGE AND THE REPEOPLING OF THE EARTH.*

Once upon a time there was a head man who had many thousands of people to rule. The time came when his wife was to give birth to four children in the form of something like that of the horse. When this came to pass the head man was displeased, and got some one to carry the young monsters away; but they grew rapidly, and it made the chief fell badly. Up to this time the people had been in the habit of wandering from one place to another, but the time had now come when they could not get around without being injured by these monsters. They went around under the monsters' feet, and when they tried to go on further the monsters would reach down and get them and swallow them. The monsters, who were called Standing-in-Water (Hoskakakadiki), faced north, east, south, and west.

The time came when the chief selected a certain man to go due northwest, to see a certain being who, though but a small man, had

---
*Told by Ahahe (Waco).

great powers. The chief told his errand man to keep pretty well hidden from these monsters while on the journey, so as to get away safely. The man with powers could grow to be an old man and then turn young again. When the chief's errand man made the visit the little man asked him to state the object of his coming; and the chief's man said that he was sent there by the chief of all the people, because everything was going wrong, and the people were being injured by four living monsters, and nothing could be done to hinder them from getting the people. Then the little man with powers told the chief's man that certain things were to happen, which would indicate that certain other things were going to happen. When the chief's man returned he had to use the same care as he had done before to keep out of sight of the monster. After his return he went to the chief's place and made it known that he had returned. Then the chief called the people to his place, so that the man could tell the story of his visit to the man with powers. The people gathered around the chief's place and were called together to hear the man's story. The chief's man said that he was told by the man with powers that there would be something done to destroy the monsters; that the time would come when there would be some sign given so that the people would know that something was about to happen; that when the time should come it would begin from the north; that the flocks of fowls of the air, and the animals from the plains and woods, would appear as clouds; and that a big water-monster (Turtle) would be sent to destroy the four monsters. Some were afraid, but others were glad that it was going to happen. After a while there came to the people some signs, which showed that there was something in the north that looked like clouds; and the fowls of the air came, and the animals of the plains and woods were seen. All of this indicated that something was to happen. The clouds that were seen in the north were a deluge.

The deluge was all over the face of the earth. When the deluge came the water-monster, of course, was under the feet of the four monsters. After the Turtle got to moving around every place was so smooth that it was impossible for the monsters to stand. The one in the south said to his brothers that he was getting tired and would have to fall; and so he fell, and as he was falling he said that the direction he fell in should be called South (Idikuts—Changing-Weather). Then the one facing the west said that he was like the one who had been in the south, that he was getting tired and would have to fall; and as he fell he said that the direction in which he was falling should be called West (Nesakisudi—Where-the-Sun-goes). The one facing north got tired and said that he would have to fall; and so when he fell he said that the direction in which he fell should be called North (Itarakadara—North-Room). There was only one more of these monsters. This one, of course, could not talk to any one else, so he said aloud to himself that he was tired and would have to fall; and while he was falling he said the direction in which he fell should be called East (Naasakaskidi—Where-the-Sun-rises). The time came, after these monsters were destroyed by the flood, when the land was to be divided from the water; for there were but two things known which had not been destroyed, namely, the Wind (Newerah), and a party which was away under the water before the flood, and known as Medicine-Men (Hareneze). Everything else on the face of the earth was destroyed. The land was then just floating. It happened that the Wind got to traveling around, drying up the land, and there were streaks of foam left on the land, which remained as mountains. The Wind still went around drying until he found that there was somebody else left on earth beside himself, which was the Medicine-Man. Of course, he still continued in going from place to place. Once upon a time he stopped, facing toward the west, and he saw something like rain falling from above. This attracted his attention, and he went on his way to see what was there. When he came to this place he saw a woman lying on the ground, with her head to the west and her feet to the east. After seeing this he still continued his traveling. The next time he visited the place he noticed that the woman had the form of one pregnant, and he went on again, drying up the land. The next time he visited the place he saw a child lying on the side of this woman, as of to-day. When he made his second visit he noticed that the woman had changed; and she did not look as she did when he first saw her. So the Wind continued his journey, going around and around, and it happened that he made his third visit to the place, and saw the child and the woman. At this time he could hardly see the woman, so he made up his mind to take the child. When reaching for the child it screamed, and the Wind heard some one from above saying that he should let this child alone. "This," he thought to himself, "must be the child of Man-never-known-on-Earth" (Kinikasias). He made up his mind that he would go again, going from one place to another. The time came again when he made another visit to this place, and he saw the child, and picked it up and went on his way to a place where he knew there were some people living. When he took the child he noticed that it was a girl. When he reached the place he took the child and gave her to the people to raise. At this time everything progressed pretty fast, so the child grew rapidly.

When the Wind first got the child, on the fourth visit, there was the child, and no woman, so he called the woman the Earth, the mother of the first woman born after the deluge, and this is why we call the Earth "mother." The girl grew pretty rapidly, and her name was Dream-Girl (Aitskasawnats). As time passed, she became old enough to marry; and in the place where she was raised there was a man who became her husband, and after a time there was a child born to them who was a boy. The boy grew, and after a while he went off from the place where they were living, and, of course, being the first boy born, he had wonderful powers to create other things that were now on the face of the earth. He went around every day doing all of this, and he commanded things to exist. At one time, on his return, he brought back with him four sticks, that his father might make arrows, and he brought another stick for a bow for his own use. Now, the boy told his father and mother to move out of the place that they were living in; so the woman went out and fixed up another place to live in, and the boy still continued his work every day. He told his father and mother not to do him wrong until he had completed all things that he wanted to do. In going out every day he would always have something with him. Once, on his return, his father and mother noticed that he had a pipe, and that he had a big bundle, in which he carried everything for his own use. He now came to be a young man, and he still told his father and mother not to do him wrong until he had finished all the things he wanted to do. Once upon a time, on his return, before reaching home, he spoke to his father and mother, saying: "You have done me wrong; so that you both have caused my work to cease, and I will not come to live with you." He told his people that he would go in the direction of the east, and he was to become the Morning-Star (Harseiryarsenarar.)

After Morning-Star had left his father and mother, another child was born to them, which was a girl. Again time passed, and another child was born to them, which was a boy. Time passed and the two children grew up. They became husband and wife; and from this on, there came to be a great many people. The father of the Morning-Star in having a great many people, said to his wife that he would do like his son, and go off. This man's name was Clearness-after-Rain (Iakadakiwitse). So he went on his way toward the northwest, becoming Clearness-after-Rain. Before leaving, he commanded the people that they should say after the rain that Never-stop-to-see-what-is-in-the-Way (Kidiahosaihiristas) was coming. The wife of this man never knew what became of him.

THE THIRD PERIOD: THE PRESENT.

57. THE WOMAN WHO MARRIED A STAR.*

One night a long time ago, after the stars in the heavens were created, some bright and some dim, just as we see them now, there was a certain woman looking up in the sky watching the stars. She noticed that some of the stars were bright and some very dim. Those that were bright she thought to have once existed as fine-looking men. The dim ones she thought might have been old people. As she was looking at the stars she pointed out one bright star, and said: "That star twinkles so bright, it must have been a fine-looking young man. I wish I could have him for my husband." After saying this she watched the rest of the stars. On the same night, after she had gone to bed and to sleep, it seems that in her dream she was with this man whom she had pointed out and desired for her husband. When she awoke she found herself in a strange place, and sitting there by the fire was an old man. There she sat, not knowing what to do. Finally the old man woke up and spoke to her, saying: "My woman, I am the star that twinkled so bright at night when you were looking at the stars in the sky, and whom you selected as a fine-looking man. All the brightest stars are old people, and the dim ones are young people. You made a mistake when you desired me. Hereafter you shall be my wife."

The woman had to stay there and live with the star, and was his wife. Some time afterward the woman noticed a large rock lying on the ground, and this she was told never to move. One time she decided to remove the rock, and when she looked down she could see the earth, but she was far away from the earth. Then she moved the rock back into its place. She began to study what to do in order to get down. In some way she found bunches of soapweed, which she cut and braided so that it was strong enough to hold her whenever she wanted to go down. Of course, it took lots of soapweed, though they were very stout. It took her a long time to make the rope. When she thought that it was long enough to reach to the ground she tied it to the stone, knowing that the stone could not go down. Then she let herself down on the rope. It is not known how long it took her to climb down to the end of it, but when she reached the ground she found that she could barely reach the tops of the highest trees. She could only hang there. In time a Buzzard flew close to her and asked her if she was still alive.

*Told by Burgess Hunt (Wichita).

She told the Buzzard that she was still alive. The Buzzard told her that he was going to let her down and that she must be ready to get hold of his neck whenever he should come down. The Buzzard commenced to fly higher and higher, then he sailed down slowly. When he was ready he told the woman to be ready. Then he came down to her and she got on his back and went down to the ground, though the Buzzard first flew a long way with her. When he had let her down he asked her if she knew the way to her home. She told him that she did. He then told her that on the way she wouud find a dead buffalo to eat, to give her strength to reach home; that she must never repeat her talk about the stars; that had it not been for him she would have starved. Some other powers she got from the Buzzard after he had saved her life. She then left the Buzzard, but it would still fly around to see if she got home safe. She came to where the dead buffalo was lying and took what she needed and went toward her home.

Arrived home, her parents asked her where she had been. She told them that through her foolishness she had been up in the sky and had been married to a star. She was asked how she got up there. She replied that in the fore part of the night when she had disappeared she had looked at the stars while lying in bed and pointed out a star, saying: "I wish that star were my husband;" and that she had thought that perhaps the brightest stars we see had once been fine-looking young men in this world. She continued: "I went to sleep, and when I awoke I found myself up in the heavens. There I saw an old man who told me that he was the bright star that I had seen and had wished for my husband. The star forbade me to move a rock that I had seen, but once I thought I would see what it was, so I moved the rock. I felt the wind and saw this earthly world of ours. I made a rope from soapweed by which to descend. When I had made the rope I tied one end to the rock, knowing that the rock could not come down on me. Thus I made my escape. I had thought the rope long enough, but when I came to its end I found myself above the tallest trees. It happened that a Buzzard flew around me and asked me if I was still alive. I told it that I was still alive, so he took me down and showed me my way here. He told me where there was a dead buffalo that I could eat, and he also guided me on my way home."

Ever since this time the people have feared to talk as the girl had talked about the stars, for fear that they might die, for the woman by her foolish talk and desire for the bright star for her husband was taken to the sky. Nor to this day do the people count the stars. They do not express desires about them, lest the thing desired happen.

58. THE MAN WHO WENT TO SPIRIT-LAND.*

The real time of this story is after horses were known in this country, many hundred years ago, while the people were living down here.

Once upon a time there were two young men who had grown up together and were of the same age. In their early days they were playmates, and the older they grew the better they liked each other. When they became grown, they went with war-parties like other men. They then became real friends, for they had made an agreement that each should share the home of the other. They offered their homes to each other's people and they lived as one family, simply because they were fast friends. By their agreement they were both to die at the same time. If one of them was killed in battle, the other was to die, so that both should die at the same time, instead of one having to mourn for the other. They were always together, and whenever there was a war-party sent out they would go to war. According to Indian custom, any persons making this kind of an agreement were called brothers, and this is the way people regarded them. One of these brothers got married, but that did not have anything to do with their friendship; the other one always remained single.

In those times there were a good many men who would get up a war-party and stay out on the war-path, one party after another. The two brothers would always be in the same party and would never part from one another, on account of the agreement they had made between them. While out on an expedition, whatever they did in time of battle they would be together, and would not leave one another, and if they killed any enemy, the one who did the killing would present the scalp to the other. In these times a scalp was a fine gift, and many men made friends by presenting scalps to one another. On their return from the war-path, the one who had scalps would present them to his people. If a man was married he would present the scalp to his wife. When the brothers were out on the war-path together their people at home would keep the wife of the married brother and help her in the lodge at all times. A woman had to wear moccasins at all times during the absence of her man. She would have to go to the creek for an early morning bath. She was not to look around, but to look straight ahead. While going to or coming from the creek she was never to speak to any one, especially to the men folks, until her man came back

*Told by Towakoni Jim (Towakoni).

from the war-path. By doing all of these things a woman gave good luck to her husband who was gone on the war-path. When a woman did not do these things something often happened to her husband. Finally there was born to the married friend a boy baby, and during this time a war-party was sent out, and the married man's friend went with the party. On account of the birth of the child, the married man remained home. This war-party, on meeting some enemies, fought them, and the unmarried brother lost his life. When the battle was over the warriors returned home. On their arrival the news regarding the death of the unmarried brother spread. The married brother was left to mourn his friend. He thought to himself: "Now, if I had been there I surely would have died with him." He often thought of committing suicide; but because he knew that if he committed suicide he would never get to see any of his people in the other world, he was prevented from doing that. Besides this, he loved his wife and child; but still he mourned for the loss of his best friend. Whenever any war-party was sent out he would go along, expecting to die in some way, so that he could see his friend and be near him all the time, instead of mourning for him.

When the child was older his mother became sick and died. The father now mourned for both his friend and his wife. Of course, the grandparents took care of the child while the father went off by himself and mourned for the loss of his wife and friend. He would sometimes go to his wife's grave and mourn there, and he would sometimes stay there all night, and time after time he went to his wife's grave. No one knew how many times he went to the grave, but once when he went to the grave and was weeping he went to sleep and, in a dream, his friend appeared to him and talked. While they were talking, he wished that the dream would come true. They were talking about how lonesome the boy's father was. While the man was dreaming of this he was asked if he had thought a great deal of his wife while she was living. The man, in his dream, replied that he loved his wife, because she brought him the boy who was left with him in the world, and he loved the child because it was the only thing left him. His dead friend then asked him if he wanted to live with his wife again, and told the dreaming man that if he wanted to he could. The man said he would like to see his wife again and live with her forever. Then the dead friend said to the man that he had come after him, but that he must first say that he loved his wife; that at this time the women were having their Turkey-dance; that before he (the dead man) should take him there he should instruct him about some things.

The dead man then said: "When arriving at the place where the dancing is going on I shall leave you to see your wife dance, and every time she dances around you must take one of the four mud balls that will be given you to throw at her. Every time you throw the ball at her you will hit her, and the fourth time you hit her with the mud ball she will leave the dancing and go off. You must follow her to her home, and on arriving at her home, the women and your wife's people will pay no attention to you. On entering you must get along the best you can and seat yourself somewhere apart from your wife, and wait until your wife's father speaks to you. The very first thing he will ask you will be, if you can shoot good. He will tell you to get on a horse and go out to a certain place where there are four buffalo, in the open timber, and you will have to do pretty good shooting to kill one of these buffalo. If you wait a little too long the buffalo will get into the timber before you have a chance to shoot any of them. He will tell you to take a lump of fat from the shoulder of the buffalo, after killing the buffalo. You will have this for your use while there, for you are to do this four times. Four days you will be allowed to stay there, and after you have done all this you will be allowed to bring your wife back into the world. There is a little more for you to go through after you have taken your wife, and that is, to present scalps after your return to your home. Your father-in-law will send you four times on the war-path, successively, and during these times you must have nothing to do with other women, for, if you do, your wife will know it right away. If you go through all these things, you can do as you like afterward."

While the married man was getting his instructions he wished that the dream would come true. He soon woke up and there was his friend standing before him. His friend touched his eyes, and he found himself in another world, still with his friend. Around him, as far as his eye could see, he saw lodges. They entered the homes of the dead, and finally came to the place where the dance was, and there the dead man left his friend. The live man saw his wife dancing, and as she came around, he threw one of the mud balls at her and hit her, as he had been told to do. She went around the pole that they were dancing around and when she came around again he threw another mud ball at her and hit her again. Every time she came around he threw at her, until he had thrown the last ball. Then she left the dance and went off to her home, and the live man followed her. When she entered her home he followed her in. Her people looked at him and put their heads down. Finally his father-in-law spoke to him, and asked him if he had come to see his wife, and the man told him that he had. The live man's father-in-law then told him that on the next morning he would have to go on a buffalo hunt; that there would be a horse ready for him to ride; that there was a bow and arrows that he was to use to kill the buffalo; that after killing one buffalo he must cut some fat off of the shoulder, then with his foot he must kick the buffalo from behind, when the buffalo would come to life, rise, and go off. Besides this, the father-in-law told the man that he must sleep with his wife, but not be covered with the same blankets; that he was not to touch her in any way. He remained all that day and night. The next morning he obeyed his father-in-law's instructions and started out for the buffalo. He went to the timber, where he was told that he would find the four buffalo lying down. As soon as he came to an open place he saw the buffalo, and he made the horse run at full speed, in order to reach them before they had a chance to get well away from him. Before they reached the timber he shot one, and the buffalo fell to the ground. The man then took his sharp flint knife and cut the buffalo open, as he had been told. He took the fat, then kicked the buffalo behind, as he had been told to do. Then the buffalo rose and ran to the woods where the other buffalo had gone. The man brought the fat to his wife's home, and kept it there for his own use while he was at his wife's home. Late in the evening of that day he was told to go to the water to take a bath, and after taking a bath, to rub the fat all over his body.

The man went on a buffalo hunt every morning for four mornings, and after the fourth morning he was told that he could live with his wife the same as he had done on earth. The next thing for the man to do was to take his wife home. The last thing he was required to do was to send out war-parties, after he should get home, and when coming home from war he must bring a scalp every time he should go out on the war-path. He was not to be afraid of getting hurt, for there was some one who would carry him through without injury. He must go on the war-path four times. During the dances after his return from the war-path he was not to associate with other women if he wanted to live with his wife again on earth. If he did associate with them he could not keep his wife, but if he should do as he was told in everything, he could do as he pleased thereafter. They were then told to go, for their child was crying for his father, and some of the people at home were getting uneasy because they suspected that he had committed suicide.

The next thing he knew, he found himself on earth. He and his wife waited until night before they entered their home. About dark the woman asked her husband to go on home and have the place cleaned up, and to have the grass-lodge smoked with burning sage. He must tell his folks not to weep when she should enter, for that was a command they had to obey. The man went on to his home, and his people asked him where he had been. He told his mother to clean up the place and smoke the room; that he was going to bring his wife in; that when she should come in no one should weep; but they must be glad to see her again. He told them that if they wept they would do him wrong. The man's mother at once began cleaning up the place and had it smoked up. Then the young man went after his wife and they went to his home, and the people were glad to see the woman, for they knew that it made the young man happy to have his wife back from the world of the dead.

They had been at home but a few days when the young man got up a war-party and set out on the war-path. They were gone about ten or fifteen days, when they found some enemies and defeated them, and scalped many. On their return they entered their homes in triumph, and the young man's name was on everybody's lips and he was highly praised. When the dancing was going on at night he remembered about what he had been told to do.

It was not very long before he sent out another war-party, and many of the men were anxious to go with him, so that a great war-party was led out by the man who had come from Spirit-Land. They met some enemies, and without losing any of their men they gained another great victory, having been on the war-path about twenty days. On his arrival he delivered some more scalps. He saved one to take to his wife's people up above. The night after his return he took the scalp and placed it where he had placed the other, so that his wife's people could get it. After he had offered the scalp to the dead people he returned to his home and joined in all of the dances. The dances continued from morning till night, and from night till morning. He and his wife would go together to the dance, and the man's wife would join in with some other women and dance with them. Usually the men did the singing, especially at the dances of the women. Long after the dancing ceased the young man sent out another war-party, and at this time a good many more men accompanied him, because they all knew that there was no doubt as to his winning a victory when he met the enemy. Again they returned home victorious, having met some of the enemy and fought with them without losing any of their own men. When they came home, their people met them before entering the village, and they presented the people with scalps, as they had always done when coming home from war.

On the night following their return the man who had sent out the war-party went to offer his scalp to his wife's dead parents. After doing this he returned to his home. The dance was going on and the people were having great times, in honor of their warriors. After he had eaten he went to the place where the people were having their victory dances. In these times a good many of the people would part from one another when any one would bring scalps home from war. The people called this "cutting-girths-from-the-saddle" (garlesteyosgox), which means, throwing the saddle off from a horse, for the men would throw one another away from a woman. The young man knew that his wife was not there to see him, and so he thought that while he had a chance to deceive her he would do it. He met a woman who was courting him since he made himself famous by going on the war-path and he stayed nearly all night with her. That night while he was asleep his wife, without telling him that she knew what he had done, left him permanently and went back to her dead people, for her man had done her wrong. If the man had gone with the woman after he had gone four times on the war-path and had presented scalps four times to his wife's dead people, he would have won what his wife's dead people had offered him. The next morning, the young man found that he was alone in bed, and he knew that his wife had left him and that now he had only his wife's child. From that time on he went back to his wife's grave, but there was no sign of anybody appearing to him, for he had not done what he had been told to do. When the people found out what he had done they came around to see him and to tell him that he had done wrong. He told the people that he had been in another world; that a great many people were there; that he saw many people whom he did not know; that the people up there carried on the same customs that they did down here; but that the place was better than the earth. He also told them that those who died in battle and went there would enter that place happier than a person who had died of sickness. On account of this the men, when going out to war, fought bravely, so as to enter into another world happy instead of dying with sickness. The man told a good many other things that a person had to do and a good many things that were done at the dead man's home. He lived many years afterward, and he mourned all the time during his life, but could never find out about his wife again. Nor did he ever dream about his wife or friend. When he died the people supposed that he had reached the homes of our dead people to live forever with his wife.

59. THE MAN WHO RESCUED HIS WIFE FROM SPIRIT-LAND.*

There was a time when a boy grew up with another person of the same age as himself. In their boyhood they were always good friends. Wherever one went the other had to go. They were always together, and like other boys, became warriors. When they had grown to be young men they still continued to go around together. When they started on their life as warriors they never parted. When they went to many battles they were together fighting, and would help one another. When any two persons did this in times of war, people used usually to call them fast friends; and especially, when they were in battle together or gave scalps to one another, or horses that they had stolen, they were known as Nawadi. The boys were both single. When at home they would stay first at the home of one, then at the home of the other. In these homes they were considered as brothers, as they had been together so long as friends.

One of them finally got married, and the other man remained unmarried. When the one was married the other went about by himself, thinking that his friend had not fulfilled his promise to him that they were never to part so long as they lived, so that when the young man got married it somewhat dissolved their partnership. The young man would be on the war-path by himself and would still think of his friend. Once upon a time when the single man was to be with a party that went out on the war-path he undertook to die in battle, so that he might cease to think about his friend. When they found the enemy, they fought, and he was killed in the battle. When the rest of the warriors returned home they brought the married man the news that his friend had been killed in battle. The married man mourned constantly for his friend, and people asked him why he had not gone along to see his friend die in battle and be with him when he died, and die, too, so he would not have to mourn for him; it being the custom that after two had formed a friendship of this kind, wherever one went the other was expected to go, and if one had to die in battle the other would die also, so that one would not have to mourn the other.

Now the married young man's wife died and left him with one child. This grieved him still more. He mourned continually for the loss of his wife and for his friend. He would go to his wife's grave, sometimes remain there all night, and come back to his home the next day. Then he would go back again. While he was there he fell asleep, and in his dream his friend appeared to him, saying to him: "Do you

*Told by Killed-Enemy-in-Water (Wichita).

love your wife, and do you love me?" The married man said: "Yes, I love you both." In his dream he thought to himself: "I wish this would come true and that I might see my friend and wife." So the dead man said to him: "It is true; wake up." So he woke up and there was his friend standing right by him. His friend told him to come on with him. As they were going along he saw that he was in a large village, and it reached farther than his eye could see. Before entering the place his friend told him there was a dance there, and that his wife was dancing in a fine war dress, having a shield on her head; that when they should reach the place where the dance was he (the unmarried man) would leave him and let him watch his wife dance; that he would be given four hard, round clay balls to throw at his wife, each one of which, when thrown, could not fail to hit her; that when the last ball had been thrown, his wife would leave the dance without paying any attention to him and would go home; that he should follow his wife, and finally he would find her; that he must not say a word, but must sit down anywhere near the door inside the lodge; that for a while, people would not recognize him, and finally would ask him if he wanted to live with his wife; that when this question was asked he must say: "Yes, and I want my wife;" that he would be told to go to a certain place where there were four buffalo in an open place, and even though he were a good marksman, he would fail to kill one of the buffalo; that he must get on a horse, and run the horse at full speed in order to get to them while they were getting up. The dead man also told the young man that the reason why the folks in the other world would not pay any attention to him was, that the people in the other world had a very different scent from the people in this world. So when they reached the place, the young man saw a dance called the Turkey-dance, which was being danced by women. There he saw his wife, and when she went around the pole to the side he was on he threw a ball of clay at her and hit her. When she came around again he threw another ball of clay and hit her again. The third time he threw another ball and hit her again. When she came around the fourth time he hit her again. The song ended and she left the dance.

The woman went to her home, and her husband followed her. When she entered he entered the place, too, and sat down by the door of the tipi. The folks now recognized him, and he sat there for a long time before any of the folks said anything to him. The father of this woman finally spoke to the man and asked him if he was looking for his wife. He answered, saying: "Yes, I was looking for her." His father-in-law asked him many questions; if he would be true to his wife, and if he would not think of any other wife but her. The young man said he would be true to his wife, because he loved her and he mourned her all his life until he had come to where they were, and he was anxious to live with her again, and would not for anything mistreat her if he could live with her again. The young husband was told to go outside; that there he would find a horse tied; that he must ride to a certain open place surrounded by timber, where there were some buffalo; that he must get on a horse and go and kill one of the buffalo; that after killing it he must cut it open along the back, take the fat off from the hump, then kick the buffalo once on the back and tell it to get on its feet and go. The young man went out where the horse was, with the bow and arrows and quiver that were given him. When he reached the smooth, open circular place surrounded by timber he saw in the middle of it four great, big buffalo sitting down. He made haste to reach them before they should rise. Now, it is natural for the buffalo, when he gets up, always to stretch before making any movement. When the young man reached the buffalo they started to run. The man cut one off from the group and shot it. The buffalo died. Then he did as he had been told to do, cutting the buffalo's back open and taking a piece of fat off from the hump, then kicking the dead buffalo once on the back and asking it to get up, for it was fast asleep. Then the buffalo rose and ran into the timber. When the man reached home he turned the horse loose and delivered the fat to his father-in-law. Still his wife made no sign of speaking to him. When the right time came the man was told to take a sweat bath; then bathe his body in incense; then use the fat, rubbing it all over him. This he did every day for four days, and when the four days had passed the man's father-in-law told him that he could take his wife back to his home, for their child was lonesome; that the child was crying every day for want of his father; that when he returned to his home he must get up a war-party and go out with it, and on his return bring back a scalp and put it away where the people could not find it before the proper time; that he must continue this until he had done it four times; that then he might live with his wife; that he was forbidden to have any other woman than his wife during this time. The young man was to secure four scalps for his wife's people before he could live with his wife. The young man and his wife started for home. The woman ordered her husband to go ahead and have the grass-lodge swept out clean, and to have it smoked with white sage; then, after this was done, to come back after her, when they would both go on home. So the young man went on to his home and had these things done and at once turned

back to go after his wife, having told his people that he had his wife
back and that he had been for several days amongst the dead people.
So they went on home, and reached the young man's lodge. The very
next day he got up a war-party, to be sent out by himself. Before starting out they took a piece of rawhide, in the place of a drum, and sang
the war-party songs that we to-day still use. It was not very long before the young man met some of his enemies, whom he killed and
scalped. On his return he brought a scalp. The rest of the war-party
also had scalps. On their return they entered the village victorious.
It being the custom to dance when a war-party returned they had all
kinds of dances that night, and some dances in the daytime. So the
young man had an easy time sending out war-parties, because he had
aid from the dead people. It was customary in those times with a
good many to dance with the husbands or wives of others instead of
their own husbands or wives, and then to remain parted. Another war-
party would be sent out, and on its return others would become husbands and wives. When the young man returned from his journey
he, of course, in order that he might remain with his wife, avoided other
women for a while. When the dances ceased, the young man again
called forth his men, and when the men came together he announced
to them that he wanted to go out on the war-path again. A good many
wanted to accompany him on the war-path again; for they knew that
he had some power by which they could easily win their battle, as long
as he was with them. That night he ordered a man to get a rawhide,
and sticks with which to beat it. They at once began to sing the war
songs, and all those men who were present at the singing were to go on
the war-party, this being the general rule among the men.

On the next morning the young man started off with his men.
They were gone for about a month, when they found some of their
enemies. The young man had foretold that they would find some of
their enemies in a few days. According to custom, when they stopped
for a night's rest they smoked. First, the chief man, called the Head-
Warrior (Tahadez), then his two other men, called Second-leading-
warrior (Neeskaa), would pass the pipe around for his men to smoke.
The young man had a war bundle, given him by his wife's dead relatives. That is how he came to know so much about what he was to
meet, and if he were safe or in danger. So when they met their enemies
the battle was easily won, and they scalped their enemies. They then
returned to their homes, and on their arrival the people praised them
for their victory. At night they again commenced their victory dances,
continuing to dance all night. The next day, the young man did as he

had been told to do, taking the scalp off to some place where there was no one and putting it away for his wife's dead relatives. When he returned home the dancing was already going on, and it lasted all that day. When night came the young man thought to himself: "Well, my wife would never know anything about it if I should dance with some other woman; suppose I try it." He said to himself: "My wife is on earth; she will not leave me again." The dance continued, and he danced with another woman and that night was with her. When he left her he went back home, and his wife was gone. The young man supposed his wife to have gone off somewhere with some other woman to dance. The next morning she did not return; for she knew what he had been doing just the same as if she had been with him. He began to mourn again and went to his wife's grave, but there was no sign of anyone appearing to him as his friend had done. So this was the man who told that there was such a thing as death and life again after death. He also told that a man who dies in battle will enter into the Above-happy-when-he-gets-there and be happy. This man lived for a while and finally died.

60. THE CRIPPLED BOY WHO DISOBEYED THE GODS.*

Many hundreds of years ago, when our people came from the north on their way to this point where we are living, there was a village called Windy-Village-on-Hill-side (Setsketskalikatatish). In this village lived Wrist-Guard-on-each-Wrist (Wychastaqual). When but a small boy he was crippled, and after he was grown up he was the ugliest man in the village. He was of no account for anything. During these times there were many men who had got great powers by visiting Windy-Village-on-Hill-side. Wrist-Guard-on-each-Wrist took a notion to visit this place. It took men one whole day to go there, and a day to come back; but it took Wrist-Guard-on-each-Wrist two days to go there. On his arrival at the foot of the mountain he began to pray to the gods who were supposed to live in this mountain. He climbed the mountain and on reaching the summit he stayed there four days without anything to eat or drink. During the first night, before he went to sleep he could hear human beings talking, but could not see any one. While asleep he had all sorts of dreams, and when he woke up, about daylight, he could hear two stars talking together regarding him. They said to one another: "Well, we will all have to go on as long as the darkness continues." Wrist-Guard-on-each-Wrist then

*Told by Towakoni Jim (Towakoni).

rose from the place where he was sleeping and began to pray to the stars and the animal gods (Itsyascha). whom he thought would have mercy upon him and help him to become a famous man, and would give him power to become a better-looking man. He stayed another day until night. When darkness came he could hear some human beings talking. He understood every word that they uttered, until he went to sleep. He had not seen any one coming to take pity on him. About daylight he woke up and heard the animal gods talking about him; then he heard them say that they would have to go on, because it was nearly daylight. After hearing all these things again, he rose from the place where he was sleeping and began to pray as before. During the day he had nothing to eat or drink, and this was his second day's fasting up on the mountain. When night came again he sat up until late, then went to sleep, having first heard some human being talking about his being there. He had a good many dreams, and about daylight he woke up. Then he could hear the animal gods talking to one another, going on to where they were all headed, for it was nearly daylight. Again he began to pray to the things that he had been praying to. He intended to stay until these animal gods did something for him, and so he prayed all day again, praying with all his might, but during the day he could see no sign of anybody who could take pity on him and give him some powers. Here he remained all day again, until night. As soon as darkness came he heard a good many people coming around where he was, but no one seemed to come close enough to be seen. Every one seemed to want to keep out of sight. When he grew tired of waiting for some one to come around he went to sleep on the same spot where he had been sleeping during the first two nights. He had a good many dreams, but none seemed true. At pretty near daylight he woke, and he could see the stars going, and every one seemed to talk about his still staying at the summit of the mountain seeking powers from the animal gods. They then said to one another that they wished some one would hurry and take pity upon him, instead of leaving him waiting so long. They then talked to one another about having to go along, for it was nearly daylight. Wrist-Guard-on-each-Wrist then arose and began to pray with all his might to the animal gods, asking for mercy. He was about starved when two men came around where he was, saying to one another: "You go and see him, and tell him what we want." Finally, one of these men came where he was and told him to rise, and insisted that he go along with them. When he came to his real senses he was following these two men, who took him to a large room in the side of the mountain.

Upon entering the room he saw a great many men. He was asked to take a seat in the rear part of the room, in front of a man whom he thought was the head man of the animal gods. All at once the head man of the place touched his eyes, and he saw in place of the men who were all around him, all sorts of beasts and fowls of the air. The man who was sitting back of him was painted on his chin, and wore a sort of black robe. The different animals and birds were wearing robes of all colors. Some of the robes were of a sort of black and gray, while others were of dark gray. In this crowd he saw all kinds of eagles, and among them the bald head. The men who brought him down to this place were of rather dark complexion, for they were Crows, of two different kinds; one was called the Raven (Kawitarh—Buffalo-Crow), and the other was a common kind of Crow (Kawi). The two men asked the other men to do whatever they expected to do for Wrist-Guard-on-each-Wrist, and to make haste in doing it. Then, one at a time, these men (the beasts and fowls of the air) took their turn to give this poor man, Wrist-Guard-on-each-Wrist, their powers. The man who was sitting back of him was a Bear, and he did the first work in giving him his powers. He gave him power to have good hearing and powers to send out war-parties and to cure sick people. Others gave him power to travel faster and not be troubled with lameness any more. Each of these beasts and fowls of the air gave him powers of all kinds, and gave him presents for his use in time of need, such things as war-bonnet, quiver with bow and arrows with it, and shield. The shield was made of the hide of the Buffalo bull who presented him with the shield. It was painted in all colors for his use. Now he had all sorts of powers, and great ones, too. Then they gave him something to eat and water to drink. After they had done all this he was told to return to his home, and to wear everything that he had, but that he was not to arrive home during daylight, but at night, so that no one would see him or know who he was. They then told him that he should not have intercourse with a woman, and they warned him, saying that since his looks were changed women might notice him.

Wrist-Guard-on-each-Wrist started home with all his gifts, but on account of having these powers the load was easy for him to carry. While he was on the way home he would look at his war-bonnet and the other things that had been given to him. He would try a good many things to prove his powers, and he wondered how he could in some way get a look at himself, to see if his looks were the same as when he left the mountains. When he came to a creek he looked for a still place in the water, and there he looked at himself and found that he was handsome.   As soon as he saw himself and found himself to be a fine-looking young man he began to think of women, and of whom he should choose for his wife.   On the following day he stopped for a while, trying to decide whether to wait until night, or to enter the village during the daytime.   He thought this over and over again, deciding whether he should remain until night or whether to enter the village during daylight.   He decided to enter the village during the daytime, and to make himself known to the people, and tell them where he had been since he had disappeared.   He saw with his own eyes, on the edge of the village, men and women playing all kinds of games, arrow games, shinny games, and double-ball games.   He especially wanted to pass near the double-ball game, because that is a woman's game, and he could get a close view of the young women and be seen; then, when night should come, he knew that some one would come around where he was.   After thinking all this over he went on to the village instead of obeying the animals who had forbidden him to enter the village during the daytime, and to have any thought of women.

When he arrived at the place where all of the games were being played he had on all his fine dress, his war-bonnet, shield, quiver, and a good many other things that he was carrying.   Every woman turned and looked at him, to see who he was; but he was unknown to them. When he got right in the middle of the crowd he turned to the young men and young women and told them who he was and where he had been for the four days since he had disappeared; that he had great powers from the animal gods, including all the things he had and the change of his looks.   He had been forbidden to tell this.   When he reached home he told his people that he was Wrist-Guard-on-each-Wrist, once a crippled boy; but since he had been to Windy-Village-on-Hill-side he would no more be a cripple, for he had fasted upon the top of the mountain four long days and had received powers.   He then put his things away, because he was now at home and thought no one could ever take away his things or his powers, since he was so far from the place where he had got his powers.   At night great crowds of men came to visit him to see what sort of a man he was since being away.   Women came and stood around outside, so that they might see him and get to marry him.   That night, after everybody had gone out of the place, woman after woman came around, and they were refused entrance.   Finally, a certain woman he wished for came around and went right to bed with him, for she thought that she was getting in bed with a fine young man.   After they had gone to sleep all of his powers were taken away from him, and his good looks were changed, so that he became ugly as at first. He did not feel the change, and he knew nothing of it, nor did the woman know anything about it until the next morning. As soon as the woman saw whom she was sleeping with she left for her home, and was as ashamed as she could be. When Wrist-Guard-on-each-Wrist woke again his wife was gone, his powers and presents were all taken away from him, and he was again an ugly and crippled boy.

Long afterward Wrist-Guard-on-each-Wrist thought that he would go back to the mountain and get back his powers; but when he visited the place there was no sign of anybody to take pity upon him, for he had lost all of his powers through foolish thoughts. Wrist-Guard-on-each-Wrist lived a long while. He was always ugly and crippled and never got any more aid of any kind.

APPENDIX.

The following tale was told to Dr. John Sibley, in 1811, by a distinguished Wichita chief at Natchitoches. The tale is interpolated in a copy of Captain Anthony Glass, "Journal of a Voyage from Nackitosh into the Interior of Louisiana on the Waters of the Red River . . . between the First of July, 1808, and May, 1809," Silliman Family Papers, Manuscripts and Archives, Yale University Library, and reprinted by permission. It is reproduced as it appears in the original manuscript.

A MIGRATION TALE

They have a story of the Orphan which they often repeat, in order to preserve a kind of traditional record from generation to generation. They say some ages ago when they lived on the river Platt that falls into the Missouri they had been so harassed by their wars with the Ozages and some other tribes that they resolved to move to the south so far that their enemies could not find them. Accordingly prepared and satt off. There was a little Orphan Boy whose parents and Relations had all been killed by their Enemies. As they were leaving their Village forever, no pervision had been thought of to take the little boy along. Everyone seemed already to have too many encumbearaces. An old man who had no family offered to take him and they sett off on foot, for at that time they had no horses, in all possible haste as though they were flying from the Enemy, and proceded through the tall grass, the Prairies resembling the Ocean, every one getting along as he could. The little boy was too small to walk and the Old Man had to carry him. They made a halt after a long march and collected some Buffalo droppings to make a fire, this only fuel these immense meadows afford—and after resting a short time and fearful of being overtaken by an enemy sett off again. The old man being extremely fatigued and nearly exhausted delayed in setting off with the main band, thinking he would rest a few minutes longer and remained by the fire till the Company were out of sight, and to amuse his little Comrade began to sing a song. The boy joined him and soon fell

315

asleep. The poor old man finding himself all alone and separated from his people, expecting the Enemy might be on the trace every moment to appear in sight was in the utmost perplexity of mind. Exhausted as he was, to carry the boy and overtake the company was impossible. To remain with him, both would be lost. He looked upon the sleeping Orphan and wept at the resolution he was about forming to go and leave him. He kissed him and wept over him, turned his back, advanced in the Path a few steps, turned Back resolved and resolved at length after one great effort satt off. The Company after some time mising the old man and his charge made a halt, the old man came up, a thousand tongues Instantaneously demanded what have you done with the little Orphan Boy? The Old Man almost breathless, interrupted by sighs and tears, told them that he had left him asleep by the fire where they had stopped. Every young man volunteered their services to go back and bring him, all the women and his little comrades calling out to those setting off to make haste. They soon found the fire and saw the prints where the boy had slept; believing he had awakened and strayed off in the tall grass they divided to search for him in every direction. In vain they sought and were about giving it out under the belief that some wild beast had taken him off bodily when they heard him singing the same song he was singing with the old man when he fell asleep. Their hearts were gladdened, thinking in an instant they would have him and be on their return, but on pursuing the voice they could not find him. After hunting for some time, become frightened and were about tracing their way back to the Company waiting when they heard the Voice of the Boy, directing them to go to an Eminence in sight and look beyond it. They did so and saw (as they supposed) an immense Valley covered with ice. Being more and more alarmed, it being in summer and the weather warm, they regarded the ice as a miracle; being about to leave it, they heard the voice of the Boy again tell them what they saw was not ice but something the Great Spirit had placed there for the good of mankind. They tasted and found it salt. The voice spoke again and told them to carry some of it to their Company and search no more for him for he was no longer mortal and was with the Great Spirit. The party returned to their company in waiting and narrated the story. Some of them took a Journey every year to the Great Saline which they call the Miracle and every night to this day sing the song of the Orphan.

ABSTRACTS.

FIRST PERIOD: CREATION.

1. THE FIRST CREATION.

Man-never-known-on-Earth creates land and water. Darkness everywhere. He makes man, Having-Power-to-carry-Light, and woman, Bright-Shining-Woman. They receive things through dreams. Woman is given Mother-Corn, to be food for people. Having-Power-to-carry-Light is drawn by man in grass-lodge toward east. There is light in lodge. Man of grass-lodge says more people will exist. While men are talking voice tells them to come and shoot deer. They are only to shoot last deer, which is half black and half white. Man of grass-lodge makes arrows. White deer, black deer, and black and white deer come out of water and man shoots last one. He follows deer and becomes Star-that-is-always-moving. Shooting black and white deer signifies there shall be days and nights. Having-Power-to-carry-Light sees man across water who says he shall be called Man-Reflecting (Sun) who will give light. Having-Power-to-carry-Light sees sun coming up. He returns home and has light to travel in. When darkness comes he sees three stars which are three deer, and fourth star which is man who wounded deer. Villages spring up. Having-Power-to-carry-Light and woman go from village to village teaching people how to make and use things. Man tells them about bow and arrows and gives men ball with string to it and teaches them how to play game. Teaches them shinny game. He tells them how to travel fast on arrows and ball. Man travels like spirit, is at place at once. Woman gives women Mother-Corn to plant to eat. They are to offer food to Man-never-known-on-Earth and rub over children before eating. The woman teaches them double-ball game and tells them use of ball in traveling. Says she will become something else, and that by her they will know whether they are pregnant. She teaches them to foretell things about to happen, and to make offerings to heavenly bodies and earth powers. Woman disappears and becomes Moon. Man tells men that in bringing game from hunt they are to offer to heavenly bodies and earth powers. Says if children bathe before daylight they will get powers. Man tells them he will sometimes be seen in early morning as star and his name will be "Bringer-of-the-Daylight."

SECOND PERIOD: TRANSFORMATION.

2. THE DEEDS OF THE COYOTE AND YOUNG-STAR.

Coyote finds Young-Star and takes him home to play with his boy. Young-Star is wonderful boy and will not say where he is from. He and Coyote's boy find black horse. They ride it home. Coyote tells family it is dangerous animal. Young-Star explains its use. Coyote thinks of moving to village to show off wonderful boy and wonderful animal. Young-Star goes off and Coyote starts east with old woman and children on horse. He whips horse to make it jump across canyon, and when it jumps family fall off and are killed. Young-Star takes blame on himself for not telling Coyote to look out for low place. Young-Star and Coyote go to village and are entertained by chief. Chief has pretty sisters, and Coyote desires to have them for wives. Next morning Young-Star sends Coyote to man and his sister living toward the north to beg for their powers. They have blue complexions. Man gives Coyote bow and sends him to cut four arrows, four dogwoods that say "me" first. All dogwoods cry out together and Coyote cuts armful. Man chooses four and sends Coyote back with remainder. Man makes some arrows for Coyote and gives him shield and war-bonnet. Tells Coyote not to think of any woman while he has these things; that enemy will attack village four times; that Coyote and son will have to do all the fighting, and that at end of four days he may do as he pleases about women. Man rubs Coyote's eyes and he can see everything. Coyote has man's blue complexion. He cannot be hit by enemies. Man says he belongs to Jay-Birds. Coyote stays in lodge with chief's sisters. When he goes to bed women talk about him. In morning he hears cries that enemy attacking. As he goes through door one woman catches him and asks him his name. He says Owner-of-Flint-Knife-Quarries. He and Young-Star kill four enemies and each presents scalp to chief. After victory dances Coyote pays no attention to women. In morning there is same alarm, and Coyote starts out. Woman speaks to him as Hanging-Knife, and he says she is spoiling his name. Coyote and his son again take four scalps and present them to chief. Coyote joins in dances and on returning goes to bed of chief's sister. In morning enemy again attack. Coyote and son again secure scalp for chief. Coyote notices some blue gone from himself to woman with whom he had slept. He and Young-Star join in dancing, but Coyote slips away early and goes to bed Women take turns to sleep with him. He hears arrows and bow talking about his not keeping agreement, and toward morning hears wind blowing inside lodge. He becomes real coyote and runs away when awakened by woman's screams. His powers leave him. Young-Star leaves village, but gives bow, arrows, and other things and powers to be used by warriors. He becomes Morning-Star. Chief's sisters bring forth young dogs, which people take home for pets.

3. THE COYOTE AND HIS MAGIC SHIELD AND ARROWS.

Coyote can not kill enough game to last long, as his children eat all meat as fast as he brings it. Goes to west, where man living by himself. Man gives him meat to eat. Coyote sees pole outside and asks man to give him one like it. Man tells him to come back next day. Next day Coyote goes back. Man tells him if he is brave and fast runner to go south to hill where three Buffalo of different sizes are sitting. He is to select Buffalo according to size of shield he wants. Coyote goes and asks for largest Buffalo to go with him. Buffalo chases him to man's place. Man tells him to jerk Buffalo by horns. After three unsuccessful attempts Coyote jerks Buffalo and has shield. He then has bow and arrows given him. He shoots arrows in four directions and they kill buffalo and bring them to Coyote. He is warned to jerk Buffalo before sunrise and told that his arrows have life. Coyote returns home with shield, and bow and arrows. After eating he four times commands arrows to hunt, and they have plenty to eat. On his way to certain village Coyote meets man carrying large bow and arrow with blunt point. He asks if arrow is any good. Persuades man to shoot at him and goes good way off. Man shoots and Coyote tries to dodge arrow, but it goes through his back and out of his mouth. Coyote asks for power to be fine-looking and to have large bow and arrow. They go to stream, into which man throws Coyote, and he becomes fine-looking man. Man who appears to Coyote is Sun. Coyote journeys to village, where he finds high tipi. In morning he jerks Buffalo and has his shield. He is challenged by man to dive in river to find out who can remain longer under water. Man had thus killed many of his enemies. Coyote dives and finds beavers' lodge, in which he remains. In evening Coyote's enemy appears, and the Coyote appears. Man asks Coyote not to be in hurry to kill him and then goes into air. Coyote shoots his large arrow, which brings man down. He burns body and pokes fire with stick, and many men who had been killed jump out. Chief makes Coyote one of head men and gives him sister for wife. Every morning Coyote jerks Buffalo by horns and makes shield, and commands arrows to go hunting. After time he lets Buffalo stand until sun gets up high, that more people may see shield. Buffalo gets angry and Coyote fails to throw him. Bow and arrows tell Coyote to go back home, as his children's and wife's food is neatly exhausted. He will not listen and Buffalo kills him. He then becomes ordinary coyote. His wife and children starve to death.

4. THE COYOTE AND HIS MAGIC SHIELD AND ARROWS.

Coyote resolves to go somewhere and starts toward west. He comes to tipi and sees large buffalo standing near. Swallow comes out, grabs buffalo between horns and shakes it, and there is shield. Coyote enters tipi and Swallow gives him food. Swallow's spittle is blue, and inside of his mouth greenish blue. Coyote asks him to give him powers. Swallow asks if he is brave, gives him meat to take to his family, and tells him to come back. Coyote takes meat to family and returns to Swallow. Swallow asks if he is good runner. Tells him how to get shield, as in myth No. 3, and Coyote throws shield on pole. Swallow makes him four arrows and bow and instructs him how to use them and shield. He then takes Coyote to flowing water and throws him in. On coming out he is like Swallow, and his spittle blue. Coyote goes home and uses his powers, making his arrows hunt Buffalo. His family scream at seeing Buffalo standing at door of tipi. Coyote grabs it between horns and it becomes shield, which he lays on pole. When he has enough meat for his family Coyote goes again to Swallow and says he is going on journey. Swallow tells him that arrows will let him know when meat at home is gone and he must then return at once. Coyote meets Sun, man with large bow and blunt arrow, which he obtains, after experiencing its powers as in myth No. 3. He goes on to the village, chief of which entertains him. He turns Buffalo into shield and every one comes to see him. Next morning he sends his arrows to hunt buffalo, and whole village is then fed. Chief gives Coyote his sister for wife. Soon afterward bow and arrows and everything he got from him run away, and he is killed by Buffalo, as is related in myth No. 3.

5. THE GREAT SOUTH-STAR, THE PROTECTOR OF WARRIORS.

Healthy-Flint-Stone-Man lives in village of many names with family of father, mother, sisters, and wife. He is a great hunter and warrior, and he sends war-parties against the Trickster people. When his wife is pregnant he tells her what to do when child is born; that he is to be called Young-Flint-Stone, and is not to know where his father is until he is old enough. Healthy-Flint-Stone-Man sets out on war expedition and goes so far that his men die of old age on the way, until only four are left. He keeps going on until these men give out one after another. He then goes on alone until he reaches cave, which he makes his permanent home. From here he goes to attack his enemies, whose heads he cuts off and hangs on a long pole. Son is born and grows rapidly. When he becomes man he asks mother about father. She says he has gone long distance to live. Boy asks mother to grind meal enough to take him to his father. This she does and boy starts in search of father. He finds trail and after long while comes to man who had given out. Man is angry, but boy puts meal in man's mouth. Man says it reminds him of village he had come from, and that boy is Young-Flint-Stone. Boy goes on and comes to second, third, and fourth men, each of whom is angry, but after tasting meal knows him. Fourth man tells him where his father lives, and that he will have to sneak around to get to his dwelling place or his father will kill him. Young-Flint-Stone goes on and manages to get in. Father will not believe him to be his son and tries to throw him. Young-Flint-Stone at last succeeds in putting meal in his father's mouth. This reminds him of his village and he recognizes his son. He tells him he has come there to be near his enemies, and that he can not go back. His hair is turning to flint stones. Young-Flint-Stone sees pole on which hang many skulls, old and fresh. He goes with father to attack enemy and each kills man. Young-Flint-Stone does not remain long. Father sends word to people that in next generation his place will be known as the Protector-of-Warriors, and that he will be seen as Great-South-Star. When they send out war-parties they are to offer him smoke for good fortune and victory. He sends scalp for his family. Young-Flint-Stone on his way home sees four men again, but they remain where they are. He reaches home safe, much to surprise of people, to whom he delivers scalp and gives account of his adventures. Young-Flint-Stone becomes a great warrior as his father, Great-South-Star, to whom he offers smoke. Young-Flint-Stone becomes a Star, Flint-Stone-lying-down-Above.

6. THE GREAT SOUTH-STAR, THE PROTECTOR OF WARRIORS.

In a village named as in myth No. 5, is famous man named Wearing-Flint-Stone-on-Top-of-Head. His father is chief of village, and he has mother and sister. Sister is married to famous warrior and becomes pregnant. He tells sister her child is to be called Young-Flint-Stone-Yelling-Boy, and that he will follow in footsteps of uncle. As in myth No. 5, this man goes out with great war-party. He goes so far that all return but four men, who gradually give out, however, and he goes on alone until he comes to hill, not far from village of enemies, where he lives alone. His nephew is born and grows so fast that he soon sends out war-parties. Other men tell him about his uncle's going south and not returning. He tells mother he is going to look for his uncle, and that she is to make him two pairs of moccasins and grind some corn to remind his uncle of home. He takes them and some tobacco and sets out. After traveling far he comes in succession to four men who had given out, as in myth No. 5. They remember after smoking, and fourth man warns him of danger, that uncle is about to turn to something, as his head is covered with flint stones instead of hair. Nephew enters place when uncle is asleep and gets hold of him as he awakes. Uncle will not believe he is his nephew until he tastes meal which nephew puts in his mouth. Nephew then gives uncle pipe of tobacco to smoke. Uncle tells nephew why he has come there and next day takes him to attack enemy's village. Nephew takes scalp of man with white hair dyed red. Uncle tells nephew about his powers and about his followers who are to think of him when on war-path. Generations to come will not have so great powers as he has. When going through Leader-of-War ceremonies they are to offer him smoke. He will be seen by them as South-Star. Uncle gives nephew red scalp for mother, which nephew takes home. Great bright star then seen, which nephew says is his uncle. He tells people of his adventures, and afterward shows them powers given him by his uncle. Nephew afterward seen ascending into sky and becomes Star.

7. THE GREAT SOUTH-STAR, THE PROTECTOR OF WARRIORS.

The same as myth No. 5, with slight variation in names of village, etc. Hero is named "Protector-of-Warriors" instead of "Healthy-Flint-Stone-Man."

8. THE SEVEN BROTHERS AND THE WOMAN.

Man named Mixed-Timber has power to change his looks, so that at some times he appears young, at others old and ugly. He goes to village to carry off chief's wife, and appears as young man. He reaches chief's place, and wife sees him when she steps out for wood. She notices fragrant odor which comes from Mixed-Timber and she starts to see who he is. He keeps backing off and woman follows until they reach end of village. They go outside of village and Mixed-Timber then stops and says he has come long journey for her. They start off homeward, west, and travel three days, and then come to lodge which woman is told not to enter until bidden. When she goes in she sees Mixed-Timber as old, ugly man, and his mother sitting by fireplace. After they have eaten together Mixed-Timber starts out on another hunting trip and mother tells woman that he drinks human blood out of a skull, and is a cannibal, and that if he gets hold of her hand she will be slain and butchered. Man returns next evening and old woman gives him human flesh for supper. After meal he asks woman to bring him fresh water. She goes to spring and finds skull, which she dips in blood and carries to man. Mixed-Timber reaches for her hand, which she jerks away. While Mixed-Timber is away mother tells woman that next time he goes hunting she should make her escape, as he intends to kill her. He returns again and sends woman for blood-water and he again tries to seize her hand. Man goes on hunting trip next day and woman is told to make her escape. She is given double-ball and stick to go on. She puts water on fire, and as smoke goes up she goes up with it. Old woman tells her she will have to cross river and go to small hill where is little boy whom she must beg to save her life, for his people have great power. After woman lights on ground she runs for a while, and tosses double-ball, with which she goes up into air. Old woman tells man at distance of woman's escape. Then she kills herself with club. Man returns and sees mother dead. He makes circuit and at last finds woman's trail. He loses it where she tossed the ball. This she does four times, and after getting on feet again she runs a long way and comes to river. She finds Crane, on whose neck she crosses river. She sees Big-Belly-Boy and asks him to save her. He walks around, but agrees to do so, as Mixed-Timber comes in sight of her. They go to great stone, which boy removes, and in room is Man-with-Supernatural-Powers. Mixed-Timber arrives, and when people will not give up woman he begins to destroy little hill in which they are. Boy tells Man-with-Supernatural-Powers to make haste. Old man takes string from neck, which has something tied to it, and throws it up, killing man outside instantly. When Mixed-Timber is dead old man tells woman to go, but at boy's request she is allowed to remain. Old man tells woman his six sons will be in soon. When they come they stop and ask what is in lodge. Boy persuades them to come, and as they enter lodge they fall dead. Old man restores them to life and they are surprised to see what was done, as they had never seen a woman before. Woman explains to boy about husband and wife. She tells brothers, and woman is married to seven brothers. Boy is born to them. Six brothers go hunting and are killed by two Double-Faced-Monsters. Old man brings them into lodge and brings them to life again. While walking around with boy, woman and child find lot of young Double-Faced-Monsters in cave. Their lungs are hanging on line across cave; boy punches them with arrow point, and all young ones fall dead. Woman tells boy about children's games and persuades him to move lodge and others consent. They move toward the north. At dark, Man-with-Supernatural-Powers makes first grass-lodge by blowing in bunch of grass. Late on fourth day they reach woman's village and old man makes grass-lodge to live in. They remain for a long while and boys marry. Child makes little boy cry, and as Man-with-Supernatural-Powers does not like it he says they had better move again. He takes them to sky, and woman goes with them. They are the Seven Stars (Ursa Major), and old man himself is North-Star.

9. THE SEVEN BROTHERS AND THE SISTER.

Seven brothers with their five sisters live with their father and mother. Brothers great hunters and warriors and have great powers on war-path. At home they play games, chiefly hoop-and-javelin. Each brother has a special power, and they are named accordingly. Large crowds go with them against the Tricksters. Woman comes to bed of oldest brother while at home. He marks her on back with white clay. Next day all women play double-ball game. He notices that his oldest sister bears mark. Next night sister comes to bed again and man strikes her all over with points of arrows. Woman goes away north and becomes Bear-Woman-having-great-Powers and carries off people to eat. Brother Great-Prophet says some beast has killed all people but their youngest sister. Good-Sight looks and says it is Bear. Brothers keep watch of Bear and sister. Sister comes with sack for Indian turnips and short stick to kill jack rabbit. She tells brothers when Bear sleeps and that she can be killed by shooting in hands and feet. Bear suspicious that brothers have helped sister to get turnips and rabbit and makes her repeat killing of rabbit. Next time girl tells brother Bear is asleep. Sister goes north with Fast-Runner and other brothers go to where Bear is sleeping with hands and feet up. Four of them shoot at once, hitting her under feet, and then run north. Bear follows and gains on them. Oldest brother throws turtle shell on ground and many turtles crawl around. Bear stops to collect turtles and brothers and sister get long way ahead. She again chases and gains on them. Eldest brother throws red-colored stone on ground, and place is full of red-colored stones, which Bear wants for painting. Bear piles up stones and then pursues again. Eldest brother throws on ground fine dust from arrows, and there are big bushes from which arrows are made. Bear wants them and cuts them with teeth. She again pursues and gains on them and oldest brother says if she succeeds in passing next place they will have to die. He passes bow-string through left hand four times and throws it on ground. Deep canyon appears. Bear comes, and finding high cedar tree standing near canyon, she jumps on tree and climbs down. She climbs up another cedar tree and gets to other side of canyon. She again gives chase, and when party hear her talking they stop and sit down facing south. When Bear arrives she sits down and rolls up to them and stops them. Oldest brother takes feather from head and blows it. As it goes up, seven brothers and sister go up with it to sky, where they live as Seven-Stars, or Dipper. Bear scolds herself for not killing them at once, and goes back to canyon. In north are worlds of bears, because Bear went there and never returned. Brothers leave their power on earth for benefit of people.

10. THE SEVEN BROTHERS AND THE SISTER.

Coyote, who has power to trick people, wanders west and sees grass-lodge. He enters and sees woman alone. Woman gives him food and asks if he has any children. He says he has daughter about her age and resembling her. Woman asks him to bring daughter to live with her as she is alone during day. Her brothers come from hunt at night. Coyote promises to send daughter, and goes home with plenty of meat. He forgets what woman told him, as he has no daughter. Some time after, he leaves home to go to her. He goes into river and dives four times and becomes full-grown woman and similar to other woman. He puts robe around him after the manner of woman. Goes to lodge and makes noise to atract woman, who comes out. Coyote woman pretends to be shy and woman takes her into lodge, gives her food, and asks why father has not come. Brothers return from hunt and ask what smells so badly in lodge. Sister says she has woman to live with her while they are away. At last they go into lodge and see woman. When men look at her she is ashamed, but she is enamoured of them. After eating they go to bed, two women sleeping together. As time goes on woman asks Coyote woman how people obtain children. She says man and woman have to marry. After further conversation woman offers her brothers to Coyote woman to marry. Sister speaks to brothers, who refuse to marry Coyote woman, but finally they agree to have woman between them. Men take turns in sleeping with Coyote woman. Child is born and Coyote woman says what has to be done and that men not to enter lodge for four days. On fifth day they come in and see child in cradle. Child grows fast and Coyote woman thinks of leaving people to marry chief of tribe. She goes away with child, but woman follows and takes them back. Next day she goes away again with child toward north. Woman tries to find them and fails. When brothers return they find sister crying. She tells them of woman's desertion, and oldest brother says he always knew she was fooled. Next morning oldest brother asks sister for pot of water. They stand in group and pour water on fire, and as smoke goes up they go up too. When up high they see Coyote woman and boy and go after them. They overtake them and get child. Brothers and sister with child go up into sky and become stars of Dipper. Sister also becomes star, but does not stay with brothers. Child is small star which is first with one of seven stars and then with another. Coyote jumps, but finds she is coyote again. He returns home, but sees only hair and bones, the remains of his family. He goes off to prairie and cries as coyotes cry.

11. THE OWNER OF BLACK-AND-WHITE-KNIVES AND HIS SON.

Father, mother, and daughter live out by themselves. Woman goes out after wood. Arrow which she picks up is claimed by fine-looking young man Owner-of-Black-and-White-Flint-Knives. She refuses to give it up and young man starts back toward west. She follows, and when man stops she can not turn back, he having charmed her. At night man makes her lie down by herself. At end of fourth day they arrive at home of man. He has mother and four sisters. Man and sisters have different meat from old woman's. Old woman and stranger sleep together. Next morning young man goes hunting and sisters go swimming. Old woman tells young woman that her children eat human flesh and that son has great power to attack human beings. One day old woman and young woman pound corn into meal and after others have gone to sleep they put meal into young man's mouth and make him eat it. He says they have taken away his powers and afterwards he hunts all kinds of game. Four women go to lake and cease to return. Young man calls together wild animals and fowls. He tells them he wants his sisters, and whoever gets their clothes and brings sisters home shall have them for wives, but that they will have to run hard, as if overtaken they will die. All agree, and Jack-Rabbit tries first. He runs away with clothes, but women overtake and kill him. Four women are ducks, and fast runners and swimmers. Hawk tries his luck, but is killed. Small-Hawk takes clothes and being fastest runner known gets into lodge with them just as women pass door. They come and beg for clothes, but brother tells them they must come in. They do so and Small-Hawk becomes their husband. Brother's wife, who has come long distance, is pregnant and he thinks he will take her back home. They start on journey, and when they stop, man tells wife to get much wood, as some one will be around at night to fight him and they must keep fire burning all night. He says, as he has lost power, he will be killed, and instructs her how to do about the child, who is to be called Young-Flint-Knife. At night creature comes and tries to pull man from fire. They struggle all night and at dawn they part. Next day they go on, and in afternoon gather much wood. At night foe, who is Double-Faced-Monster, comes again. This occurs again next night, and on following day man tells wife she will have to go home alone as he will be carried off. He says she is not to tell his son about him until he is old enough, and he is to have father's elk-horn bow and arrows to play with. Double-Faced-Monster comes again at dark and after struggle carries man off, fire having gone out. Wife reaches home and tells them what has happened. Child is born and is called Young-Flint-Knife. He sits down and calls for something to eat. Mother gives him black stone and white stone, which she says is his food. He grows and becomes famous and has great powers. When he hears that his father has been carried away he asks mother for meal and starts in search of him. He finds trail of Double-Faced-Monster and follows it to deep canyon. He sees father and slides down steep wall to him. They go to caves and see young Double-Faced-Monsters. Their hearts are hanging up and Young-Flint-Knife sticks his arrow into them, one after another, asking whose they are, and all are killed. Young-Flint-Knife goes with father to deepest place in creek and asks him to dive in. He does so and comes out of water same in appearance as when carried away. They go to home of young man, who is now much stronger than his father. Soon after Owner-of-Black-and-White-Flint-Knives asks his son to come with him and become something else. At night they go up into the sky and become stars and are called "Flint-Stone-Lying-down-above."

12. THE DEEDS OF AFTER-BIRTH-BOY.

Two villages are near together. Chief of one village has girl, that of other village has boy. Boy and girl are attracted to each other and marry contrary to custom of families. They leave and start on journey to look for new home. They select place near river with timber. Woman builds grass-lodge and man becomes hunter. Woman becomes pregnant. One day man tells wife that she is to fix meat for some one who will come and eat when he is gone. She is not to look at him, but is to get into bed and cover herself up. Man goes hunting. Wife hears some one coming and covers herself up in bed. Person enters and eats meat and then goes away. This takes place every day. At last woman has in mind to try to look at person. She bores hole through robe and puts piece of hollow grass through. Person comes and eats and as he starts away woman peeps through grass. She sees that man has double face and mouth on back of neck. Man turns back and says she has looked at him. He comes to her, kills her, and cuts her open, taking child out of womb. He wraps child in robe and then thrusts stick into after-birth and throws it into water. Man returns from hunting and finds wife dead. Takes her body some distance and lays it on ground. Coming back he hears child crying. Finds boy and he grows rapidly. Takes it with him when going hunting until old enough to play alone. Man then makes bow and arrows for him and shinny ball and stick. Man now leaves boy at home. Another boy comes to play arrow game with him. Strange boy wins all arrows from other boy and then goes off into water. Tells lodge boy they are brothers and that he is not to tell father of his coming. When father comes back he asks what boy has done with arrows. Boy says he has lost them, but refuses to go with father to look for them. Man makes fresh arrows. Next day man goes hunting and strange boy comes again to play. He wins all lodge boy's arrows and goes to water again. Father on return asks boy what he has done with arrows and he says he has lost them shooting birds. Father believes him and makes other arrows. Strange boy comes third day with same result as before. When father asks boy about arrows he tells him about strange boy—that he has tail like poker stick, and goes into water, and calls him brother. His name is "After-birth-Boy." Father finds out that strange boy is his son and arranges with son to attack him and make him stay at home. Next day father stays at home and tells son to invite strange boy into lodge and while examining his head hold him by hair. Father then turns into fire-stick. Strange boy comes, but when he enters lodge he detects father and goes back into water. Next day before "After-birth-Boy" comes father hides behind door and turns into stem of grass. After-birth-Boy comes and is enticed into lodge to eat. They examine each other's heads and lodge boy tangles After-birth-Boy's hair. Takes hold of it and calls father. After-birth-Boy drags them to river, but then consents to live with them. When released he jumps into river and comes back with arm full of arrows. Father makes shinny ball and two sticks and more arrows with netted ring. Tells boys not to roll it toward west, and forbids them to go to place of Spider-Woman, Thunderbird, Double-Faced-Monster, and Headless-Man. Soon after After-birth-Boy asks brother to go with him to Spider-Woman. They shoot birds and give them to Spider-Woman. She puts them into pail of boiling water, but they upset it and scald her to death. Boys go to see Thunderbird's nest. After-birth-Boy climbs tree and Thunderbird tears off all his limbs. He reaches nest and kills two of young birds. He slides down tree and brother puts his legs on again. Boys find long stone on ground and take it to father to sharpen knife on. He tells them it is their mother and makes them take it back again. Next day boys go to caves of Double-Faced-Monsters. They find young ones. They see lungs hanging in cave. After-birth-Boy strikes them with point of arrow and kills all Double-Faced-Monsters but one young one. This they take home as pet for father, but he makes them take it back again. Several days afterward they take shinny ball and sticks and go to where Headless-Man is. He tells them they must play shinny game, and die if they lose. After-birth-Boy sends brother west and says they will send ball back and forth to wear Headless-Man out. They do so and when Headless-Man is tired After-birth-Boy knocks ball over creek, which is goal. Then he passes bow-string four times through his hands and kills Headless-Man with it. Boys' ball and sticks green, representing spring of year. Boys take netted ring and roll it toward west. They run after it and can not stop. Ring rolls into lake and boys find themselves inside great water-monster. Father finds they have gone, and he becomes star in sky. Boys stay long in monster and then After-birth-Boy passes bow-string four times through left hand and swings it around. Monster goes up and falls on dry land. They get out and find it is great fish. Boys start for home. Find no trace of father. Vines grown over lodge. At last After-birth-Boy finds father's track and at night they see his star in sky. After-birth-Boy shoots arrow into sky and drop of blood falls on his hand, showing that star is father. He then shoots two arrows, by which boys climb up into sky to their father. They are boys who killed all meanest beings that lived in those times.

13. THE THUNDERBIRD AND THE WATER-MONSTER.

In village are two chiefs. On east side Thunderbird is chief, and is liked by all but Evil-Spirited-Persons. In games life of person is wagered. Coyote, nephew of Thunderbird, goes to play hand-game and asks uncle to go with him.

Uncle long refuses, but at last consents. On entering lodge where hand-game is going on, Thunderbird is asked to sit on high hump which is covered up. After game people leave and Thunderbird starts to rise, but finds he is stuck to hump, which begins to move. It is water-monster and moves toward lake. Thunderbird tells Coyote that so long as he can see tassel at end of bow he will know that his uncle is alive. Monster goes to bottom of lake, and water goes over head of Thunderbird and then tassel at end of bow disappears. Soon afterward every one leaves village. Only old man and woman and two grandsons remain. Boys shoot birds near lake for fun. One day they hear singing. They tell grandparents, and old man tells them of drowning of Thunderbird, who must be singing. He says if there is any flesh on him he is still alive. Old man instructs boys to heat many rocks and throw them into lake. They do so and lake dries up, showing water-monster. All go to lake and cut up monster. Inside are bones of Thunderbird. They find some pieces of flesh on bones of fingers. Bones are put in grass-lodge, which is set on fire. Old man calls on Thunderbird to come out, and fourth time he comes out same as before and having his bow and arrows. He asks first where people are. Thunderbird goes hunting every day and when boys grow he gives them power to become great hunters. Many people gradually return to village, Coyote among them. He finds his uncle alive and they are first and second chief. All people remain human beings, except those who went off and never returned.

14. THE DEEDS OF WETS-THE-BED.

Three chiefs who paint themselves differently live in village. War-parties go out against Tricksters to entertain themselves. Old man and old woman, who are very poor, have grandson, Wets-the-Bed. Boy hears of war-party and determines to go. He follows trail. Is ordered back, but chief allows him to accompany them. When near enemy's village men take off robes and leave them in charge of Wets-the-Bed. When they have gone he jumps into creek and comes out changed to man. He goes on to village, enters ahead of war-party, having red war bonnet and carrying war-club. He goes through village fighting people, and returns to creek, dives in and comes out as he was before. People talk about strange man seen in lead. Long after there is another war-party and Wets-the-Bed again follows. Leader tells people to keep their eyes on person who should be in lead on attack. Again men leave robes with Wets-the-Bed, who again changes himself and heads attack on village as before. This happens four times. Leader wonders who it can be who is faster runner than himself. He calls all men together and offers his girls to man who can prove he arrived at village before rest of warriors. Wets-the-Bed proves he was the man. Oldest girl does not like him and allows younger girl to live with him. One day while men are slaughtering buffalo Wets-the-Bed sends grandfather to bring him some intestines. He grabs intestines and as punishment holes are bored through cheeks and hide tied through them. He returns to boy, who goes and dives in creek, coming out same as when with war-party. He goes and finds man who cut his grandfather's cheeks and serves him in same way. After reminding people of what he had done he goes to creek and again changes himself. People talk and chief has largest tipi prepared for grandparents of Wets-the-Bed, who goes back to wives. He takes his young wife to creek, and after diving in he throws her in and they are both changed. When older sister sees change she wants to sleep with Wets-the-Bed. She has to be satisfied to lie near bed and make a step for them. Wets-the-Bed recognized as good son-in-law. Finally chief appoints him head chief in his place. He treats everybody right. Chiefs paint themselves differently. Wets-the-Bed has war-bonnet of hair, dyed red and yellow. He is troubled about old chief's oldest daughter and announces he wants to go where he came from, and wants people to do as they please about themselves. He calls himself Red-Star and says he got his powers from Shooting-Star. Other chiefs turn into Swift-Hawk, Buffalo-Crow, Eagle, Black-Eagle, respectively. People pour water on fire, and smoke goes up. Some fly into air, others go as animals, some to timber, some to prairie, and some to water. Those that remain continue human beings.

15. THE DEEDS OF WETS-THE-BED.

Wets-the-Bed lives with grandparents, who are abused by Coyote. Young-Man-Chief is only friend of Wets-the-Bed, who is also called Corn-Meal-Boy, because he eats at mortar where corn is grinding. Four beautiful girls, sisters, tell grandfather they want to form war-party against the Tricksters. He shows the contents of four war bundles and explains use of pipe. He fills pipe with tobacco and girls take it to Young-Man-Chief. He smokes it and becomes leader. Corn-Meal-Boy tells old folks he wants to go with war-party, as sisters promise to be wives of one who first sees enemy. He follows war-party, but Coyote sends him back. Young-Man-Chief and Coyote go in advance as spies and Corn-Meal-Boy gets before them. They try to drive him back, but he persists in following and chief carries him on back. Spies rest and Corn-Meal-Boy goes on and sees smoke. There is village of Tricksters and Coyote begs Young-Man-Chief to tell young women that Coyote had found enemies. Young-Man-Chief tells story of discovery and gives credit to Corn-Meal-Boy. Three older sisters refuse to accept him as husband, but youngest one takes him and they are married on war-path. Village is attacked and Corn-Meal-Boy gets in first. Young-Man-Chief gives prisoner to him and his wife. Other sisters object so much to Corn-Meal-Boy that his wife moves to where he lives. He sends his grandfather to get some tripe at buffalo killing, and some one cuts his hands and bores hole in cheek and ties string through. When Corn-Meal-Boy sees this he dives in water and comes out a fine-looking man having war-bonnet and short club. He pounds on chief's doors, hits Coyote in ribs, and bores hole in cheek of man who had cut his grandfather and ties string through it. Chiefs offer pipes to Corn-Meal-Boy, but he will smoke only at request of Young-Man-Chief. New home is built for Corn-Meal-Boy's people and he takes wife to water. When she comes out her appearance is changed. When sisters hear they go to see her. They want Corn-Meal-Boy for husband, but wife objects. He is seen by people only when they go on war-path. Coyote claims to be first to attack, but it is always Corn-Meal-Boy. Shows dirty string he wore around neck as Wets-the-Bed, and it is his war-bonnet. It shines like fire when he goes in lead of war-party. When Corn-Meal-Boy has shown many supernatural powers and given powers to men he goes up in sky. He is called "First-seen-by-War-parties," and appears to people as shooting-star.

16. THE THUNDERBIRD WOMAN.

Three people live together in grass-lodge, in front of north door of which stands large cottonwood tree. They are Thunderbird-Woman, Little-Big-Belly-Boy, and the Libertine. Libertine hunts and is very strong, but can not lift little things. Piece of grass falls on his back. He asks boy to help him, but for fun boy lets it stay until Libertine gives out. Then boy takes it off. To cure soreness Libertine takes cottonwood tree out by roots and stands it on his back, with other wood, and sets it on fire. Next morning he goes hunting and brings home live buffalo. Buffalo will not let boy out of lodge. At last Libertine takes buffalo and makes robe out of it for boy. Boy catches mouse and ties it by neck near door. Libertine is afraid and asks boy to release mouse. Boy remains in bed and laughs at Libertine, but finally, at his request, takes mouse, shakes it and makes robe for Libertine. Robe is too heavy for him and boy has to remove it. Boy tells Libertine something is coming to carry him off. Libertine shoots arrow through tree but boy says that is not enough. Sun-Buzzard, having body covered with sharp flint stones, comes and carries off Libertine, who tries, but fails, to shoot it. He carries Libertine to his nest. Young ones pick at him and he kills two of them. He descends tree and by means of string parts water and runs across place. Libertine returns home. Sun-Buzzard comes again and Libertine leads other two to mountains, through which he carries them on his back. Sun-Buzzard follows them, but it falls down and Libertine kills it. Libertine is afraid something will happen to them again, and so he goes to woods and becomes Big-Red-Water-Worm. Thunderbird-Woman goes north and calls herself Rain-Woman, and Little-Big-Belly-Boy flies toward prairie and becomes Linnet-Bird, or Dry-Grass-Bird.

17. HEALTHY-FLINT-STONE-MAN AND WOMAN HAVING-POWERS-IN-THE-WATER.

Flint-Stone-Man marries pretty woman in village. Strange woman comes and asks wife to go with her to get wood. She goes with Litle-Old-Woman and cuts wood for both. Little-Old-Woman kneels and wife helps her with her pile and then she helps wife. They return home. Little-Old-Woman comes second time and they go further away to get wood. Wife cuts two piles of wood and Little-Old-Woman helps her first with her pile. Little-Old-Woman tells wife if she will go with her to fetch wood four times, she will need no more help from her. Third time wife goes with Little-Old-Woman and they go much further to get wood. Little-Old-Woman comes fourth time. They go twice as far as before. When wife cuts wood, wife tries to persuade other to kneel first by pile. Finally wife kneels and old woman tightens carrying ropes around her neck, so that she falls dead. Then she blows into top of her head and blows skin from her, hair and all. Old woman then puts on skin and by stretching makes it fit her. She then throws body into flowing water. Old woman takes pile of wood to her new home. Chief does not discover change, as old woman knows all about wife's ways. Time comes for skin to decay and hair to come off. Old woman pretends to be sick, but refuses to be doctored, and chief hires servant, Buffalo-Crow-Man, to doctor her. He says she is fraud, and after singing song four times decayed hide comes off from her. Men take old woman and kill her. Man says he has seen choking of wife by old woman and tells where she has thrown body. Chief goes to place and stays all night and next day weeping. He goes again and third time he hears singing coming from river. He goes and listens. It is his wife's voice. She sings song four times, and then he sees wife standing in river. She tells his parents to clean grass-lodge and purify room by burning sage, and then he is to return for her. That is done and he takes her home and they live long together. Finally Flint-Stone-Man goes toward south to become flint stone. His wife becomes Woman-having-Powers-in-the-Water, and many people become flint arrows and animals, some remaining as human beings.

18. THE HAWK AND HIS FOUR DOGS.

Near village lives man, wife, daughter, and son. Son has four dogs, white, black, red, and copper color. Dogs always kept tied up. Boy hunts, and tells father, mother, and sisters if dogs get uneasy they are to be untied, as boy will then be in danger. Boy meets two good-looking women, with tattooed faces, and wearing buffalo robe. They ask him to go with them. On their way north, they ask him what he can do to escape if attacked by enemy. He tells them of his powers. They see herd of Buffalo, and when they are near women become Buffalo and boy disappears. Women tell Buffalo they must stamp ground where young man disappeared. They stamped ground, but he has become ant and crawled away and then gets on his feet and runs for his life. Buffalo run after him and he becomes small bird. Women tell Buffalo again to stamp ground, but he has crawled away and again run away. Buffalo run after him and they see him shoot his arrows, which carry him along with them. When last arrow used young man climbs elm tree. Buffalo gather around and hook tree. Young man's dogs grow restless and father cuts ropes and they go to his rescue. As tree falls dogs come and chase Buffalo away. Young man goes home, but never sees dogs again. After a while, to prevent further accident, he and father, mother, and sisters fly away and become hawks. Then old home is changed to tree, and meat to bark of tree.

19. THE STORY OF CHILD-OF-A-DOG.

Old woman and granddaughter are living apart by themselves. Granddaughter has small dog. Old woman tells granddaughter that if man asks her to be his wife she is not to refuse, as she will have child. Dog becomes pregnant and is put in small grass-lodge. Girl goes and peeps into lodge and sees child, instead of puppies. They make bed for dog in lodge. Child-of-a-Dog is cared for by girl and soon begins to walk. Has bow and arrows and shoots birds, and when young man goes hunting two women come and ask to be engaged to Child-of-a-Dog. He rejects them, but afterward follows them. They request Child-of-a-Dog to shoot Squirrel. He does so, but it catches limb of tree. He climbs tree to get squirrel, but his hands and feet stick and women leave him to starve to death. His father, Wind, comes and releases him. Tells him not to follow women, but he does so and they take him home. They say he can have other two sisters for wives. Their brother tells him that other two women are married to four brothers, who eat human beings. Further that he will have to run race against four brothers. Two sisters advise him about race and give him seven things to aid him, and also soft, white feather. They tell him not to drink from gourds of sisters, and to shoot his opponents. In morning Child-of-a-Dog takes bath and then goes to meet opponents. Objects to starting-point three times as not being far enough. Brother-in-law does first part of race: Then Child-of-a-Dog begins race and, to get before brothers, drops comb, which causes thick burrs. These impede brothers, who command wind to blow. Child-of-a-Dog can not travel rapidly now, and he makes wind to go into gourd. Child-of-a-Dog overtakes brothers and he throws piece of clay, which makes boggy place for other men. They again overtake Child-of-a-Dog and command it to snow. This contest of powers goes on until final race, when Child-of-a-Dog puts waving feather on head, which makes him light. He runs against oldest brother, who has to pack him on his back and soon gives out. The same result attends race with other brothers, and Child-of-a-Dog wins. Two women offer him drink from their gourds, but he refuses it and his wives give him drink. Child-of-a-Dog turns back and shoots his opponents and makes them Buffalo. Two women and two wives contend for him by hauling wood and carrying water, and wives win. Bad women become Dog and Hawk, that they may have man to themselves. Child-of-a-Dog goes on visit to other village and when he sits down on robe he falls into pit. He hears them tell people to bring hot ashes to throw into pit. He digs hole on side and is safe. People go hunting, leaving him to die. People in timber remove ashes and get Child-of-a-Dog out of pit. He goes to creek, dives in and is as before. He remains with people to hunt for them and then follows those who have done him harm. He catches up with them, and after dark whistles four times. Dog who was former wife comes and he then shoots four arrows in different directions. Fire comes up. Dog tells him that mother and old woman are dead and that young woman is in danger of being killed by husband. Child-of-a-dog at once departs for home. East of house he sees woman sitting on bank of pond watching ducks swim. He shoots duck. Woman sees it is her son's arrow and turns around. He takes her home. When husband comes in Child-of-a-Dog takes bow-string and casts man into ground and he is Wood-Rat-Man. Woman sees six deer, which Child-of-a-Dog follows and kills. While cooking meat, two women come and ask for food. Older woman asks for liver before it is ready to be eaten. She asks for more meat and finally whole deer eaten. When two deer have been eaten woman says man shall be her son-in-law. When they have eaten third deer, woman goes out and other woman tells him about older woman and her daughters, who have teeth in their vaginas. Woman returns and again asks for meat, but before fifth deer eaten daylight appears. Child-of-a-Dog goes with women and is taken to place where two young women live. Old woman sends him for dead burnt log to burn while she is asleep. He goes to other woman's place and she gives him ear of black corn and tells him it will turn to log and he is to push it into lodge. She also tells him not to sleep first night, as old woman will come to kill him if girls do not. He takes log, and as he pushes it into lodge woman tries to hit him on head with club. At sundown young people go to bed and old woman snores, but during night she comes to see if girls have caused man's death. He does not have intercourse and gets up early and goes out. Next day old woman sends him to get two logs, and he is given two ears of black corn, also two long hard stones to use on girls. After killing one he can escape with other to high hill westward, where is woman with many children, who can save them. Woman puts ears of

corn on fire and says this will make old woman go to sleep and she will not wake
until he is long way off. Child-of-a-Dog is also given long feather to use over
fire. If it goes up in air, they will go with it. He takes ears of corn which
girls take into lodge. Some time after they have gone to bed, old woman sleeps
and snores. Child-of-a-Dog uses stone on more cruel girl and kills her. He
renders other girl harmless and tells her she is to be his wife, but they have to
leave place. They stand near fire, and when Child-of-a-Dog puts feather over fire
feather flies up and they go up in air with it toward west. When they have gone,
woman who gave power to Child-of-a-Dog deserts her home and jumps from tree
to tree and causes old woman to lose her trail. Child-of-a-Dog shoots his arrows
and he and girl fly with them. His power is exhausted and they hear old woman
at a distance saying she has found their trail. Woman then throws double-balls,
and they travel on them. She does this four times and then they see place of their
retreat. Little-Spider-Woman arrives and threatens to kill woman if she helps
Child-of-a-Dog and his wife. Buzzard-Woman gets under old woman and flies
into air with her. She flies higher and higher until they can not see them any
more. Then they hear something fall, and Little-Spider-Woman falls to ground
dead. Child-of-a-Dog and wife go to his home. Wife tells her of troubles with
Little-Spider-Woman and that her parents are Raccoons and that parents of other
girl are Owls. The woman who helps them to escape is Squirrel-Woman.
Woman comes and goes off with child into ground. Child-of-a-Dog searches
for him without success. He and wife go to west and wife finds trail. He
draws feathered part of arrow along ground and they see woman and child
down in ground. Child-of-a-Dog goes down and drags woman out and says
she is always to live in ground as Mole. Child at once begins to cry and can not
be stopped crying until father says he will tell child all about his life and hard
times he has had. Father tells tale of his and mother's life. They then say they
will be something else and escape further trouble. Child-of-a-Dog becomes Wind
and his boy small Wind. Wife becomes Raccoon. Other woman pours water
on fire, goes up with smoke and becomes Black-Eagle.

20. THE OLD-AGE-DOG, WHO RESCUED THE CHIEF'S SON.

Young-Man-Chief is admired by everybody, but refuses to marry. People are
afraid of Tricksters, so women who haul wood are accompanied by armed men.
Young-Man-Chief remains when women return home. Sees woman behind who
calls him to her and gets hold of him. They are there for long time and are
attacked by Tricksters. Man escapes and leaves woman to be taken away.
Young-Man-Chief is sorry for woman and determines to go and seek her.
He finds home of Tricksters and at night walks into village and looks into every
lodge. Sees woman in tipi, makes hole and punches woman's back with piece
of grass. Woman walks out and Young-Man-Chief asks her to return home.
She insists on going into tipi again. She tells husband about him, seeking
revenge for leaving her to be captured. Young-Man-Chief is captured, tied to
pole by fire, and burned to death during victory dance. People move next day,
leaving old dog behind. Dog finds body of Young-Man-Chief and thinks he will
save him. Dog howls and tells him to get up. At fourth howl Young-Man-Chief
rises from dead. Dog makes him dive four times in deepest part of stream. He
comes out healed and with his arrows. They return to man's home, and people

hug Young-Man-Chief and the dog. He relates what has taken place and wants to send war-party against Tricksters. War-party go, and on way come to hole into which dog dives and comes out young. Dog goes on top of hill and howls. Other dogs come and he tells them to take away Tricksters' weapons, chew off bow-strings and carry away war-clubs, as war-party wants to attack Tricksters. Dogs do so, and when Young-Man-Chief learns he returns to camp. Next morning attack is made. Young-Man-Chief kills woman who had put him to death and captures fine-looking young woman to give to her father. Party returns victorious and father is satisfied. Young-Man-Chief marries, and he, wife, and Old-Age-Dog sleep together. Dog tells him that he is jealous. Young-Man-Chief goes with war-party and leaves dog in care of wife. He returns safely through powers of dog. He goes again, and man comes to wife's bed. She kicks dog off from bed. Dog will not eat and gradually goes from tipi to hill, where war-party appears when returning. Young-Man-Chief finds dog there and learns from him what has taken place. They remain together and gradually turn to stone.

21. THE OLD-AGE-DOG, WHO RESCUED THE CHIEF'S SON.

Woman catches hold of Chief's-Son, as in No. 20, and is captured by Tricksters. Chief's-Son goes in search of her and is captured and burned to death, but brought to life again by Old-Age-Dog, who becomes White-Dog. Chief's-Son and White-Dog are now brothers. They take war-party against Tricksters. White-Dog incites dogs to destroy bow-strings. White-Dog kills woman, and Chief's-Son kills husband and captures young woman as adopted daughter for woman's father. Chief's-Son marries and forbids wife to strike dog. He goes on war-path and leaves woman in care of dog, which stays at foot of bed. Man comes to wife's bed and she kicks dog off bed. Dog goes and lies by door and refuses to eat. Dog moves away from village and gradually reaches hill. People are uneasy about Chief's-Son. He returns and finds dog. On hearing what has occurred he says he will do as dog wants. They remain there and turn to sandstone. People all remain human beings.

22. YOUNG-BOY-CHIEF, WHO BECAME AN OTTER.

Chief of one village has boy, and chief of another village has girl. Older men sing to boy, and women can not get near him. His name is Young-Boy-Chief. Girl is watched so that no man can come around. Father has company every day and girl cooks for them. Her bed is set on high poles, and to reach it she has to take ladder. Chief's-Son has same kind of bed, so that young women can not get to him. Chief's-Son goes at night to place where girl is. He calls her and finally goes to bed with her. He repeats visit and tells her what things he will furnish her with should she become pregnant. Girl becomes pregnant and Chief's-Son does not return to her. She refuses to say whom child belongs to. Child is born and girl waits for Chief's-Son to bring things he promised. Men continue to sing for young man. Girl's parents say she must leave place or say whose is the child. She gets tired of waiting for promised things and takes child to place where men are singing for Chief's-Son. She places child on his arms and goes away. Singing stops, and Chief's-Son follows woman. She refuses to stay and goes to lake, takes off her clothing, and flies away over lake as Eagle. Her garments turn into grapevines. Man and child cry and go to sleep. Woman comes back with another man she has married. Both are Eagles. They take child away while Chief's-Son is asleep. On waking he looks for child and sees it with others, flying over him. Woman Eagle sings song about things promised for child and then song of feathers. Each Eagle sends down three feathers to young man and then they fly toward east. Chief's-Son takes feathers and goes home. He finds everybody gone, and he goes to river and turns into Otter. The feathers he throws into brush of which arrows are made, for benefit of next generation.

23. YOUNG-BOY-CHIEF, WHO BECAME AN OTTER.

Village is divided into two parts, each of which has chief. Chief of north division has son named Chief's-Son, for whom prominent men sing and who has no thought of marrying. Chief of south village has daughter, who has not thought of men. She does most of cooking for father's visitors. Chief's-Son and chief's daughter go to see each other at same time. They meet and decide to go away together. They return home for necessary things and then start south. At end of fourth day they find suitable place. Chief's-Son tells wife what things he will get for child. Boy is born. Some time afterward young man thinks of home. He leaves wife and child. At home he resumes former life, as if unmarried, and men sing for him. When chief's daughter tired of living alone she starts for village and goes to home of Chief's-Son, who is seated on lap of man singing for him. She puts child on lap of Chief's-Son and walks away toward north. Chief's-Son follows with child. Woman will not stop, but sings about things promised for child's use in cradle. She comes to lake, takes off robe, flies over lake and becomes Eagle. Her robe turns to grapevine. She marries Eagle and they fly around until Chief's-Son goes to sleep. Eagle-woman takes child away. Chief's-Son awakes and there are three Eagles. Chief's-Son asks to be taken up, but Eagle-woman sings and shakes feather down to him. Twice again she sings, and Eagle-man and young one shake down feathers. Eagles fly away, and Chief's-Son returns home, but finds tall weeds instead of village. He goes to river and throws feathers into bushes for feathering arrows. He then becomes Otter.

24. THE MAN WHO BECAME A FLAMINGO.

Chief has five daughters, who refuse to marry. Man-having-greater-Powers-than-any-other-Man thinks he will play trick on daughters of chief, who at certain time go to bring water from river for bath. He puts pipe bone on path for them to pick up. Eldest of sisters finds relic and picks it up and puts in front of her under blanket. She tries to find it on reaching home, but fails. After a time she becomes pregnant and tells father she does not know to whom child belongs. Child cries all day, and chief directs men to present arrows and bows to child. He whose bow and arrows are accepted by child is to be husband of child's mother. Men pass around chief's lodge to offer bows and arrows, but child keeps on crying. Coyote's turn comes and child stops crying, and Coyote thinks he will be chief's son-in-law, but child begins again. Child is handed to Man-having-greater-Powers-than-any-other-Man, who speaks to it. Child stops crying and plays with bow and arrow, and father becomes chief's son-in-law. He removes his things to home of child and next day starts to hunt for whole family. Chief tells people that men are to go hunting and that any one killing red turkey and bringing it to him shall have his next daughter. Man-having-greater-Powers-than-any-other-Man kills red turkey. Coyote kills white turkey and paints it red, thinking he will become chief's son-in-law. Daughter is given to other man, who also wins third daughter for having prettiest war-bonnet, although Coyote tries to coax daughter to choose his bonnet. Long afterward chief offers his two remaining daughters to funniest dancer. Coyote tries to make them laugh at him, but they laugh at Opossum, who becomes chief's son-in-law. Opossum is worried at having two wives and splits his membrum. Chief's first grandson, Child-sprung-from-Relic, disappears. Chief announces that any one finding child shall be chief of whole village. Man-having-greater-Powers-than-any-other-Man finds his child has been taken into water, and will not leave river banks, and becomes Flamingo. Chief says he wants to become something else, and some become birds, others wild animals, and some remain human beings.

25. THE SPIDERS WHO RECOVERED THE CHIEF'S GRANDSON.

Two villages divided by street have two chiefs. One chief has son and the other has daughter, who will not marry in their own families. In chiefs' families young people have high sleeping places, entered by means of ladder, which parents remove to keep any one from getting to the bed. The chief's son and the chief's daughter on the same night think of going to see each other. They meet, and after explanation they go to young man's home. Next morning young man's mother finds girl in bed with him and tells them to come to breakfast. Chief's daughter is sought for and Coyote finds her. Chief is satisfied when he knows that she has married other chief's son. Boy is born to them. Child is taken around to other lodges and brought home to mother to nurse. Old woman comes for child, which mother hands to her out of cradle. It is not returned and can not be found. Spider-Woman comes and finds that old woman has gone underground with child, but loses her trail. People accompany chief on hunting trip. Coyote remains at home and takes family into timber. While trying to shoot fish, some one behind speaks to him. It is Spider-Man. Coyote asks if he may dress like him, and he dumps Coyote into water. When he comes out he is like Spider-Man. Spider-Man gives him food, which increases as it is turned round on stick. Asks Coyote if he is brave, as he wants him to go after chief's grandchild, which has been scorched nearly to death. Coyote takes meat to his wife and tells her how to increase it. Spider-Man sends him back to tell wife they are now to be brother and sister. Spider-Man tells Coyote he will meet four dangerous men and gives him instructions how to proceed on trip to place where child is. Coyote comes to four Headless-Men, in succession, and manages to get around them facing the north, and sticks their feet in ground. He comes to village where child is and shoots four arrows in different directions, causing fires. Makes dash for child, and people scatter, thinking Spider-Man has come. He takes child from pole, runs quickly and escapes thunder and lightning. On his way home he kills Headless-Men. Spider-Man throws child into water and on taking it out sends Coyote for his child of same age. Spider-Man throws Coyote's child into water and the two children are alike. Coyote receives powers like Spider-Man's and is to have nothing to do with women. Coyote goes to chief's place and asks him to call people together. He tells story of loss of child and of his recovery. Chief sends men for child, but they can not find place. Coyote goes with them and they bring two children who are alike, and Coyote's child is adopted by chief's son and daughter. Coyote has new home given him with power to become great chief. Women try to marry him, but he refuses. Long time after Woman-who-wears-Shell-Rattles comes and Coyote allows her to lie down. Spider-Man knows and takes away Coyote's powers. In morning he is true coyote and goes out into wilderness. Chief calls people together and says that as other wrong may befall him, they may become animals if they wish. Some in families become birds of air, some wild animals. Chief and family remain human beings.

26. THE ORIGIN OF THE EAGLES.

Young-Boy-Chief is leader in all expeditions. He helps everybody when help is needed. War-party goes against Tricksters, who are Prairie-chickens. On return Young-Boy-Chief waits at river longer than others. Old woman comes and he offers to take her across. He packs her across on his back, and on other side she refuses to come off. He carries her to village, and she then says that as he has refused to marry any one, she is going to be his wife and remain on his back. He lies down and old woman is such a nuisance people think he is going to die. Coyote gets four men to try to pull old woman off, but they fail. Boy out shooting at birds hears old man, Ears-painted-Red (Turtle), say he can get old woman off. Boy tells chief, who sends Coyote for the Turtle, who says he can take woman off. Sends four men for buffalo fat and then makes bow and arrows and gets some paint. Next morning the Turtle sings song about Young-Boy-Chief, who is seated on buffalo robe. He shoots arrow and woman's right hand comes off. With other arrows he shoots off her left foot, her left hand, and her right foot in succession. Then Coyote clubs old woman to death. She is green tree. The Turtle rubs buffalo fat over sore places on Young-Boy-Chief, and then puts red paint on them and he is healed. Chief fears something else may occur and tells people they can leave their homes next day if they please. They go by families and some become birds and others beasts of woods and plains. Chief's family go up with smoke and become Eagles. Some people remain in village.

27. THE COYOTE AND THE BUFFALO.

Chief called Wolf controls village of hunters. Their swiftest runner is Black-Wolf. Buffalo disappear and Coyote goes to find their trail. In four days he comes to lodge in which live man and family who have plenty of meat. To find out where meat is kept he changes to little dog and crawls into lodge after dark. Children play with him and take him to bed. Old man in morning goes hunting. Coyote follows and sees man go to large stone lying on side of hill. Man commands stone to go aside and calls to fattest buffalo to come out. When buffalo comes man shoots it and takes all lean meat and tells buffalo to go back in hole. Stone then moves to its place again. When man, who is Raven, goes home with meat Coyote goes to stone and commands it to move to one side. It does so and a great herd of buffalo comes out. He drives buffalo to place where he came from and tells chief. People kill buffalo and people have plenty to eat. Chief Wolf announces that as they may have hard times again they should become what they were. They remain in their lodge as Wolves, Coyote, and Black-Wolf.

28. HALF-A-BOY, WHO OVERCAME THE GAMBLER.

Half-a-Boy lives in village where all kinds of games are played. He goes to another village where is man who plays wheel game very well. Is directed to tipi of chief. Chief warns boy that he will have to play with cruel man who lives there, and after losing all he has will have to bet his life. He plays next day and loses all his things. Man tells him he has to bet his life. His body is equal to three bets, right side, left side, and backbone. He loses two of these bets by time sun goes down and finally persuades man to spare his life until next day. Man calls him Half-a-Boy because he lost part of his body by gambling. He remains at grounds and when everybody is asleep two women come and call him. He goes with them and they become Buffalo-cows. They come to where grandfather and grandmother are taking smoke. Women tell old people to give him powers. Obtains black and red sticks from old Buffalo bull and song from old woman Buffalo. He receives instructions as to play. Boy returns to village and in morning his opponent comes to win rest of his body. He asks to see his opponent's stick and passes it through his left hand four times. Boy hits man's stick and breaks it in two. Chief goes to tipi for boy's sticks and hands red stick to opponent. Black stick always finds wheel. Boy wins back third of his body and then doubles his bet. He wins everything in opponent's village, then kills all his people. He bets his life against life of man, who is Shadow-of-the-Sun. Boy wins first, second, and third part of body of Shadow-Man. As stick enters wheel two big buffalo arise and chase man, who is torn to pieces and body burned up. As fire dies down boy pokes it and men killed by Shadow-Man jump out. Half-a-Boy refuses to be chief and turns into Blackbird and goes to buffalo in north.

29. YOUNG-BOY-CHIEF, WHO MARRIED A BUFFALO.

Village is divided into two parts, each governed by chief. In space between parts games are played. Young-Boy-Chief is son of chief of south village. Other chief has daughter. Boy spends his time in watching other boys play. Girl always stays at home. Young-Buffalo-Woman comes, and on way finds piece of dry grass like white, soft feather. She is dressed differently from other women and is tattooed on face. Young woman goes to ground and sees Young-Boy-Chief, who is on lookout for chief's daughter. She drops dry grass and wind rolls it toward young man. She plays in double-ball game and always is ahead. Dry grass rolls between legs of Young-Boy-Chief, and when he throws it away it returns. It bothers him, and he takes it with him to lodge. Woman leaves game and goes to tipi, after bathing in creek. People have no food, and woman brings kidney and corn bread from her left side and gives them to eat. She puts back fat and then takes same things from her right side and eats them. Young-Boy-Chief searches for woman and finds her in last lodge. He tells woman he has mistaken her for daughter of chief, but they begin to live as husband and wife. He says his marriage is to be kept secret. They live together long time, but when she is pregnant Young-Boy-Chief ceases to go to see her. Child is born and woman waits for him to come and see it. Boy grows and asks who father is. Woman will not say, but finally takes him to Young-Boy-Chief's home, where many older men sitting around him. Child calls him father and he asks men to remove woman and child. Woman takes child on back and starts toward north. When away from village they become Buffalo. Young-Boy-Chief follows and overtakes them. Woman gives him kidney and bread to eat and tells him of troubles he will have at her home. He will have to meet her four husbands, who are brothers, and that her younger sister will offer herself as wife. He will have to pick out from other buffalo his wife, his wife's uncles, father, and mother, and his child. She tells him how to distinguish each of them. On fourth day they come to wife's home in buffalo village on high hill. Young-Boy-Chief is asked to have sister for wife, but pays no attention. Next day he performs all tasks required of him and is permitted to retain his wife. Young-Boy-Chief likes new home better than old one. Long afterward Buffalo chief goes to other people to trade. People are to wear their best dresses when killing Buffalo. If meat only taken and hide left Buffalo live again, and best dresses belong to Buffalo. Young-Boy-Chief has to do as other Buffalo. He has many children by Buffalo wife. Whenever Buffalo come to people they show their desire to trade.

30. THE SWIFT-HAWKS AND SHADOW-OF-THE-SUN.

Village is divided into two parts, each ruled over by chief, one good, other bad. In another place is boy who lives with father, mother, and three younger brothers. Boy decides to visit village, which he comes to on fourth day after leaving home. He is directed to tipi of chief, where he is told that he will be called to enter foot race. Next morning he is called to race by other chief, Shadow-of-the-Sun. Boy and other chief take bath and then go to scene of race. Shadow-of-the-Sun runs first with the chief, then with Coyote, who are beaten. Then boy, Swift-Hawk, runs until he comes to deep canyon which he can not pass, and Shadow-of-the-Sun kills him with club. Another of four Swift-Hawks goes to same village, has similar experience to his brothers', and meets same fate. This happens to four brothers in succession, all of whom are killed by Shadow-of-the-Sun. Other chief offers his life to him, but he refuses it, and after race carries off lot of chief's people. Father knows what has happened to boys and goes to village of two chiefs. Before starting he puts water and white clay into shell and tells wife that if blood appears in shell it indicates that he is dead and she is to leave place. He reaches villages in four days, goes to chief's tipi, and is told he will have to run foot race. Next morning he is called by Shadow-of-the-Sun. He, with chief and Coyote, go for bath, and old man comes out of water just like his four sons. He comes with Shadow-of-the-Sun, gets on right side of him, then on left side, and finally gets on his right shoulder and then on his left shoulder. When they come to canyon, old man, being on shoulder of Shadow-of-the-Sun, kicks him on breast and then in back and then goes on and leaves him behind. When he wins race he takes bow-string and pulls it through his left hand four times and kills cruel chief with it. Body is burned and old man calls his boys to come out. Men jump out of fire and old man and his boys go back home. Old man insists family shall leave place because what has happened may happen again. They go and become Swift-Hawks.

31. THE SWIFT-HAWKS AND SHADOW-OF-THE-SUN.

Family of Hawks, consisting of father and three boys, live by themselves away from village. Oldest boy goes to visit village and sees people playing games. He puts up at lodge of chief, who tells him that there are evil-spirited people whose chief, Shadow-of-the-Sun, will challenge him to foot-race. Early next morning young man is challenged to foot-race by Shadow-of-the-Sun. Boy takes bath and then goes with good chief to ground. Race is run and boy is beaten and killed with club by Shadow-of-the-Sun. Good chief offers his life, but it is refused, as it is through his visitors other chief gets his fun. Father knows what has become of boy, but he lets second boy go to look for his brother. He goes to village, is received by good chief, and recognizes brother's things. He is invited to run race with Shadow-of-the-Sun, is defeated and killed. Two other brothers go to village successively and meet same fate. Father goes in search of boys, first coloring water in bowl with white clay in which wife will see blood color if he is slain. Reaches village evening of fourth day and is directed to chief's tipi. He sees his boys' weapons and things hung up near bed. In morning he is called to race, but first jumps into flowing water, from which he comes changed to young man. Chief goes with him to race, but he refuses to run from the starting place. Old man and Shadow-of-the-Sun run, and at fifth time old man turns into hawk and lights on chief's shoulder. He kicks chief on breast and enters village first. Shadow-of-the-Sun begs for his life, and being refused goes up into sky. Old man shoots arrow in direction he has gone and chief falls to ground, dead. His body and all human bones found are burned, and as those killed by Shadow-of-the-Sun are called they jump out of fire. Good chief tells people they have had such hard times they had better not exist longer as human beings. Some people fly away, some into timber, some into prairies. Chief becomes Eagle. Father takes boys home and they turn into Hawks.

32. YOUNG-BOY-CHIEF AND HIS SISTER, WHO BECAME EAGLES.

Young-Boy-Chief and his sister live by themselves. They have Little-Dog. Sister sees deer and she calls Young-Boy-Chief four times to come and shoot it. He shoots at deer but all his arrows break to pieces. Deer carries Young-Boy-Chief off on his antlers. It is Big-Hail-Deer. Sister searches for Young-Boy-Chief and finds broken arrows. Long while after she resolves to go and look for brother. She takes the meal and leaves the meat and gourd of water for Little-Dog. While on journey she sings and weeps alternately. Person on hill tries to keep her from passing. She pours out corn meal, and he then tells her about her brother. He is Mountain-Lion, and he tells her to go on. She continues journey and travels with double-ball and stick until she comes to another man on hill. He does as first man until she pours out some meal, and then tells her to go on to next man, who has great powers. He is Headless-

Man. Third man is Bear-having-great-Powers, and when woman pours out meal he tells her her brother must be nearly dead now, as deer has hardly time to stop. He tells her to go on to next man, who will aid her. She is to pack on her back little child she sees playing, and take him in to old man's place and give corn meal to child. She travels on and sees dug-out on small hill and little boy playing. She carries child into lodge and gives it corn meal. Old man is Old-scabby-Bull, and he finally agrees to help her, but she must not weep when she sees brother. She hears him singing, but he is nearly dead. Old man makes small bow and arrow. Next day they go to meet deer. Woman hides herself and old man turns into Snowbird. Deer comes, and as he approaches old man passes bow-string through his left hand four times and clubs deer with it. He helps Young-Boy-Chief off his antlers and then piles wood over deer and sets it on fire. Old man makes Young-Boy-Chief dive in creek, and he comes out with four arrows and bow after being called four times. They go on to man's home, where Young-Boy-Chief hunts until people have much meat. Young-Boy-Chief and sister travel home fast by means of double-ball and arrows. They come to turkeys dancing and laughing because their enemy, Young-Boy-Chief, is dead, and he throws ashes on their heads. They see woman in tree crying because when Young-Boy-Chief was living she had plenty to eat. She is Red-Bird, and Young-Boy-Chief commands tree to bear wild grapes. Bunch of Deer tell him they are happy because of Young-Boy-Chief's death, and he pulls their ears out long, then scares them, making their eyes wide open. He commands tree to bear fruit for man who is weeping on account. of Young-Boy-Chief's death. Man is Opossum, and tree bears persimmons. When they reach home they find only hair and bones of Little-Dog, which sister throws into creek. She then calls it and dog comes out happy as can be. Young-Boy-Chief fears something else may happen to him, so they pour water on fire and go up with smoke and become Eagles. Little-Dog remains as he is.

33. THE STORY OF NOT-KNOW-WHO-YOU-ARE.

In large village after celebration of return of war-party Not-know-who-you-are hears crying. This occurs on next celebration, and he learns that some one is carried off by some animal. He thinks he will have war-dance, and perhaps he can kill animal after dance. He gets up war-party and on return he joins in dance and keeps watch. He sees nothing, but suddenly people cry out that somebody is carried off. He takes his parents and sister to another village. He gets up war-party, and many scalps are brought back. While people dance screaming is heard by some one carried off. Before going to look for being man cuts two long poles, which he marks toward top and sticks up. He intends to cut off front feet of strange being and tie them on ends of poles. He says that woman who can guess what poles are for and why he has come to the village shall become his wife. There is family of father, mother, and four girls, called Horned-Owls. Three oldest daughters go to guess, ugly youngest staying at home. Father tells youngest what man has in mind. She goes to guessing place and is successful. Girl is taken into man's lodge. At dark they go to creek, girl jumps in and comes out better looking. Man finds beast and asks it to guess what poles are for. Animal tells man what he has done, and says poles have nothing to do with intention. Man then tells meaning of poles and kills animal, which is Mountain-Lion, with bow-string. He cuts off hoofs of animal and puts them on poles. Man returns home and sticks poles by his lodge. People in village remain there without further molestation.

34. EARLY-MORNING-DEER-SLAYER, WHO OVERCAME ELK.

Five villages are in line from west to east. In last village toward east lives chief, Early-Morning-Deer-Slayer, with his mother and sister. Chief is Mountain-Lion and great hunter of deer. He finds out that something is going to take his life, and he is so troubled he stays in bed all the time. Powerful animal appears in village toward west. People shoot at it, but arrows drop off. Animal goes through four villages unharmed and enters last village. Chief gets up and takes his bow and four arrows, two painted red and two painted black. He goes to meet enemy and shoots him with arrows, but animal is uninjured. It is Elk. Elk takes chief on his horns and turns back to where he came from. Man from each village follows to see where chief is taken to. Elk travels so fast that he leaves men far behind, and man bends bow around his head and causes animal to go slower, so that men catch up again. They see high place where Elk lives in great cave with his children. When Elk reaches this place it stops to dump chief off, and he kicks it in back of head and down both go. Elk is first and is eaten by his children. Chief gets hold of root of tree half way down. Men come and look down and chief tells them to dig hole big enough for them to lie in. Then, swinging bow-string, he causes north wind to blow until it blows him out of place and there stops. Chief says he will return to place he came from. He asks men from village if they will go back. They say it is too far, so chief throws them away, and man from first village becomes Sparrow, man from second village becomes Yellowhammer, third man becomes Towhee, and fourth man Red-Bird. Chief sees people dancing because their enemy is killed, and he throws ashes on their heads. His arrows come back to him and he kills deer. Two Opossum come and eat with him. He sees sister and shoots arrow over her that she may see it. Sister is packing Coyote's children and chief destroys them. He makes Coyote pack sister and string splits him in two. He shoots arrows to four directions to be used by other generations. Arrows cause fire which burns his village. Chief and sister are Mountain-Lions.

35. TROUBLE AMONG THE CHIEF'S CHILDREN.

Chief of village has son and daughter, both of whom refuse to marry. Man-fond-of-Deer-Meat comes to daughter and is found in bed with her. He is only hunter, and father tells daughter she must either go elsewhere to live with him or send him away. Man and woman go away together, and after seven days' travel they find a place to live in. They make home and live there for a long while, having plenty of meat and corn. Man shoots at deer sitting down and misses it. Deer runs and man looks for arrow, but can not find it. Next day he goes in search of arrow instead of hunting. He does this every day, without success, and they eat up everything they have. Then man cuts the flesh from body until he is nearly nothing but bones. Person comes and tells wife that man will never find arrow. Big-Hail-Deer has taken notion to ruin him, and that she should make her escape, as it is her day to die. He gives her stick and double-ball, armful of deer hair, bark from dogwood tree, and pieces of red stone for painting, and explains their use. Woman goes out. She tosses ball up in air and is on it. Late in evening she hears man talking about eating her. He finds her trail and nearly overtakes her. She throws deer's hair on ground, and when man gets to place he chases deer. He starts after her again and she throws down dogwood bark. There are big bushes, and man commences to cut them down, removes bark, and straightens them. He continues chase, and woman empties bundle of red stones. When man comes to place he gathers stones, but is reminded of his chase and starts after wife again. She hears him coming and strikes ground with stick, making deep canyon. Woman is now near her home. From top of hill she sees man coming after her. It is late in evening. She goes right on into grass-lodge of father and goes straight to him. They hear man outside asking that she may be turned out. Woman's father begins to tell story. It is about herself. When story completed it is daylight, and man falls dead just outside of lodge.

36. THE TURTLE'S WAR-PARTY.

Daughter of chief offers herself to any man who can bring her a scalp that has red hair. Many men try, but all fail to get scalp. Turtle gets meal from mother and goes on war-path to get red-haired scalp. He meets Rat and takes him along. They meet Horned-Beetle and afterward Locust, who asks to join them. All say it is easy to get such a scalp. They go toward the south, meet Coyote, who laughs at them. When he hears they are going on war-path he asks to join them, but they refuse him because he is coward. He offers to do spying and is allowed to join. He brings news of enemy's village, and Turtle tells men they will attack it. Coyote is scared, but at night when most people asleep, they enter village. They go from tipi to tipi looking for man with red hair. They see one in large tipi where great men are sitting up to pass time. When everybody has gone to sleep men go in and Turtle cuts man's throat and takes his scalp. They go out and Coyote, who has been scared nearly to death, joins them again. They start home, but before they are out of village Turtle begins to sing victory songs and wakes everybody up. They find chief killed, pursue war-party. Four hide themselves in grass and enemies pursue Coyote and kill him. When enemy gone home war-party come together again. They go on and find Coyote dead, full of arrow wounds. Turtle puts him on his feet and tells him to rise, he has slept too soundly. Coyote rises and Turtle says he knew he was coward. On reaching home chief's daughter given scalp and Turtle is given woman. Not long afterward chief calls all people to hear Turtle, who says that for their sakes he has saved men from having to send war-parties to get scalp and he wants never to live as human being again. He goes to prairie and turns into Prairie-Turtle, and many people go off and turn into something else.

37. THE TURTLE'S WAR-PARTY.

Chief of village where Turtle lives offers his daughter to one who gets red-haired scalp. Red-haired people are Wasps. They have White-Geese for spies, and every one, therefore, fails to get such scalp. Turtle tells mother he is going after red-haired scalp. She tries to dissuade him, but finally makes him pair of moccasins and prepares meal for him. Turtle starts west and sees smoke coming from high point. He finds Mole, who says he has induced him to come and will aid him to get scalp. Turtle stays there and Mole goes under ground and locates red-haired men, without being seen by Geese. He notifies Turtle, and then both go under ground to red-haired people's homes. When they are all asleep mole locates chief, and Turtle goes and cuts off his head. Turtle goes back home and gives scalp to chief, who tells him he can live there and have his daughter for a wife.

38. LITTLE-CROW, WHO BECAME A SPARROW-HAWK.

Four brothers, noted warriors, live with mother in village. Oldest brother says that if they have to meet the enemy and any one fails he shall wear woman's clothes and help mother to do cooking. Little-Crow goes next morning to have bath, and while in water sees woman standing where his things are. He remains in water for her to go away, but she stays long time, and then asks why he does not go to battle then going on. He remembers agreement and comes out of water and takes his things. He runs as fast as he can and meets man who says all enemy have been killed. He goes on and meets brother, who says only one enemy left and brothers are after him. Little-Crow goes and meets his brothers, who tell him to go back, as only enemy left is hard one to fight. He goes on and enemy turns to meet him. They shoot at each other, use war-clubs, and then wrestle, one on top trying to get arrow to stick other with. This Little-Crow succeeds in doing and kills enemy. To convince his brothers that he has really killed man he carries home body on his back. While standing outside he hears his brothers talking about him, and saying that he must have died. Little-Crow then sings song about his life and of his going for bath and woman finding him, and of his fight with enemy and carrying his body home at daylight. He calls on his brothers to come out and see whether he has not killed person they had failed to kill. They come and say it is so. People give great victory dance, which is the beginning of victory dances. Long time after they begin to teach people their powers. Then they throw water on fire and all four brothers go up with smoke and become Sparrow-Hawks.

39. THE LITTLE-BROWN-HAWKS.

Family of father, mother, and four boys, who are alike, live by themselves. They are called Swift-Hawks. Father tells boys not to go to village north of their home. Oldest boy goes to village, taking him four days. He goes to visitor's place, and Coyote, servant of dangerous man, comes and sees him. Next morning he is called to shinny-ball game, the loser to forfeit his life. He loses game and is clubbed to death with shinny club. Second brother goes to look for him, and on reaching village is thought to be same man. He plays and loses game and forfeits his life. The third and fourth brothers meet the same fate in turn. Father knows where sons have gone, and determines to try his turn. He goes to village and in tipi sees his children's weapons. In morning he takes bath and looks much younger. He plays and loses game and is clubbed to death. Old woman takes bath and hears noise in water. She becomes pregnant and boy is born to her. Boy grows rapidly and when young man goes to recover rest of family. He arrives at village and after bath is called to shinny ground. He has club and ball. His ball is used and he tosses it up. Hail falls instead of ball and kills dangerous man. Young man stops hail. Body of dangerous man is burned up and men whom he has killed come to life, among them Swift-Hawks and their father. Soon after reaching home they pour water on fire and go up with smoke and turn into Little-Brown-Hawks.

40. THE COYOTE WHO LOST HIS POWER.

Two villages are situate same distance apart. Both send out war-parties, but while on return of party from east village people have good times, in west village there is crying. Coyote goes to this village to find out cause of crying. Goes with war-party from west village. When they stop men gather wood and cut some dogwood. After sunset man asks from distance way to fire. He comes and Coyote is afraid of him, he is dressed so peculiarly. He is Shooting-Star, and as human being has great powers. He has plenty of dogwood. Men use dogwood sticks to count number of enemies they have killed. Stranger counts beyond any of others, and when man has told all his war tales stranger kills him. Men become very few about daylight and then Coyote goes. Coyote meets Little-Man, who agrees to give him power to kill stranger. He gives Coyote bow and arrows, tells him to have dress made after fashion of stranger's, and says that when he has got ahead of stranger in story telling there will be foot-race, in which he is to run above ground, and when he has beaten stranger he is to kill him. When Coyote has accomplished all he is not to marry. Little-Man instructs Coyote how to bring dead men back by burning bodies. Coyote tells people what has happened and what he is going to do. They make him clothes and bonnet, and Little-Man gives clothing appearance of that of stranger. Coyote goes to place where everybody dies and mimics men in getting wood and dogwood sticks. At dark stranger comes to camp-fire. He is surprised to see that Coyote's dress resembles his own. They begin to tell war tales and Coyote tells more than the stranger. Stranger tells true stories and Coyote stories only half true. Daylight comes and stranger has told all his war tales. Coyote prepares to kill him, but stranger says they have to run race, and he can run on top of ground or under ground. Coyote decides on top and they run for high point. Coyote receives power from Little-Man and reaches point first. When stranger arrives he offers Coyote his power, but Coyote kills him with bow and arrows. He drags body to camp-fire and gathers human bones lying around and burns them. He calls names of men who have been killed there and they come out of fire. Men go home. At suggestion of chief people build Coyote new dwelling-place and give him wives. Prominent men come to visit Coyote, and his wives cook for them. Wives become pregnant. Little-Man sends whirlwind to take away Coyote's powers and leave him as at first, because he has disobeyed his order. Next morning wives find coyote instead of human being. They scream and awake coyote, who runs away from village. Wives' children are coyotes, and the people take them home for pets.

41. THE BOY WHO LED WAR-PARTIES AND BECAME A HAWK.

Chief has two boys. The older one is called Bad-Boy. Father is wishful to give him power, but he will not stay at home. Chief is tired of his doings and announces to people that if they see Bad-Boy among their lodges they shall kill him or whip him. Bad-Boy hears, and being afraid, goes home to bed. Next day he is quiet and asks father to instruct him regarding war bundle. Father takes down War-secrets-Bundle and spreads things before Bad-Boy. He instructs him particularly what to do if he wants to set out on war-path. One foggy day Bad-Boy thinks he will send out war-party. He fills pipe with tobacco and goes to select man to serve under him. Man accepts pipe and asks when they are to start. He says in a few days. Next day he leaves home and goes to village where young men playing shinny game. Lives in tipi of old man, old woman, and small child, and begins to do things he has done in father's village. Goes with people on hunt, but returns to get things he has left in cave. He dresses himself and follows people on hunt. He meets young women who laugh at him. He drives them from hunting party and asks them to go on war-party. They are willing and make camp. Bad-Boy follows instructions given by father. Next day they start and travel fourteen days. Every time they camp two women, Second-leading-Warriors, have to go through tobacco rite. Bad-Boy goes spying, and on return women form circle, which he enters, gives whoop, and says he has seen it. They sit down and Bad-Boy tells his story, and after telling his intention they rise and go in direction of enemy. They see Trickster, who shoots at them until Bad-Boy clubs him and takes his scalp. They start off home and people dance all night in honor of Bad-Boy. He sends out more war-parties, of men instead of women. He remains single, and when old he tells people he is going to leave them and become something else. He flies away as Hawk.

42. THE COYOTE AND THE WARRIOR.

Coyote sees man on war-path and asks if he can go. Coyote says he is brave, and man lets him go, although he knows he is a coward. First night they stop at place called Where-Scalped-Man-sits-by-the-Fire. They kill buffalo and after eating most of the meat they rest. Coyote cuts pieces from largest part of heart and fits it on his knee. He goes to sleep and when he awakes he thinks Scalped-Man is sitting before him. He strikes with club and hits his own knee, which pains him and swells up. Next night they are to camp at place called Where-cooked-Meat-flies-around. Coyote says knee is feeling better. They come to place. When they have caught all they want meat stops flying around. Next night they are to stay at Where-Arrows-fly-around and Coyote complains of sore leg hurting him. His knee becomes worse and they stop to rest. Arrows begin to fly around. Man catches some, but Coyote dodges and is hit in arm. Man kicks Coyote's feet and tells him to get up. While eating, man tells Coyote next stopping place is Where-Women-visit-the-Men. Coyote wishes next day might come quickly. Next morning he does cooking and says knee does not hurt. When they camp next night two women come. Coyote cooks tripe and eats it with woman to find out whether she is young or old. In eating she makes noise and Coyote tells her to leave him, as she is too old. She arises and her apparel rattles like that of young women and Coyote finds he has made mistake. Woman walks off and will not pay any attention to Coyote. Man keeps other woman to himself. Man says next stopping place is Where-War-clubs-Fly-around, and Coyote's leg begins to pain him again. They camp next evening and they hear war-clubs flying around. Coyote begins to dodge them and one hits him on head. Man secures two good ones and flying ceases. He kicks Coyote's feet and tells him to get up. While sitting, man tells Coyote they will next stop at place called Where-Vaginas-fly-around. Coyote asks various questions and sleeps little. In morning he is in good condition to walk and leaves man behind. In evening they encamp, and while eating objects begin to fly around and Coyote catches one in his quiver. Man says they will come to real place next time called Where-Enemies-Attack-their-Foes. Coyote's knee pains him next day. They travel till late and they start next morning. They are attacked by enemies. Coyote tries to run away but enemy kills him. After fight man goes to Coyote and finds him on ground scalped. He kicks Coyote's feet and brings him to life. Coyote runs away from man and becomes wild. Man is Chicken-Hawk.

43. THE END OF THE TRICKSTER-CHEATER.

Village ruled by old man, who has wife, daughter, and four boys. Old man and wife become blind and boys become head of village. Four brothers announce hunting trip, and tell people to get ready in four days. Father thinks it useless for him, wife, and daughter to go, and chiefs have them removed to safe place near timber and water. When people have left village Trickster-Spies come and find no one in village. Among them is Trickster-Spy, who finds old folks and daughter living in timber. When warriors go away he goes with them, but when good way off he leaves them and returns. He kills buffalo, takes meat to where folks are living. When girl steps out he motions for her to come for meat. She goes and tells father and he finally tells her to see what man wants. She goes and man returns with her, carrying meat. Father tells mother and daughter to do what man asks. Man makes up mind to stay and marry girl. He has great powers and always brings home meat. If he sees enemies he turns to deer or coyote. He sees four brothers and people coming and tells his wife. Brothers return and accept him as brother-in-law. His wife has boy called Son-of-the-Trickster-Spy. Trickster-Spy always takes son hunting. Once when boy heavy he paints his head with white clay and leaves him in tree. Tricksters come and take child away. Trickster-Spy follows and overtakes them. He joins party, carries child in his turn, lets crowd go on and turns back with child. When old enough, child has as great powers as his father. Trickster-Spy lives with four chiefs long while, then beats wife and has to fly, leaving wife and boy. Trickster's son is angry at father and looks out to kill him. War-party is sent against Tricksters, and Trickster's son goes out to spy. He and father see each other and turn to deer, but are afraid to meet. War-party returns home. While on hunting trip, Trickster's son accidentally sees some one who has killed game. He finds it is his father and turns into buck deer. He turns back, attacks father before he knows, and kills him. He takes father's scalp and gives it to people, who dance for joy over death of their meanest enemy.

44. THE COYOTE, PRAIRIE TURTLE, AND SQUIRREL.

Prairie-Turtle wishes to cross creek, but it is swollen. Buffalo offers to take him across on his hoofs, or back, or between his horns, but Turtle declines. Then Buffalo suggests anus and Turtle gets in. He eats part of intestines and Buffalo drops dead when across creek. Turtle calls for some one with knife to butcher Buffalo, and Coyote hears. Turtle denies he has called for butcher. Coyote sees Buffalo on ground and asks what it is. Turtle insists it is his robe, but admits it is Buffalo he has killed. Coyote offers to butcher for half beef. Turtle consents. When through, Coyote suggests that they run race for all meat. Turtle is beaten and Coyote leaves him to watch meat while Coyote goes for wife and children. Squirrel comes and suggests playing trick on Coyote. They carry all meat to tree and Squirrel takes meat and then Turtle up into tree, which spreads over creek. Coyote returns and finds meat gone. He sees Turtle and Squirrel reflected in water. They smile and Coyote jumps into water, but can not reach them. He comes out and still sees them smiling. Coyote ties stone on neck and dives. Excrement floats and Coyote's children call for intestines, as he has told them to do. Turtle and Squirrel tell them they have drowned their father. Squirrel pours boiling hot soup on them and they run in different directions. This is why Coyotes do not stay together. Squirrel brings Turtle down to ground and they part.

45. THE COYOTE, RABBIT, AND SCALPED-MAN.

Coyote and Rabbit plan to get Scalped-Man's bonnet, not knowing what sort of head he has. They take calumet pipe to him and say they have come to give him dance. One sings while other dances and they take turns in singing. Scalped-Man comes with gifts of things to wear. He first tells war-story. When all his things are gone, Coyote and Rabbit call for bonnet. Scalped-Man refuses and they will not stop dancing and singing. Finally Scalped-Man comes running with his bonnet off and Coyote and Rabbit are so afraid they run away. Scalped-Man follows them and seizes Rabbit by feet. He overtakes Coyote and throws Rabbit in his face. When Rabbit and Coyote meet they talk about man's head and things they have at Scalped-Man's place, which they are afraid to go after. They laugh over their sport.

46. THE COYOTE AND SKUNK INAUGURATE THE FEAST.

Coyote, who is a notorious coward, while hunting finds Skunk, and says he must kill him. Skunk tells Coyote that Beavers are having medicine dance near by and together they can kill lot of them. He instructs Coyote what to do. Coyote goes and finds Beavers having medicine-men's dance. He tells them his partner is sick and asks for man to doctor him. He is told to take his choice, and he selects fattest. Medicine-man asks what part of sick man's body hurts him. Skunk turns over, and while medicine-man is examining anus Skunk defecates, blinding him. Coyote kills him with club and hauls him off to distance. After cleaning ground Coyote goes again to Beavers. He pretends that first medicine-man has failed to cure sick man, has gone to look for different medicine. He asks for another medicine-man, as his partner is nearly dead, and selects fattest man. They go to where Skunk pretends to be dying and Coyote kills him as first one. By this trick four Beavers are killed and Coyote carries them home. He tells wife his friends are coming to feast and she is to cook for them. When cooking is done Coyote orders family to go to creek until feast is over. Family go and Coyote raps on door and pretends that some one is coming in and then talks as though seating his friends. Coyote then eats from place to place, eating most at first place, less at next, and so on. When he has eaten he talks again as though to his friends. After a while, calls for his family. He tells them some of his friends were not very hungry. Coyote's family eats rest of meat. He then commands them to move away and be coyotes and that in after generations there shall be making of feasts for friends.

47. THE COYOTE WHO BECAME A BUFFALO.

Coyote sees big Buffalo grazing and asks him for powers to live like Buffalo. Finally Buffalo says Coyote can become Buffalo if he is brave. He tells Coyote to stand and let Buffalo run against him and he will get up great Buffalo bull. Coyote goes and stands facing Buffalo, who runs toward him as hard as he can. Coyote steps out of way. This takes place three times, but fourth time Coyote shuts his eyes and Buffalo runs over him. When Coyote stands up he is great Buffalo bull. Buffalo tells him he can go where he wants to, but must not hurt any one. Coyote-Buffalo sees another Coyote and tells him he can be changed to Buffalo bull and live as he is doing. Coyote consents and Coyote-Buffalo starts to run over him. Coyote jumps out of way three times, but fourth time Coyote-Buffalo runs over him and they are both coyotes—Coyote-Buffalo for trying to make another Coyote into Buffalo.

48. THE COYOTE AND THE ARTICHOKE.

Coyote goes to hunt and meets people who are going to dig artichokes. He joins party, and seeing people eat as they go digging, he commences to eat. He is told to throw away piece so that it will grow again. People go, but Coyote thinks he will stay. He kept on eating artichokes and finally eats every bit without saving piece. He gets so full that he expels flatus, which bounces him up, and finally he bounces up into hollow stump. Coyote can not get out and remains there several days. People come back and they hear him calling. They cut down timber and release him. He goes away home, where he finds his family starved to death. He goes off howling.

49. THE COYOTE AND THE WILD-CAT.

Coyote is hungry and finds some dry bones. He takes rib and makes fire to cook it. While he sleeps Wild-cat comes along and eats meat. He fills Coyote's teeth with meat, greases his hands and knife, and puts bones before him. Wild-cat then goes off and sleeps. Coyote wakes and thinks he must have eaten, but is still hungry. He sees tracks of Wild-cat and trails him. Finds Wild-cat and takes him to creek, where he leaves him on high bluff. Coyote goes away and finds another dry bone and goes to sleep again. Wild-cat wakes up and rolls into creek. He finds Coyote's tracks and follows them to where Coyote is asleep. He puts Coyote on his back and carries him to creek, where he fixes Coyote up to spoil his looks. Coyote wakes and finds he is different. He suspects Wild-cat, finds him asleep and changes him by making face round and shortening tail. When Wild-cat wakes he goes to creek to see himself and sees he has ugly face. He again traces Coyote and finds him sound asleep. He places him in hole in old burnt tree and leaves him entirely. Coyote wakes up, finds himself in tree and can not get down. He calls for birds with largest axe to help him. Finally Woodpecker comes and succeeds in getting him down. Woodpecker's axe is his nose. Coyote roams over prairie and has hard times to get something to eat.

50. THE COYOTE, THE OPOSSUM, AND THE CROW.

Coyote, Opossum, and Crow meet and ask one another meanings of their names. After hearing Opossum and Crow on their names, Coyote says he has four names, all of which are connected with war. Their names are nothing to his. They all add word "Wets" (man or bold) to their names.

51. THE COYOTE AND THE FISH-HAWK.

Coyote sees man fishing in creek by means of string-like thing on his head. Coyote asks man to give him same power. Man tells him he will have to look for place just like that and to follow instructions, or he will get into trouble. The thing was put on his head for line. Man says Coyote must never call for largest fish in water. Coyote finds place and catches all the fish he wants. Thereafter he follows that way of fishing, but food does not last long. Coyote wants to catch largest fish, that it may last longer. He calls for largest fish. It bites and he can not pull it out. It pulls on line and finally takes whole of scalp off Coyote's head. Coyote cries and runs home. His family are afraid of him and run away. Coyote then dies. Man who gave Coyote power is Fish-Hawk.

52. THE COYOTE AND THE BEAR.

Coyote goes north before daylight and hears Bear coming, threatening to kill him. Coyote thinks he will play Bear trick and orders him to stop and not kill him until his father looks at him. Bear stays and Coyote rushes toward him, as Sun rises. Coyote tells him to make haste or he will kill Bear. Bear gives up all hopes of living, as he has tried to kill son of the Sun. Coyote pushes him back and Bear finally promises if he is not killed to go home with Coyote and do all the work and hunt to feed children. Coyote agrees and rides home on Bear's back. Before reaching home Coyote orders Bear to hunt. Bear catches deer and takes it to Coyote's place. Coyote makes Bear cook meat and burns him with stick when he sits down to rest. Bear supports Coyote's family for long while. Children ill-treat him and ride him about. Somebody tells Bear while hunting that Coyote is not child of Sun and has no powers. Bear returns without anything and kills whole family of Coyotes.

53. THE COYOTE AND THE SMALLEST SNAKE.

Coyote on prairie finds little Snake Never-grows-larger. He teases it for
being so small and asks it to show its teeth. Coyote shows his teeth and
challenges Snake to bite. They bite each other and Coyote says he will go little
way and they shall call to each other. Coyote calls to Snake and Snake answers
weakly. Coyote is called and answers pretty low. They keep calling one another
and Coyote's body begins to swell. At last Coyote answers very faintly and
Snake very loud. Finally Coyote does not answer and Snake goes to him and
finds him dead.

54. THE COYOTE AND THE TURKEY.

Coyote attacks Turkey. He pulls all his feathers off and puts them around
Turkey's neck. He asks Turkey if he is honest, and when he says he is, Coyote
sends him to Coyote's wife to tell her to cook him and save Coyote wing.
Turkey goes and tells wife that Coyote has sent him to copulate with her. She
sends children out and Turkey notices arrow-sticks and sinew are hung up.
Woman is treated turkey fashion and then Turkey tells her Coyote wants her
to break arrow-sticks and cook sinew with them. Coyote returns home and
after talk with wife goes out again in search of Turkey. He finds Turkey up in
tree and tries to coax him down, without success. Coyote returns home and
finds his children and wife starved to death, so he goes off and cries.

55. THE DELUGE AND THE REPEOPLING OF THE EARTH.

Formerly people had many supernatural powers. There was no death and
people remained old or young. Wife of chief brings forth four little monsters
who have four feet. Many men wish them to be killed, but mother objects.
Man who is prophet says their birth is sign that something dreadful is going
to happen. Monsters play with other children and run over them. When older
they eat buffalo robes, upturn tipis, and, finally, eat children. People try to
kill them, but can not harm them. Monsters go to middle of village and stand
together facing east, south, west, and north. They all grow together and grow
higher and higher. Prophet is told to get tall cane and place between joints
all kinds of seeds, grass, corn, etc., and then he is to select in pairs good
animals. When everything ready he is to set up pole in ground and crawl into
it. Prophet goes to man in north, who says sign indicating dire things will
be coming of animals from north to south. Animals appear and prophet crawls
into cane. Flood comes and drowns bad people and all not in cane. Man in
north sends with flood Turtle which gets under feet of monsters, who fall, one
after another, toward four directions, and are drowned. Flood disappears, leaving prophet and wife on high point. After long while prophet is told to go down
mountain. He finds trees for their use. Things come out of cane and go from
place to place. Woman goes to sleep. In morning Morning-Corn has grown.
Voice gives them directions for use of things. They find grass-lodge and four
corn stalks. Corn is to be always used, and if time comes that after planting
corn something else comes up it will be sign of end of world.

56. THE DELUGE AND THE REPEOPLING OF THE EARTH.

Wife of head man gives birth to four children in form of a horse. Head man sends them away. The monsters grow and swallow people who go away from their feet. They are called Standing-in-the-Water and face four directions. Chief sends errand man to northwest to see small man who has great powers. On return man says something will be done to destroy monsters; it will begin in north; fowls of air and animals will appear as clouds and water-monster (Turtle) will be sent to destroy four monsters. After a while fowls of air and animals come and flood is all over earth. Turtle is under feet of four monsters and they fall, one after another, in four directions. Wind and Medicine-men are not destroyed. Wind dries up land and streams of foam remain as mountains. Wind sees something like rain falling in west. He goes and sees woman lying on ground. He goes again and notices that woman is pregnant. Next time child is lying on side of woman. He can hardly see woman and is taking child when some one above tells him to let it alone. Thinks it is child of Man-never-known-on-Earth. Wind makes another visit to place and takes child, which is girl, to place where are people. He calls mother of child Earth. Girl grows rapidly and takes man for husband. Boy is born and being first boy he has power to create things. He tells his parents not to do him wrong until he has completed all the things he wants to do. On returning once he tells them they have done him wrong and he goes east and becomes Morning-Star. Afterward girl is born and then boy, who, when they grow up, become husband and wife. Father goes toward northwest and becomes Clearness-after-Rain.

THIRD PERIOD: THE PRESENT.

57. THE WOMAN WHO MARRIED A STAR.

Long while ago woman watching stars notices some are bright and some dim. She thinks bright stars are fine-looking young men and dim stars old men. She wishes she could have particular bright star for husband. When asleep she is with this man. In morning she is in strange place and old man sitting by fire. He wakes and tells her he is the bright star she selected. Dim stars are young men. Woman becomes wife of star. She is told not to move large rock lying on ground. She does so and sees earth below. She studies how to get down and cuts and braids soapweed into rope. She ties it to rock and lets herself down. When at end of rope she is near top of highest trees. Buzzard takes her down on his back and sees her safely home. Parents ask where she has been and she tells them about star and getting back. People since afraid to express desires about stars.

58. THE MAN WHO WENT TO SPIRIT-LAND.

There are two young men of same age who are playmates. When they are grown they become real friends and agree to die at same time. They are regarded as brothers. One of them marries. They go on war-path together and present each other with scalps they take. Boy baby is born to married friend and he stays at home, while unmarried friend goes on war-path and is killed.

Married friend mourns brother and goes on war-path to die. Mother of child dies and he goes to wife's grave to mourn. While there he goes to sleep and has dream, in which his friend appears. Friend asks if he throught a great deal of his wife while she was living, and says he can live with her again if he wishes. Dead man tells him what he will have to go through to bring this about. He wakes up and friend is standing there. Friend touches his eyes and he finds himself in other world. They see lodges and come to place where dance is. Friend leaves live man, who sees his wife dancing. As she comes around he throws mud balls at her and fourth time she leaves dance and goes home. He follows her and enters home. Father-in-law asks if he has come to see his wife, and then tells him that next morning he must go buffalo hunting, kill buffalo and cut fat from shoulder, then he must kick buffalo and it will come to life again. Next morning he obeys his father-in-law's instructions and brings fat to wife's home. He is told to take bath and rub fat all over his body. He goes on buffalo hunt four mornings and then is told he can live with his wife same as on earth. Getting back home he is to send out war-party four times and bring scalp every time. During dances after return from war-path he is not to associate with other women. If he does he can not keep wife, but afterward he can do as he pleases. He finds himself on earth with his wife. She tells him to have lodge cleaned and smoked with sage, and that his folks are not to weep when she enters. When place is ready, young man and wife go to home. Soon afterward young man goes with war-party, which returns with scalps. During dancing he remembers what he was told. He goes out with another war-party, which is victorious. He places scalp where wife's dead people can get it and goes with wife to dance. Long after, young man sends out another war-party. They return home victorious and young man offers scalp to wife's dead parents. He goes to dance and wife is not there. He meets woman who has courted him and stays nearly all night with her. His wife knows what he has done and leaves him permanently while he is asleep and returns to her dead people. He goes to her grave, but no one appears to him. He tells people that he has been in another world and that those who die in battle are happier than those who die of sickness. Man lives long afterward, but never finds out about his wife again.

59. THE MAN WHO RESCUED HIS WIFE FROM SPIRIT-LAND.

Two boys become friends and go to battle together. In their homes they are considered brothers. One gets married. Other boy goes on war-path by himself and dies in battle, that he may cease to think of friend. Married man's wife dies, leaving him child. He mourns continually for loss of wife and friend. While at wife's grave he falls asleep and dreams of friend. He wakes and sees friend. They go together to large village and enter dance place. Friend instructs him what to do, and he throws four mud balls at wife while dancing and follows her to her father's lodge, as in No. 58. Father asks him many questions and then tells him he must go and kill buffalo, take fat from hump and kick buffalo on back and tell it to go. He does so and delivers fat to father-in-law. Man is to take sweat bath, bathe his body in incense, and rub fat over him every day. At end of four days man is told to take wife. He is instructed to go on war-path and secure four scalps. On return home wife directs him to have grass-lodge cleaned and smoked before she enters. Next day young man gets up war-party, who takes rawhide, in place of drum, and sings songs. They obtain scalps and on return home they dance. Young man soon goes on another war-party. He has war bundle given him by his wife's dead relatives. They again return victorious and young man puts scalp away. At night, thinking his wife will not know, he dances with another woman and stays with her all night. When he goes back home his wife is gone. He mourns again, but no one appears to him.

60. THE CRIPPLE WHO DISOBEYED THE GODS.

Small crippled boy has notion of visiting Village-on-Hill-side to get powers. He goes and fasts on mountain-top. He hears stars talk about him and he plays to stars and animal gods to help him to become a famous and better-looking man. This continues three days, and early on fourth day two men come who take him into large room inside of mountain. He sees many men. Head man touches his eyes and he sees all sorts of beasts and fowls of air. They wear robes of all colors. There are all kinds of Coyotes, Raven, and Crow, who bring him there and ask other men to make haste and do for him. Bear gives him power to have good hearing, to send out war-parties, and to cure sick people. Each gives him powers and presents. He is then told to return home and to wear everything he has, but to arrive at home at night, so that no one will see him or know who he is, and that he is not to have intercourse with women. He starts home and looks into water and sees he is handsome. He begins to think whom he shall choose as wife. He decides to enter village by daylight and make himself known. He watches people playing games, especially woman's double-ball game. When he arrives at place he goes in middle of crowd and tells them who he is, and where he has been since he disappeared. He reaches home and tells his people. At night crowds of men go to see him and many women stand outside to marry him, but are refused entrance. Certain woman comes and goes right to bed with him. After he has gone to sleep all his powers are taken from him. He becomes ugly as at first.